STORIES DONE

WRITINGS
ON THE
1960s
AND ITS
DISCONTENTS

Mikal Gilmore

FREE PRESS
New York
London
Toronto
Sydney

FREE PRESS
A Division of Simon & Schuster, Inc.
1230 Avenue of the Americas
New York, NY 10020

First Free Press hardcover edition November 2008

FREE PRESS and colophon are trademarks of Simon & Schuster, Inc.

For information about special discounts for bulk purchases,
please contact Simon & Schuster Special Sales at 1-800-456-6798 or
business@simonandschuster.com

DESIGNED BY ERICH HOBBING

Permission credits appear on pages 377–378

Manufactured in the United States of America

1   3   5   7   9   10   8   6   4   2

Library of Congress Cataloging-in-Publication Data
Gilmore, Mikal.
Stories done: writings on the 1960s and its discontents / Mikal Gilmore.
p. cm.
1. Musicians—Biography. 2. Beat generation—Biography. 3. Popular music—Social aspects—
History—20th century. 4. Popular music—History and criticism. I. Title.
ML394.G55   2008
780.92'2—dc22
[B]   2008024119

ISBN-13: 978-0-7432-8745-6
ISBN-10:   0-7432-8745-2

To Elaine Schock,
who let me into her heart

CONTENTS

INTRODUCTION

This book is a collection of stories about people who helped carry a time and a motion—people largely identified with the 1960s. The motion that I refer to here had, of course, begun years earlier in isolated discoveries, and would carry over to shattering cultural and political disputes. Some of it was born from the liberties asserted by Elvis Presley, some of it by the Beat movement and its impeachment of postwar America's aesthetics and ideology. Some of it came from an audacious wave of drug experiments, conducted by everybody from respected scientists, doctors, writers, artists, actors, musicians and professors to less sanguine types within the CIA and the U.S. military. Some of it was from a spirit born in the hard and heroic campaign for civil rights, and some of it by a growing reaction against Western liberal democracy's battle with international communism (which would culminate in the argument over the American debacle in Vietnam). It was carried along by folk singers, blues revisionists, British rock & roll usurpers, American soul singers and groundbreaking jazz musicians, and it was picked up by rebel authors, student activists, community settlers, teenage dancers, drug users, sexual explorers, spiritual surveyors, street rebels, black militants and reformist politicians. In the end, the movement was a confluence of music, film, poetry, theater, literature, art, science, society, politics, war and revolt, almost all of it driven by vision and mania, by hope and anguish. An epoch happened between the mid-1950s and the early 1970s: it was intense and it was fast, and it seemed in its moment that it could lead to a transfigured world.

Then, that momentum came undone. By the early 1970s, most of the significant components of the 1960s dream had come apart or had been subsumed, from both internal and external pressures. Illumination, defeat, genius, madness, joy, death and misspent permission all exacted their toll. From there, I guess, you measure how much we've learned, or how much we've lost.

This volume clearly isn't a formal history of the 1960s; for one thing, it doesn't attempt to chronicle the era's momentous political unrest (though the effect of that disruption is indivisible from perhaps every subject and theme covered here). Rather, *Stories Done* is an attempt to look at some of what was at risk in those times, through the lives of a handful of notable people and events that were elemental to the period's arts and arguments. There are, I admit, some obvious shortcomings here: There is nothing in this survey about female figures of importance, nor about R&B and jazz musicians, all of whom were critical to the period under survey. (I also have other regrets: There is nothing here about John Coltrane, Miles Davis, the Velvet Underground or Tim Buckley, whose musical realizations mattered especially to me.) Still, the persons and occasions that I was able to address in these pages certainly changed the stakes of our lives and ideals and even the possibilities of our future; they were part of a major historical shift that not only challenged the cultural and social values of that age, but also, for an astonishing term, almost preempted the real power and polemics of the era. As I note more than once in these stories, almost all the arguments that have mattered in our culture and politics these last forty years have been a reaction to the brink that those times approached.

Going back through these stories, I didn't expect anything about them to surprise me, though something did: the amount of writing about drugs (including alcohol) and their toll. Drugs and alcohol of themselves likely wouldn't persuade me enough to make them a recurring thematic interest, despite my own experiences; what drew my interest to any of the subjects was their lives and the consequence of their work or moment. But after selecting and reviewing the various pieces for this collection, I came to see that drug or alcohol use figured significantly in almost every one of these histories. Clearly, this wasn't just coincidental, and it bears some consideration.

For more than half of the subjects here, including Ken Kesey, Timothy Leary and the Haight-Ashbury, psychedelics were a major factor in their lives and in any story about them. These were people and a place on a frontier, and all were exploring how these largely unknown quantities might affect the mind or spirituality or community. They chose those particular drugs as an important part of their purpose, and they were willing to accept whatever the ramifications might be. Those choices made them famous and influential, but also feared or despised. Leary and Kesey incurred criminal reputations, which hindered them somewhat but not altogether; certainly, drugs didn't kill them. But drugs did kill Haight-Ashbury. While psychedelics made the district an attraction for dealers and starry-eyed pilgrims and runaways, the drugs also transformed the area's freewheeling idealism from dream into farce.

This doesn't mean that psychedelic experimentation in the Sixties wasn't useful; the hallucinatory state had an extraordinary effect on the era's creativity. I'd certainly argue that there was momentous writing from Ken Kesey, and wonderful music made by the Grateful Dead, the Beatles, the Doors and Pink Floyd, that would not have happened if not for the LSD experience. But then, in Pink Floyd's case, it is fair to say that LSD certainly hastened the brilliant Syd Barrett's decline. This raises a question worth asking: If Pink Floyd's remarkable early music owed anything to Barrett's drug use, then . . . was that splendor worth its cost? Clearly, psychedelic daring could produce real ruin. I worked for several years in the 1970s as a counselor in drug and alcohol treatment programs in Portland, Oregon, and although I saw far worse and more plentiful injury resulting from the use of heroin, amphetamines and alcohol—including more deaths of young people than I ever want to remember—I remember feeling a special sympathy for those who seemed misplaced or lessened by psychedelics. I'd taken LSD and mescaline myself, yet had no personal experience of heroin or speed. I'd also had a fearful incident with LSD (as I mention in this book's Leary story), so I knew something of how it felt when your consciousness ran into a place where it seemed to fall apart into holes and particles and God knows what. I never regretted using psychedelics, but I respect the prospect that they might invert you in considerable ways, and I understand that some psychologies could never bear that inversion.

Many of the figures in these pages were transformed by other intoxicants (including alcohol, opiates and amphetamines) that, in the cases of Johnny Cash, Phil Ochs, Hunter S. Thompson, Jim Morrison, Gregg Allman and Jimmy Page, were addictive and ran high risks of fatality. The effects on these men were frequently awful. Some—Cash, Allman, Page—survived and reformed, while others—Ochs, Thompson, Morrison and Led Zeppelin's John Bonham—had their possibilities cut short.

Why did all this happen? Was it attributable to the times? One of the Sixties' most defining shifts in attitude was a growing sense, among great numbers of young people and others (including politicos), that the existing value system was not necessarily trustworthy, and that we no longer had to defer to dominant social conventions and ideologies. To put it more pointedly, we no longer had to ask permission for our choices and convictions. This shift changed everything and led to much that was remarkable.

But because it happened so swiftly—within two or three years, really—and opened up so many chances in so much uncertain territory, this hands-off creed conjured risks. As Carolyn Adams (who was close to Ken Kesey and was once married to Jerry Garcia) notes in the Haight-Ashbury chapter, this new ideal of freedom also became a permission to fuck up, sometimes badly enough so as to induce harm. Getting stoned could feel great, but the simple science of these drugs was that taking too many too often, or among an unregulated public, could lead to awful effects. There were real differences between psychedelics or marijuana and drugs like amphetamines, cocaine and heroin; many of us in that time regarded the former grouping as something that enabled lofty possibilities and the latter as the means of a death trip. However, many of the subjects in this book did not draw that same line, and their pursuit of freedom often led to a terrible downfall. The freedom to fuck up could prove wonderful, but it could also mean fucking up for good.

It's clear that much of the drug use born of the 1960s was terribly foolhardy, though the punitive and hysterical reactions to drugs that have swelled since then have had too little real effect other than helping to spread unjust harm. The 1960s will always have to bear repute for its leniency regarding drugs. That's not entirely unfair, but it's also a loaded charge. Intoxicants have been with us forever, causing pleasure, enlightenment, addiction and fatality. But just as drugs delimit some lives, they may also help extend life for others who long for something to make their days and nights more bearable.

The commonality of the role of drugs and alcohol in these stories could hardly be coincidental, and though that trait also wasn't what attracted me to those stories, I now understand that what drew me was something else. Almost every person featured in this book, including George Harrison and John Lennon, suffered from depression at various times and in varying degrees. Depression and intoxication, of course, have forged bonds for hundreds of years. Drugs and alcohol can seem to make depression more tolerable or even truant, though in truth they also invariably deepen it, sometimes within the high itself and almost always after that state fades. Drugs or alcohol promise to stave off that despondency—that is, until the high or inebriation wears off again. Add to this rotation the snare of physical addiction, and it can prove overwhelming to find a way out.

This was all going on well before the 1960s. Though many narratives of that time—and of the present—brand the predicament wholly in terms of illegal drugs, in truth legal intoxicants and narcotics (including drink, tobacco and prescription drugs) accounted for vastly more addiction and mortal loss over recent decades. Drugs will always be with us because they address tendencies and needs—some psychological, some cultural—that can't be wholly eradicated. You do the best to save whom you can, including yourself, but you can't cure the prospect of human fucked-upness and you can't force deliverance.

Most of the people I've chronicled here produced something remarkable despite themselves, despite whatever broke or finished them or perhaps even made them ignoble. The merits that came from their fucked-upness are, I believe, what made them great; it's what made their names and their works lasting, no matter how much they were failing themselves or others. We still save whatever blessings they left us.

With most of these stories, I've been mindful of writing about unruly lives and aspirations in the period during which the George W. Bush administration has controlled the helm of American power. These have been maddening and disheartening years, in which the dominating ideology proved in some ways more unwavering, more impregnable, than was the case even in the 1950s, when rock & roll was among those forces that began to assault established modes of institution. For the last couple of generations, elements of popular culture often had an insurgent and remedial effect: the wonderful, undermining strength of scorn. But in the new century's first decade, the presiding power worked in ways that were more cunning and perhaps more uncompromising. The Bush ideology—horrible and ruinous, though lamentably brilliant—managed to ride roughshod over the prospects of derision and dissent, and to a terrible degree, it managed to sabotage the dignity of the disreputable.

Though I've written about the impetus of the 1960s in these pages, my purpose isn't to say that the Sixties or its music and artists were somehow superior to what we have today. That isn't the case; there's always far more extraordinary and brave new music—of all sorts—than most of us are able to keep up with. What I am saying, though, is that there is now a social and political mind-set that never again wants to see youth culture and its arts empowered as they were in recent generations. This isn't to say that popular culture can no longer subvert hegemony. But the sort of youth power that the Beatles and Bob Dylan, among others, helped awaken, and that I've written about at various points in this book, is simply no longer even considered in its former sweeping terms. The cultural perspective that defines youth has changed, drastically. Today's youth are often seen as children whose judgments are immature, who have to be protected from influences that may steer them in directions that threaten decency and social authority. It's true that the same things were said about teenagers in the 1950s and 1960s, but our ambition then *was* to dispute mores and intimidate ideology: We meant to be a threat, though we weren't always judicious about our purposes or impact. Today, the pressures against such instincts for adolescents come from within both their peer group and the culture at large. As a result, the more conservative outlook of recent years has largely stigmatized the sort of insurrectionary spirit that the Beatles and others manifested in much of their 1960s music.

Over two millennia ago, the Greek philosopher Plato wrote: "Forms and rhythms in music are never changed without producing changes in the most important political forms and ways. . . . The new style quietly insinuates . . . a greater force . . . goes on to attack laws and constitutions, displaying the utmost impudence, until it ends by over-throwing everything, both in public and in private." Is this still possible? Does it still happen? Of course it does—just witness the disturbances caused by hip-hop in the last many years. Yet cultural, commercial and media mechanisms have become more adept at assimilating or discrediting pop culture's threats or at confining those threats to mere affronts of modesty and good manners. Spring breaks, clubbing, and *American Idol*'s instant democracy don't really constitute a riot going on. I worry that even after the Bush years have ended, the remnant of this time's ideology will have become habitual and systemic enough to still curb the underlying tremors that could be facilitated by popular cultural disturbances.

I don't live in the past, nor do I long to see it reenacted; I want to know what is possible tomorrow, what can be justly broken, and what might be made anew. But I will always be grateful for the period and events that I've had the chance to write about here. Coming together in that time, around rock & roll or for political action, felt like we were forming a kinship, brimming with expectation and desire. It's amazing to realize how much power actually coalesced in those American days and nights, whether we understood it or not.

A final note: Most of what appears here has been published in some form, but was not previously collected, though I've imported four pieces—about Timothy Leary, Allen Ginsberg, the Allman Brothers, and Jerry Garcia and the Grateful Dead—and sundry other passages from an earlier book of mine, *Night Beat*; given the purpose of this current volume, it felt right to me to give them this new context, and I want to thank Doubleday and Anchor Books for allowing their inclusion. Although a couple of profiles are included here, by and large these stories are historical overviews or syntheses. There's a fair amount of overlap between various articles that cover related or synchronous subjects (for example, several pieces cover LSD usage in the 1960s), though I've done my best to eliminate unnecessary repetition.

These writings are largely the product of opportunities afforded me by *Rolling Stone*, where I began writing in 1976. The magazine remains a force committed to championing popular culture's power to partake in political change, and I'm honored to have been able to contribute to its pages. I'm also more grateful than I know how to say for the times and events covered in this collection that I have managed to share or learn from.

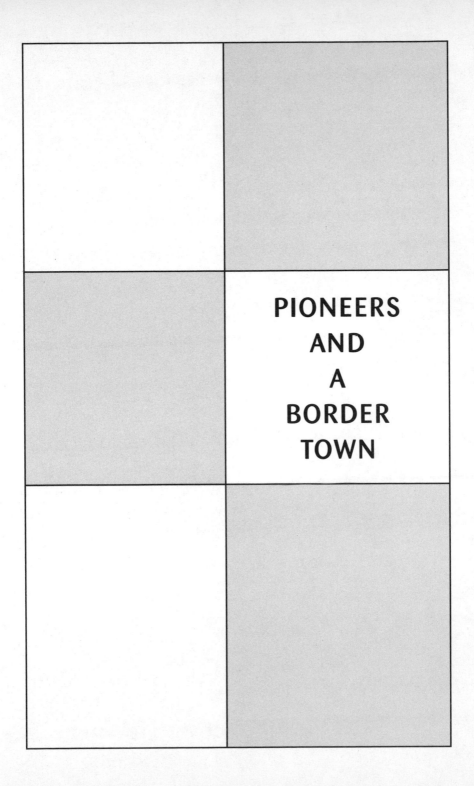

PIONEERS
AND
A
BORDER
TOWN

ALLEN GINSBERG:
HOLY MAN

Allen Ginsberg had been contemplating the meanings that come from death's inevitability for nearly the entirety of his writing career. In 1959, in "Kaddish," his narrative-poem about his mother's decline and death, Ginsberg said to his mother's memory: "Death let you out, Death had the Mercy, you're done with your century...." And in 1992, he wrote of himself: "Sleepless I stay up & / think about my Death ... / If I don't get some rest I'll die faster." As it turned out it was only seven days before his death, on April 5, 1997, at age seventy, that Ginsberg learned that the illness of his last few years had turned worse—that it was now inoperable liver cancer. Hearing the news, Ginsberg returned to his apartment in New York's East Village and proceeded to do what he had always done: He sat down and wrote a body of poems about the experiences of his life—in this case, about the imminence of his end. One of these poems—a long, hilarious and heart-affecting piece called "Death & Fame"—ran in *The New Yorker* the week following his demise. In the poem, Ginsberg envisioned hundreds of friends, admirers and lovers gathered at his "big funeral," and he hoped that among the eulogies, someone would testify: "He gave great head."

In those last few days, Ginsberg also talked to friends—his lifetime compeer, author William Burroughs; his lover of several decades, Peter Orlovsky; poet Gregory Corso, among others—and he wrote a letter to President Bill Clinton (to be sent via George Stephanopoulos, another Ginsberg friend), demanding, in jest, some sort of medal of recognition. At one point during his last week, he listened to a recording of "C.C. Rider" by 1920s blues vocalist Ma Rainey—the first voice Ginsberg said he remembered hearing as a child. He sang along with it, according to one report, then vomited and said: "Gee, I've never done that before." By Friday, he had slipped into a coma. Surrounded by a few close friends, Ginsberg died early Saturday morning, April 5, 1997.

A quiet closing to a mighty life. Not since the 1977 death of Elvis Presley and the 1980 murder of John Lennon had a certain segment of popular culture have to come to terms with the realization of such an epochal ending. Allen Ginsberg not only made history—by writing poems that jarred America's consciousness and by insuring that the 1950s Beat movement would be remembered as a considerable literary force—but he also lived through and embodied some of the most remarkable cultural mutations of the last half century. As much as Presley, as much as the Beatles, Bob Dylan or the Sex Pistols, Allen Ginsberg helped set loose something wonderful, risky and unyielding in the psyche and dreams of our times. Perhaps only Martin Luther King Jr.'s brave and costly quest had a more genuinely liberating impact upon the realities of modern history, upon the freeing up of people and voices that much of established society wanted kept on the margins. Just as Dylan would later change what popular songs could say and do, Ginsberg changed what poetry might accomplish: how it could speak, what it would articulate, and whom it would speak to and for. Ginsberg's words—his performances of his words and how he carried their meanings into his life and actions—gave poetry a political and cultural relevance it had not known since the 1840s' Transcendentalists (Ralph Waldo Emerson and Henry Thoreau among them) or since the shocking publication of Walt Whitman's 1855 classic, *Leaves of Grass*. Indeed, in Ginsberg's hands, poetry proved to be something a great deal more than a vocation or the province of refined wordsmiths and critics. Ginsberg transformed his gift for language into a mission—"trying to save and heal the spirit of America," as he wrote in the introduction to fellow poet Anne Waldman's *The Beat Book*. In the process, he not only influenced subsequent writers like Bob Dylan, John Lennon, Lou Reed, Patti Smith and Jim Carroll, but Ginsberg's effect could also be found in Norman Mailer's *Advertisements for Myself,* in the writings and deeds of Czechoslovakian president Vaclav Havel, in the lives and exploits of 1960s insurrectionists like Timothy Leary, Tom Hayden and Abbie Hoffman. One can also hear Ginsberg's effect on later-generation artists such as Sonic Youth, Beck, U2 and several of our finer hip-hop poets.

Ginsberg was also, of course, simply a man—at turns generous and competitive, self-aware yet self-aggrandizing, old in his wisdom, juvenile in his tastes and affections, and relentlessly promiscuous though deeply faithful. More than anything, though, Ginsberg was someone who once summoned the bravery to speak hidden truths about unspeakable things, and some people took consolation and courage from his example. That example—that insistence that he would not simply *shut up*, and that one should not accept delimited values or experiences—is perhaps Ginsberg's greatest gift to us. Today, there are many other artists who have carried on in that tradition—from Dylan, Smith and Reed, to Eminem or, for that matter, the Dixie Chicks, as well as numerous others—and so in that way, Ginsberg's death does not rob us of unfulfilled possibilities, as happened in the horrid deaths of Kurt Cobain, Tupac Shakur and the Notorious B.I.G. That's because Ginsberg's entire life was a process of opening himself (and us) up to possibilities. Still, Ginsberg's loss counts as enormous. There is no question: A giant passed from our times. It is only fitting to look back on what he did for us and for our land.

Allen Ginsberg was born in 1926, the son of politically radical Russian-born Jewish parents who were also aesthetic progressives (Allen's older brother, Eugene, was named after labor organizer Eugene V. Debs; Ginsberg also recalled that the music of Ma Rainey, Beethoven and Bessie Smith filled the family's home in Paterson, New Jersey). Allen's father, Louis, was a published and respected poet. Louis and Allen would have many arguments over the years regarding poetry's language and structure, though in his father's last few years, the two men often shared stages together, exchanging poems and genuine respect and affection.

But it was Ginsberg's mother, Naomi, who proved in many ways to have a more profound and haunting effect on her son's life, mentality and writing. By 1919, she had already experienced an episode of schizophrenia. She recovered for a while and returned to her life as an activist and mother, but when Allen was three, Naomi experienced an intense relapse. She committed herself to a sanitarium, and for much of the rest of her life, she moved from one psychiatric institution to another. During the times she returned home, she would often declaim frightened fantasies about a pact between her husband, Hitler, Mussolini and President Roosevelt, all involved in an attempt to seize control of her mind. Also, she took to walking around the house nude. Allen—who was kept home from school to take care of his mother on her bad days—would sit reading, trying to ignore Naomi's nakedness and ravings.

Growing up witnessing painful madness and missing the attendance of a loving mother had an enormous impact on Ginsberg. For one thing, it taught him a certain way of preparing for and dealing with hard realities. In Jerry Aronson's film *The Life and Times of Allen Ginsberg*, Ginsberg stated:

"I've had almost like this screen built so I could hear people dying and get on with it. . . . I could survive without tears, in a sense, so that the tears would come out in a poem later, rather than in an immediate breakup of my world. My world already was broken up long ago."

Naomi's problems—and her absence from the home—also brought out a neediness and uncertainty that stayed with Ginsberg in many ways his entire life, and that affected how, as a child, he made connections between erotic incentives and emotional fulfillment. Ginsberg often related how, during the lonely nights when his mother was away, he would cuddle up against his father, Louis, Allen rubbing his erect penis against the back of his father's leg while Louis tried to sleep and ignore the activity. Finally, Naomi's mental problems also made Ginsberg both more afraid of his own possible madness and also more sympathetic about the troubles of others—and it left him with a fear of shadows and ghosts and as a person prone to seeing visions. By the time he was eleven, Allen was already writing about these matters in his early journals, and he discovered something that gave him a certain comfort and strength: Words, unlike so much that surrounded him as a child, were something he could have dominion over, something that could express his thoughts, something he could take pride in.

But for all the loneliness and fearfulness that characterized his childhood family life, Ginsberg also inherited his parents' clear intelligence and much of their political compassion. By the time he was sixteen, he was also coming to the realization that he was attracted to men sexually; in particular, he worshipped a high school classmate who left Paterson for Columbia University, in New York City. In 1943 Ginsberg received a scholarship from the Young Men's Hebrew Association of Paterson, and he promptly headed for Columbia.

Ginsberg arrived at the university planning to study to become a labor lawyer, but two differing intellectual milieus changed that course. The first was Columbia's formidable English studies department, which then included Pulitzer Prize–winning poet Mark Van Doren and literary critic Lionel Trilling; Ginsberg became enamored of these men as mentors and soon changed his major to literature. Over the course of the next year or so, Ginsberg also met another group of men—some of them fellow Columbia students, closer to his own age—and it was this fraternity that turned his life around and that would function as a sort of secondary family for much of the rest of his life. Among these men were William S. Burroughs, Lucien Carr, and a football star with literary aspirations named Jack Kerouac. The bond that developed among them transformed not only their own destinies, but also those of future generations. In particular, Ginsberg and Kerouac seemed to share a special connection. Both were haunted by their child-hoods—Kerouac had an older brother, Gerard, who had died young, and Kerouac's mother used to hold Jack as a child and tell him, "*You* should have died, not Gerard." But the most important thing these men shared was a sense that, in the mid-1940s, there were great secrets lurking at America's heart, that there were still rich and daring ways of exploring the nation's arts and soul—and that there was a great adventure and transcendence to be found by doing so. Indeed, America *was* about to change dramatically, but the significance of that change wouldn't be fully understood or reckoned with for another twenty years. In 1945, the nation emerged victorious from the horrors of World War II and would enter a long era of new prosperity and opportunity; the new American life, many politicians and critics declared, was now the world standard of the *good* life. But all this came at unexpected psychic costs: The knowledge of the prospect of nuclear devas-tation changed all the possibilities of the future. Plus, for all the nation's vic-tories abroad, there were still many battles unwaged at home—including the delicate question of minority rights. Ginsberg, Kerouac, Burroughs and the rest of their crowd were beginning to be drawn to some decidedly different ideals and hopes. They heard the music of bebop alto saxophonist Charlie Parker and pianist Thelonious Monk, they tasted the visions of marijuana and benzedrine, they prowled the late-night reality of Times Square. A new world—a world still largely underground—was being born, and they had keen eyes and a keen need for it.

The friendship that developed among them was complex, sometimes tense, sometimes loving, but what held it together for so long was a shared desire to inquire—in matters of the mind, of aesthetics and of the senses. In time, this group became the nexus for a literary and artistic community known as the Beat Generation—the first countercultural movement that would have a major impact on America's popular culture. But all this was still years away, for before Beat became a movement or style, it was simply the way these men chose to live their lives, to examine their own experi-ences and their view of things both internal—like the spirit—and external, like the night and music and sex. Sometimes these men related to each other sexually (Ginsberg later told stories of him and Kerouac jacking each other off after a night of drinking; years later, Ginsberg also had an affair with Burroughs). Mainly, the group would spend nights consuming alcohol and mild drugs (though Burroughs soon turned to heroin), staying up until dawn, talking about the poetry, visions and madness of Blake, Whitman, Rimbaud, Dostoyevsky, Céline, Genet and Baudelaire; about how language might learn from jazz; about what was truly holy and what was truly allowed in one's life. Along the way, the group derived a certain ethos and aesthetic that they called the New Vision: It relied on stretching one's experiences, finding truths in distorted realities, in sexual pursuits, finding spirituality in the lower depths of life, and, most important, in making a commitment to an extemporized manner of living, writing, talking and risking. Somewhere during this time another friend of the group, a bisexual junkie prostitute, Herbert Huncke, referred to them as "beat," meaning *beat down, wasted.* Kerouac saw in the word another possibility: *beatific.* In time, the term went both ways: Beat came to stand for the idea that to discover one's true self and the self's liberation, you first had to descend into some of the most secret, used-up and bereft parts of your heart, soul, body and consciousness. Consequently, Beat became hardboiled and loving at the same time, erotic and spiritual. Later, Ginsberg would write Kerouac: "I can't believe that between us . . . we have the nucleus of a totally new historically important generation."

But the budding movement also could lead to costly excesses. In August 1944, Lucien Carr stabbed to death a friend of his, David Kammerer, after a night of drinking and arguing. Carr was a beautiful young man, and Kammerer had been obsessed with him, and relentlessly pursued and pushed Carr. After the stabbing, Carr went directly to Burroughs's apartment and admitted what he had done. Burroughs advised Carr to turn himself in to the police. Carr then went and awakened Kerouac and repeated his confession. Kerouac helped Carr get rid of the knife. In a few days, Carr did turn himself in to the authorities, and Burroughs and Kerouac were arrested as accessories after the fact. Ginsberg as well was castigated for being part of such a dangerous crowd. In truth, Ginsberg felt that in some way the group's "libertine" attitudes had helped make the tragedy possible—and that understanding made Allen much more careful, in years to come, about any excesses that might lead to violence. Eventually, Carr was sent to prison (he served two years), and for a short time, the old crowd dispersed. A few months later, Ginsberg was found in his Columbia dormitory in bed with Kerouac; for that infraction, and for having written offensive graffiti in the dust of a windowsill, Allen was suspended from the university for a year. Things went up and down for the group for a few years. People drifted in and out of

New York, and then in 1949, Ginsberg got involved in the life of Herbert Huncke, drug addict and thief. That association resulted later in Ginsberg's arrest for possessing stolen property and his being committed to the Columbia Presbyterian Psychiatric Institute—a turn of events that would in time have great effect on his poetry writing.

Prior to that, though, in late 1946, a new figure showed up in the Beat circle—and his involvement with the crowd had a seismic impact on both Ginsberg and Kerouac. Neal Cassady was a sharp-featured, handsome, fast-talking, brilliant natural prodigy. He didn't so much write (in fact, he wrote very little), but it seemed to others that he lived his life as if it were a novel. He drove across America relentlessly, loved to masturbate frequently each day and also fucked a good number of the beautiful women (and some of the men) he met along the way. He became involved with Carolyn Robinson, and the couple eventually settled down in Denver for a time. Kerouac was taken by Cassady's intense, fast-clip language—like a spoken version of bebop—and with Cassady's willingness to go as far as he could with the sensual experience and sensory rush of life. Ginsberg was impressed by the same traits, but he was also entranced by Cassady's beauty. One night, following a party, Ginsberg and Cassady found themselves sharing the same bed. Ginsberg was scared of his own desires, he later admitted, but Cassady put his arm around Allen and pulled him close, in a gentle motion. It was the first time in his life that Ginsberg felt truly loved, and it was also his first passionate sexual experience.

Ginsberg fell in love with Cassady, and his pursuit of that love—and the intensity of how wrong it all went—proved a key episode in leading to his development as an artist. Cassady, in the meantime, started to discourage the attraction. Ginsberg was undaunted and followed Neal to Colorado. Though he and Neal still had occasional sex, he knew it meant little to Cassady. He returned to New York, devastated, and later went on to fall into trouble with Huncke.

By the early 1950s, Ginsberg had gone through severe pain over his loss of Cassady, and had also gone through psychiatric treatment. He didn't know what he wanted to do with his life and was working in an advertising agency in Manhattan. One day, discussing this matter, Ginsberg's therapist asked him what he *really* wanted to do with his life. Ginsberg replied: quit his job and write poetry. The therapist said: "Well, why don't you?" Then, in 1954, the old crowd started to reassemble in the San Francisco Bay Area. Cassady and Robinson had moved to San Jose, and Kerouac settled in for a visit. In San Francisco itself, a poetry movement was beginning to burgeon, inspired in part by the success of local poets Kenneth Rexroth and Lawrence Ferlinghetti—the latter of whom had just opened the nation's first all-paperback bookstore, City Lights, and who had started to publish local poets. Allen headed for San Jose. He was thinking about poetry, but he was also still thinking about Neal. One afternoon, Carolyn walked into her home to see Neal and Allen in bed, Ginsberg sucking Cassady's penis. She ordered Ginsberg from their home, drove him to San Francisco, gave him twenty dollars and left him there.

It was the best thing that ever happened to Ginsberg. He soon fell in with the poet crowd in San Francisco's North Beach area, and he met a man that he would stay involved with for decades, Peter Orlovsky. All the hopes and visions that had formed years before in New York were starting to come to fruition for some of the old crowd—especially for Kerouac, who had finished two novels, and for Ginsberg, who was ready for something to break loose in his poetry. One afternoon in August 1955, Ginsberg sat down at a typewriter in his tiny apartment and attempted to write a poem for his own ear, but also a poem that would catch the free-flowing style that he had seen Kerouac hit upon in his own recent writing. Ginsberg wrote the whole day, thinking about many things: his lost loves, his found loves, the discarded people of America, the discarded promises of America, the fear that was just behind him, the fear that lay ahead for all.

Two months later, in October, Ginsberg—with help from Kenneth Rexroth—organized a poetry reading, to be given at a cooperative art gallery, the Six Gallery, to showcase a handful of the scene's poets. Six poets read that evening—including Gary Snyder, Michael McClure and Philip Lamantia—to a crowd of maybe one hundred to two hundred people, with Kerouac sitting on the gallery's floor, drinking and tapping out rhythms on a wine jug, urging "Go! Go!" to the cadences of the poets' words. Ginsberg was the last to read, and as he began *Howl*—the poem he had written in one sitting two months earlier—the crowd was transfixed from its first lines, about visionary outcasts ravaged by their own revelations: the same people who were now hearing the poem. Ginsberg went on to describe the fearsome evil that he saw America becoming—"Moloch whose blood is running money! Moloch whose fingers are ten armies!"— and when he finished, the crowd exploded in applause. "All of a sudden," Rexroth later said, "Ginsberg read this thing that he had been keeping to himself all this while, and it just blew things up completely. Things would never be quite the same again."

Howl was one of the most incandescent events in post–World War II literary history or popular culture, and its arrival would later insure the
Beats their place on the map of modern times. Also, because *Howl* was a
poem that had such force when read aloud by Ginsberg, it marked a return
of poetry to the art of vocalization. But most important, *Howl* was the first
major American work of the era that spoke for the outcasts, for the mad
and the lost, and about what would soon happen in the nation's soul. In the
context of those times, in the midst of a frightened new patriotism that was
being defined by fears of socialism and communism and a desperate need
to believe in the assurance of the family structure and traditional mores,
Howl battered at the heart of the American ideal of civilization. It was a
heroic work, on many levels. America was hardly prepared to admit that
homosexuality might be anything other than a form of madness; for a
poet—for anybody—to declare pride or pleasure to be queer was to run a
monumental risk. To talk about—to cherish those who "let themselves be
fucked in the ass by saintly motorcyclists, and screamed with joy"—was no
small matter. In effect, it meant aligning oneself with madness, with inex-
pressible values. To find grace and worthy companionship and celebration
in the company of junkies, prostitutes and black jazz revolutionaries only
pushed the ante more. Something opened up in America's culture and in its
future the day that Ginsberg gave utterance to these thoughts with *Howl*.
The following year, working from quite different quarters, Elvis Presley in
his own way helped push the gates open as well. "We liked Elvis," poet Gregory Corso later said of the night he and Kerouac watched Presley on *The
Ed Sullivan Show*. "We identified with the sexual wiggling of his body."

Howl and Presley. Nothing would ever be the same after that. America's
libido, America's likelihood, had been ripped wide open.

This isn't to say that *Howl* was immediately or widely read or praised.
Quite the contrary: The reaction of some people was that *Howl* should
never be widely read. In 1957, Lawrence Ferlinghetti (who published the
first editions of *Howl*) and a City Lights bookstore employee were arrested
for knowingly selling obscenity and put on trial. The prosecutor was a Bay
Area district attorney, Ralph McIntosh, bent on closing down porn shops
and prohibiting the sale of magazines with nudity. The ACLU, Grove Press,
Evergreen Review and poet Kenneth Patchen, among others, offered their
support to Ferlinghetti, Ginsberg and *Howl*. Among those testifying on
behalf of the poem's serious merits were Rexroth and author Walter Van
Tilburg Clark. In his final argument, McIntosh asked Judge Clayton W.

Horn: "Your Honor, how far are we going to license the use of filthy, vulgar, obscene, and disgusting language? How far can we go?"

Horn ruled that *Howl* was not lacking in social relevance, and therefore could not be ruled obscene. In delivering his decision, Horn also offered what may be the single best succinct review that *Howl* received: "The first part of *Howl* presents a picture of a nightmare world, the second part is an indictment of those elements in modern society destructive of the best qualities of human nature; such elements are predominantly identified as materialism, conformity, and mechanization leading toward war. The third part presents a picture of an individual who is a specific representation of what the author conceives as a general condition. . . . 'Footnote to *Howl*' seems to be a declamation that everything in the world is holy, including parts of the body by name. It ends in a plea for holy living."

Though Ginsberg was vindicated and suddenly famous, he was determined not to arrive as the Beats' sole writer-hero. Over the years, he helped Jack Kerouac in his long quest to publish *On the Road*—a book about Kerouac's adventures with Neal Cassady (who was called Dean Moriarty in the published text)—which had been turned down by numerous major publishers since 1951. The book was finally published by Viking, in 1957, as a result of Ginsberg's efforts, and went on to both good commercial and critical reception, and is now recognized as a milestone novel in modern literature. Ginsberg also championed the cause of William S. Burroughs—a much tougher sell, because Burroughs was a drug user who wrote radical prose (such as *Junky*), and because he had killed his wife in a shooting accident in Mexico in 1951. Ginsberg understood that his old friend felt a tremendous guilt, and Ginsberg also believed Burroughs might never redeem himself unless he could concentrate his soul and mind on his writing. Ginsberg later helped Burroughs assemble the final draft of *Naked Lunch*, and worked tirelessly until the book was published in the United States. (Which resulted in *Naked Lunch*'s own obscenity trial and another ruling that the book could not be held to be called obscene.)

The Beats were—at least for a brief time—a force in American arts and letters, but there remained many who were incensed by their words and beliefs. In 1960 FBI director J. Edgar Hoover stood before the Republican National Convention and declared that "Beatniks" were among America's major menaces. In addition, Norman Podhoretz—an old classmate of Ginsberg's at Columbia and by 1958 the editor of *Commentary* magazine—asserted that the Beats were an affront to the nation's central ideals. By the end of the decade, the Beats had been sidelined, declared a silly aberration by moralist critics on both the right and left. But despite all the resistance and disdain, Ginsberg continued to grow and thrive as a poet—and to remain undaunted. At the conclusion of one of his most defiant works, "America," he wrote: "America I'm putting my queer shoulder to the wheel."

Then, in 1959, after a night of taking benzedrine, listening to the rhythm & blues of Ray Charles, and walking New York's streets, Ginsberg sat down to write "Kaddish." It was his tribute to his mother Naomi, whose mental pain had grown so horrifying that, in the late 1950s, Ginsberg signed papers allowing doctors to perform a lobotomy on her. Ginsberg never truly got over the guilt of that decision, and he would never enjoy the union and relationship with his mother that he'd longed for his entire life. In 1956 Allen sent Naomi a published copy of *Howl*. Naomi died shortly thereafter. A few days after learning of her death, he received her last letter: "I received your poetry," she wrote, "I'd like to send it to Louis for criticism. . . . As for myself, I still have the wire on my head. The doctors know about it. They are cutting the flesh and bone. . . . I do wish you were back east so I could see you. . . . I wish I were out of here and home at the same time you were young; then I would be young."

In "Kaddish," Ginsberg remembered everything about his mother— tender things, scary things, the amazing perceptions that sometimes blazed through her madness—and with enormous love and compassion, he finally found her place in his heart (and recognized his in hers) and let her go to her death. It was most likely Ginsberg's finest moment as a poet, and it is impossible to hear any of his readings of that work and not be moved by how profoundly "Kaddish" measures just how much that people, families and nations can lose as their hopes and fates unwind.

For the next three decades, Allen Ginsberg would remain an important artist and active force. Indeed, more than any other figure from the Beat era, he made the transition from the styles and concerns of the 1950s to those of the decades that followed. Jack Kerouac died in 1969, after living an embittered and alcoholic final few years at his mother's home in Massachusetts. (His mother hated Ginsberg and came between the two men's friendship whenever possible.) Neal Cassady went on to become a popular figure in San Francisco's mid- and late-1960s Haight-Ashbury scene; he became the driver for Ken Kesey and the Merry Pranksters' legendary cross-country bus trek, and he also became a driver and companion to the Grateful Dead. But Cassady pushed his spirited self a bit hard. One day in 1968, after leaving a wedding in a small Mexican town, Cassady collapsed while walking alongside some railroad tracks. He died the next day, just short of his forty-second birthday.

Ginsberg not only survived, but kept pace with the spirit and needs of the times, with the permutations of youth culture; also, he kept faith with the humane and impassioned ideals that had made *Howl* so powerful in the first place. In 1965 he became friendly with the Beatles and Bob Dylan. Ginsberg's and the Beats' work already had meaning and effect for these artists. Dylan recalled that after reading Kerouac and Ginsberg, he realized that there were people like himself somewhere in the land—and indeed, when he made his startling transition to the electric, free-association style of music found in *Highway 61 Revisited* and *Blonde on Blonde* (and again later with *Blood on the Tracks*), Dylan was taking the language, cadences and imagery of the Beats and applying it to a new form. The impact of this melding on 1960s music—like the effect of Ginsberg's *Howl* on the 1950s— was colossal. (In fact, one of the early proposed cover photos for *Blonde on Blonde* showed Dylan standing with Ginsberg and poet-playwright Michael McClure.) In addition, John Lennon had read the Beats in his years as an art student in Liverpool and changed his spelling of the group's name, Bee- tles, to Beatles, in part as tribute to the spirit of that inspired artistry. Dylan and the Beatles changed not just a specific art form—that is, rock & roll—but also transformed the perceptions and aspirations of youth and popular culture at large. Without the earlier work of Ginsberg and Kerouac, it is possible that these 1960s artists might not have hit upon quite the same path of creativity—or at least might not have been able to work in the same atmosphere of permission and invention.

Ginsberg also became increasingly involved and influential in the polit- ical concerns of the 1960s and thereafter—though he did so in a way that made plain his own conviction in a politics of nonviolence and joy, rather than of destruction and hatred. In some ways, in fact, the 1960s culture of the hippies and radicals amounted to the realization of what the Beats began to envision and prophesy in the late 1940s (interestingly, "hippie" was a term first coined by the Beats, meaning "half-hip," and the phrase "flower power" was first verbalized by Allen Ginsberg). In the summer of 1968, Ginsberg helped organize Chicago's Festival of Life (along with the Yippies, Abbie Hoffman, Jerry Rubin, Tom Hayden and members of the Black Pan- thers), in protest against the Democratic Party's sponsorship of the Vietnam War, and as a rebuke to Hubert Humphrey's capitulation to the party's hawkish elements. But when the events of those few days turned suddenly brutal and bloody—with policemen clubbing young people, old people, anything in their path, and demonstrators began tossing bricks at, and taunting, the already enraged cops—Ginsberg turned sickened and horrified. On one occasion, as police raged though a crowd bashing protesters, a policeman came upon Ginsberg, seated in the lotus position, softy chanting. The policeman raised his club to crash it down on Ginsberg's head. The poet looked up at the officer, smiled and said: "Go in peace, brother." The cop lowered his club. "Fucking hippie," he declared, then moved on. In 1970, when several of the key Chicago activists—known as the Chicago Seven, including Tom Hayden, Abbie Hoffman, Jerry Rubin and Bobby Seale—were brought up on federal charges of conspiring to riot, defense attorney William Kunstler called Ginsberg to the witness stand. At Kunstler's request, Ginsberg recited parts of *Howl*. When he reached the poem's climax— "Moloch the vast stone of war! Moloch the stunned governments!"—he turned in his chair and pointed at the judge who had been so hostile to the defendants, Julius Hoffman (ironically, the same judge who years earlier declared William Burroughs's *Naked Lunch* not obscene).

In addition, Ginsberg became a key player in the 1960s' argument over psychedelic drugs, such as LSD. He had, of course, taken several drugs in his days with the Beats, and already had some psychedelic experience. But in the early 1960s, Ginsberg heard about a Harvard professor, Dr. Timothy Leary, who was conducting authorized research at the university and sharing the drug psilocybin with his project's volunteers. Ginsberg contacted Leary and arranged for a visit to experiment with the drug. Leary and Ginsberg struck up an immediate friendship and had considerable influence on each other's thinking. Ginsberg believed strongly (in contrast to most of Leary's cohorts) that it was a good idea to move psychedelics from the domain of a small elitist group and share them with artists, writers, poets and musicians—and as a result, hallucinogenic drugs and their visions made inroads into the arts, and later helped transmute the aesthetics and ideals of late-twentieth-century music, literature and painting, film and video. Ginsberg also convinced Leary that psychedelics could be a way of enabling people to examine and transform their own minds, and that it would be the young who would prove most receptive to such possibilities.

Ginsberg later forswore psychedelics, but his friendship with Leary continued off and on for more than thirty-five years. During the last few weeks of Leary's life, in the spring of 1996, the two men spoke often. Leary knew that Ginsberg had planned a trip to Los Angeles, in July, to attend an art show featuring Burroughs's work. Though Leary's health was daily diminishing as his body succumbed to prostate cancer, he hoped to live until Ginsberg's visit and made the date the last mark on his calendar. Leary would die without seeing his friend one last time. But in the hours preceding his death, Ginsberg's Buddhist teacher, Gelek Rinpoche, managed to reach Leary, uttering a final prayer for his passage into death.

Ginsberg stayed active in politics, arts and popular and renegade culture for the remainder of his life. In the mid-1970s, he toured with Bob Dylan and his Rolling Thunder Revue, singing and reading poetry. A few years later, he released his own sets of songs and collaborations with such artists as Dylan and the Clash—and it proved as exhilarating as his best poetry had a generation earlier. Throughout the 1970s, 1980s and 1990s, Ginsberg befriended and encouraged many other poets, punks and rap artists.

Of course, as time went along, the role of the renegade has grown more assimilated to some degree in mainstream culture. What was shocking in the 1950s was less shocking in the 1970s; what was disruptive in the 1970s was commonplace and profitable by the 1990s. Ginsberg understood this inevitable progression of how radical works and impulses are first resisted, then gradually diffused, and in his own way he had fun with that fact and mocked it a bit. He took to wearing suits and ties as he grew older—in part, it gave his pronouncements more authority, more respectability for some critics, but the other thing was: Ginsberg looked *great* in suits and ties. But for all his venerability and respectability, there was a part of Ginsberg that would never be domesticated, much less silenced. In 1979 the National Arts Club awarded him a gold medal for literary merit. At the awards dinner, according to Burroughs's biographer Ted Morgan, Ginsberg bemusedly read a poem called "Cocksucker Blues," to the genuine consternation of his audience. He also remained a relentless supporter of author Burroughs. In the late 1970s, after his own 1973 induction into the rarefied ranks of the American Academy and Institute of Arts and Letters, Ginsberg began a campaign to have Burroughs inducted as well. Ginsberg met with a great deal of refusal—Burroughs was *not* a writer that several of the other fine authors wanted in their company—but the poet persisted. It took six years, but Ginsberg won Burroughs's entry into the Institute, in 1983. Also, Ginsberg remained a fierce advocate of free speech. In his later years he even took up a defense of NAMBLA, an organization dedicated to lowering the age of consensual sex between men and boys. Ginsberg's involvement with the outfit outraged many of his longstanding admirers, but Ginsberg would not be cowed. "It's a free speech issue," he said repeatedly, pointing out that to stifle the ability to discuss such a matter in a free society was perhaps its own kind of outrage. Also, apparently, he stayed as sexually active as he could. In "Death & Fame" in *The New Yorker*, Ginsberg boasted about the many men he had seduced throughout his lifetime, and he detailed what it was he liked about his sexual intimacy with these partners. But for all that Ginsberg did or attempted to do, to this day *Howl* still cannot be played over America's airwaves during the day, due to the efforts of the Federal Communications Commission.

And so he is gone. In the days following Ginsberg's death I saw and heard countless tributes to his grace, power, skills and generosity—but I also saw and heard just as many disparaging remarks: what a shoddy writer he was; what a failure the legacy of his Beat Generation and the 1960s generation turned out to be; what an old lecher the guy was. Perhaps all this vitriol isn't such a bad thing. Maybe it's another tribute of sorts: Allen Ginsberg never lost his ability to rub certain nerves the wrong way when it came to matters about propriety, aesthetics, morality and politics.

But I also know this: Allen Ginsberg *won*—against the formidable odds of his own madness-scarred childhood, against all his soul-crippling doubts of self, against all those stern, bristling, authoritarian forces that looked at this man and saw only a bearded radical faggot that they could not abide. Ginsberg won in a very simple yet irrefutable way: He raised his voice. He looked at the horror that was crawling out from the American subconscious of the 1950s—the same horror that would later allow the nation to sacrifice so many of its children in the 1960s to a vile and pointless military action— and he called that demon by its name: "Moloch!" He looked at the crazed and the despairing, those people hurting for a fix, for a fuck of love, for the obliteration of intoxicated visions, and he saw in them something to adore and kiss, something to be treasured and learned from. And Ginsberg looked at himself, and for all his hard-earned pride, lust, vanity and audacity, he would not shut up even in the face of his own vulnerability.

In an evening, long ago—an evening caught between two Americas, the America of the past and the America that was to follow, an afternoon where America was truly found, realized and celebrated—a nervous, scared young homosexual Jewish man stood before a crowd, and he raised his voice. He said things that nobody had ever said before in quite the same terms to a crowd in this nation—filthy things, beautiful things—and when he was finished, he had become a braver man. He had, in fact, in that hour, transformed himself into the most eventful American poet of the century. When Lawrence Ferlinghetti—who was in the room that night and who brought *Howl* to the world—heard that his old friend was dying, he wrote the following: "A great poet is dying / But his voice won't die / His voice is on the land."

Ginsberg's voice will never leave us. Its truths and purposes will echo across our future as a clarion call of courage for the misfits, the fucked up, the fucking and the dying. And we—all of us, whether we understand it or not—are better for it.

Good-bye, Allen Ginsberg. Thank you for illuminating our history—thank you for the gentle yet fierce, slow-burning flame you ignited on that evening so long ago. Thank you for what you brought to our times, our nerve and our lives.

Go in peace, brother. Your graceful, heavy, loving heart has earned it.

TIMOTHY LEARY:
THE DEATH OF THE
MOST DANGEROUS MAN

It is a late afternoon toward the end of spring 1996. I am seated with several other people on the floor of a bedroom in a ranch house, high up in the hills of Benedict Canyon. Through the plate glass doors on one side of the room, you can see the day's light starting to fade, and a breeze soughs through the trees and bushes in the house's backyard. On the bed before us lies a gaunt, aged man, covered in a red blanket, sleeping a restive sleep.

We have all gathered into this room for the same purpose: We are here to watch this man as he takes sleep's journey to death. It is not the sort of thing that many of us have done before.

The man who is dying is Dr. Timothy Leary—one of the most controversial and influential psychologists of the last forty years, and a guiding iconic figure of the countercultural tumult of the 1960s and 1970s. It was Leary who, as a young promising clinical researcher, helped develop the theory of transactional analysis—effectively changing the doctor-patient relationship in modern psychology—and it was Leary, who only a few years later, conducted a provocative series of psychedelic experiments at Harvard University that helped pave the way for an era of cultural and psychosocial upheaval.

But nothing Leary had done in the years since stirred as much reaction as how he had been preparing for his death. A year and a half earlier, Leary learned that he had fatal prostate cancer—and he promptly did the one thing almost nobody does in such a situation: He celebrated the news. Leary announced to family, friends and media that he intended to explore the consciousness of dying the same way he once explored the alternative realities afforded by drugs: with daring and with humor. As time went along, though, Leary's proclamations became more audacious. At one point he suggested that when the efforts of maintaining his life no longer seemed worth it, he might take one last psychedelic, drink a suicide cocktail, and have the whole affair broadcast on his website. Then, following his death, a crew of cryonics technicians would come in and freeze his body, later removing and preserving his brain. Needless to say, these sorts of hints have attracted a fair amount of media interest and have also stirred disdain and criticism from various quarters—even from a few right-to-death advocates who felt Leary wasn't taking dying somberly enough. "They'd have me suffer in silence," he once told me, "so I can save them the pain."

But when all was said and done, Leary was *not* dying outrageously. Rather, he was dying quietly and bravely, surrounded by people he loves and who love him.

Even as he is dying, though, he is still Timothy Leary, and he still has something to say.

Around 6:30 in the evening he wakes, blinks, wincing momentarily in pain. He looks around him, seeing familiar people, including his stepson, Zachary Leary, and his former wife, Rosemary, who once helped him escape a California State prison and flee the United States. He winks at Rosemary, then—looking at the rest of us—says: "Why?"

He smiles, tilts his head, then says: "Why *not*?"

A couple of people in the room laugh and repeat the phrase back to him.

It goes on like that for a few minutes, Leary saying "Why not?" over and over, in different inflections, sometimes funny, sometimes sad. At one point he says, "*Esperando*"—Spanish for "waiting." A few moments later, after another litany of "*Why nots*," he will say, "Where's the proof?" And still later "Go now."

He looks back to Rosemary and mouths: "I love you," and she mouths the same back to him. Finally, barely above a whisper, he says "Why?" twice more, then drifts back into his heavy sleep.

I first met Timothy Leary only a few weeks before his death. I approached him nervously.

Like many of the people I knew who came of age in the 1960s, I had been influenced by Leary's spirit and by his teachings. As a result, I had taken psychedelics—mainly mescaline and LSD—with the idea that I might see visions that would change my life, and once or twice, I guess that's what happened. I remember one night I went looking for God (a required acid activity at some point or another) and came back realizing that God was indeed dead—or that at least if God was a divine power that might judge and condemn us for our frailties and desires and madnesses, then he was dead in my own heart and conscience. Exit God. Hasn't been seen since.

Another time, I took acid not long after a brother of mine had died following surgery (I know: not such a good idea), and I plunged into what was called (appropriately, I decided) a bad trip. That night I saw the death of my lineage—the deaths of my ancestors, the deaths of my parents and brothers, the deaths of the children I had not yet had (and still have not had), and, of course, the death of myself. I sat in a dark-red oversize chair that night and watched death move before me and in and out of my being, and I gripped tight to the arms of that chair until the morning came. It was the only sunrise I have ever been happy to see. I was not the same for days after. Maybe I was not ever the same again.

That was 1971, and it was the last time I took acid. It wasn't that I didn't like the psychedelic experience—I'd loved it, and had much wonderful fun with it over the years. It's just that I didn't fancy the idea of running into death any more than necessary.

And so when I went to see Leary the first time, I wasn't sure what I was getting into. I was fascinated by his history and had things I wanted to ask him, but there was this problem: The man was dying, and that meant getting close to death.

You could say I was unprepared for what I found. Death had already been welcomed into Timothy Leary's house, and it was being teased relentlessly, even joyfully. The place, in fact, was full of life. About a dozen staff members and friends—most in their twenties—were in and out of the house constantly. Some of them—a crew called Retina Logic—were in the garage, busy working on Leary's website. It was a cause that was close to Leary's heart: He planned to have all his writings and various memoirs stored on it in perpetuity, and he was thinking of maybe even dying there, on an internet telecast. Other house regulars, such as Trudy Truelove and Vicki Marshall, were busy making Leary's schedule for him, slating him for a steady stream of interviews, visits with friends, dinner parties and rock & roll concerts. Clearly, death did not hold the upper hand in this house—at least not yet.

As I waited for Leary in his front room—full of brightly colored art pieces—I noticed a contraption in the corner alongside his large glass patio doors. It was the cryonics coffin he was supposed to be placed in at the hour of his death. His blood would later be drained and replaced with antifreeze compounds, so that his brain might be preserved. It might have been a creepy thing to stumble across, except it was actually sort of comical. Somebody had draped it with Christmas lights and plastic toys, and a Yoda mask had been placed on the coffin's head pillow.

Leary entered the room seated in his motorized wheelchair. He was pretty adept with the thing, able to make sharp, quick turns and wiggle his way in and out of tight spots, though sometimes he would collide head-on with his big, beautiful golden retriever, Bo, who was blind as a bat. Bo wandered Leary's house and yard constantly, bumping into tables, doors, people, trees—a sweet, majestic Zen-style guard dog.

I learned quickly that it was almost impossible to conduct anything resembling a linear interview with Leary. It had nothing to do with his temperament. I found him always cheerful, funny and eager to talk. But he was easily distracted. He'd break off suddenly to focus on whatever was happening around him or to gaze appreciatively at the short skirts that one or two of the women around him wore. "I'm senile," he told me on that first visit, "and I make it work for me." Some of the distraction, I suspect, was the byproduct of the steady stream of painkillers and euphorics that he availed himself of—including morphine patches, marijuana biscuits, Dilaudid tablets, glasses of wine and balloons of nitrous oxide, his seeming favorite. I was glad he had the stuff. In those moments when I saw him doubled over, cringing in pain, I could only imagine how much worse it might have been without his calmatives.

Other days, I found him completely lucid and focused. One afternoon we were talking about, well, death. I had been telling him about my last acid trip. He winked at me and laughed. "But of course," he said. "Everybody says it's a dying, *death* experience. If you don't die, you didn't get your money's worth from your dealer. Dying was built right into it. Why do you think we were using *The Tibetan Book of the Dead* as our guiding text?"

I understood then that I was talking with a man who had already died many times over his years. It's like he said: that was one of acid's core truths. It could take you into all kinds of deaths—deaths of ego, deaths of misconceptions—and you could then walk back alive. More or less.

I asked him what he thought real death would be like.

He reached over to his nitrous tank, filled a large black balloon and sat quietly for a few moments. "I don't think of it," he said, looking a little surprised at his own answer. "I mean, yes, every now and then, I go: *'Shit!'* You know, every now and then. The other night I was looking around and I thought, 'Good God, my friends here—their lives have been changed by this. The *enormity* of it.' But I just take it as the natural thing to do."

He took a sip from his balloon, and seemed to be looking off into his own thoughts. "It's true that I've been looking forward to it for a long time," he said. "The two minutes between body death and brain death, the two to thirteen minutes there while your brain is still alive—*that's* the territory. That's the unexplored area that fascinates me. So I'm kind of looking forward to that."

Leary stopped talking for a moment, clenching at his stomach, his face crumpled in pain. After several seconds, he gained his breath and returned to his balloon.

"The worst that can happen," he said, his voice husky from the nitrous, "is that nothing happens, and at least that's, um, interesting. I'll just go, 'Oh, shit! Back to the Tibetan scorecard!' But yes, it's an experiment that I've been looking forward to for a long, long time. After all, it's the ultimate mystery."

Timothy Leary was fond of pointing out that the probable date of his conception was January 17, 1920: the day after the start of Prohibition, the official beginning of America's troubled attempts to regulate intoxicants and mind-altering substances in the twentieth century. Born in Springfield, Massachusetts, on October 22, 1920, Leary was the only child of his Irish American parents. His father, Timothy—also known as Tote—had been an officer at West Point and later became a fairly successful dentist who spent most of his earnings on alcohol. In 1934, when Timothy was thirteen, Tote got severely drunk one night and abandoned his family. Timothy would not see him again for twenty-three years. In the most recent (and best) of his autobiographies, *Flashbacks* (1983), Leary wrote: "I have always felt warmth and respect for this distant male-man who special-delivered me. During the thirteen years we lived together he never stunted me with expectations." But his father also served as a "model of the loner," and for all his charming and gregarious ways, Leary would have trouble in his life maintaining intimate relations with family members—a problem that would not disappear until his last several years.

By contrast, Leary's mother, Abigail, was a beautiful but dour woman who was often disappointed by what she saw as her son's laxity and recklessness. In her own way, though, she also served as a model. In *Flashbacks*, Leary wrote: "I determined to seek women who were exactly the opposite to Abigail in temperament. Since then, I have always sought the wildest, funniest, most high-fashion, big-city girl in town."

For years, Leary seemed prone to the wayward life that his mother feared so much. He studied at Holy Cross College, at West Point and at the

University of Alabama, and had serious problems at each establishment (in fact, he was more or less driven out of West Point for his role in a drunken spree), though he finally received a bachelor's degree during his army service in World War II. Then his life took a turn. In 1944, while working as a clinical psychologist in Butler, Pennsylvania., Leary fell in love with and married a woman named Marianne. After the war, the couple moved to California's Bay Area, and had two children, Susan and Jack. It was at this point that Timothy's career began to show some promise. In 1950 he earned a doctorate in psychology from the University of California at Berkeley, and during the next several years, along with a fellow psychologist, Frank Barron, Leary conducted some research that yielded a remarkable discovery. By testing a wide range of subjects over an extensive period, they learned that one-third of the patients who received psychotherapy got better, one-third got worse and one-third stayed the same. In essence, Leary and Barron proved that psychotherapy—at least in its conventional applications—couldn't really be proven to work. Leary wanted to discover what *would* work, what methods might provide people with a genuine healing moment or growth experience. He began exploring the idea of group therapy as a possible viable solution, and he also started developing a theory of existential-transactional analysis that was later popularized in psychiatrist Eric Berne's *Games People Play*.

By the mid-1950s Leary was teaching at Berkeley and had been appointed director of Psychological Research at the Kaiser Foundation in Oakland, California. He had also produced a book, *The Interpersonal Diagnosis of Personality*, which would enjoy wide-ranging praise and influence. But behind all the outward success, Leary's life was headed for a cataclysm. After the birth of Susan, in 1947, Timothy's wife, Marianne, went through a bad bout of postpartum depression and became increasingly withdrawn from the world and, according to Timothy, from her husband and family. As time went along, both Marianne and Timothy began drinking heavily and fighting regularly. The source of their arguments was often the same: For two years, Leary had been conducting an affair with a friend's wife at a rented apartment on Berkeley's Telegraph Avenue. The affair, combined with the drinking, the quarreling and Marianne's depression, became increasingly painful for her.

On a Saturday morning in October 1955—on Timothy Leary's thirty-fifth birthday—he awoke to find himself alone in bed. He stumbled around the house, groggy from a hangover, calling Marianne's name. A few minutes later he found her inside the family's car, in a closed garage, with the motor running and exhaust clouding around her. She was already cold to the touch. Leary called to his startled children, who were standing in the driveway, to run to the nearby firehouse for help, but it was too late. Marianne had withdrawn for the last time.

Leary's hair turned gray within a short time.

"He took a lot of the blame on himself," said Frank Barron. "After that, Tim was looking for things that would be more transformative, that would go deeper than therapy. He was looking, more or less, for answers."

By the end of the 1950s, Leary had quit his posts at Berkeley and the Kaiser Foundation, and moved with his two children to the southern coast of Spain. He was, by his own description, in a "black depression" and felt at a loss about both his past and his future. In January 1959, in Torremolinos, he later wrote, he went through his first thorough breakdown and breakthrough. One afternoon, he suddenly fell into a strange feverish illness. His face grew so swollen with water blisters that his eyelids were forced shut and encrusted with dried pus. Over the next few days, the disease got worse: His hands became paralyzed and he couldn't walk. One night, he sat awake for hours in the darkness of his hotel room, and after a while, he began to smell his own decay. In his book *High Priest*, he described it as his first death: "I slowly let every tie to my old life slip away. My career, my ambitions, my home. My identity. The guilts. The wants.

"With a sudden snap, all the ropes of my social life were gone. I was a thirty-eight-year-old male animal with two cubs. High, completely free."

The next morning, the illness had abated. Timothy Leary was about to be reborn.

In the spring of 1959, Leary was living with his children in Florence, Italy, when Barron paid a visit. Barron brought with him two bits of information. First, during a recent research trip to Mexico, he had located some of the rare "sacred mushrooms" that had been alleged to provide hallucinations and visions to ancient Aztec priests and the holy men of various Indian tribes in Latin American. Back at his home in Berkeley, Barron had eaten the mushrooms—and had a full-blown, William Blake–quality mystical experience. He thought that perhaps these mushrooms might be the elusive means to psychological metamorphosis that he and Leary had been seeking for years. Leary was put off by his friend's story, and, as he later wrote, "warned him against the possibility of losing his scientific credibility if he babbled this way among our colleagues."

Barron's other news was more mundane but of greater appeal to Leary:

The director of the Harvard Center for Personality Research, Professor David McClelland, was on sabbatical in Florence and would probably be willing to interview Leary for a teaching post. Leary visited McClelland the next day and explained his emerging theories of existential psychology. McClelland listened and read Leary's manuscript on the subject, then said: "What you're suggesting . . . is a drastic change in the role of the scientist, teacher, and therapist. Instead of processing patients by uniform and recognized standards, we should take an egalitarian or information-exchange approach. Is that it?" Leary said, yes, that's what he had in mind. McClelland hired him on the spot. "There's no question," he said, "that what you're advocating is going to be the future of American psychology. You're spelling out front-line tactics. You're just what we need to shake things up at Harvard."

Leary began his career at the Harvard Center for Personality Research in early 1960. That summer, he took his son on vacation to Cuernavaca, Mexico. For the first time in several years, life felt rewarding. Things were good at Harvard. Leary was enjoying his research and teachings, and was also enjoying the esteem of his colleagues. One day an anthropologist friend stopped by the villa where Leary was staying. The friend, like Barron, had been seeking the region's legendary sacred mushrooms and asked if he would be willing to try some. Leary was reminded of Barron's statement— that perhaps mushrooms could be the key to the sort of psychological transformation they had been searching for—and his curiosity got the better of him. A week later, he found himself staring into a bowl of ugly, foul-smelling black mushrooms. Reluctantly, he chewed on one, washed back its terrible taste with some beer and waited for the much-touted visions to come. They came, hard and beautiful—and in the next few hours, Leary's life changed powerfully and irrevocably. "I gave way to delight, as mystics have for centuries . . . ," he wrote in *Flashbacks*. "Mystics come back raving about higher levels of perception where one sees realities a hundred times more beautiful and meaningful than the reassuringly familiar scripts of normal life. . . . We discover abruptly that . . . everything we accept as reality is just social fabrication."

Leary decided that mushrooms could be the tool to reprogram the brain. If used under the right kind of supervision, he thought, they could free an individual from painful self-conceptions and stultifying social archetypes, and might prove the means to the transformation of human personality and behavior, for as far as individuals were willing to go. It took some work, but Leary persuaded Harvard to allow him to order a supply of psilocybin—the synthesized equivalent of the active ingredient in the magic mushrooms—from the Swiss firm Sandoz Pharmaceuticals. Leary also joined forces with Barron (who had been invited by McClelland to spend a year teaching at Harvard). Leary and Barron created what would become known as the Harvard Drug Research Program. In that strange and unlikely moment in educational and psychological history, the seeds of a movement were born that would transfigure not just Leary's life but the social dynamics of modern America for years and years to come.

Leary, of course, was not the first psychologist or modern philosopher to explore the potential effect of psychedelics, which is the term that had been given to thought-altering hallucinogenic drugs. The respected British author Aldous Huxley had already written two volumes on the subject, *The Doors of Perception* and *Heaven and Hell*, and other philosophers and psychiatrists, including Gerald Heard, Sidney Cohen and Oscar Janiger (the latter's Los Angeles practice included such renowned patients as Cary Grant and Anaïs Nin), had been working toward various modes of psychedelic therapy and had achieved some notable results in treating conditions such as neurosis and alcoholism. More notoriously, the CIA and the U.S. Army Chemical Corps had conducted covert research using powerful hallucinogens with the aim of incapacitating foreign and domestic enemies or driving them insane.

But three factors set Leary's work apart. One was the incorporation of his transactional analysis theories into the overall experimental model: Therapists would not administer drugs to patients and then sit by and note their reactions but would, in fact, engage in the drug state along with the subjects. Another element was Leary's implementation of an environmental condition that became known as "set and setting": If you prepared the drug taker with the proper mind-set and provided reassuring surroundings, then you increased the likelihood that the person might achieve a significant opportunity for a healthy psychological reorganization. But the final component that set Leary apart from all other psychedelic researchers was simply Leary himself—his intense charisma, confidence, passion, anger and indomitability. He was a man set ablaze by his calling, and though that fieriness would sometimes lead him into a kind of living purgatory, it also emblazoned him as a real force in modern history.

For the first two years, things went well with the Harvard experiments. Along with Barron and other researchers, Leary administered varying doses of psilocybin to several dozen subjects, including graduate students. He also gave the drug to prisoners and divinity students, with noteworthy results: The prisoners' recidivism rate was cut dramatically, and the divinity students, for the first time in their lives, had what they described as true spiritual experiences. In addition, Leary made two important contacts outside the university: Aldous Huxley and poet Allen Ginsberg. With Huxley, Leary probed into the metaphysical fine points of the psilocybin mind state and debated whether psychedelics should remain the property of a small, select group of poets, artists, philosophers and doctors, who would take the insights they learned from the drug and use them for the benefit of humanity and psychology. With Ginsberg, though, Leary settled the debate. Like Huxley, Ginsberg was convinced that it was indeed a keen idea to share the drug with writers and artists—and in fact arranged for Leary to do so with Robert Lowell, William Burroughs, Thelonious Monk and Jack Kerouac, among others. But Ginsberg also believed in what became known as "the egalitarian ideal": If psychedelics had any real hope of enriching humankind, then they should be shared with more than just an aristocracy of intellectuals and aesthetes. Leary came to agree—fervently. Psychedelics, he believed, could be a way of empowering people to inquire into and transmute their own minds, and he suspected that probably the people who were most open to such an experience, who could benefit from it the most, were the young.

In the fall of 1961, Frank Barron returned to his job at Berkeley, and Leary found a new chief ally: a good-humored and ambitious assistant professor named Richard Alpert who had a penchant for fine clothes and high living. From the beginning, Alpert and Leary shared a special bond. "I had never met a mind like Tim's," says Alpert. "He was like a breath of fresh air because he was raising questions from philosophical points of view. I was absolutely charmed by that. And there was a way in which our kind of symbiosis worked—our chemistry of the Jewish and the Irish, or the responsible, grounded, solid person and the wild, creative spirit. I thought that I was at Harvard by shrewd politicking rather than by intellect, therefore I didn't expect anything creative to come out of me. And then I found that Timothy was freeing me from a whole set of values."

But for some others at Harvard, it seemed as though Timothy might be freeing up just a few too many values. Some professors found the whole thing too unsavory—the very idea of giving students drugs that apparently took them out of their rational minds, under the auspices of the university. Also, McClelland was growing uncomfortable with what were seen as the increasingly "religious" overtones of the enterprise. Leary, Alpert and others began touting once obscure Eastern sacred texts, such as the Tibetan

Book of the Dead, the Bhagavad Gita and Zen Buddhist scripture. What was Leary doing, McClelland wanted to know, advancing the values of societies that had been backward for hundreds of years?

Leary's supervisor McClelland scheduled an open staff meeting in the spring of 1962 to debate the merits of continuing the drug project. The day before the event, McClelland called Alpert into his office. "'Dick, we can't save Timothy,'" Alpert recalls McClelland saying. "'He's too outrageous. But we can save you. So just shut up at tomorrow's meeting.'" Alpert gave McClelland's advice some thought. "Being a Harvard professor," he says, "gives you a lot of keys to the kingdom, to play the way you want to play. Society is honoring you with that role."

The meeting turned out to be more like a prosecution session than a discussion. Some of the professors tore into Leary with a vitriol rarely seen at Harvard meetings. They insisted that if he was to continue his project, he would have to surrender the drugs to the university's control and only administer them in the environment of a mental hospital. To Leary, it would mean retreating to the medical standard of the doctor as authority and the subject as lab rat—the same model that Leary had sworn to bring down. "Timothy was blown away by all the vehemence and vindictiveness," Alpert says. "He was, for once, speechless. At the end there was a silence in the room. And at that moment, I stood up and said, 'I would like to answer on behalf of our project.' I looked at Dave McClelland, and Dave just shrugged, and that was the beginning of the process that would result in our end at Harvard."

In 1963, in a move that made front-page news across the nation, Timothy Leary was "relieved" of his teaching duties and Richard Alpert was dismissed for having shared psilocybin with an undergraduate, though psychedelics were still legal to possess and use at the time. (At the time, Alpert and Leary were reported to be the only professors to be fired from the university in the century.) "I remember being at that press conference," says Alpert, "surrounded by people who saw me as a loser, but in my heart, I knew we'd won."

Leary also wasn't distressed at the idea that his Harvard career was finished. He had, in fact, found a new passion. In the spring of 1962, a British philosophy student named Michael Hollingshead paid a visit to Leary and had brought with him an ominous gift. Hollingshead is perhaps the most mysterious figure in Leary's entire story. Alpert describes him as "a scoundrel—manipulative and immoral." But it was Hollingshead who first brought a jar of powdered sugar laced with LSD—an intensely psychedelic solution whose psychoactive properties had been accidentally discovered in the 1940s by a Swiss scientist, Dr. Albert Hoffman—into Leary's home and taunted Tim by ridiculing psilocybin as "just pretty colors," compared to the extraordinary power of LSD. Leary resisted the bait at first, as he had with the magic mushrooms, but one weekend he finally caved in. "It took about a half hour to hit," he later wrote. "And it came suddenly and irresistibly. Tumbling and spinning, down soft fibrous avenues of light that were emitted from some central point. Merged with its pulsing ray I could look out and see the entire cosmic drama. Past and future. . . . My previous psychedelic sessions had opened up sensory awareness, pushed consciousness out to the membranes. . . . But LSD was something different. It was the most shattering experience of my life."

Hollingshead would come and go in Leary's life, sometimes valued, often reviled. But Hollingshead's gift, the LSD—that was a gift that stayed.

Despite their fall from Harvard, Leary and Alpert intended to continue their research into psychedelics, now focused primarily on the far more potent drug, LSD. In the fall of 1963, a friend and benefactor, Peggy Hitchcock, helped provide them with a sixty-four-room mansion that sat on a sprawling estate two hours up the Hudson River from Manhattan, a place called Millbrook. From 1963 to early 1967, Millbrook would serve as a philosophic-hedonistic retreat for the curious, the hip and the defiant. Jazz musicians lived there; poets, authors and painters visited; journalists scouted the halls; and actors and actresses flocked to the weekend parties. Some came for visions, some for the hope of an orgy, some to illuminate the voids in their souls. All of them left with an experience they never forgot.

This was a time of immense change in America's cultural and political terrain. It was, on one hand, an epoch of great dread and violence: The bloody civil rights battles, the assassination of President John F. Kennedy and the rising anger over the war in Vietnam made it plain that America had quickly become a place of high risks. At the same time, youth culture was beginning to create for itself a sense of identity and empowerment that was unprecedented. The new music coming from Bob Dylan, the Beatles, the Motown and Southern soul artists, and San Francisco bands like the Grateful Dead and Jefferson Airplane only deepened the idea that an emerging generation was trying to live by its own rules and integrity, and was feeling increasingly cut off from the conventions and privileges of the dominant mainstream culture. More and more, drugs were becoming a part of that sense of empowerment—a means of staking out a consciousness apart from that of the "straight world," a way of participating in private, forbidden experiences.

It was during this time of strange possibilities (and the fear of strange possibilities) that LSD began to become the subject of a frenzied social concern. Despite the best efforts of such qualified experts as Frank Barron and Oscar Janiger, LSD was seen as a major threat to the nation's young, and therefore to America's future. Newspaper and television reports were full of sensationalistic accounts of kids trying to fly off buildings or ending up in emergency rooms, howling at the horrors of their own newly found psychoses. The level of hysteria drove Leary nuts. "Booze casualties were epidemic," he wrote in *Flashbacks,* "so the jaded press paid no attention to the misadventures of one drunk. Their attitude was different with psychedelic drugs. Only one out of every thousand LSD users reported a negative experience, yet the press dug up a thousand lurid stories of bark-eating Princeton grads."

Nevertheless, for some in the psychiatric community, Leary had become part of the problem. By the nature of his flamboyance and his disdain for the medical model, they felt he had single-handedly given psychedelics a bad name and that he was endangering the chance for further valid research. "It was easy," says Frank Barron, "for Tim to say, 'There are people who are going to have psychoses under these circumstances; if they have that within them they should let it out.' These are brave words, but Tim and I had plush training in psychology. We had personal analysis. We were well prepared. But if you have an adolescent in the middle of an identity crisis and you give him LSD, he can be really shaken. And I think that's where some of the more serious casualties occurred."

Indeed, Leary became indelibly identified with what *Time* magazine termed "the LSD Epidemic," and he was under fire from several quarters. When he appeared before the 1966 Senate hearings on LSD, Senator Ted Kennedy held him up to sustained ridicule. It was then, Leary realized, that before much longer LSD would be declared illegal and its users would be criminalized. At the same time, things in his personal life were going through momentous change. In late 1964 he married Nena von Schlebrügge. By the time the couple returned from their honeymoon a few months later, both the marriage and Millbrook were in trouble. Leary felt that Alpert had let the place get out of hand. The two friends argued over various grievances—including Leary's apparent discomfort with Alpert's homosexuality—and Alpert ended up cast out from Millbrook and, for a time, from Leary's life. Alpert went on to change his name to Baba Ram

Dass and became one of America's most respected teachers of Eastern disciplines. In time, the rift between him and Leary healed, but they were never again the fast partners they'd once been.

Then in the summer of 1965, Leary became close to a woman named Rosemary Woodruff, whom he eventually married in late 1967. The romance with Rosemary would prove to be perhaps the most meaningful of Leary's life, but it would also prove to be the one most beset by difficulties. During the week following Christmas 1965, Tim and Rosemary shut down Millbrook for the season and set out, along with Leary's children, in a station wagon, bound for a Mexico vacation. The couple had thoughts of changing their lives: Rosemary had hopes that perhaps they would have a child of their own, and Timothy entertained notions of returning to his studies and writings. At the Mexican border, however, they were denied entrance, and as they attempted to reenter America near Laredo, they were ordered out of the car. They were searched and a matron found a silver box with marijuana in Susan Leary's possession; she was then eighteen. Leary didn't hesitate. "I'll take responsibility for the marijuana," he said. The consequences of that moment reverberated through Leary's life for years. He was arrested for violating the marijuana laws in one of the most conservative jurisdictions in the nation. When his lawyer advised him to repent before the judge, Leary said he didn't know what the word meant. Eventually, he was given a thirty-year sentence and a $30,000 fine—the longest sentence ever imposed for possession of marijuana. Susan got five years. In 1969 the U.S. Supreme Court overturned the conviction because Leary had been tried under antiquated tax-violation laws. The Laredo prosecutor simply retried Leary for illegal possession and sentenced him to ten years.

Timothy Leary quickly became a national symbol for both sides of the drug law dispute, and he did his best to rise to the occasion with wit and grace, but also with a certain recklessness. While free during his appeal of the Laredo conviction, he gave lectures and interviews around the country about drugs. He was invited as an honored guest to the Gathering of the Tribes festival, in San Francisco's Golden Gate Park, and he and Rosemary sang and clapped along at John Lennon and Yoko Ono's recording session for "Give Peace a Chance." He also recorded his own album of chants with Jimi Hendrix, Buddy Miles, Stephen Stills and John Sebastian as sidemen. It all made for heady days and high nights, but it also made Leary the most obvious target for the country's rising mood of anger about drugs. President Richard Nixon told the American people that Timothy Leary was "the most dangerous man alive," and the directive couldn't be more plain: Both Leary and his philosophies should be brought down.

And, more or less, that's what happened. Back in New York, a local assistant district attorney, G. Gordon Liddy, organized a raid on Millbrook. The charges were soon dismissed, but another raid followed—and those charges stuck. The raids had the desired effect of finishing Millbrook for good. Leary moved Rosemary and his family to Laguna Beach, California, but the day after Christmas 1968, he was arrested again for marijuana possession, this time along with Rosemary and his son, Jack. (Leary always claimed that the arresting officer had planted the joints.) At the trial in January 1970, Rosemary and Jack were given probation, but Timothy was sentenced to ten years. In an extraordinary move, the judge, declaring Leary a menace to society and angrily waving a recent *Playboy* article written by the ex-Harvard professor, ordered him to jail immediately, without an appeal bond.

Leary was forty-nine years old, and his future appeared certain. He was going to spend the rest of his life in jail for the possession of a small amount of marijuana that—even in the furor of the 1960s—rarely netted most offenders more than a six-month sentence.

Upon entering the California State Prison at Chino, Leary was administered an intelligence test to determine where he should be placed within the state's prison strata. The test happened to be based on psychological standards that Leary himself had largely authored during his groundbreaking work in the 1950s. He knew how to use it to his advantage. He marked all the answers that, in his own words, would make him seem "normal, nonimpulsive, docile, conforming." As a result he was transferred to California Men's Colony-West at San Luis Obispo, a minimum-security prison.

On the evening of September 12, 1970, following a carefully mapped plan that depended on exact timing, Leary methodically made his way from his cellblock along a complex maze of twists and turns into a prison yard that was regularly swept by a spotlight. Dodging the light, he crossed the yard to a tree, climbed it and then dropped down to a rooftop covering one of the prison's corridors. He crept along until he came to a cable that stretched to a telephone pole outside the walls of the jail. Wrapping his arms and legs around the cable, he began to shimmy its length until, only a third of the way across, he stopped, exhausted, gasping for breath, barely able to keep his grasp. A patrol car passed underneath him. "I wanted Errol Flynn and out came Harold Lloyd," he wrote in *Flashbacks.* "I felt very alone. . . . There was no fear—only a nagging embarrassment. Such an undignified way to die, nailed like a sloth on a branch!" Then, some hidden reserves of strength and desire kicked in, and Leary grappled his way to the outside pole and descended to freedom.

A few weeks later, Timothy and Rosemary surfaced in Algiers, Algeria, where they had been offered asylum and protection by Eldridge Cleaver and other members of the Black Panther Party. Cleaver and Black Panthers who were with him had fled the United States after a 1968 shoot-out with policemen in Oakland and had been recognized by the socialist-Islamic Algerians as the American government-in-exile. At first Leary was excited at the idea of setting up a radical coalition abroad with Cleaver, but he soon lost favor with the Panthers. Writing in *Rolling Stone* in the spring of 1971, Cleaver declared that it had been necessary for the Panthers to place Timothy and Rosemary Leary under house arrest in Algiers, claiming that Timothy had become a danger to himself and to his hosts with his uncurbed appetite for LSD. Such drug use, Cleaver stated, was counterproductive to bringing about true revolutionary change—and what's more, he thought it had damaged Leary's once brilliant mind. "To all those who look to Dr. Leary for inspiration or even leadership," Cleaver wrote, "we want to say that your god is dead because his mind has been blown by acid." Leary, for his part, claimed that Cleaver simply wanted to flex some muscle and to demonstrate to his guests what it was like to live under oppression and bondage.

Looking back at the episode, Rosemary would feel a great sadness that the experiment between Leary and the Panthers failed. "That's always haunted me," she said, "the idea that we had the possibility for some kinship. I think Eldridge and the others wanted us to recognize the experiences that had brought them there, and how different it was from the experiences that they thought had brought *us* there. They recognized that we weren't going to be killed in any confrontation with the law. The Black Panthers, though, *had* been killed. We were so naïve, so stupid. At the same time, we were frightened. Eldridge was very dictatorial. He kept me away from the women and the children, and then the Panthers threatened us and kept us in a dirty room in an ugly place for three days. So what were we to do?"

The only thing they could do: flee. Next stop: Geneva, Switzerland, where they enjoyed a short respite until the Swiss arrested Leary after the U.S. government filed extradition papers. Leary was in the Lausanne prison for six weeks—"the best prison in the world," he once told me, "like a class hotel"—until the Swiss, following the petitions of Allen Ginsberg and others, refused the Nixon administration's requests for deportation. By this time, though, all the years of harassment, fear, flight and incarceration—plus the lost opportunities for any stable and real family life of their own—had taken a toll on Rosemary, and she decided to part temporarily from Leary. "I had always felt it was my job to protect Tim—that seemed to be the role that I played. But Tim . . . he was Sisyphus: he was the mythic hero chained to the rock, and he was always going to be pushing that rock. He seemed to thrive on notoriety. He'd become a celebrity during those years, and that carries its own weight with it. It's not the lifestyle *I* would have chosen. I'd always wanted the quiet life, and with Tim, there simply wasn't the possibility for it.

"Did I regret having chosen Tim to love? I don't think so. He was always the most interesting person. Everyone else seemed boring, by comparison. Of course, by the time I wanted boredom, it was too late."

By late 1972, Leary had become a man without a country and without recourse. The United States was exerting sizable pressure on foreign governments not to harbor the former professor—indeed, an Orange Country DA announced he had indicted Leary on nineteen counts of drug trafficking, branding him as the head of the largest drug-smuggling enterprise in the world—and the Swiss would not extend him further asylum. Accompanied by his new girlfriend, Joanna Harcourt-Smith, Leary fled to Afghanistan, but he was arrested at the Kabul airport by an American embassy attaché and turned over to US Drug Enforcement agents. He was brought back to Orange County, tried for escape and sentenced to five years, in addition to his two previous ten-year sentences. He was also facing eleven counts from the second Millbrook bust and nineteen conspiracy counts related to his indictment as the head of a drug-smuggling outfit.

The US government had succeeded in its campaign. LSD had been declared illegal and its most influential researcher and proponent had been pursued across the world, arrested, brought home, and put behind bars once again—bigger bars this time, in fact. The psychedelic movement had been shut down, and for decades after, Timothy Leary would be vilified for the inquiring and defiant spirit that he had helped set loose upon the 1960s. Looking back on the collapse of that experiment, writer Robert Anton Wilson, a longtime friend of Leary's and author of *The Illuminatus Trilogy*, says: "A lot of psychologists I've known over the years agreed with Leary—they acknowledged in private that LSD was an incredibly valuable tool for analyzing and effecting positive personality change in people. But these same psychologists backed off gradually as the heat from the government increased, until they all became as silent as moonlight on a tombstone. And Tim was still out there with his angry Irish temper, denouncing the government and fighting on alone.

"I don't want to discount that there are people whose lives have been destroyed by drugs," Wilson continues, "but are they the results of Timothy Leary's research, or the result of government policies? Leary's research was shut down and the media stopped quoting him a long time ago. Most people don't even understand what Leary's opinions were, or what it was he was trying to communicate. By contrast, the government's policies have been carried out for thirty years, and now we have a major drug disaster in this country. Nobody, of course, thinks it's the government's fault—they think it's Leary's for trying to prevent it, for trying to have scientific controls over the thing.

"He deserves a better legacy than that."

In 1975 some nasty and frightening reports began to circulate about Timothy Leary. According to stories that appeared in *Rolling Stone* and other publications, Leary was talking to the FBI and was willing to give them information about radical activists and drug principals he had known, in exchange for his freedom.

The rumors were hard to confirm—the FBI was moving Leary from prison to prison on a regular basis, and few friends saw or communicated with him for roughly a year—but even the idea had a chill-effect on many of Leary's former compatriots. Allen Ginsberg, Ram Dass, Jerry Rubin and Leary's own son, Jack, held a press conference denouncing Leary for collaborating and asserting that his testimony shouldn't be trusted by the courts. In *Flashbacks*, Leary wrote that essentially he led the FBI on a wild goose chase and that nobody was imprisoned because of his statements— though he admitted that he had made declarations about certain people to a grand jury.

In any event, Leary was released from the California prison system in 1976, his reputation pretty much in tatters. Many of his old friends would no longer speak to him. "There was no question he was no longer the Tim I'd known before," says Frank Barron. "Prison doesn't improve anybody very much, and he'd suffered for it. His sense of invulnerability was gone. But he was determined to come back into the public and to reassert his mission."

Gradually, Leary rehabilitated his image. Shortly after his release, he separated from Joanna Harcourt-Smith, whom some thought had been an unfortunate influence in the whole FBI matter. He settled into Los Angeles and became a regular at Hollywood parties. In 1978 he married his fourth wife, Barbara Chase, and took her young son, Zachary, as his own. Though Timothy and Barbara would divorce fifteen years later, he would stay close to Zachary. It seemed that with Zachary, Leary found the sort of relationship that he had not been able to achieve with his son, Jack—who stopped talking to Leary in 1975 and who only briefly saw him again two months before his death.

"It was a time for him to do it again," says Zachary, "and see if the whole domesticity of having a family was something really applicable to his life, and he found that it was. He was happy about that, because the sadness of his earlier family had been so great. So I think it was great for him, in his late fifties and sixties, to be a father again with a little kid, taking me to the ballparks and playing sports in the backyard. Young people—that's really what kept him going, that's what kept his theories alive. And I think that the biggest moral ground that he covered for me was communication: 'Never try and shut anything down,' he told me. I'm only starting to realize now the magnitude of the environment that I was lucky enough to grow up in. I really do consider Tim my father."

Leary went on to other interests. Primarily he became a champion of computer and communications technology, and was among the first to declare that these new developments—particularly the rapidly growing internet—had the same sort of potential to empower creativity on a mass level and to threaten authority structures as psychedelics had once had in the 1960s.

In time, the old friends came back. Ginsberg, Ram Dass and others made peace with the man with whom they had once shared such phenomenal adventures. "When people ask me why it is I treasure and respect Timothy," says Ram Dass, "I say it's because he taught me how to play with life rather than be played *upon* by life. That's the closest I've gotten to stating what it feels like. Timothy plays with life. People are offended by that because they think it doesn't give life its due respect. But I think it's quite a liberating thing."

In 1990 the newfound equanimity of Timothy Leary's life was shattered. His daughter, Susan Leary Martino, forty-two, had been arrested in Los Angeles for firing a bullet into her boyfriend's head as he slept. Twice she was ruled mentally unfit to stand trial. Then one morning she was found dead in her jail cell. She had tied a shoelace around her neck and hanged herself.

Some people close to Leary believe that Susan had never been the same since the Laredo arrest and trial—that she held herself to blame for her father's subsequent troubles, and that, like her mother, she had grown depressed and withdrawn over the years. Others claim that Susan had always loved her father powerfully, and that all the years and events that kept him from her—the arrests, the flights, all the many girlfriends and wives— ate away at her. Regardless of the causes, Susan's suicide hit Leary hard, a blow that many of those close to him feel he never really recovered from. "I don't think he could push that one away so easily," says Ram Dass. "I remember speaking with him on the phone and feeling a surprising vulnerability in Tim that I wasn't used to hearing."

The news of Susan's death also came as a terrible blow to Rosemary, who had been living on the East Coast under an assumed name, still a fugitive. "I'd been angry with him for a long time," she says, "but I'd been having dreams about them prior to her death, about Susan and Tim and myself in some bucolic setting with streams running and the three of us very happy. Which wasn't the case when the three of us were together. So I knew I was being taught something, or told something, about Tim and Susan, and about my heart. And then, when she died, it was so *hard*. And I knew how hard it would be for him."

Rosemary, who hadn't spoken with Timothy or anybody close to him since 1972, called Ram Dass, who put her in touch with Tim. "We met in Golden Gate Park," she says. "It was a great romantic meeting. When I left him in Switzerland, we were quarreling, so to meet him and find that our love was still there—the love that we had for one another—was just incredible. It validated so much for me to know that about him and about myself, and to have given up the anger and the hurt that I had felt. The emotion involved in all that just opened the way for me to love Tim again."

Timothy put Rosemary in touch with a lawyer and helped her resolve her fugitive status. "I had lived such a remarkable life for so long, never sure who to trust or what to say." Rosemary says, "It was liberating to be free of all that. I just got my California driver's license with my name on it."

Rosemary began to see Tim often. She was impressed, she said, by how open his heart now seemed. But she also saw other changes. "I could tell he wasn't feeling wonderful. He'd always had an amazing constitution; I'd never known him to be ill, even with a cold." And then, around Christmas 1994, after a strenuous lecture tour, Leary was felled by a bout of pneumonia. "It was his first taste of mortality in terms of his body," says Rosemary, "and I think it was devastating for him to find himself so ill, and then not to bounce back from it."

It turned out to be more than pneumonia. The doctors had determined that Leary had developed prostate cancer, and it was inoperable. With the right treatment, they might be able to keep him alive for a year or two. Leary later told reporters he was "exhilarated" by the news. This would be the start of his greatest adventure: a conscious and loving journey into death. He called his friends—Rosemary, Ram Dass, author Ken Kesey, Allen Ginsberg and many others—and shared with them his excitement. "That's just the epitome of his personality," says his stepson Zach. "I guess it made perfect sense that he would feel that way about it. But when he was first disclosing it, I felt, 'God, how could you *feel* like that?' But to him it was just another card in the hand—the death card. And now I have to say I've learned so much from him in these last few months."

Indeed, it seems the knowledge of his death brought out a gentle and transcendent quality in Timothy Leary. "He's more emotionally available now," says Ram Dass, "which is remarkable, because he's never handled his emotions at all. I mean, he's always been a very friendly person—fun and vibrant and stimulating, and all that—but deep emotions have been delicate to play with historically with Timothy. He's lived more on the surface of events and things rather than the slower, deeper rhythms of emotions. The last few times I saw him, he was very much there, and that thrilled me. When we would look into each other's eyes, he was looking at me about death. It gave me the conviction that he isn't afraid of death. He knows he's going after one of the darkest secrets of the society, and it's humbled him in an interesting way."

There's also something about Leary's awareness of death's imminence that heightened his sense of play. In the last few months, there was nonstop activity around his home, and much of it was geared to fun stuff: dinners, outings to midnight rock & roll shows, around-the-clock visits by well-wishers and friends. "Silly silliness is being performed as a high art here," he told me one afternoon, with utter joy.

A good example of Leary's latter-day high-art silliness is an event that became known as "Wheelchair Day." One day Leary decided to round up as many wheelchairs as possible, load his staff and friends into them and hold wheelchair races on Sunset Strip, then wheel into the House of Blues for a luncheon designed on the model of Da Vinci's *The Last Supper*. After the event, Leary was riding back to his house in the rented convertible of his friend, internet rights activist and former Grateful Dead lyricist John Perry Barlow, with two of the young women from his staff, Trudy Truelove and Camella Grace, in the backseat. The radio was blasting as they headed west on Sunset, and Trudy and Camella were sitting on the car's trunk, goofing and making dancing gestures. Leary looked at Barlow, smiled and shouted, "Life is good!" That was when Barlow glanced into his rearview mirror and saw the flashing red and yellow lights of a Beverly Hills police car—and realized that the car he was driving was perhaps not entirely free of illegal substances. "Shit," he thought to himself, "Tim Leary's last bust."

Barlow rolled down his window and said to the officer: "I know what we were doing was wrong. But you see, my friend here is dying, and we're trying to show him a good time." Barlow later told me he'd never forget the look that Tim gave the policeman: "Caught in the act of dying like he had his hand in the cookie jar."

The officer smiled back at Leary, then turned to Trudy and Camella. "I'd be lying if I didn't say that looks like fun," he said, "but just because *he's* dying doesn't mean you should. Now get down in the seat and buckle up and I'll let you go."

When they pulled back into traffic, Leary turned to Barlow, laughed and said: "What a fucking gift *that* was!"

Not everybody, though, was enamored of the gallows humor of Leary and his troop.

On the night of the wheelchair-race caper, I arrived at Leary's to find an ambulance outside his house, being loaded with his cryonics coffin. It turned out that a short time before, a team from CryoCare—the outfit that was to undertake the freezing and preservation of Leary's brain upon his death—had come in to remove all their equipment.

For some time, a tension had been building up between the CryoCare representatives and Leary's crew. CryoCare felt that Leary's folks had shown disrespect for their equipment by decorating it with lights and toys, and also believed that some people at the house had been trying to keep Cryo-Care's technicians away from Leary. More important, CryoCare's Mike Darwin had grown alarmed about Leary's pronouncements about his plan to commit suicide live (so to speak) on the World Wide Web. Darwin did not feel that his organization (whose brochure bears the motto, "Many are cold, but few are frozen") could afford to be involved in what he termed a potential crime scene, or that they should leave their equipment in a house where illegal drugs may be present or used.

For their part, the Leary folks had become increasingly put off by what they regarded as CryoCare's ghoulish interest in obtaining the head of Timothy Leary. The problem was only exacerbated when they learned that a CryoCare official who would be involved with the decapitation and freezing process, Charles Platt, had an assignment to write about the operation for *Wired* magazine. (Platt had also been sending serial email to various parties, expressing his disdain for the Leary staff and his impatience with Leary for not dying as soon as had been expected. "What insane will to live," he wrote in one letter.)

In any event, CryoCare's actions left Leary with a decision to make: He could either sign on quickly with another cryonics outfit, or he could accept that his death would be final—that his brain would not be preserved for some indeterminate future attempt at reanimation. In the end, he decided against cryonics. "I have no real great desire to do it," he told me. "I just felt it was my duty to futurism and the process of smart dying."

Leary's decision was not a small thing for him. He once told me that he did not believe that anything human survived beyond death, and that if we possess a soul, then the soul is our mind, and the brain is the soul's home. By forgoing cryonics, Timothy Leary decided that even if he could, he would not return. His immortality, instead, would be his work and his legend, and it was his hope that those things would find an ongoing life on the website that had become his most prized dream in his final season.

It was not long after this that the end came. One afternoon I had to drop something by Tim's place and we had a brief conversation. He was in the best spirits and most cogent form I'd seen him in. He told me touching stories about his relationship with John Lennon and Yoko Ono—about how Lennon had written "Come Together" for Leary, who was contemplating a California gubernatorial candidacy, but then thought twice about it and kept it for the Beatles. Leary also talked about how he had tried to warn Ono that New York's Dakota was too risky a place—too exposed, too accessible—for a man like Lennon to live. "I wish I'd been wrong about that one," he said, looking at the large photo above his bed of himself and Rosemary with Lennon and Ono during the recording of "Give Peace a Chance." I left that day looking forward to visiting and talking with him some more.

A few days later I received a call from Zachary. "It looks like Tim is going today. You should come up soon if you want to say good-bye."

Zach later told me: "Tim just decided he couldn't live in that body anymore and he wanted to get out. The key moment for him was when he went to take a shower last week and he stopped and looked at himself in the mirror, naked. That was all he needed to know. He was very clear and lucid and he looked at his body and saw it was pathetic and it was below his quality of life." That night Leary called Zach and the house staff around him at the table and said: "Can you go on without me?"

"It was like he was asking for our permission," said Zach.

The morning that Zach called me, Tim had got out of bed and climbed into his motorized wheelchair and rode all over his ranch house. He stopped in the backyard where he sat drinking a cup of coffee, looking at the flowers that were coming to bloom in his garden. Then he said, "I'm tired. I'm going to take a nap," and wheeled back into his bedroom. A short while later his nurse summoned Zach and told him he should notify anybody who might want to see him one last time.

I sat for about an hour with several other people that afternoon and watched Leary as he slept. Occasionally he woke, smiled, took sips on the ice that the nurse gave him, and once or twice tried to say something. At one point, he opened his eyes wide and said: "Flash!"

Later, around 9:00 p.m., I made another visit to his bedroom. The only illumination in the room was a string of Christmas lights, on the wall above Leary's bed. Zach sat close, holding his stepfather's hand. Tim opened his eyes briefly at one point, looked at Zach, smiled and said softly, "Beautiful."

It was the last thing Timothy Leary said.

A few hours later, around 2:30 a.m., I received another call, telling me that Tim had died at 12:45. I headed back to his house.

The lights were still dim in his bedroom. On a nearby chair sat Trudy Truelove, staring at Tim. "I've decided to stay with him until they remove him. I've decided to be his guardian."

Tim was laid on his back, dressed in white, the red blanket turned down. His mouth was wide open, frozen in his last exhaled breath. It looked as if he was calling out silently. Somebody had placed a large orange flower in his hand, its petals reaching up to his face.

Soon, the room filled with several people. We stood there for a long time in silence, until we were told that it was time to say our good-byes. The mortuary people had come to claim Tim's corpse.

One by one, the people in the room approached Tim, some touching and kissing him, others whispering last words. When it was my turn I went up to the bed and looked down at him. I hadn't been able to tell before, from the darkness in the room, but his eyes were wide open, and when you looked into them, it was if they were looking back into you. I bent over, gave him my kiss and then turned and left the room.

•   •   •

One night not long before Leary's death, I took LSD for the first time in twenty-five years. I guess I'd just grown curious after spending so much time around Tim, but I felt I also owed it to myself. I'd left psychedelics on bad terms, and that had never felt right. It was time, once again, to see what they held for me, what might be revealed after so much time.

I lay on my bed in the dark, listening to Bach's *Goldberg Variations*, and once more, death came to visit. I saw what seemed thousands of faces. They were all in agony, and then they died, and were swimming in straits of grace. Their suffering, I saw, was inevitable. And so was their dying. And so was their release. Once more I saw death move around and through me, and this time I did not try to hide from it. I lay there and cried, and somehow I felt a great comfort in what I'd seen.

I thought about this experience as I sat in Leary's bedroom at three in the morning and studied him in his death. As I implied earlier, I'd always been terrified of death—even to be near it. When I visited the funeral homes to see my father, my mother, my brother, lying in their coffins, I took short glances and got away quickly. I never touched my loved ones as they lay dead. I don't think I could have.

Sitting with Leary, I realized something had changed—and maybe it had been a gift on his part. His greatest achievement, I believe, was to ask the people he knew to face the darkest part of themselves, and to be willing to be there with them—to interact with them, to guide them—when they reached that place. I can't say whether he ever faced the darkest parts within himself in that same way; maybe it never really happened until that last day and night. And if that was the time, I'm glad there were good people there for him.

Being around Leary had taught me what nothing else had: that encountering death did not always have to be an experience of freezing horror. In those last hours, Timothy Leary could still be a good therapist.

I looked at Tim lying there in his death, his eyes hollow, the skin on his face already sinking, and I was reminded of something Rosemary once told me. It was a story about one of the last times she saw Leary before he fell ill. "I'd gone to New Mexico with him," she said. "He was lecturing there. He'd gone to the bar to pick up some drinks, and I was standing out of the light. And just the way the light hit him in the bar, and illuminated the planes of his face—he was so beautiful. And it was the old face. I mean, the one from years ago. I don't know why. It was just the way the lighting hit him. Beautiful bones."

I sat there in the dark, looking at Tim, thinking of Rosemary's words. Beautiful bones, I thought. Even in death, beautiful bones.

THE END OF JERRY GARCIA AND THE GRATEFUL DEAD

He was the unlikeliest of pop stars and the most reticent of cultural icons. Onstage, he wore plain clothes—usually a sacklike T-shirt and loose jeans, to fit his heavy frame—and he rarely spoke to the audience that watched his every move. Even his guitar lines—complex, lovely, rhapsodic but never flashy—as well as his strained, weatherworn vocal style had a subdued, colloquial quality about them. Offstage, he kept to family and friends, and when he sat to talk with interviewers about his remarkable music, he often did so in sly-witted, self-deprecating ways. "I feel like I'm stumbling along," he said once, "and a lot of people are watching me or stumbling along with me or allowing me to stumble for them." It was as if Jerry Garcia—who, as the lead guitarist and singer of the Grateful Dead, lived at the center of one of popular culture's most extraordinary epic adventures—was bemused by the circumstances of his own renown.

And yet, when he died on August 9, 1995, a week after his fifty-third birthday, at a rehabilitation clinic in Forest Knolls, California, the news of his death set off immense waves of emotional reaction. Politicians, newscasters, poets and artists eulogized the late guitarist throughout the day and night; fans of all ages gathered spontaneously in parks around the nation; and in the streets of San Francisco's Haight-Ashbury—the neighborhood where the Grateful Dead lived at the height of the hippie epoch—mourners assembled by the hundreds, singing songs, building makeshift altars, consoling one another and jamming the streets for blocks around. Across town at San Francisco city hall a tie-dyed flag was flown on the middle flagpole.

Chances are Garcia himself would have been embarrassed, maybe even repelled, by all the commotion. He wasn't much given to mythologizing his own reputation. In some of his closing words in his last interview in *Rolling Stone*, in 1993, he said: "I'm hoping to leave a clean field—nothing, not a thing. I'm hoping they burn it all with me. . . . I'd rather have my immortality here while I'm alive. I don't care if it lasts beyond me at all. I'd just as soon it didn't."

Jerome John Garcia was born in 1942, in San Francisco's Mission district. His father, a Spanish immigrant named Jose "Joe" Garcia, had been a jazz clarinetist and Dixieland band leader in the 1930s, and he named his new son after his favorite Broadway composer, Jerome Kern. In the spring of 1948, while on a fishing trip, Jerry saw his father swept to his death in a California river. "I never saw him play with his band," Garcia told *Rolling Stone* in 1991, "but I remember him playing me to sleep at night. I just barely remember the sound of it."

After his father's death, Garcia spent a few years living with his mother's parents in one of San Francisco's working-class districts. His grandmother had the habit of listening to Nashville's Grand Ole Opry radio broadcasts on Saturday nights, and it was in those hours, Garcia would later say, that he developed his fondness for country music forms—particularly the deft, blues-inflected mandolin playing and mournful, high-lonesome vocal style of bluegrass's principal founder, Bill Monroe. When Garcia was ten, his mother, Ruth, brought him to live with her at a sailor's hotel and bar that she ran near the city's waterfront. He spent much of his childhood there, listening to the boozy, fanciful stories that the hotel's old tenants told, or sitting alone, reading Disney and horror comics, and poring through science-fiction novels.

When Garcia was fifteen, his older brother Tiff—the same brother who, a few years earlier, had accidentally lopped off part of Jerry's right-hand middle finger while the two were chopping wood—introduced him to early rock & roll and rhythm & blues music. Garcia was quickly drawn to the music's funky rhythms and rough-hewn textures, but what captivated him most was the lead-guitar sounds—especially the bluesy mellifluence of players like T-Bone Walker and Chuck Berry. It was otherworldly-sounding music, he later said, unlike anything he had heard before. Garcia decided he wanted to learn how to make those same sounds. He went to his mother and proclaimed that he wanted an electric guitar for his upcoming birthday. "Actually," he later said, "she got me an *accordion,* and I went nuts. *Aggghhh, no, no, no!* I railed and raved, and she finally turned it in, and I got a pawnshop electric guitar and an amplifier. I was just beside myself with joy."

During this same period, the Beat scene was in full swing in the Bay Area, and it held great sway at the North Beach arts school where Garcia took some courses and at the city's coffeehouses, where he heard poets like

Lawrence Ferlinghetti and Kenneth Rexroth read their venturesome works. "I was a high school kid and a wannabe beatnik!" he said in 1993. "Rock & roll at that time was *not* respectable. I mean, beatniks didn't like rock & roll. . . . Rock & roll wasn't cool, but I *loved* rock & roll. I used to have these fantasies about 'I want rock & roll to be like *respectable* music.' I wanted it to be like *art*. . . . I used to try to think of ways to make that work. I wanted to do something that fit in with the art institute, that kind of self-conscious art—'art' as opposed to 'popular culture.' Back then, they didn't even talk about popular culture—I mean, rock & roll was so *not legit,* you know? It was completely out of the picture. I don't know what they thought it was, like white-trash music or kids' music."

By the early 1960s, Garcia was living in Palo Alto, hanging out and playing in the folk music clubs around Stanford University. He was also working part-time at Dana Morgan's Music Store, where he met several of the musicians that would eventually dominate the San Francisco music scene. In 1963 Garcia formed a jug band, Mother McCree's Uptown Jug Champions. Its lineup included a young folk guitarist named Bob Weir and a blues aficionado, Ron McKernan, known to his friends as "Pigpen" for his often-unkempt appearance. The group played a mix of blues, country and folk, and Pigpen became the front man, singing Jimmy Reed and Lightnin' Hopkins tunes.

Then, in February 1964, the Beatles made their historic appearance on *The Ed Sullivan Show,* and virtually overnight an entire young generation was instilled with a new spirit and sense of differentness. Garcia understood the group's promise after seeing their first film, *A Hard Day's Night.* For the first time since Elvis Presley—and the first time for an audience that had largely rejected contemporary rock & roll as seeming too trivial and inconsequential—pop music could be seen to hold bold, significant and thoroughly exhilarating possibilities that even the ultraserious, socially aware folk scene could not offer. This became even more apparent a year later, when Bob Dylan—who had been the folk scene's reigning hero—played an assailing set of his defiant new electric music at the Newport Folk Festival. As a result, the folky purism of Mother McCree's all-acoustic format began to seem rather limited and uninteresting to Garcia and many of the other band members, and before long, the ensemble was transformed into an electric unit, the Warlocks. A couple of the jug band members dropped out, and two new musicians joined: Bill Kreutzmann, who worked at Dana Morgan's Music Store, on drums, and on bass, classically trained musician Phil Lesh, who, like Garcia, had been radicalized by the music of the Beatles and

Dylan. "We had big ideas," Garcia told *Rolling Stone* in 1993. "I mean, as far as we were concerned, we were going to be the next Beatles or something— we were on a trip, definitely. We had enough of that kind of crazy faith in ourselves. . . . [The] first time we played in public, we had a huge crowd of people from the local high school, and they went fuckin' *nuts!* The next time we played, it was packed to the rafters. It was a pizza place. We said, 'Hey, can we play in here on Wednesday night? We won't bother anybody. Just let us set up in the corner.' It was *pandemonium,* immediately."

It was around this time that Garcia and some of the group's other members also began an experimentation with drugs that would forever transform the nature of the band's story. This wasn't the first time drugs had been used in music for artistic inspiration or had found their way into an American cultural movement. Many jazz and blues artists (not to mention several country-western players) had been using marijuana and various narcotics to intensify their music making for several decades, and in the 1950s the Beats had extolled marijuana as an assertion of their nonconformism. But the drugs that began cropping up in the youth and music scenes in the mid-1960s were of a much different, more exotic, sort. Veterans Hospital near Stanford University had been the site of government-sanctioned experiments with LSD—a drug that induced hallucinations in those who ingested it, and that, for many, also inspired something remarkably close to the patterns of religious experience. Among those who had taken the drug at Veterans Hospital were Robert Hunter, a folksinger and poet who would later become Garcia's songwriting partner, and Ken Kesey, author of *One Flew Over the Cuckoo's Nest* and *Sometimes a Great Notion.* Kesey had been working on an idea about group LSD experiments and had staffed a loosely knit gang of artists and rogues, called the Merry Pranksters, dedicated to this adventure. Kesey's crew included a large number of intellectual dropouts like himself and eccentric rebels like Neal Cassady (the inspiration for Dean Moriarty in Jack Kerouac's *On the Road*) and Carolyn Adams (later known as Mountain Girl, who eventually married Garcia and had two children with him).

When the Pranksters began holding acid parties at a house in the nearby town of La Honda, California, the Grateful Dead—as the Warlocks were now called—became the house band for these collective drug experiments, known as the Acid Tests. These events became the model for what would shortly become known as the "Grateful Dead trip." In the years that followed, the Dead would never really forsake the philosophy of the Acid Tests. Right until the end, the band would encourage its audience to be involved with both the music and the sense of camaraderie that came from and fueled the music. Plus, more than any other band of the era, the Grateful Dead succeeded in making music that seemed to emanate from the hallucinogenic experience—music like 1969's *Aoxomoxoa,* which managed to prove both chilling and heartening in varying moments. In the process, the Dead made music that epitomized psychedelia at its brainiest and brawniest, and also helped make possible the sort of fusion of jazz structure and blues sensibility that would later help shape bands like the Allman Brothers.

"I wouldn't want to say this music was written on acid," says Robert Hunter, who penned some of the album's lyrics. "Over the years, I've denied it had any influence that way. But as I get older, I begin to understand that we were reporting on what we saw and experienced—like the layers below layers, which became real to me. I would say that *Aoxomoxoa* was a report on what it's like to be up—or down—there in those layers. I guess it is, I'll be honest about it. Looking back and judging, those were pretty weird times. We were very, very far-out."

By 1966 the spirit of the Acid Tests was spilling over into the streets and clubs of San Francisco—and well beyond. A new community of largely young people—many sharing similar ideals about drugs, music, politics and sex—had taken root in the Haight-Ashbury district, where Garcia and the Grateful Dead now shared a house. In addition, a thriving club and dance-hall scene—found mainly at Chet Helms's Avalon Ballroom and Bill Graham's Fillmore—had sprung up around the city, drawing the notice of the media, police and various political forces. In part, all the public attention and judgment made life in the Haight difficult and risky. But there was also a certain boon that came from all the new publicity: The music and ethos of the San Francisco scene had begun to draw the interest of East Coast and British musicians, and all of this was starting to affect the thinking of artists like the Beatles and Bob Dylan—the same artists who, only a year or two before, had exerted such a major influence on groups like the Grateful Dead. For that matter, San Francisco bands were having an impact on not just pop and fashion styles, but also on social mores and even the political dialogue of the times. Several other bands, of course, participated in the creation of this scene, and some—including Jefferson Airplane, Quicksilver Messenger Service and Janis Joplin with Big Brother and the Holding Company—would make music every bit as inventive and memorable as the Dead's.

Because of its reputation as a youth haven, the Haight was soon overrun with runaways, and the sort of health and shelter problems that a community of mainly white middle-class expatriates had never had to face before. By 1967's Summer of Love, there were bad drugs on the streets, there were rapes and murders, and there was a surfeit of starry-eyed newcomers who arrived in the neighborhood without any means of support and were expecting the scene to feed and nurture them. Garcia and the Dead had seen the trouble coming and were among those who tried to prompt the city to prepare for it. "You could feed large numbers of people," Garcia later said, "but only so large. You could feed one thousand, but not twenty thousand. We were unable to convince the San Francisco officials of what was going to happen. We said there would be more people in the city than the city could hold." Not long after, the Dead left the Haight for individual residences in Marin County, north of San Francisco.

By 1970 the idealism surrounding the Bay Area music scene—and much of the counterculture—had largely evaporated. The drug scene had turned creepy and risky; much of the peace movement had given way to violent rhetoric; and the quixotic dream of a Woodstock generation, bound together by the virtues of love and music, had been irreparably damaged, first by the Manson Family murders, in the summer of 1969, and then, a few months later, by a tragic and brutal event at the Altamont Speedway, just outside San Francisco. The occasion was a free concert featuring the Rolling Stones. Following either the example or the suggestion of the Grateful Dead (there is still disagreement on this), the Stones hired the Hell's Angels as a security force. It proved to be a day of horrific violence. The Angels battered numerous people, usually for little reason, and in the evening, as the Stones performed, the bikers stabbed a young black man to death in front of the stage. "It was completely unexpected," Garcia later said. "And that was the hard part—the hard lesson there—that you can have good people and good energy and work on a project and really want it to happen right and still have it all weird. It's the thing of knowing less than you should have. Youthful folly."

The record the band followed with, *Workingman's Dead,* was a statement about the changing and badly frayed sense of community in both America and its counterculture, and as such, it was a work by and about a group of men being tested and pressured at a time when they could have easily splintered from all the madness and stress and disappointment. The music reflected that struggle—particularly in songs like "Uncle John's Band," a parable about America that was also the band's confession of how it nearly fell apart—and "New Speedway Boogie," about Altamont. "One way or another, this darkness has got to give," Garcia sang in the latter song, in a voice full of fear, fragility and hard-earned courage. *Workingman's Dead* and the record that followed it, *American Beauty*, made plain how the Grateful Dead found the heart and courage and talent to stick together, and to make something new and meaningful from their association. "Making the record became like going to a job," Garcia said. "It was something we had to do, and it was also something we did to keep our minds off some of these problems, even if the music is about those problems."

As a result, *Workingman's Dead* and *American Beauty* are records that explored the idea of how one could forge meaningful values in disillusioning times. Says Robert Hunter: "When the Jefferson Airplane came up with that idea, 'Up against the wall,' I was up against them. It may have been true, but look at the results: blood in the streets. It seems the Airplane was feeling the power of their ability to send the troops into the field, and I wanted to stand back from the grenades and knives and blood in the street. Stand way back. There's a better way. There has to be education, and the education has to come from the poets and musicians, because it has to touch the heart rather than the intellect, it has to get in there deeply. That was a decision. That was a conscious decision."

Sometimes, adds Hunter, it was difficult to hold on to that conviction. "When *American Beauty* came out," he says, "there was a photograph due to go on the back which showed the band with pistols. They were getting into guns at the time, going over to Mickey's ranch, target shooting. It wasn't anything revolutionary; they were just enjoying shooting pistols. For example, we got a gold record and went and shot it up.

"I saw that photo and that was one of the few times that I ever really asserted myself with the band and said, 'No—no picture of a band with guns on the back cover.' These were incendiary and revolutionary times, and I did not want this band to be making that statement. I wanted us to counter the rising violence of that time. I knew that we had a tool to do it, and we just didn't dare go the other way. Us and the Airplane: We could have been the final match that lit the fuse, and we went real consciously the other way."

In addition, with their countryish lilt and bluesy impulses, *Workingman's Dead* and *American Beauty* were attempts to return to the musical sources that had fueled the band's passions in the first place. "*Workingman's Dead* was our first true studio album," Garcia told me in 1987, "insofar as we went in there to say, 'These are the limitations of the studio for us as performers; let's play inside those limitations.' That is, we decided to play more or less straight-ahead songs and not get hung up with effects and weirdness. For me, the models were music that I'd liked before that was basically simply constructed but terribly effective—like the old Buck Owens records from Bakersfield. Those records were basic rock & roll: nice, raw, simple, straight-ahead music, with good vocals and substantial instrumentation, but nothing flashy. *Workingman's Dead* was our attempt to say, 'We can play this kind of music—we can play music that's heartland music. It's something we do as well as we do anything.'"

In a conversation I had with Robert Hunter in 1989, he revealed something else that he thought had affected Garcia's singing in that period and made it so affecting. "It wasn't only because of the gathering awareness of what we were doing," he said, "but Jerry's mother had died in an automobile accident while we were recording *American Beauty*, and there's a lot of heartbreak on that record, especially on 'Brokedown Palace,' which is, I think, his release at that time. The pathos in Jerry's voice on those songs, I think, has a lot to do with that experience. When the pathos is there, I've always thought Jerry is the best. The man can get inside some of those lines and turn them inside out, and he makes those songs entirely his. There is no emotion more appealing than the bittersweet when it's truly, truly spoken."

With *Workingman's Dead* and *American Beauty*, the Grateful Dead hit a creative peak and turned an important corner. For one thing, the two records sold better than anything the group had issued before, and as a result, the band was able to begin working its way free of many of the crushing debts it had accrued. More important, the Dead now had a body of fine new songs to perform onstage for its rapidly expanding audience. With the next album, a double live set, *Grateful Dead* (originally entitled *Skullfuck*, until Warner Bros. balked), the band issued an invitation to its fans: "Send us your name and address and we'll keep you informed." It was the sort of standard fan club pitch that countless pop acts had indulged in before, but what it set in motion for the Dead would prove unprecedented: the biggest prolonged fan reaction in pop music history. (According to *The New Yorker*, there were 110,000 Deadheads on the band's mailing list in 1995.) Clearly, the group had a devoted and far-flung following that, more than anything else, simply wanted to see the Grateful Dead live. One of the aphorisms of the time was: "There's nothing like a Grateful Dead show," and though that adage sometimes backfired in unintended ways—such as those occasions when the band turned in a protracted, meandering and largely out-of-tune performance—often as not, the claim was justified. On those nights when the group was *on*—propelled by the double drumming of Bill Kreutzmann and Mickey Hart, and the dizzying melodic communion of Garcia's and Weir's guitars and Lesh's bass—the Grateful Dead's verve and imagination proved matchless.

It was this dedication to live performance, and a penchant for near-incessant touring, that formed the groundwork for the Grateful Dead's extraordinary success for a period of more than twenty years. Even a costly failed attempt at starting the band's own autonomous recording label in the early 1970s, plus the deaths of three consecutive keyboardists—Pigpen McKernan, of alcohol-induced cirrhosis of the liver, in 1973; Keith Godchaux, in a fatal car accident in 1980, a year after leaving the band; and Brent Mydland, of a morphine and cocaine overdose in 1990—never really deterred the Dead's momentum as a live act. By the summer of 1987, when the group enjoyed its first and only Top Ten single ("Touch of Grey") and album (*In the Dark*), the commercial breakthrough was almost beside the fact in any objective assessment of the band's stature. The Grateful Dead had been the top concert draw in America for several years and in fact had probably played before more people over the years than any other performing act in history. But the nature of the band's success went well beyond big numbers and high finances: From the late 1960s to the mid-1990s, the Grateful Dead enjoyed a union with its audience that was unrivaled and unshakable. Indeed, the Dead and its followers formed the only self-sustained, ongoing fellowship that pop music has ever produced—a commonwealth that lasted more than a quarter century.

At the same time, Jerry Garcia and the other members of the Grateful Dead paid a considerable price for their singular accomplishment. By largely forswearing studio recordings after the 1970s (the band released only two collections of all-new music in the period from 1980 to 1995), and by never returning to the sort of songwriting impetus that made works like *Workingman's Dead* and *American Beauty* so notable, the Dead lost the interest of much of the mainstream and cutting-edge pop audiences of the last two decades. To the band's fans, the Dead's magic lay in their live extravaganzas, where the group's improvisational bents melded with their audience's willful devotion, to achieve the sort of bouts of musical-communal ecstasy that few other rock & roll performers ever managed to equal. As a result, for many years, the Dead tended to play out their career, and make their meanings, almost entirely in the live moment, in the process attracting a mass-cult audience for whom the group functioned as the only ongoing force to keep faith with the dreams of collective utopia popularized in the 1960s. To the group's detractors, though, the Grateful Dead often appeared as little more than a 1960s relic, a band frozen in the sensibility of exhausted ideals, playing to a gullible cult audience that, like the group itself, was out of touch with the changing temper of the times. Or as one critic put it, the Grateful Dead was a group of "nostalgia mongerers . . . offering facile reminiscences to an audience with no memory of its own."

Garcia and the other members of the Dead heard this sort of criticism plenty over the years, and it had to have cut deep into their pride. "It's mortifying to think of yourself as a 'nostalgia' act when you've never quit playing," said Robert Hunter. "For years and years we drew an audience of nineteen- or twenty-year-old kids. Can you have a nostalgia for a time you didn't live in? I think some of our music appeals to some sort of idealism in people, and hopefully it's universal enough to make those songs continue to exist over the years."

Perhaps the general pop world's disregard and outright ridicule took a certain toll on the spirits of the various band members. In any event, something began to wear on Jerry Garcia in the mid-1980s, and whatever it was, it never really let up on him. By 1984, rumors were making the rounds among the Deadheads—which was one of the best networked communities on the planet—that Garcia's guitar playing had lost much of its wit and edge, that his singing had grown lackadaisical and that, in fact, he was suffering from drug problems. The rumors proved true. Garcia had been using cocaine and heroin for several years—in fact, had developed a serious addiction—and according to some observers, his use had started to affect the spirit and unity of the band itself. "He got so trashed out," said the Dead's sound engineer, Dan Healy, "that he just wasn't really playing. Having him not give a shit—that was devastating."

Watching from his home in Wyoming, Garcia's friend John Barlow thought he was witnessing the probable end of the Grateful Dead. "I was very afraid that Garcia was going to die. In fact, I'd reached a point where I'd just figured it was a matter of time before I'd turn on my radio and there, on the hour, I'd hear, 'Jerry Garcia, famous in the '60s, has died.' I didn't even allow myself to think it wasn't possible. That's a pretty morbid way to look at something. When you've got one person that is absolutely critical, and you don't think he's going to make it, then you start to disengage emotionally, and I had. For a while, I couldn't see where it was all headed. I mean, I could see the people in the audience getting off, but I couldn't see any of us getting off enough to make it worthwhile.

"And it wasn't just Garcia," Barlow says. "There were a lot of things that were wrong. I don't want to tell any tales out of school, but I think our adherents have a more than slightly idealistic notion of what goes on inside the Grateful Dead, and just how enlightened we all are.

"What happened with Garcia was not unique."

It was not long after this time that I had my only lengthy conversation with Jerry Garcia. It was during a period of high activity and high risks for the Grateful Dead. The band was putting the finishing touches on its first album of new songs in several years, *In the Dark,* which, in turn, would launch the band's only Top Ten single, "Touch of Grey," a touching song about aging, decline, rebirth and recommitment. At the same time, the Dead were beginning rehearsals with Bob Dylan for a nationwide tour that would make for a series of performances that were, at times, disorderly at best, and other times, full of surprising ferocity.

Garcia and I met on an uncommonly warm evening in the spring of 1987, in the band's San Rafael recording studio. When our conversation began, we had just finished viewing a video documentary about the band called *So Far,* which was shot nearly two years before. *So Far* is an adventurous and impressive work that, in its grandest moments, attests to the much-touted spirit of community that the Dead shared with their audience. Yet certain passages of the hour-long production seemed to be rough viewing on this night for Garcia, who looked rather heavy and fatigued during the project's taping. At the time *So Far* was made, Garcia was deeply entangled in the drug problem that, before much longer, would not only imperil his own health but also threaten the stability of the band.

That fact lends a certain affecting tension to the better performances in *So Far*—in particular, the group's doleful reading of "Uncle John's Band." The song, with its country-style singalong about people pulling together into a brave community in frightening times, had long been among the band's signature tunes, yet in *So Far*, the Dead render it as if they were aiming to test its meanings anew. In the video, Garcia and rhythm guitarist Bob Weir face off in a dimly lighted concert hall, working their way through the lyrics with an air of frayed fraternity, as if this might be their last chance to make good on the music's promise of a hard-earned bond. "When life looks like easy street, there is danger at your door," they sing to each other, and from the look that passes between them in that moment, it's impossible to tell whether they are about to pull together or come apart.

It is a raggedy but utterly remarkable performance, and on the occasion of our meeting, it seems to leave Garcia a bit uneasy. "There were so many people who cared about me," he tells me, "and I was just fucking around. . . . Drug use is kind of a cul-de-sac: It's one of those places you turn with your problems, and pretty soon, all your problems have simply become that one problem. Then it's just you and drugs."

It is now late in the evening. The other band members have all gone home, and only a couple of assistants linger in a nearby room, making arrangements for the next day's rehearsals with Dylan. Garcia looks tired on this night—it has been a long day, and the next one promises to be a longer one—but as he sips at a rum and Coke and begins to talk about the rough history of the previous years, his voice sounds surprisingly youthful.

"There was something I needed or thought I needed from drugs," he says directly. "Drugs are like trade-offs in a way—they can be, at any rate. There was something there for me. I don't know what it was, exactly. Maybe it was the thing of being able to distance myself a little from the world. But there was something there I needed for a while, and it wasn't an entirely negative experience. . . . But after awhile, it was just the drugs running me, and that's an intolerable situation.

"I was never an overdose kind of junkie. I've never enjoyed the extremes of getting high. I never used to like to sit around and smoke freebase until I was wired out of my mind, know what I mean? For me, it was the thing of just getting pleasantly comfortable and grooving at that level. But of course, that level doesn't stay the same. It requires larger and larger amounts of drugs. So after a few years of that, pretty soon you've taken a lot of fucking drugs and not experiencing much. It's a black hole. I went down that black hole, really. Luckily, my friends pulled me out. Without them, I don't think I ever would have had the strength to do it myself."

In fact, says Garcia, it was the Grateful Dead who made the first move to resolve his drug problem. "Classically," he says, "the band has had a laissez-faire attitude in terms of what anybody wants to do. If somebody wants to drink or take drugs, as long as it doesn't seriously affect everybody else or affect the music, we can sort of let it go. We've all had our excursions. Just before I got busted, everybody came over to my house and said, 'Hey, Garcia, you got to cool it; you're starting to scare us.'"

The problem became so acute that one day in January of 1985 the other members of the Grateful Dead paid Garcia a visit and told him they were afraid he was killing himself. They also reportedly issued the sort of warning they had never before issued to a bandmate: Garcia would have to choose between his involvement with drugs and the band. The members wanted Garcia to understand that they loved him, but they also wanted him to choose his allegiance.

"Garcia was the captain of his own ship," Bob Weir says of that period, "and if he was going to check out, that was up to him. But you know, if somebody looks real off-course, we might take it upon ourselves to bump up against him and try to push him a little more in a right direction."

Perhaps, in that confrontation, Garcia was reminded of something he had once said about the Grateful Dead's original lead singer, Pigpen, in 1972, after it had been disclosed that Pigpen had severely damaged his liver from drinking. "He survived it," Garcia told *Rolling Stone*, "and now he's got the option of being a juicer or not being a juicer. To be a juicer means to die, so now he's being able to choose whether to live or die. And if I know Pigpen, he'll choose to live." The following year, Pigpen was found dead. According to most reports, he had never really returned to drinking but had simply suffered too much damage to continue living.

In any event, Garcia reportedly made a decision: He promised the band he would quit drugs and would seek rehabilitative treatment within a few days. As it developed, he never got the chance. On January 18, 1985, while parked in his BMW in Golden Gate Park, Garcia was spotted by a policeman who noticed the lapsed registration on the vehicle. As the policeman approached the car, he reportedly smelled a strong burning odor and noticed Garcia trying to hide something between the driver and passenger seats. The policeman asked Garcia to get out of the car, and when Garcia did, the policeman saw an open briefcase on the passenger seat, full of twenty-three packets of "brown and white substances."

Garcia was arrested on suspicion of possessing cocaine and heroin, and about a month later, a municipal court judge agreed to let the guitarist enter a Marin Country drug-diversion program.

Looking back at the experience, Garcia was almost thankful. "I'm the sort of person," he says, "that will just keep going along until something stops me. For me and drugs, the bust helped. It reminded me how vulnerable you are when you're drug dependent. It caught my attention. It was like 'Oh, right: illegal.' And of all the things I don't want to do, spending time in jail is one of those things I least want to do. It was as if this was telling me it was time to start doing something different. It took me about a year to finally get off drugs completely after the bust, but it was something that needed to happen."

Garcia pauses to light a cigarette, then studies its burning end thoughtfully. "I can't speak for other people," he says after a few moments, "and I certainly don't have advice to give about drugs one way or another. I think it's purely a personal matter. I haven't changed in that regard. . . . It was one of those things where the pain it cost my friends, the worry that I put people through, was out of proportion to whatever it was I thought I needed from drugs. For me, it became a dead end."

Following Garcia's drug treatment, the band resumed a full-time touring schedule that included several 1986 summer dates with Bob Dylan and Tom Petty and the Heartbreakers. "I felt better after cleaning up, oddly enough, until that tour," Garcia says. "And then, I didn't realize it, but I was dehydrated and tired. That was all I felt, really. I didn't feel any pain. I didn't feel sick. I just felt tired. Then when we got back from that tour, I was just *really* tired. One day, I couldn't move anymore, so I sat down. A week later, I woke up in a hospital, and I didn't know what had happened. It was really weird."

Actually, it was worse than that: Though he had never been previously diagnosed for diabetes, when Garcia sat down at his San Rafael home on that July evening in 1986, he slipped into a diabetic coma that lasted five days and nearly claimed his life. "I must say, my experience never suggested to me that I was anywhere near death," says Garcia. "For me, it had just been this weird experience of being shut off. Later on, I found out how scary it was for everybody, and then I started to realize how serious it had all been. The doctors said I was so dehydrated, my blood was like mud.

"It was another one of those things to grab my attention. It was like my physical being saying, 'Hey, you're going to have to put in some time here if you want to keep on living.'" Garcia still seems startled by this realization. "Actually," he says, "it was a thought that had never entered my mind. I'd been lucky enough to have an exceptionally rugged constitution, but just the thing of getting older, and basically having a life of benign neglect, had caught up with me. And possibly the experience of quitting drugs may have put my body through a lot of quick changes."

At first, though, there were no guarantees that Garcia would be able to live as effectively as before. There were fears that he might suffer memory lapses and that his muscular coordination might never again be sharp enough for him to play guitar. "When I was in the hospital," he says, "all I could think was 'God, just give me a chance to do stuff—give me a chance to go back to being productive and playing music and doing the stuff I love to do.' And one of the first things I did—once I started to be able to make coherent sentences—was to get a guitar in there to see if I could play. But when I started playing, I thought, 'Oh, man, this is going to take a long time and a lot of patience.'"

After his release from the hospital, Garcia began spending afternoons with an old friend, Bay Area jazz and rhythm & blues keyboardist Merl Saunders, trying to rebuild his musical deftness. "I said, 'God, I can't do this,'" says Garcia. "Merl was very encouraging. He would run me through these tunes that had sophisticated harmonic changes, so I had to think. It was like learning music again, in a way. Slowly, I started to gain some confidence, and pretty soon, it all started coming back. It was about a three-month process, I would say, before I felt like 'Okay, now I'm ready to go out and play.' The first few gigs were sort of shaky, but . . ." Garcia's voice turns thick, and he looks away for a moment. "Ah, shit," he says, "it was incredible. There wasn't a dry eye in the house. It was great. It was just great. I was so happy to play."

Garcia smiles and shakes his head. "I am not a believer in the invisible," he says, "but I got such an incredible outpouring. The mail I got in the hospital was so soulful. All the Deadheads—it was kind of like brotherly, sisterly, motherly, fatherly advice from people. Every conceivable kind of healing vibe was just pouring into that place. I mean, the doctors did what they could to keep me alive, but as far as knowing what was wrong with me and knowing how to fix it—it's not something medicine knows how to do. And after I'd left, the doctors were saying my recovery was incredible. They couldn't believe it.

"I really feel that the fans put life into me . . . and that feeling reinforced a lot of things. It was like 'Okay, I've been away for a while, folks, but I'm back.' It's that kind of thing. It's just great to be involved in something that doesn't hurt anybody. If it provides some uplift and some comfort in people's lives, it's just that much nicer. So I'm ready for anything now."

In the years following that 1987 conversation with Garcia, the Grateful Dead went on to enjoy the greatest commercial successes of their career. More important, though, was the symbiosis that developed between the band and its audience—a reciprocity likely unequaled in pop history. At the heart of this connection was the Dead themselves and their self-built business organization—the latter of which did a largely independent, in-house job of handling the booking and staging of the band's near-incessant tours, and which also bypassed conventional ticket-sales systems as much as possible by selling roughly 50 percent of the band's tickets through a company-run mail-order department. This model of an autonomous cooperative helped spawn what was perhaps the largest genuine alternative communion in all of rock: a sprawling coalition of fans, entrepreneurs and homegrown media that surrounded the band and promoted it as the center for a worldwide community of idealists. What's more, that community thrived largely without the involvement or support of the established music industry or music press.

But any meaningful example of cooperative community isn't without its problems, and by the early 1990s, the Deadhead scene was increasingly beset by serious dilemmas. As far back as the mid-1980s, some of the group's more reckless and unfaithworthy fans—particularly the ones who gathered in parking lots outside the band's shows, begging for free tickets, sometimes selling various drugs and often disrupting the peace and security of nearby neighborhoods—had grown so prevalent that some concert halls, local police departments and city councils were forced to pronounce the Dead and their audience as unwelcome visitors. The Dead often tried to dissuade its followers from this sort of behavior, but it wasn't until the summer of 1995—following some serious bottle throwing and gate crashings that resulted in riot incidents—that the situation reached a crisis level and provoked a severe response from the band. The Dead issued an edict, in the form of fliers, demanding that fans without tickets stay away from the show sites, and advising that any further violent mass actions might result in the band canceling future tours. "A few more scenes like Sunday night," the band wrote, "and we'll quite simply be unable to play . . . And when you hear somebody say 'Fuck you, we'll do what we want,' remember something. That applies to us, too." In response, Garcia received a death threat that was taken seriously by not only the band and its entourage, but by law enforcement officials as well. After events such as these, according to some observers in the Dead's camp, Garcia and the band had seriously started to question whether many of the people they were playing to truly made up the sort of community they wanted to preserve.

But there was a graver problem at hand. Garcia's health continued to be a problem in the years after his 1986 coma, and according to some accounts, so did his appetite for drugs. He collapsed from exhaustion in 1992, resulting in the Dead canceling many of the performances on their tour. After his 1993 recovery, Garcia dedicated himself to a regimen of diet and exercise. At first, the pledge seemed to work: He shed over 60 pounds from his former 300-pound weight, and he often appeared renewed and better focused onstage. There were other positive changes at work: He had become a father again in recent years and was attempting to spend more time as a parent, and in 1994, he entered into his third marriage, with filmmaker Deborah Koons. Plus, to the pleasure of numerous Deadheads, he had recently written several of his best new songs in years with his longtime friend Robert Hunter, in preparation for a new Grateful Dead album.

These were all brave efforts for a man past fifty with considerable health problems and a troubled drug history. In the end, though, they weren't enough to carry him further. In mid-July 1995 he checked into the Betty Ford Center in Rancho Mirage, California, for one more go at overcoming his heroin use. According to one report, he wanted to be clean when he gave away his oldest daughter, Heather, at her upcoming wedding. He checked out several days later, so he could spend his fifty-third birthday on August 1, with family and friends. A week later he went into a different clinic, Serenity Knolls in Marin County. He was already clean, most sources report; he just wanted to be in sound shape. This time, Jerry Garcia did not walk out and return to the loving fraternity of his band, his fans and his family. At 4:00 a.m., Wednesday, August 9, 1995, he was found unconscious by a clinic counselor. In his sleep, it seems, he had suffered a fatal heart attack. According to his wife, he died with a smile on his face.

Jerry Garcia and the Grateful Dead were so active for so long, and were so heartening for the audience that loved them, that it seemed somewhat astonishing to realize that the band's adventure was now over. Of course, anybody paying attention—anybody aware of the up and downs in Garcia's well-being—might have seen it coming. Still, endings are always tough things to be braced for.

"He was like the boy who cried wolf," says John Barlow. "He'd come so close so many times that I think people gradually stopped taking the possibility as seriously as they otherwise would have. Or maybe we felt so certain that this would happen someday that we had managed—as a group—to go into a kind of collective denial about it. I mean, I looked at this event so many times, and shrank back from it in fear so many times, that I erected a new callus against it each time I did so. Now that I'm here at the thing itself, I hardly know what to think of it. Every deposition of every imagined version of it is now standing in the way of being able to understand and appreciate the real thing.

"But this is a very large death," says Barlow. "There are a lot of levels on which to be affected here, all the way from the fact that I'm going to miss terribly the opportunity to spend time in conversation with one of the smartest and most playful minds I've ever run up against, to the fact that there will never truly be another Grateful Dead concert. I never thought of myself as a Deadhead, exactly, but that's been a pretty fundamental part of my life—of all our lives—for the past thirty years."

It was, indeed, a big end. To see the Grateful Dead onstage was to see a band that clearly understood the meaning of playing together from the perspective of the long haul. Interestingly, that's something we've seen fairly little of in rock & roll, since rock is an art form, the most valuable and essential pleasures of which—including inspiration, meaning and concord—are founded in the knowledge that such moments cannot hold forever. The Grateful Dead, like any great rock & roll band, lived up to that ideal, but they also shattered it, or at least bent it to their own purposes. At their best, they were a band capable of surprising both themselves and their audience, while at the same time playing as if they had spent their whole lives learning to make music as a way of talking to one another, and as if music were the language of their sodality, and therefore their history. No doubt it was. What the Grateful Dead understood—probably better than any other band in pop music—was that nobody in the group could succeed as well, or mean as much, outside the context of the entire group, and that the group itself could not succeed without its individuals. It was a band that needed all its members playing and thinking together to keep things inspiring. Just as important, it was a band that realized that it also needed its audience to keep things significant. Indeed, it would probably be fair to say that, for the last twenty years, the Dead's audience informed the group's worth as much as their music did.

In the hours after I learned of Garcia's death, I went online to the Well, the Bay Area computer conference system that thrived in no small part due to its large contingent of Deadheads. I wanted to see how the fans were doing, and what they were saying, in the recognition of their loss. For the most part—at least in those first hours that I scanned the messages—what I found were well-meaning, blithe comments, people sending each other "beams" (which are like positive extrasensory wishes) and fantasies of group hugs. They were sentiments that many people I know would retch at, and I must admit, they proved too maudlin for my own sensibility. Still, one of the things I had to recognize about the Deadheads years ago was that this was a group of people for whom good cheer wasn't just a shared disposition but also an act of conscious dissent: a protest against the anger and malice that seems to characterize so much of our social and artistic temper these days. The Deadheads may sometimes seem like naïfs, but I'm not convinced their vision of community is such an undesirable thing. After all, there are worse sustained visions around—for example, the conservative and neoconservative ideologies that have engendered disaster in the nation since the 1980s and that still scourge any community of the misfit or helpless.

In any event, for my tastes I saw far too little attention paid—by both the Deadheads and the media—to just how much darkness there was that made its way into Garcia and the Dead's music, and how strong and interesting that darkness was. For that matter, there was always a good deal more darkness in the whole 1960s adventure than many people have been comfortable acknowledging—and I don't mean simply all the drug casualties, political ruin and violence of the period. There was also a willingness to explore risky psychic terrain, a realization that your best hopes could also cost you some terrible losses, and I think that those possibilities were realized in the Dead's music and history as meaningfully as they were anywhere.

In fact, the darkness crept in early in the Dead's saga. It could be found in the insinuation of the band's name—which many fans in the early San Francisco scene cited as being too creepy and disturbing as a moniker for a rock group. It could also be found deep down in much of the band's best music—in the strange layers and swirls that made parts of *Aoxomoxoa* such a vivid and frightening aural portrayal of the psychedelic experience, and in the meditations about death and damage that the band turned into hardboiled anthems of hope on *Workingman's Dead*. And of course, there was also all the darkness in the band's history that ended up bringing so many of its members to their deaths.

Not all darkness is negative. In fact, sometimes wonderful and kind things can come from it, and if there's one thing that was apparent to everybody about Jerry Garcia, it was that he was a good-humored man with generous instincts. But there was much more to him than that, and it wasn't always apparent on the surface. In a conversation I had several years ago with Robert Hunter about Garcia, Hunter told me: "Garcia is a cheery and resilient man, but I always felt that under his warmth and friendliness there was a deep well of despair—or at least a recognition that at the heart of the world, there may be more darkness, despair and absurdity than any sane and compassionate heart could stand."

In his last interview with *Rolling Stone*, in 1993, Garcia had this to say about his own dark side: "I definitely have a component in my personality which is not exactly self-destructive, but it's certainly ornery. It's like . . . 'Try to get healthy'—'*Fuck* you, man . . .' I don't know what it comes from. I've always clung to it, see, because I felt it's part of what makes me *me*. Being anarchic, having that anarchist streak, serves me on other levels—artistically, certainly. So I don't want to eliminate that aspect of my personality. But I see that on some levels it's working against me.

"They're gifts, some of these aspects of your personality. They're helpful and useful and powerful, but they also have this other side. They're indiscriminate. They don't make judgments."

Garcia, of course, made his own choices, and whatever they may have cost him, I would argue that in some ways they were still brave, worthy choices. Maybe they were even essential to the wondrous products of his life's work. His achievements, in fact, were enormous. He helped inspire and nurture a community that, in some form or another, survived for thirty years and that may even outlast his death; he cowrote a fine collection of songs about America's myths, pleasures and troubles; and, as the Grateful Dead's most familiar and endearing member, he accomplished something that no other rock star has ever accomplished: He attracted an active following that only grew larger in size and devotion with each passing decade, from the 1960s to the 1990s. You would have to look to the careers of people like Louis Armstrong, Duke Ellington, Count Basie, Miles Davis or Charles Mingus to find the equivalent of Garcia's musical longevity and growth in the history of American bandleaders.

Most important, though, he was a man who remained true to ideals and perceptions that many of the rest of us long ago found easy to discard—and maybe in the end that is a bigger part of our loss at this point than the death of Garcia himself.

My favorite Grateful Dead song of the last decade or so is "Black Muddy River." It's a song about living one's life in spite of all the heartbreak and devastation that life can bring, and in its most affecting verse, Garcia sang: "When it seems like the night will last forever / And there's nothing left to do but count the years / When the strings of my heart begin to sever / Stones fall from my eyes instead of tears / I will walk alone by the black muddy river / Dream me a dream of my own / I will walk alone by the black muddy river . . . and sing me a song of my own."

Those were among the last words Garcia sang at the Grateful Dead's final show, at Chicago's Soldier Field, in early July 1995. Not bad, as far as farewells—or a summing-up of the man's purpose—might go. When Garcia died, a certain world was lost, a lingering ideal was finally gone. That hope of community that he and the Dead represented fast dissipated. The dream had long been a misapprehension, of course—at least for somebody as disenchanted as myself. Still, I would trade almost anything to be in the midst of that fool's paradise once again. It was an experience too remarkable ever to forswear.

KEN KESEY'S
GREAT AMERICAN TRIP

It is possible that one of the great American literary works of the last forty years wasn't a novel after all—not in any conventional sense, anyway. Instead, this particular great story—which is to say, a captivating tale that enriches our understanding of not just our nation but also a nation of ideas—may have been a writer's life, as much as his books. Make no mistake: Ken Kesey—who died on November 10, 2001, at age sixty-six, following complications from surgery for liver cancer—was indeed a great American novelist. His first celebrated book, *One Flew Over the Cuckoo's Nest*, proved as innovative as it did indelible, and it anticipated a great change in both a nation's and generation's outlook. But Kesey was something beyond an author: He was a considerable cultural force who helped transform modern history as much through how he lived his life as through the words that he wrote. Indeed, following his death, some obituaries seemed to view Kesey as a man who had forsworn his considerable literary talents in exchange for his mid-1960s drug-obsessed exploits with the Merry Pranksters (a loose crew of friends and like-minded explorers) and the Grateful Dead (his key partners in a notorious series of West Coast event-concerts known as the Acid Tests). In other words, Kesey could have grabbed the golden ring in American letters, but somewhere, somehow, he made a different choice: He decided to challenge America's psychic landscape in ways that risked not just his own reputation but that also seemed to jeopardize our social sanity.

The interesting part is, Kesey realized all along that he was imperiling his own standing, and he seemed as delighted as he did perplexed by the turns he made in his life. In a letter he wrote in the late 1960s to novelist Larry McMurtry during a brief fugitive flight to Mexico to avoid prison on drug charges, Kesey wrote: "What was it that had brought a man so high of promise to so low a state in so short a time? Well, the answer can be found in just one short word, my friends, in just one all-too-well-used syllable:

"Dope!

"And while it may be claimed by some of the addled advocates of these chemicals that our hero is known to have indulged in drugs before his literary success, we must point out that there was evidence of his literary prowess well before the advent of the so-called psychedelic into his life but no evidence at all of any of the lunatic thinking that we find thereafter!"

That letter appears in Tom Wolfe's *The Electric Kool-Aid Acid Test*—a rollicking and meticulous documentation of Kesey's adventures. Wolfe was himself shattering journalistic and novelistic traditions in the form-breaking way in which he crafted his account. Even so, Kesey was among those who had broken the mold that allowed writers like Wolfe to explore new styles and chancy subject matter. Tom Wolfe had the good sense to recognize that Kesey was living a terrific novel in that time, not writing one. Kesey, though, is the one who had the sense (good, bad or neither) to live the risks of his tale.

Kesey was raised as what might be called an all-American boy. He was born in La Junta, Colorado, to dairy farmers Fred and Geneva Kesey, on September 17, 1935. The family later moved to Springfield, Oregon. Fred Kesey—who would found one of Oregon's largest dairy cooperatives—was a man who imbued in his sons a love of outdoor life (shooting, running the rapids of the Willamette River) and a passion for sports; Kesey was an outstanding runner and a star football player and wrestler in high school. Fred also taught Kesey what were viewed as essential masculine values: to be ambitious, independent, tough and fearless. Consequently, Kesey grew up confident and as something of a natural leader. His Springfield high school voted him the "most likely to succeed" among his graduating class, and at the University of Oregon he was popular in fraternities and enjoyed success as a wrestler and actor. Kesey later spent time in Los Angeles, thinking about becoming an actor, but mainly he wanted to write.

In 1958 he attended Stanford University's graduate writing program on a creative-writing fellowship, where his teachers included Wallace Stegner and Malcolm Cowley (the latter had been William Faulkner's editor and also edited Jack Kerouac's *On the Road*). Kesey and his wife, Faye (the two had been high school sweethearts and married in 1956), settled into an area in Palo Alto known as Perry Lane, famed as a bohemian neighborhood. Many of the hip sophisticates on Perry Lane took Kesey as an Oregon hayseed—a young man with farm-bred ways and rough table manners, even though he was a perceptive student of literature. But another Perry Lane resident—a psychology student, Vic Lovell—thought Kesey possessed a keen and curious mind. Lovell told Kesey about a series of experiments under way at the Veterans Hospital in nearby Menlo Park: Psychologists and clinicians were paying volunteers $75 a session to take "psychomimetic" drugs that induced short-term but powerful shifts in consciousness—everything from hallucinations to what the doctors termed temporary psychosis. Kesey volunteered for the program in 1959, and that was when everything in his life began to change, on all levels.

Kesey immediately realized two things as he began taking the drugs (which included LSD and peyote, a cactus bud used in American Indian religious rites). For one, the drugs that he was taking had wild and ecstatic effects—maybe close to madness, but also rife with insights that could alter one's fundamental understandings of life and mind. The other thing was, the doctors who were administering these drugs—who were trying to measure mental states by checking blood pressure, taking temperatures, asking dispassionate questions and making detached observations—didn't really grasp the significance of their own experiments, and surely didn't grasp the potential sociopsychological impact of a drug like LSD. The clinicians were on the outside of the experience; Kesey was on the *inside:* He was observing more valuable truths about these drugs, he believed, than the doctors did. Kesey also believed that these experiences were too good to be kept secret. They should be shared outside the setting of hospitals and free of the controls and survey of psychologists and medical students. Somehow, the drugs—which soon became generically known as psychedelics—began to find their way out of the Veterans Hospital and into the bodies, minds and lives of Kesey's friends and his neighbors on Perry Lane. After that, nobody thought of Ken Kesey as a hayseed. They thought of him as the most daring guy around, with keys to an unimaginably rich new kingdom. They began to think of him as a pioneer.

By this time, Kesey had already started work on a novel, *Zoo,* about the remnants of Beat life in San Francisco's North Beach district. He took a job at Menlo Park's psychiatric ward, as a night attendant. In part, the job gave him time to think about his novel, and it also gave him greater access to the drugs he wanted for himself and his friends. Sometimes he would go to work under the influence of LSD, and as he did he started to see something wrong in the approach of the hospital's doctors and nurses to the psychiatric patients: They were, in fact, often treating patients in antitherapeutic ways that served to deepen their fears and psychological instability rather than to help them. As a result, some patients learned that to be judged "sane" they essentially had to fake a version of mental health that matched social expectations. His experience with drugs, Kesey later told *Paris Review*, "gave me a different perspective on the people in the mental hospital, a sense that maybe they were not so crazy or as bad as the sterile environment they were living in."

These observations—fused with his ongoing drug experiences—inspired Kesey to set aside the novel he was working on and produce a whole new one. He wrote parts of it under the influence of psychedelics, and then, when the drugs had worn off, he would go back through his pages, keeping the passages that conveyed distorted mental states and rewriting the parts that the drugs had made excessive. The result was *One Flew Over the Cuckoo's Nest*. One of the most legendary and influential novels of the last half century, *Cuckoo's Nest* was the story of Randle Patrick McMurphy, a defiant man in a madhouse where madness was the only affirming and clarifying response to the dehumanizing tyranny of an authority figure like Nurse Ratched. *Cuckoo's Nest* was published in February 1962 and was an instant commercial and critical success. Jack Kerouac called Kesey "a great new American novelist," and it seemed as if Kerouac was passing to the younger writer the torch of iconoclasm in American fiction. (Indeed, Kesey has often been viewed as the key transitional figure between the Beats of the 1950s and the hippies of the 1960s.) *Cuckoo's Nest* has never lost its power for American readers and audiences: It became a smash play (successfully revived by Gary Sinise in 2001) and was made into an Academy Award–winning film by Milos Forman in 1975 (though Kesey hated the film). Writing about the book in her *New Yorker* review of the film, Pauline Kael observed that "the novel preceded the university turmoil, Vietnam, drugs, the counterculture. Yet it contained the prophetic essence of that whole period of revolutionary politics going psychedelic. Much of what it said has entered the consciousness of many—possibly most—Americans."

Kesey was already at work on the second major novel of his career: *Sometimes a Great Notion*—an epic about a tough-minded family of loggers in Oregon, and in some ways a tribute to the values he had learned years before from his father. But something even bigger and more lasting was brewing in the author's life and creativity. He and his family had moved from Palo Alto to nearby La Honda, and thanks to his newfound fame as America's most promising young author and the gradually spreading news of his drug passions among an underground of intellectuals and cultural daredevils, Kesey began to draw a burgeoning crop of colorful characters to his home, among them Neal Cassady.

Kesey had finished *Sometimes a Great Notion*, and along with several of his companions—including Cassady and an old Stanford friend, Ken Babbs—Kesey hit on an interesting plan to celebrate the new novel's release. They bought a 1939 International Harvester school bus that had been out-fitted as a home-on-wheels for a family, painted it in garish colors, loaded it up with a crew of cohort upstarts—a team that became dubbed the Merry Pranksters—and set off to New York, to arrive in time for the book's publi-cation. After all the interior journeys LSD had provided, Kesey and this close-knit group were lighting out for larger territory: They would dis-cover America—they would take a reading on its values and learn if it was ready for the sea-change they saw coming—and they would get very, very stoned on a regular (that is, daily) basis. Neal Cassady was at the wheel, driv-ing at times on acid, at other times on speed. On the front of the bus Kesey and crew painted the declaration: "Furthur." On the back, they wrote: "Weird Load." It proved quite a trip. Along the way, the Merry Pranksters enchanted some Americans, disgusted others, bewildered various police-men, and worked on what is one of the more legendary unreleased films of the last century (Kesey was reported to be working on the film's final edit at the time of his death).

The bus and its Pranksters arrived in New York just as reviews for *Some-times a Great Notion* began to appear. The critics were of mixed opinion on the book—some thought it extended the genius implicit in *Cuckoo's Nest*, others saw it as pretentious and messy—but Kesey was growing less inter-ested in what the novel form offered him. He began talking about writing as being old-fangled and limited. Years later, he told *Rolling Stone* that he had found the paradigm for this new view in Neal Cassady. "I saw that Cas-sady does everything a novel does, except he did it better 'cause he was livin' it and not writin' about it."

Near the end of their stay on the East Coast, Kesey and the Pranksters vis-ited Millbrook, an experimental, drug-fixated community in upstate New York. Millbrook was headed by ex-Harvard professors Timothy Leary and Richard Alpert (the latter later known as Baba Ram Dass), who had gained unwanted notoriety for conducting drug experiments with college stu-dents and losing their tenure as a result. (Leary had long been studying the therapeutic use of psychedelics.) Kesey and the Pranksters saw Leary, Alpert and the others at Millbrook as sympathetic comrades, but when Furthur pulled into the grounds at the stately Millbrook mansion, with the Pranksters setting off green smoke bombs, they received a chilly welcome. In part this was because the two groups differed strongly in their views of how psychedelics should be administered. It's true that Leary, like Kesey, believed that therapists should not administer drugs to patients and then sit by and note their reactions but should, in fact, engage in the drug state along with the subjects. But he also strongly favored implementation of an environmental condition that became known as "set and setting": If you prepared the drug taker with the proper mind-set and provided reassuring surroundings, then you increased the likelihood that the person might achieve a significant opportunity for a healthy psychological reorganization. Kesey, by contrast, believed in a Wild West approach: Let people take the drugs in any variety of social or public settings and just see what happens. In short, Leary and Alpert's Millbrook assembly saw the Pranksters as frivolous and irresponsible and gave them a cold reception. Leary, the Pranksters were told, was sequestered in a three-day LSD experiment upstairs in the mansion, and he couldn't receive visitors. Kesey and crew left miffed, convinced that their Eastern counterparts—even when high on psychedelics—were stuffy. Still, Leary and Alpert had a point: By the time Furthur arrived back in La Honda, at least two of the Pranksters had gone through mental anguish or disassociation intense enough to require concentrated help.

Furthur's journey was a turning point for Kesey—his first attempt at breaking through what his friend and colleague Robert Stone called "the artifice between the artist and the public." That quest would drive Kesey, in varying ways, for the rest of his days. It would also win him a hell of a lot of fame and trouble in the process.

The Furthur bus trip became the stuff of myth for the hippie nation that would soon form in America. It also solidified the bond between Kesey and the Merry Pranksters. For the Pranksters, Kesey became a central guiding force—the most important and inspired partner in their enterprise. For Kesey, the Pranksters' experimental community became the primary vehicle for his new living-art form of artistic and literary ambition. Together, they felt they constructed a "group mind" that—despite inevitable tensions and a few nervous breakdowns—worked with a near-unanimity of instinct, or at least with mutual tolerance. Today, such a description probably sounds like a recipe for a cult of frightening potential. But Kesey was wise and honest enough to tone down his perceived role as a leader. He was hardly without ego, temper or bad judgment, but he purported to harbor no ambitions to be a prophet or savior, even if that image sometimes followed him. In addition, Kesey poured all of his earnings from his books into supporting the Pranksters' life and to funding their ongoing movie.

Back in La Honda, the word of Kesey and company's drug intake and communal lifestyle was now an open secret. Citizens became alarmed about what was going on down the road from them, and local law enforcement put Kesey's house under surveillance—all to the amusement of the Pranksters. Then, on an April night in 1965, police raided Kesey's home. Kesey busted one officer in the face and was arrested for resisting arrest. He was also arraigned on possession of marijuana—a charge that could yield serious prison time. None of this impeded Kesey or the Pranksters. Kesey was released on bail, and a few months later rewarded the citizens of La Honda by inviting the Hells' Angels to a three-day beer-and-acid getting-to-know-each-other affair at his home. The police kept a close watch, but there was no trouble. The Angels admired Kesey's self-determination and audacity, and Kesey admired the Angels' acceptance of their outlaw status (a romantic view that would have serious repercussions later when the real—rather than the idealized—Angels wreaked havoc at the Rolling Stones' tragic Altamont concert, in late 1969).

In the fall of 1965, an organization called the Vietnam Day Committee staged a huge antiwar rally at the University of California in Berkeley, and invited Kesey and the Pranksters to participate—but their involvement didn't turn out as expected. When Kesey took his turn at the microphone, he lampooned the other speakers and the rally's aims, rebuking the crowd for what he deemed their own warlike belligerence. "Holding rallies and having marches . . . ," he said, between blowing blasts of "Home on the Range" on his harmonica, "you're playing their game . . . There's only one thing to do . . . And that's everybody just look at it, look at the war, and turn your back and say . . . Fuck it . . ." The committee was outraged. "Who the hell invited this bastard?" somebody yelled. Paul Krassner—the editor of *The Realist* and one of the organizers of the event—first met Kesey that day and became a lifelong friend. He recalls: "Kesey was in this unusual position, for him, of bringing people down. I said I disagreed with his position because I was an antiwar activist, but I really admired his willingness to be politically incorrect, especially in front of this audience which was gung-ho to march. And so at a benefit the next night, I played the harmonica and parodied his position, and he was in the audience and he jumped up onto the stage with a twinkle in his eyes, and he just said, 'I protest.' I thought that he was a political animal; however, he was not doctrinaire . . . his dope activism was extremely political."

Kesey was about to become even more an activist in that regard. In considering the potential effects of the use of psychedelics, Kesey stated:

"When you've got something like we've got, you can't just sit on it . . . and possess it, you've got to move off it and give it to other people." Kesey and the Pranksters—whose group now included Carolyn Adams (also known as Mountain Girl, who would later marry Jerry Garcia), began to think of a way to make this experience more public, more accessible. They conceived a series of parties, to be known as the Acid Tests, and they distributed leaflets around the Bay Area, bearing the question: "Can *you* pass the Acid Test?" The idea was to see what would happen when people took LSD in a setting where there were no regulations or predetermined situations. At Kesey's invitation, a local musical group, the Grateful Dead, became the house band for these collective drug experiments. The Dead would play for hours as the Pranksters filmed the goings-on—everything from freak-outs to religious revelations to group sex. The Acid Tests were meant to be acts of cultural, spiritual and psychic revolt, and their importance to much of what would follow—the development of hippie community and ethos, the growth and importance of the Grateful Dead, the disposition of Kesey's own fates—cannot be overestimated.

The Acid Tests ran in direct contrast to the philosophy of set and setting that Timothy Leary, Richard Alpert and others had formulated for the psychedelic experience. Some people called the experience a "mindfuck," and for fair reason: More than a few participants underwent difficult, even frightening experiences at the Tests, and they weren't always treated with sympathy or concern. Consequently, there was some intense backlash against the Acid Tests within both the pro-psychedelic and antidrug movements. Up until this point, psychedelics had remained legal—Kesey and the Pranksters were breaking no laws with the Acid Tests—but all this new publicity forced the California State Legislature's hand, and the state soon made the substances illegal.

In January 1966 Kesey was sentenced to three years' probation for his prior legal trouble, but he was almost immediately arrested again on new marijuana charges. A second violation brought the possibility of an increased sentence. Combined with his probation—which now might be revoked—Kesey was facing eight years of prison time. He decided he had only one choice: to become a fugitive. "If society wants me to be an outlaw," he said, "then I'll be an outlaw, and a damned good one." With the help of Carolyn Adams and others, Kesey wrote an elaborate note and staged a fake suicide—but he had not kept his ruse private enough. Before the note was even found, everybody—friends, the FBI and the press—seemed to know where Kesey was: He had gone to Puerto Vallarta, Mexico, where a few

Pranksters occasionally visited him and found him living a nervous life, taking off on a fast run every time somebody gave him a suspicious look. On one occasion, Mexican *federales* had stopped Kesey in a car and were about to detain him when he bolted, hopped a train and ended up in Guadalajara. But Kesey shortly tired of the fugitive life. He felt he owed the Pranksters and his family a bit more valor, and he snuck back into the Bay Area, where he turned up at various events and gave clandestine interviews. "I intend to stay in this country as a fugitive, and as salt in J. Edgar Hoover's wounds," he told the *San Francisco Chronicle*.

Meanwhile, the Acid Tests continued—some in California and Oregon, under Ken Babbs's direction, and some in Mexico, with Kesey. By the time Kesey returned to the Bay area, a full-blown hippie community was thriving in San Francisco's Haight-Ashbury district. Psychedelics were rampant in the city, and various concert promoters—including Bill Graham and Chet Helms—were staging weekend "Trips Festivals" of their own, featuring the Grateful Dead and other psychedelic bands. In essence, Kesey and the Pranksters' social model had now become the norm for a new population. As Tom Wolfe wrote in *The Electric Kool-Aid Acid Test:* "All of a sudden it was like the Acid Tests had taken root and sprung up into people living the Tests like a whole lifestyle." But the results were in many ways problematic: More and more young people were being arrested on drug charges, more and more were showing up homeless and hungry in the city, and more were proving vulnerable to unpleasant versions of the psychedelic experience. Kesey began to take a new view of how things were developing. "I'm going to tell everyone to start doing it without the drugs," he announced. This turnabout upset many people in the Haight: They thought Kesey was in danger of selling out their scene.

On October 20, 1966, Kesey was pulled over on the Bayshore Freeway by FBI agents. He vaulted down an embankment, but the agents caught him. Now, he faced a total of three major charges, including unlawful flight to avoid prosecution. Since Kesey had already made known his new feelings about abusing psychedelics—"Once you've been through that door, you can't just keep going through it over and over again," he said—his lawyers turned his change of heart into a defense strategy: Kesey, they told the court, would now work his influence to discourage drug experimentation. In the end, some charges were dropped, two trials ended in hung juries, and Kesey pled guilty to a lesser charge and received a ninety-day jail sentence and a six-month sentence on a work farm, to run concurrently. In the Haight, nobody seemed to know if Kesey had become a turncoat or had run a swindle on the law. The confusion only deepened when Kesey and the Pranksters staged an Acid Graduation Ceremony. "It's time to move on to the next step in the psychedelic revolution . . . ," Kesey said. "I know we've reached a certain point, but we're not moving anymore, we're not creating anymore, and that's why we've got to move on to the next step. . . ."

Kesey moved his family back to his hometown of Springfield, Oregon. After serving his sentences, he joined them there, and various Pranksters paid regular visits over the years. Kesey lived in Springfield for the rest of his life. As the years went along, he kept his hand in cultural matters. He became one of the major forces—along with Stewart Brand and Paul Krassner—behind *The Whole Earth Catalog,* a popular educational guide to environmental and countercultural influences (later cited by Steve Jobs as an influence on the development of Web search engines and their methodology). Kesey also wrote journalism on a regular basis for many publications. He also would write more fiction—*Sailor Song* (1992, set in Alaska) and *Last Go Round: A Dime Western* (a 1994 book about an Oregon rodeo, written with Ken Babbs in the form of a pulp tale), but the critical consensus was that Kesey had perhaps blown out his literary gifts with too many years of drugs and indolence. In 1990 Kesey admitted to the *Los Angeles Times* that his drug use might have hampered his fiction. "But," he said, "if I could go back and trade in certain experiences I've had for brain cells presumably burned up, it would be a rough decision."

Mainly, Kesey stuck to his conviction that the greatest art form was a life well lived, and to the principle that it was probably a better bet to confound fans' expectations than to feel obliged to meet them. He contributed to the Oregon community where he lived, teaching writing to various classes and coaching wrestling. He also developed his own peculiar sense of libertarian politics, which sometimes placed him in seeming conflict with feminist and gay concerns, though that's not how he saw it. "Kesey told me that he was inadvertently influenced by the feminist movement when he wrote *Sometimes a Great Notion,*" says Paul Krassner. "He said: 'Women's lib has made us aware of our debauching of Mother Earth. The man who can peel off the Kentucky topsoil, gouge the land empty to get his money nuts off, then splits the conquest, leaving the ravaged land behind to raise his bastards on welfare and fortitude is different from Hugh Hefner only in that he drives his cock on diesel fuel.'"

In 1984 Kesey's son Jed was killed in a bus crash on the way to a wrestling tournament. Kesey was shattered for a long time by the event, friends of his said, and the loss may have figured into why his highly anticipated return novel, *Sailor Song,* seemed to suffer. But Kesey used the tragedy as incentive to campaign for seat belts in Oregon's school buses. "Family was essential to his life," Krassner said. "His own family and his extended family."

"I thought of him as a true patriot," Krassner added, "putting all the principles of freedom of assembly into true action. He had this American flag kerchief and he had other clothing with stars and stripes that he wore, and this was all before the current trend of mixing fashion and patriotism and gung-ho nationalism. Kesey's patriotism was intertwined with what he did—the bus trip and the ability to do these things in this country that he didn't think he could do anywhere else. He was very basically American. He had the original values of the founders, and his writing and his actions reflected that."

Ken Kesey's legacy is likely a mixed one, though also a key one. He authored a major American novel that signaled a rising generation's restlessness over deadening and authoritarian conventional ethics, and he went on to live at the center of an intense and controversial experiment that took the values of *Cuckoo's Nest* and transformed them into real-life risks. Later, when he had to face some of the costs of that risk—in his own life and in the culture around him—he stepped back into a more private form of his own story, and back into the verities of land and family that he had emerged from. This isn't to say that he retreated into convention, any more than it is to say that his earlier iconoclasm was an attempt to undermine society. It wasn't: It was a hard-fought and brave attempt to examine how people might view and support one another in a time of great peril and great possibilities. Because he made these efforts, he helped America become a different place. Whether we like it or not, we are still living in Ken Kesey's America. Chances are, it will be a long time before the effects of his life settle enough to be fully measured or easily forgotten.

HAIGHT-ASHBURY
IN THE SUMMER OF LOSS

On the unseasonably clear morning of January 14, 1967, American poets Allen Ginsberg and Gary Snyder led a prayer march in a clockwise circle around the polo field in Golden Gate Park. They were preparing the field as they walked—blessing it in a Hindu rite of purification—for an assembly of pilgrims to be known as the Gathering of the Tribes for a Human Be-In, the first major gathering of the hippie counterculture. By the early afternoon, the grounds were filled with twenty thousand celebrants, moving to the sway of loud electric music, the throb of LSD, the entrancement of newly discovered fraternity. The planners of this event—mainly the editors of San Francisco's underground newspaper *The Oracle*—intended the event for anyone who cared to attend, though primarily it would draw the psychedelic community from the Haight district and the nearby San Francisco State College. The organizers recruited the Bay Area's best bands—among them the Grateful Dead, Jefferson Airplane, Country Joe and the Fish, Big Brother and the Holding Company, Quicksilver Messenger Service and the Loading Zone—all playing for free. They also invited several of the counterculture's best known figures, such as philosopher and psychologist Alan Watts, antiwar activist Jerry Rubin, poets Ginsberg, Snyder, Michael McClure and Lenore Kandel (whose poem "To Fuck with Love" was at the heart of an obscenity charge she was facing in San Francisco), and controversial psychedelic gurus Timothy Leary and Richard Alpert. *The Oracle* also extended a special invitation to radical activists at the University of California at Berkeley, who for some time had regarded hippies and their fast-emerging alternative culture as passive and hedonistic, and too withdrawn from political interests. This gathering, its heralds believed, would show that these two disparate but sympathetic clans could meet on a common plane in mutual accord. Allen Cohen, *The Oracle*'s editor, anticipated the day in these terms: "A union of love and activism previously separated by categorical dogma and label mongering will finally occur ecstatically . . . so that a revolution of form can be filled."

The Diggers, a Haight-Ashbury-based loose collection of street-theater provocateurs and community guardians, served turkey sandwiches spiced with LSD, with both the meat and the drugs supplied by Stanley Owsley, maker of the most powerful and most refined psychedelics commonly available. He also provided "White Lightning" acid in large quantities, for the occasion. The musicians played loud and commandingly; the Bay Area's notorious Hell's Angels looked after, and played with, the children who had wandered off in the crowd; the spiritual and inspirational leaders held forth to little real attention; and through it all, two policemen sat on horseback calmly watching, as various illegal drugs were in open use around the field. The Be-In ran from 1:00 to 5:00 p.m., and when it was over the organizers and volunteers swept the field of all debris. They were glowing. The Gathering of the Tribes for a Human Be-In had demonstrated that America's outsiders were considerable in their numbers and peaceful in their intent. It showed that new mind-sets were finding a footing in the land, that there was a future to be lived in a collective dream. Foremost, the Be-In announced that San Francisco was again a frontier town, this time for an unanticipated kind of frontier.

Watching it all unfold throughout the day was Emmett Grogan, the Diggers' best-known doctrinaire and idealist. All he saw was a sham and massive trouble to come. In his autobiography, *Ringolevio,* Grogan wrote that he was angry with the Be-In's organizers for "drawing a disproportionate number of kids to the district . . . who fell for the Love Hoax and expected to live comfortably poor and expected to take their place in the district's kingdom of love." Though Allen Ginsberg had a brighter disposition, there was a moment, he later remembered, when looking at the Be-In's multitudes in their seeming incorruptibility, a shudder passed through him. Ginsberg turned to fellow poet Lawrence Ferlinghetti, who ran San Francisco's City Lights bookstore, and said: "What if we're all wrong?"

It was only the first month in a year of expected miracles.

In 1967 the San Francisco Bay Area would be the epicenter of a cultural and political upheaval that challenged not just how people viewed America's purposes and standards, but also how they understood the meanings of life, art and the mind. California had long been the American location, in myth and history, where the bold and the hopeful migrated to realize ultimate visions—that luminous shore where they might find new starts or dead ends, the place where the American dream hit its last edge. San Francisco was the twist in that dream—a city with opium, whores and outlawry in its past, an image as alluring as it was notorious. It was there, in the 1950s, in the city's North Beach district, that Allen Ginsberg wrote *Howl*—an epic poem about the discarded people and promises of America, and the fears that lay behind and ahead for all—and it was there he first read the poem aloud, at a gathering that included Gary Snyder and Jack Kerouac, author of the not yet published novel *On the Road*. *Howl* was a shocking poem, a monumental piece of resistance but also of new prospects: It opened not just new doors in America's literature and public arts, it also pounded at the nation's ideals of civilization. Nobody had ever said anything like it before; as a result, it changed what could be said. It also helped make North Beach the putative home for the Beats—the hard-living literary and philosophical movement that Ginsberg, Kerouac and William Burroughs had helped define in the late 1940s. North Beach remained largely an enclave of poets and Beats until the mid-1960s, when a younger bohemian crowd—more colorfully dressed, with longer hair and affection for the rock & roll that followed in the wake of the Beatles—began mingling in the area. The Beats called these newcomers, somewhat derisively, "hippies," which is to say diminutive hipsters. The hippies drew certain traits from the Beats—including looser attitudes about sex, plus predilections for marijuana and improvisational music—though they were decidedly more optimistic about the potential of the era. Around that same time, as strip joints and new restaurants drove up rents in North Beach, the hippies began moving to Haight-Ashbury, a largely once black but now moribund neighborhood with plenty of affordable Victorian houses, near Golden Gate Park and not far from San Francisco State College.

Two key exploits—both born outside San Francisco—had decisive bearing on how the Haight would develop its character and purposes. The first took shape in the South Bay, in La Honda and Palo Alto, where in 1965 author Ken Kesey was conducting psychedelic group events known as the Acid Tests. In 1959 Kesey had volunteered to take part in a local Veteran Hospital's experimental program studying the effects of psychomimetic drugs—that is, drugs believed to induce brief and harmless bouts of psychosis. The experiments familiarized Kesey with LSD, a drug that delivered what he believed to be a radical way of looking at life with a new hallucinatory and ecstatic perspective. For the next few years, Kesey made himself a pioneer for LSD, and with his crew of cohorts, the Merry Pranksters, he began staging large parties to see what would happen when people took the drug in settings where there were no rules. The Warlocks—later called the Grateful Dead—became the house band for these events. In those hours, Jerry Garcia would later say, the Dead's music "had a real sense of proportion to the event"—which is to say that sometimes the group's playing would seem to overshadow the event, and at other times it would function as commentary or backdrop to the action of the event itself. Either way, neither the Pranksters nor the Dead were the stars of the party. Instead, the parties' central force was formed from the union of the music and musicians with the audience, and the spirit and shape of what was happening from moment to moment—which meant that there was a blur between the performers, the event and the audience.

Kesey conducted the Acid Tests at various sites over the next year (LSD was still legal to consume in California until October 1966). Then, in late 1966, as he was facing marijuana possession charges (Kesey eventually served six months in prison), the outlaw author announced that it was time for the emerging counterculture he had helped foster to stop taking psychedelics. Along with the Pranksters, he conducted a Graduation Day event for LSD users on Halloween 1966, at a San Francisco warehouse. Most of the San Franciscans now involved in psychedelics felt that Kesey was trying to control something he could no longer control. LSD was now a vital part of the burgeoning Haight-Ashbury community.

The other development that helped form the Haight's early temperament took place at a Western-style dance hall, the Red Dog Saloon. In June 1965 a San Francisco band, the Charlatans, took up residence at the saloon. Their easygoing attitude and meandering performances, as they played sometimes under LSD's influence, set another model for public psychedelic gatherings, one much less tense and sardonic than Kesey's. In San Francisco in October 1965 a couple of Red Dog veterans, now calling themselves the Family Dog, staged an evening of dancing and bands at the Longshoreman's Hall. The event, called A Tribute to Dr. Strange, featured the Charlatans, Jefferson Airplane and the Great Society. The event spontaneously fused the lenient spirit of the Acid Tests with Red Dog's focus on dancing and proved a pivotal occasion in the psychedelic scene's history. Over the next two years, San Francisco dance ballrooms—primarily the Avalon and the Fillmore—became not merely a central metaphor for Haight-Ashbury's reinvention of community, but also a fundamental enactment of it. "In the early days," Big Brother and the Holding Company's Sam Andrew later said, "the audience and the bands were on the same plane. . . . It felt like everyone was joined by this electric current, and they were all part of it." In *Beneath the Diamond Sky: Haight-Ashbury: 1965–1970,* by Barney Hoskyns, Haight-Ashbury community leader David Simpson expanded on this idea:

"It is very important to know how closely the alternative community of San Francisco identified with the music of specific musicians. . . . They were our bands, they were our musicians. Neither they nor we felt the distinction between the artists and the people, and it gave the music great strength. . . . It was a wonderful inspired sense of oneness."

The bands that emerged in this setting—including Jefferson Airplane, Big Brother and the Holding Company, Quicksilver Messenger Service and Country Joe and the Fish—were made up largely of musicians who had come up playing in the Bay Area's numerous folk music venues. The folk crowd had been notoriously dismissive of rock & roll; they saw it as unserious and decadent, not at all committed to social or political concerns. But after the arrival of the Beatles in 1964 and Bob Dylan's transition to electric music in 1965—and after the Los Angeles band the Byrds exhibited a mellifluent and rousing example of folk rock that also included such disparate elements as Indian ragas and John Coltrane–style modal jazz—Bay Area folk musicians began to see how electric music could incorporate substantive themes and poetic language. "Rather than being some drug-induced thing," said Country Joe and the Fish guitarist Barry Melton in *Beneath the Diamond Sky,* "it was really a bunch of serious folkie musicologists who played bluegrass and blues joining forces with guys who played at the edge of town, chewed gum and couldn't put two sentences together—the rock & roll players." But as psychedelics made their way steadily into the music scene, bands couldn't help but adapt to the drugs' effects as they played together. LSD changed musicians' sense of continuity—a player could follow a melody wherever it might lead, altering the shape and function of the music's harmonic structure, transforming it into a background of reverie for improvisations—a process that the Grateful Dead's Jerry Garcia once described as "something like ordered chaos." LSD could also alter one's sense of time: The perceived moment, and not its true measurement, mattered most. In performances that sometimes meant a single song's exploration might stretch for a half hour or even much longer.

The best circumstance for hearing this new daring music was in the ballrooms. Promoter Chet Helms had taken over the Family Dog and was presenting shows regularly at the Avalon, and Bill Graham—a gruff organizer resented by some, but who fought fiercely for the community's rights to gather and hear music—ran the Fillmore. In these venues' darkened and large spaces, loud and propulsive sounds combined with vivid and kinetic images, making for an immersive environment. In particular, the dance hall scene's famous light show displays—in which artists and technicians mixed colored liquids in glass pans and swirled the blends in overhead projections, in improvised motions that fit the music—were an indispensable part of the inclusive experience.

This new music, and the life it found in the concert halls, played a considerable part in the Haight-Ashbury's early growth, and that success rapidly became a problem. In the late 1960s rock & roll was more than a powerful and strange form of music—it was a sign of an unprecedented cultural divide, marked largely along generational lines. The parents of the nation's youth had expected their children to affirm the values of a post–World War II America that was intent on expanding its prosperity and overcoming the threat of communist empire—even though it was the youth who would pay the bloodiest costs for the nation's war in Vietnam. But the youth were forging their own ideals of peace, tolerance, politics, aesthetics and community. Those ambitions were manifest in a growing opposition to Vietnam involvement and in the desire to form a new culture—the counterculture—with its own ethics and practices.

San Francisco's city hall and media saw Haight-Ashbury foremost as a society of drug users and dealers, draft evaders and indolent freeloaders—a place to be watched, contained and deprecated. Two local headlines in 1967 declared: "Mayor Warns Hippies to Stay Out of Town" and "Supervisors Back War on Hippies." The police ratcheted up pressures, shutting down dances at the Fillmore and other locales when possible, while various other city officials tried to revoke dance hall licenses and succeeded in forbidding the attendance of youth under eighteen. Meantime, the press reported often and disapprovingly on what they saw as the hippies' weirdness. Finally, in October 1966, possession of LSD became illegal. San Francisco's youth culture—and others like it—had to take its central ritual underground.

It made for a paradox. San Francisco—in the case of both the Haight and the new music emanating from the city's ballrooms—was forging a model for a freewheeling, beneficent culture. "Let me see you get together / Love one another right now," Jefferson Airplane sang on its first album, and it wasn't an orgiastic bid. But because this new ideal of commonality worked outside received notions of civic duty and the sanctions of authority, it was seen as an ominous uprising. The community's only significant public advocate was *San Francisco Chronicle* jazz critic Ralph J. Gleason (later a cofounder of *Rolling Stone*), who began covering the new music and the counterculture knowledgeably, and reported on the police harassment of Fillmore promoter Bill Graham as he tried to cope with the new under-eighteen rule. Gleason wrote: "Since the dances have started—almost exactly a year ago—the only trouble at the dance halls has been the police. . . . The trouble is, this society is terrified of youth, so it has been made illegal."

It certainly felt that way to many at the time. Haight-Ashbury and its integral psychedelic community was an experiment, on a scale that had not been seen in America since the Mormons turned Nauvoo into a city-state in 1840s Illinois. Of course, the Mormons were driven from the state for their beliefs, and by the time 1967 rolled around in Haight-Ashbury, there were many who wanted the hippies to come to a similar end.

Truth be told, there never was a Summer of Love in 1967 San Francisco. If there was such a season, it was in that spring and summer stretch of 1966, when Haight-Ashbury was taking on the aspects of a town within a city, when shops like Ron and Jay Thelin's Psychedelic Shop were opening on Haight Street and an increasing and creative population was giving new life to a once fading district. As Charles Perry wrote in *The Haight-Ashbury: A History*, "To the people involved in psychedelics . . . a whole world now revolved around the Haight-Ashbury, and was plainly growing. . . . What was happening was so big it would wash . . . imperfections away or perhaps engulf them and transform them into unexpected benefits."

But by 1967, it was a different story. It's true the year had begun with the large and peaceful Human Be-In, but it had also started with the inauguration of a new governor, Ronald Reagan, who won election largely for condemning recalcitrant youth and promising to come down hard on them. These two events were promises running in opposite directions, but what eventually happened to the Haight had nothing to do with promises. Dreams simply hit hard limits and bad faith. Indeed, Haight-Ashbury became a village of arguments after the Be-In. Already, in the year's early months, the district's population was denser, and an alarming amount of the new faces appeared to belong to high school–age runaways. But that was nothing compared to what was now anticipated. Both community leaders and police were predicting an influx of anything from fifty thousand to two hundred thousand visitors to the Haight by summer's end—numbers that, no matter how they finally tallied, could amount to a disaster.

The Diggers—the Haight's contrarian conscience—had been at odds with many of the Haight's leaders for some time. Police had stepped up drug arrests in Haight-Ashbury recently, and *The Oracle* and the hip merchants believed that opening a benevolent dialogue with the police chief and patrolling officers would increase mutual empathy and help assuage the problem. One shop owner posted a sign in his window, urging people in the neighborhood to "Take a Cop to Dinner." The Diggers saw this as a message of useless appeasement. They issued a broadside through the Haight, stating: "And so, if you own anything or don't, take a cop to dinner this week and feed his power to judge the morality of San Francisco." The Diggers were now leveling much of the blame for the impending surge at the Haight Independent Proprietors (HIP), a merchants' association that had formed in November 1966. They also aimed disapproval at the psychedelic community's newspaper, *The Oracle,* and at some of the new culture's self-appointed spokesmen, such as Timothy Leary, whose resounding call to youth to drop out of social obligations and tune in to LSD's enlightenment, they believed, was irresponsible and intentionally guileless. The Diggers believed that all these contingents' various interests were commodifying the community and despoiling its original promise. Emmett Grogan and the other Diggers had envisioned Haight-Ashbury as a self-sustained local village with its own economy and with an ethos of self-invention. *The Oracle,* by contrast, envisioned little short of a global transformation (indeed, the paper enjoyed a worldwide readership of over one hundred thousand), with an event like the January Be-In serving as a lure to a nationwide immigration that would, in the Diggers' estimation, destroy Haight-Ashbury and everything it had been trying to achieve.

Some of what happened in the months leading up to the Summer of Love took on curious, even absurd, aspects. That was because the new psychedelic vogue not only could make money but was in fact changing how marketers were responding to trends. In *The Haight-Ashbury,* Charles Perry notes an advertising executive's comments to the *Washington Post*: "People all of a sudden are becoming aware of a segment of the population having an almost controlling effect on what is bought and not bought—as though it didn't exist last year. Industry is jumping up and down and saying, 'How can we get with it? What can we put in or copy?'" Which perhaps explains why the Gray Line Bus Company began a "San Francisco Haight-Ashbury District 'Hippie-Hop' Tour"—"the only foreign tour within the continental United States." At first the Haight's residents took the tour with good humor, but they soon began to resent tourists gawking rudely, as if hippies were a zoo exhibition. Early on, the Diggers commandeered one of the buses and drove it over to the Grateful Dead's house on Ashbury— a stop that Gray Line made a regular feature of the tours. Finally, residents began following the tours, sometimes holding up mirrors to the sightseers, sometimes pelting the buses with tomatoes. In May, Gray Line canceled the tours.

But the problem of how to handle the flood of newcomers and tourists that the Haight would unwittingly invite to its streets come summer was still pressing. In early February, the Diggers and the hip merchants met to discuss how to prepare for the incursion. The Diggers had already been working to establish spaces for overnight shelters—crash pads—for runaways and itinerants, and they were surprised to learn that all that HIP had planned was access to free legal advice and a job co-op. That set off the Diggers' Emmett Grogan, who launched into an invective, charging that HIP wasn't serious about their accountability. The Diggers, though, weren't alone in trying to prepare for a mass arrival. In the spring, Episcopal ministers asked the park commission to allow temporary camping in Golden Gate Park to avert a crisis. San Francisco Police Chief Thomas Cahill (the man who had first named the new movement the "Love Generation") shut down that possibility, saying, "Any encouragement . . . tending to attract still more undesirables to the problem areas of San Francisco is a disservice to the community." The following day, San Francisco mayor John Shelley said he wanted any arriving hippies declared officially unwelcome.

Digger Peter Cohon (actor Peter Coyote) felt that though the young people arriving in the Haight that year were already encumbering the Diggers' resources, the collective felt they had no choice but to continue in their efforts. "The city," Coyote later said, "was . . . telling all these kids—our age, a lot of them younger—to get lost. And our feeling was that they were our kids. You know? This was America; these were our kids." Certainly, the Diggers understood the hazards of sheltering runaways: It might expose the neighborhood to even greater police scrutiny, running the danger of more drug arrests. But nobody—not the Diggers, not the merchants and not the Haight's residents—was about to cooperate with the authorities in their hunt for runaways. Radical activist Abbie Hoffman, who for a time saw himself as a Digger, once likened runaways to "escaping slaves." Turning them in would undermine every principle that the hippie community had built itself on.

In May a twenty-four-hour resource, the Haight-Ashbury Switchboard, opened to help people find places to sleep or eat, and to guide them through crises. The following month, the around-the-clock Free Clinic opened, staffed by thirty volunteer doctors. Still, worries persisted. In mid-

April, Haight watchdog Chester Anderson had issued the most famous and disturbing broadside in the community's history:

> Pretty little sixteen-year-old middle-class chick comes to the Haight to see what it's all about & gets picked up by a seventeen-year-old street dealer who spends all day shooting her full of speed again & again, then feeds her 300 mikes [a high dosage of LSD] & raffles off her temporarily unemployed body for the biggest Haight Street gang bang since the night before last.
>   The politics & ethics of ecstasy.
>   Rape is as common as bullshit on Haight Street.

On an earlier occasion Anderson wrote: "Are you aware that Haight Street is just as bad as the squares say it is?"

It would still be weeks until the Summer of Love.

Despite this growing sense of crisis, the ballroom scene and San Francisco's new generation of bands continued to flourish. Jefferson Airplane—comprising folk and blues players assembled by lead singer Marty Balin, who was eager to craft a folk-rock band—was the first truly popular sensation to emerge from the Haight and would consistently prove one of the Bay Area's most exhilarating live bands. In May, their second album, *Surrealistic Pillow* (their first to feature Grace Slick, from the Great Society, as a soaring co-lead vocalist, and along with *Bless Its Pointed Little Head*, the band's best album), rose to Number Three on the album chart, and yielded two remarkable singles, "Somebody to Love" and "White Rabbit" (the latter, in part, an outright paean to psychedelics). By contrast, the Grateful Dead—the band that had played Ken Kesey's Acid Tests—recorded a debut that many believed fell short of their already renowned live performances (later captured memorably on *Live Dead*). Even so, that first album, *Grateful Dead*, included a number of songs that would remain in the band's concert repertoire for the duration of its lifespan, and it was also the only brash rock & roll album the Dead ever made. Other bands were also forceful presences. Berkeley's Country Joe and the Fish was the only prominent band on the scene to put radical politics out front, and their first album, *Electric Music for the Mind and Body,* remains one of San Francisco psychedelia's most rewarding works. Though Quicksilver Messenger Service wouldn't appear on an album before 1968, the band on its best nights was the fiercest of any of the San Francisco bands, featuring long-ranging song suites and mesmeric instrumental passages, driven by John Cipollina's fleet and sinuous guitar lines and Greg Elmore's impelling drum thrusts. (In almost all cases, dynamic and inventive drummers were essential to the success of the San Francisco bands' music.)

But the Haight's dark horse proved to be Big Brother and the Holding Company, with singer Janis Joplin, as became powerfully evident at the June Monterey Pop Festival. Monterey Pop was conceived by the Mamas and the Papas' John Phillips and record producer Lou Adler as a showcase for the new sensibilities in folk and popular music and avant-garde rock & roll, but the San Francisco bands were wary of the Los Angeles–based organizers' intentions.

At first, most Bay Area artists refused to sign a release form that would grant the festival worldwide rights for the use of their performances in a film, until they understood that the film was the only way for the enterprise to recoup some of its expenses, since it was a nonprofit affair. Before it was over, most of the artists signed the release, and in the case of Big Brother and the Holding Company, that decision led to an historic moment. Though the band's musicians carried a reputation for somewhat ungainly performances, their appearance in D. A. Pennebaker's film *Monterey Pop* is searing and riveting, and Joplin's rendition of Big Mama Thornton's "Ball and Chain," in which she merged deep-felt pain with an overwhelming eroticism, was perhaps the high point of the festival—a febrile moment that instantaneously made Joplin the Haight's single biggest star. The funny hitch in this development was that Joplin herself despised psychedelics; she and some of the other members of Big Brother preferred alcohol (they referred to themselves as "alkydelics") and heroin. Later, Joplin more or less disavowed the community that had embraced her. "They're frauds," she said, "the whole goddamn culture. They bitch about brainwashing from their parents, and they do the same damn thing."

Monterey Pop took a lot of blame for spoiling the virtues of the San Francisco rock scene by fomenting stardom in what had once been a community of peers, but the judgment was neither fair nor accurate. Several of the artists—in particular Jefferson Airplane and Janis Joplin—already had ambitions that reached beyond hometown success, plus most were growing discouraged by the increasingly corrosive atmosphere in the Haight. In the end, it is the music that the scene produced that remains the single most palpable legacy of the whole experiment. It still has effect, it still has verve and life, a sense of confidence in the untried.

Indeed, that music was powerful enough in its time that it helped create and spread the vision of the Haight as a hub for epiphany to an outside world that was unaware of the neighborhood's impending crisis. For that matter, the Haight's darkening realities didn't particularly intrude on the rest of San Francisco, where many other young people felt they were in fact living the Summer of Love dream. The main venues for the new rock & roll, the Avalon and the Fillmore, existed outside the Haight, and they drew audiences from all over the Bay Area. The experience inside those dance halls was blissful, and it was what inspired Ralph Gleason, in describing the Fillmore and the Avalon, to write: "The kids and the adults there are outstanding for their peacefulness." This impression also reached young people outside of California. The national media was rendering Haight-Ashbury and San Francisco's music-centered scene as something both deplorable and fascinating, but the other, more meaningful medium—the music itself—was spreading sounds and images of transformation. It was hard for many to hear the music emerging in 1967 and not want to go to San Francisco, with its apparent promise of community founded on ideals of hope and concord—where the war didn't reach—and the possibilities of amazing psychedelic and sexual adventures. This was a new world, there for the journey.

In the final days before summer 1967, folksinger Scott McKenzie's hit single "San Francisco (Be Sure to Wear Flowers in Your Hair)," written by John Phillips of the Mamas and the Papas, was everywhere on pop radio. The naïveté of its sunshine promise was maddening—"For those who come to San Francisco / Summertime will be a love-in there / In the streets of San Francisco / Gentle people with flowers in their hair"—and yet there was something undeniably lovely, even haunting, about the song. McKenzie's voice, the way the music opens into a space of gravity as a bass pulse grounds the song's reverie, now seem to anticipate a heartbreak past the serene ideal described in the lyrics. The utopia the song envisioned was, like all utopias, illusory, but its myth was now an inexorable allure.

Truth be told, the idea of an LSD-bound community was, as much as the music, an essential part of that allure. LSD was foremost a drug that facilitated remarkable encounters with the self and other selves. In the Haight, LSD became a bonding instrument—a way of declaring a new fraternity and forging a new paradigm that stood apart from old precepts. This outlook could make the drug's effects feel like a shared insight—especially in a dark room full of music and dancers—but all of acid's peregrinations came from inside the user and for the most part ended there. Timothy

Leary understood this, and advocated preparing the LSD user with the proper mind-set and providing reassuring surroundings, for a healthy psychological experience. Of course, Ken Kesey also appreciated LSD's intense inner reality, but his idea of the right set and setting was to foment perplexity (or worse) in relatively unrestrained environments. A fair number of people came away from various Acid Tests deeply unsettled, and it seemed to some that for Kesey that was the ideal.

Kesey's model is the one that had greater bearing in the Haight, though using psychedelics in public settings—even friendly ones—always entailed a certain jeopardy. This became notoriously apparent on the day summer began, June 21, when the Diggers staged their own version of a gathering, a summer solstice festivity that would "leave be-ins to the college students, ad men and news medea [sic]." By the time the Summer of Love actually started, harder drugs had begun to pervade the Haight. According to Martin Torgoff's account in *Can't Find My Way Home: America in the Great Stoned Age, 1945–2000*, the Diggers' solstice observance was far worse. A new drug, STP, produced by Owsley Stanley, had come into circulation at a June 21 summer solstice festival. STP stood for Serenity, Tranquility, Peace, though the drug provided no such experiences. Instead, it kept users in a psychedelic state for up to three days, and it wasn't a pleasant experience for many. Torgoff claims that five thousand people took the drug at the solstice gathering, and for three days San Francisco's emergency rooms were filled with people undergoing bad experiences with STP. There was nothing that could be done for them. Thorazine, an antipsychotic with a tranquilizing effect, had been widely given to LSD users in emotional and mental trouble, but Thorazine wouldn't work with STP. Instead, it only made the psychedelic's effect horribly worse.

The event seemed to correspond to a declining interest in psychedelics in the Haight. As it developed, with the flood of newcomers also came different drug preferences. Many people in Haight-Ashbury were now shooting methedrine, an amphetamine. Numerous others were trying heroin, sometimes as a counteragent to the high-wired, agitating effects of amphetamines. All of these drugs had one thing in common: They were ways of managing the apprehension and the desolation that now filled Haight-Ashbury's streets and many of its homes as well. They were also inherently dangerous. Injecting drugs always ran risks of infection and overdose, and amphetamines—that is, speed—might also induce psychosis, even violence, far more readily than the use of psychedelics. "The criminal element was growing, and it got harder to deal with," Carolyn Adams (known as

Mountain Girl in the Haight, and once married to Jerry Garcia) told Nicholas von Hoffman in *We Are the People Our Parents Warned Us Against*. "The freedom thing was being turned into the freedom to fuck up in public—the freedom to break a bottle, the freedom to hit somebody, the freedom to step on somebody who was on the ground. . . . These powerful elements of destruction had suddenly entered this beautiful street party that had been going on ever since the Be-In." Soon, the Grateful Dead began scouting new locations to base themselves and their families.

In that same June that "San Francisco (Wear Some Flowers in Your Hair)" was a hit, *The Oracle* published an editorial that tried to defuse the imminent Summer of Love predicament. In March the paper had posed the question, "Will success spoil the Haight-Ashbury?" The writer answered: "Maybe. Probably. . . . But not if we're very, very good. And careful." Now *The Oracle*'s editors admitted that they and others had been unable to garner the help of the city's resources in caring for the young people who were about to swarm not just the Haight but much of the rest of San Francisco. They urged readers to create their own alternative communities, but not in San Francisco. If the suggestion had any effect—and perhaps it did—it wasn't at all apparent. Bad things had started, and they weren't about to stop.

In the heart of the summer of 1967 in Haight-Ashbury, there were bad drugs—drugs that weren't what they were purported to be—being sold and consumed, there were street beatings, and there were confrontations with the police. On an early July evening, a police attempt to clear a blocked intersection turned into a serious hourlong clash. It ended in nine arrests and four bad injuries, including a girl who had her jaw broken twice by a policeman's nightstick. A man attempting to walk his sheepdog was arrested, and a policeman beat the dog to death with a nightstick. The Haight was like a tinderbox, but instead of blowing up, the neighborhood steadily burned itself down.

In early August, a drug dealer was found dead in his apartment near the Haight. He had been stabbed a dozen times, and his right arm—the arm he was known to chain his briefcase to—was severed and missing. The man later arrested in the murder still had the arm with him but claimed he wasn't sure why, due to his prolonged bad history with LSD. Three days after the first murder, another slain man was found, this time in Marin County. He was a black LSD dealer who had been a familiar figure in Haight-Ashbury. In between the news of the two murders, something else happened: Beatle George Harrison and his wife, Pattie Boyd, paid the Haight a brief visit. Harrison, who was on LSD when he arrived, strolled up Haight Street to the Panhandle. It wasn't long before he was noticed and was asked to sing a song. He strummed a guitar somebody handed him, trying to find his way through "Baby You're a Rich Man," but found the experience disconcerting and made a fast retreat. Harrison later said that he had expected something a bit more urbane, like London's psychedelic scene. Instead, he felt appalled by the "hideous, spotty little teenagers" he'd found in Haight-Ashbury, and before leaving San Francisco he resolved not to take any more LSD. (Despite his experience, Harrison donated $66,000 to the Haight-Ashbury Free Clinic in 1974 and saved it from closing down.)

By the time the Summer of Love was finished in September, more than seventy-five thousand people had visited Haight-Ashbury, then left the place. There are numerous statistics and subjective claims about how many people had bad drug or health experiences during that time. For example, the Free Clinic treated more than twelve thousand patients in three months, and San Francisco's General Hospital reported a fivefold increase in acute drug episodes from February to July. Other organizations' figures vary widely; accurate research on drug use in a nomadic and suspicious community is an elusive feat. It's clear, however, that multi-thousands took LSD in San Francisco in the mid- and late 1960s (according to one commonly quoted figure, four million Americans had already taken the drug by 1964, which seems implausible beyond belief), but what the quality or results of those incidents might have been couldn't be determined. Haight-Ashbury may have been the largest laboratory for drug experimentation in America's history, but nobody was monitoring it with anything close to objectivity. Perhaps the worst of it could never have been quantified. In Joan Didion's account of the Haight during 1967, "Slouching Towards Bethlehem," she told of meeting a five-year-old girl, Susan, reading a comic book, stoned on LSD. The girl's mother, Didion wrote, had been giving her child both LSD and peyote for a year. It was an unbearable glimpse at a dream that didn't even know when it had passed into nightmare.

Come October, Ron and Jay Thelins closed the Psychedelic Shop and left a sign in its window: "Nebraska Needs You More." By then, residents were continually leaving the district for safer homes, for communes and country life. The Grateful Dead, though, didn't move quite fast enough: On October 2, police raided their house on Ashbury Street and arrested two band members (Bob Weir and Pigpen) for drug possession. Four days later, the Diggers and others led a Death of Hippie/Birth of the Free Man funeral march, bearing a cardboard coffin, to the corner of Haight and Ashbury. Not many Haight locals joined in. Some wondered why a group that attacked anybody seen to be in leadership positions was still trying to determine the community's viewpoints. Nobody much thought that the hippie movement was truly dead.

Both the Grateful Dead's arrest and the Death of Hippie procession were covered in the first issue of a new magazine, *Rolling Stone*, dated November 9, 1967. *Rolling Stone* was started by Jann Wenner, who had been a student at the University of California at Berkeley. Earlier in the year, Wenner had approached his friend Ralph J. Gleason, the *San Francisco Chronicle* columnist who been reviewing the city's new music, with an idea: He wanted to launch a new-style music magazine—one that would give rock & roll its cultural and revolutionary due. "*Rolling Stone*," Wenner wrote in the magazine's first issue, "is not just about music but about the things and attitudes that the music embraces." The magazine would cover the San Francisco scene definitively. It would also write about the news and attitudes surrounding illegal drugs, and about the new culture that was burgeoning in—and disturbing—America. This was terrain that the Haight made promising for years to come.

The Haight itself, though, was clearly finished. "It was like somebody had come through it with a flame-thrower," poet Michael McClure later said. A number of the district's more devoted inhabitants moved on to life in self-sustaining communes, some in or near cities, others in rural locations throughout California and America. (In 1968 Stewart Brand, who had been associated with Ken Kesey and the Merry Pranksters and who organized the pivotal 1966 Trips Festival, created *The Whole Earth Catalog*, which proved an imaginative and widely influential resource for the rural movement.) Many others moved across the Bay to Berkeley and areas around Oakland, where cheap rents could still be found. Berkeley—which had been a focal point for civil liberties activism and radical politics since the 1964 Free Speech Movement at the University of California—also witnessed extraordinary events in 1967, peaking in fierce October antidraft demonstrations in Oakland that proved the tipping point in America's burgeoning antiwar movement. In time, Telegraph Avenue became the new Haight Street, though Berkeley police—who conflated longhairs with the city's fervent antiwar movement—proved even more relentless in the harassment of hippies and students. Tensions turned bitter and ugly, finally culminating in May 1968, in an argument between the University at Berkeley and students over a piece of contested land, People's Park. Police ended up seizing the land in a violent confrontation. Governor Ronald Reagan praised the raid and sent in two thousand National Guard troops to suppress any further reaction. In essence, it was the final stand of what had become of the Haight-Ashbury movement.

Still others from Haight-Ashbury—musicians, former community leaders, merchants—moved north across the Golden Gate Bridge, to the spacious, largely undeveloped terrain of Marin and Sonoma counties. The most notable of these émigrés was the Grateful Dead, who had been known as the "people's band" in Haight-Ashbury—the band that cared about the following it played to, and that often staged benefits or free shows for the community's good. Long after the Haight's moment had passed, it would be the Grateful Dead—and the Dead alone among the original San Francisco bands—who would still exemplify the ideals of camaraderie and compassion that most other 1960s-bred groups had long relinquished and that many subsequent rock artists repudiated in favor of more hard-bitten ideals. Though the band left San Francisco for the pastoral relief of Marin, they also took something about the Haight's best spirit with them as they traveled the world for three decades. By and large, the people who gathered to see them weren't simply an audience, but rather a dispersed society that, by gathering, reenacted the ideal of the San Francisco ballrooms of 1966 and 1967—a possibility that still existed as long as the Dead lasted.

When Jerry Garcia died in August 1995, a tie-dyed flag was flown on the middle flagpole at San Francisco's city hall, and the surrounding flags were lowered to half-staff. It was a fitting gesture from a civic government that had once feared the movement and social changes that the Haight represented, and that now acknowledged not just the passing of a great musician and bandleader, but that the seasons of the Haight-Ashbury adventure proved one of the most notable chapters in the city's modern history. Over the years, San Francisco had come to embody some of the best of what that neighborhood had handed down.

What went wrong in Haight-Ashbury? How did an adventure that began in exploring new forms of creativity and the life of the mind turn into an environment of dread and decay? Or was it all wrong from the start, a journey in bad values and bad judgment, leading to a place of bad ends? People have been arguing over these questions for over forty years now.

Part of the Haight's rise and fall was always psychedelics and how they drew the people there into extraordinary shared experiences. "In places as

public as the Haight-Ashbury and as private as farms in the Kansas coun-
tryside," wrote David Farber in *The Age of Great Dreams: America in the
1960s*, "young people dropped acid, imagined the impossible, and then
tried to bring it to life." That was the drug's miracle, but also its curse: LSD's
effects, in the moment, could seem life changing, rich in boundless poten-
tials that might turn the world upside down. But in the end, the LSD
experience couldn't function on the scale that the Haight had facilitated. It
wasn't so much because of the damage the drug purportedly caused;
despite all the media hysteria and horror-stricken anecdotes, LSD did only
limited injury. Millions of people took it, and the lives the drug hampered
were certainly in far smaller numbers than those destroyed by the harder
drugs that took over the Haight or by the legal ruin of heavy drinking.

LSD, it has to be said, was an amazing experience. It could be great fun
and it could be edgy, even frightening. But almost all of us weathered
those mind storms—we recovered and went on. Whether we got much
from it, that's another arguing point. Still, LSD was radical. Its greatest hazard wasn't insanity nor even upheaval, but breaking the bounds of permit-
ted possibilities, not all of them beneficial, as Carolyn Adams noted when
she was speaking about "the freedom thing" that went awry in the Haight.
On communal and mass levels, LSD stood to transmute familiar notions of
order—and in late-1960s America, disrupting social conventions often
proved constructive. But the nation's dominant culture wasn't willing to
abide hallucinogenic disruptions that would reach into their homes and
schools, and into the recesses of the rational mind. LSD was just too damn
scary to America to survive as a social currency, and Haight-Ashbury's
identity with the drug inspired abhorrence among many. It seems long ago
now, that time when an urban village could disturb and excite an entire
nation. What happened in San Francisco in those seasons was seen as a fis-
sure in modern certainties—as a blight or as a wonder. In the years since,
the transformations that took place in the Haight and in similar neighborhoods, towns and college centers across the country have been denounced
as the source for many subsequent social dilemmas, including varying
drug problems and youth's endemic sexual activity. The hippie movement
of the 1960s, we have been told time and time again by conservative critics,
injured—even corrupted—American civilization: It unleashed frightening
and empowering specters that continue to haunt and harm us, say those
detractors, and the permissions that resulted need to be resisted and, where
possible, overturned. The 1960s counterculture became a scapegoat,
blamed for a social changeover that was, in some ways, already ongoing and

that developed from a complex mesh of conditions. The truth is, legal narcotic addictions were a mainstream American societal scourge long before the illegal use of marijuana and psychedelics became popular, and freedom of sexual activity became more permissible after the availability of birth control pills. In any event, an increasing open-mindedness about sexuality, as well as about the public communication of controversial ideas, were significant improvements.

There were other effects that were also clearly enriching. The powerful sense of connectivity that motivated the Haight at its best—of people being of one place and of like mind—and a growing belief among the counterculture in the primacy of the natural world over modern material-ism, soon led to a keener sense of connection to the environment human-ity depends on yet has steadily spoiled. To be sure, environmentalism was already an important concern, but the counterculture helped advance it as a global movement that has never lost its urgency. In March 1970, after a campaign around the nation and in the UN, San Francisco inaugurated an Earth Day observance that grew massively in dimension over time.

The hippie movement also had great influence on how Americans (and others in the Western world) viewed, judged and tolerated one another—though this change developed in fitful and complex ways. Initially, much of this transpired over issues of appearance. More and more men, for exam-ple, now wore their hair much longer. This fashion had started, of course, with the Beatles' arrival in America in February 1964, inspiring a trend of longer hairstyles for men over the years; high schools fought to ban the style, and countless American businesses refused to hire males with longer hair. By 1967 hair length often reached to a man's shoulders or longer. This progression incurred both public hostility and sometimes violence. Men's long hair was no small break with twentieth-century style—to some it heralded a suspicious feminization, and to many others it was an emblem of radical beliefs and practices that were seen as affronts to longstanding values. That is, long hair—along with more ornate and flowing types of clothing among young males and females alike—was seen as a deliberate flouting of more uniform postwar standards, as a breach in accepted pub-lic manners, as a disavowal of American values. (This is partly what the film *Easy Rider* was about: People could risk their lives over these differences.) But within seasons, more people gradually adopted these styles, until by the 1970s, long hair often meant little more than personal preference—even conservatives and reactionaries could look hip without danger. More signif-icantly, mass numbers of people began experimenting with marijuana, even though many of them had no particular devotion to what they saw as hippie or radical ideals. Plus, they grew more accepting of changes in sexual morality and political convictions. (By 1972 this developing new worldview largely remade the Democratic Party, after the debacle of the 1968 Chicago Convention.) Was all this progress? If not, it was certainly major change, and though various instances of deviance and nonconformity are still frequent objects of derision, open-mindedness and social liberalization made some worthy advances that have never been overturned.

This is how the spirit that is identified with 1967—or more accurately, the combined effect of the hippie movement, the changing rock & roll scene and social and political activism—spread into the world. This is how it changed the possibilities for how life and community could be lived, as well as how new forms of democracy might come from the streets and from the peripheries in American society. The Haight and the culture it represented initially bore influence through its music and its impact on similar-minded communities throughout the nation, then later—more lastingly—through its effect on ideas, attitudes and social and personal practices. This process didn't end up remaking institutions as some in the counterculture expected would happen, nor was it an unambiguous, sweeping break with the world of the past. However, to a remarkable degree it vastly reconfigured America's culture and manners for the next forty years—and, of course, it ignited a mean-witted conservative backlash that owes much of its being and fervor to the purpose of annulling the forces set free in that time.

What happened in San Francisco, and throughout much of youth culture in that time, is still with us, whether we like it or not. Now, much of it is assimilated, but in that year, in that summer, radical transformation seemed everywhere—in the music, in the streets, in the news, in our homes—and it felt startling and provoking. That atmosphere formed the central dynamic of a war of values that became the story of America in the late 1960s and early 1970s. Each side felt as if it were playing for big stakes—nothing less than the fate of the nation's soul. The story of our times since then has been a reaction, an effort to roll back the spirits of transformation and resistance of that time, and to make sure that nothing like it might happen again. But it can never be completely undone. The resonance of that disruption still informs almost every major political dispute and cultural rupture of our times. In one way or another, the arguments of San Francisco in 1967 will never end.

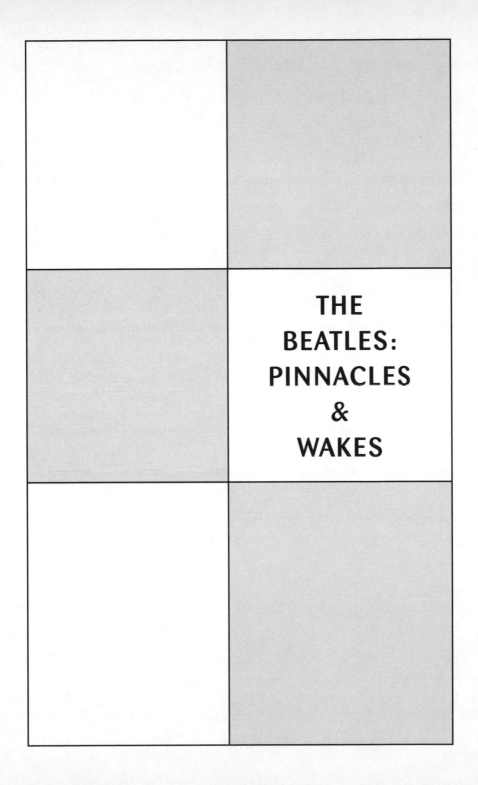

THE
BEATLES:
PINNACLES
&
WAKES

THE MYSTERY INSIDE
GEORGE HARRISON

"George himself is no mystery," John Lennon said in 1968. "But the mystery *inside* George is immense. It's watching him uncover it all little by little that's so damn interesting."

George Harrison was, in the early days of the Beatles' fame, the most unknowable personality of this sudden, inexorable force that was changing culture and history—and then later he seemed the band's most forward-looking and surprising hidden treasure. When the Beatles ended, Harrison initially reaped the greatest solo successes of any of the group's members. He made a masterful and loving epic post-Beatles solo work, and followed it with the most singular concert in rock & roll's history. He seemed a man of heartfelt and energetic goodwill. But since the mid-1970s, George receded from public view and from the popular music arena, into the massive confines of his enigmatic mansion, into carefully shielded seclusion, into reported fears, into a deliberate distance from contemporary pop vogues. Was this a retreat, or was it instead a way of arriving at some form of fulfillment? Did Harrison have no more need for the world that had once loved him so fervently, or had he in fact suffered some irreparable disappointment that made his efforts at music making—as affecting as they sometimes were—only sporadic?

"Being a Beatle was a nightmare, a horror story," Harrison once said. "I don't even like to think about it." The Beatles received an extraordinary bounty of love in their career and lives—and each of them told the world through their music that love was a key act of faith and will that could save us or make our lives worthwhile. How, then, did such gifts and such an outlook translate into a nightmare for the gift givers? I can't answer that, as much as I've puzzled over it. The one person who could died on November 29, 2001, after a brave and dignified battle not just with death, but also with life.

• • •

George Harrison sometimes referred to himself and Ringo Starr as "economy-class Beatles." It was a remark that was both self-deprecating and barbed—a way of pointing out that Paul McCartney and John Lennon were the acknowledged and envied creative center at the heart of the world's most beloved rock & roll band, not to mention its wealthiest members. By contrast, he and Starr were seen as gifted yet lucky accompanists. But there was something revealing in the comment about the Beatles' historic and class origins. Years ago it was possible to visit Liverpool and see the homes and districts where the group's members grew up, before these areas were cleaned up a bit and declared official birthplaces for tourist traffic. What one discovered from such a visit was eye-opening: John Lennon—the Beatle who most passionately promoted his working-class sympathies and identity—grew up in relative comfort compared to his bandmates. The others—especially George and Ringo—grew up in tougher, riskier, more rundown areas that would, by American standards, be considered low-income housing projects.

Apparently, though, Harrison didn't feel especially deprived in his childhood. Indeed, of all the Beatles, he probably grew up in the home that provided the greatest sense of continuity and support. His father, Harold Harrison, came from working-class Liverpool lineage. At age fourteen, Harry was already supporting himself, and by his seventeenth year, he was a steward aboard a famed ocean liner. In May 1930 Harry married Louise French. By the time he was ready to settle ashore in Liverpool with his wife in 1936, the Depression that had gripped America had spread to England and Europe, and it hit the once-respected town of Liverpool hard. For more than a year, Harry and Louise had to live on the dole, like many other proud Liverpudlians.

Harry eventually took work as a bus driver, and the family settled into a Liverpool working-class suburb. In 1931 the Harrisons' first child, Louise— named after her mother—was born. In 1934 the family gave birth to its first son, Harry, and in 1940 (the same year that John Lennon was born), the Harrisons had a second son, Peter. In those days, Goering's *Luftwaffe* was making bombing raids over the city, destroying Liverpool's famed docks. The town's citizen's were living with fear and endangerment as a daily reality, and they were also living with the necessity of rationed food supplies, scant amenities and a sense of economic limitations that—war or no war—continued to set parts of England's North apart from some of the wealthier areas of its South. It was in these circumstances that George (named after King George VI) was born on February 25, 1943, as the family's unexpected final addition. The Harrisons were strained economically in this period, and in 1949, the family moved to a council house in Speake, a nearby district known as a poor and tough area.

Later, Harrison would describe Liverpool and its surrounding environs at that time as being like New York's Bowery. Even so, the Harrisons seemed a tight family (George's mother described her youngest son as "seldom misbehaved . . . bright . . . and extremely independent"). Harry Sr. was seen as a stern but fair man (he prided himself on being Liverpool's best bus operator and later became a top union official for the city's drivers), and Louise enjoyed a reputation as a generous and convivial woman, but also somebody who, like George, had little patience for abiding people who imposed on her. In any event, the family wasn't terribly ambitious in its hopes, which was typical of Liverpudlians in the aftermath of the war. The older sons, Harry and Peter, quit school early on. George ended up as the family's only boy who made it through grammar school and, in 1954, into high school. By all accounts—including his own—he was not a distinguished or reverent student, though, like many young people in England and America at that time, his lack of interest in conventional academic and social standards was more an affirmation of his wits than it was a sign of any lack of them.

That's because George Harrison—like the other young men with whom he would soon form a famous bond—was witnessing the birth of the social and cultural upheaval that became known as rock & roll: the clamor of young people, kicking hard against the 1950s public ethos of vapid repression. In many ways, Britain was as ripe for a pop cataclysm as America had been for Elvis Presley during the ennui after world war. In England—catching the reverberations of not just Presley, but the jazz milieu of Miles Davis and Jack Kerouac—the youth scene would acquire the status of a mammoth subcultural class: the by-product of a postwar population, top-heavy with people under the age of eighteen. For those people, pop music denoted more than preferred entertainment or even stylistic rebellion: It signified the idea of autonomous society. British teenagers weren't just rejecting their parents' values—they were superseding them, though they were also acting out their eminence in American terms, in the music of Presley and rockabilly; in blues and jazz tradition.

Liverpool, more than most British metropolitan areas, was ripe for the explosion of rock & roll. American sailors were regular visitors to the city because of its naval stockyards, and—like German tourists who also occasionally came through the town—these visitors sometimes brought the latest R&B and dance singles to town. Liverpool's record stores were prone to stocking new and fresh American sounds that were either too rough or too new to have yet made an appearance on BBC radio. By the time he was thirteen, George was caught up in the new rock & roll, rockabilly and country sounds. In particular, he was enamored of the Sun recordings of Carl Perkins and Elvis Presley, and he thought Little Richard was wild beyond belief.

At this time, British schoolboys were expected to dress in neat clothes or young men's suits, but George took to wearing skin-tight pants and greased-back hair, in the manner of other Teddy Boys—the British youth contingent that adopted American rockabilly as a cause and that was seen as the UK's equivalent of juvenile delinquents. When Harry Sr. expressed concern about this rebellious appearance, George's mother expressed support for her youngest son's boldness. "There's more than enough sheep in this life," she told her husband. "Just let the boy be." George later said: "My mum did encourage me. Perhaps most of all by never discouraging me from anything I wanted to do. . . . If you tell kids not to, they're going to do it in the end anyway. . . . They let me stay out all night and have a drink when I wanted to." There were limits, however, to what his parents would allow. Though George was a successful art student, he failed most of his other courses, prompting one schoolmaster to remark that he "made no contribution to school life." George's high school, the Liverpool Institute, decided to hold him back a year, though he declined to tell his parents. Instead, he would spend afternoons visiting friends or movie theaters. When his parents finally discovered his deceit, they weren't so much angry as practical: Since George was no longer in school and not anxious to return, but was of an age where he could at least make a small living, it was time for him to find a job. At his father's insistence, George accepted an apprenticeship as an electrician at a Liverpool department store, Blackler's.

Harrison found the job tedious. He didn't want to be an electrician. He didn't want to be a laborer. By this time, a British pop star named Lonnie Donegan was helping forge a homegrown response to American rockabilly with a trend called skiffle—a merger of American folk and black forms with country textures and a distinctly British cadence. The vogue eventually became so popular that several young Liverpool males began sporting guitars about town, simply as fashion wear. When George's mother noticed he was constantly drawing sketches of guitars, she bought an inexpensive acoustic for him. He often stayed up through the nights, trying to master chords, country-western fingerpicking patterns and rock & roll riffs, and before long, he bought a more professional Hofner model. While riding on his father's bus, George had already met another Liverpool skiffle and rock & roll fan, Paul McCartney, who was a little older than Harrison. McCartney started studying guitar with George at the Harrisons' home. He was stunned at George's facility on the instrument—he could play fleet rockabilly and country riffs, and McCartney taught him some of the more complex jazz chords and riffs of legendary gypsy guitarist Django Reinhardt. Harrison, in turn, was impressed by McCartney's range and force as a vocalist—his ability to mimic the throat-busting yowls of Little Richard, as well as his talent for memorizing and conveying pop standards and ballads. The two became close friends, hitchhiking on weekends with their guitars, practicing constantly, sometimes sleeping on dirty sand or sidewalks after a long night of trying to copy the riffs of Carl Perkins or emulate the powerful yet dreamy vocal styles of the Everly Brothers and Buddy Holly. After seeing Holly and the Crickets at Liverpool's Empire Theatre, McCartney thought the two should form a duo or band of their own. George, though, was content with his role as a sideman and occasional singer.

For the next year or two, George played in various local bands—a short-lived skiffle outfit, the Rebels, and the Les Stewart Quartet. Meantime, McCartney had become enamored of another local skiffle-based outfit, the Quarry Men, led by a brash yet charismatic rhythm guitarist and singer, John Lennon. Lennon had an arrogant exterior—he was sarcastic, even rude, but it was hard to say whether these traits were signs of his confidence or vulnerability. He was also a respected student at Liverpool's Art College, though he had little patience for art school pretensions. He was another one of the local roughs who dressed as a Teddy Boy, and it seemed to many that to get close to him you had to accept that he carried a chip on his shoulder and could turn sardonic or mean without notice. Though he'd grown up in relative middle-class luxury, he wanted to be seen as a common type with a street temperament. Paul was more conventional and prudent in his manners, but Lennon's talent and showmanship fascinated Paul, and soon Lennon accepted him as a member of the Quarry Men, where McCartney effectively became second in command.

As time went along, McCartney began to lobby Lennon to bring Harrison into the Quarry Men as well. Lennon was as impressed as Paul by George's faculty on guitar, but he was leery of accepting Harrison as a peer. Harrison was three years younger than John, and Lennon told Paul he wasn't sure he wanted to let a "baby" into the group. Also, Lennon was annoyed that Harrison would tag along like an uninvited kid brother in social situations—

such as when John was seeing his girlfriend, Cynthia Powell. But John's estimation of George began to turn around when Harrison showed up at the house where Lennon lived with his aunt Mimi and she refused to let the scruffy-looking George enter her tidy home. "And why not, Mimi?" John said. "Too common for the likes of such a grand lady as you?" Lennon appreciated that Harrison's mother welcomed the young musicians into her house to practice without protest or condescension, and after John's mother Julia was killed in a car accident, he was grateful when George visited to console him. John finally caved in: George was allowed to join the group. The only catch was, the Quarry Men were breaking up just as Harrison enlisted.

By the late 1950s and early 1960s, Liverpool was perhaps the most promising music center in England. True, it was a fading port town that had slid from grandeur to dilapidation during the postwar era, and it had come to be viewed by snobbish Londoners as a demeaned place of outsiders—in a class-conscious land that was itself increasingly an outsider in modern political affairs and popular culture. But one thing Liverpool had was a brimming pop scene, made up of bands playing tough and exuberant blues and R&B-informed rock & roll—a boisterous movement that soon became known as the Merseyside scene. Numerous clubs opened up in the area, featuring such acts as Billy Fury, Gerry Marsden and the Pacemakers, and Rory Storm and the Hurricanes (who featured the flash drummer Richard Starkey, working under the stage name of Ringo Starr). Though the Quarry Men were defunct, the new core team of John Lennon, Paul McCartney and George Harrison remained committed as a music unit. Other members came and went, while the transformed group searched for a new name. One possibility: Johnny and the Moondogs. Another: the Silver Beatles. (Lennon favored the peculiar spelling of the last name in part because Merseyside bands were becoming known as beat groups, and also because he and Harrison and McCartney were fans of Jack Kerouac's *On the Road* and the American Beat literary and artistic movement that it epitomized.)

Finally, a shorter name evolved: the Beatles. An art school friend of John's, Stu Sutcliffe, soon joined the new group as bassist. George and Paul weren't thrilled with Sutcliffe's addition: Stu drew too much of John's attention for the liking of either one, and they also considered him a limited musician. Instead, they lobbied for Paul as bassist—but at the start (and for many years to come), the Beatles were in effect led by John Lennon. Sutcliffe notwithstanding, the main musical dynamic in the group was developing between Lennon and McCartney: They sang most of the leads on the group's ever-growing body of rock & roll covers, and the two were starting to compose songs of their own. In fact, they had formed a handshake deal: The two would share songwriting credits as the team of Lennon-McCartney for any songs they wrote jointly or apart. This left George as an odd man out; he had been closer to Paul for longer and he was captivated by John's charisma, but he knew he was losing Paul's loyalty to John. Also, Harrison had no burning desire to be a songwriter. Lennon would allow him the occasional lead vocal and instrumental, but George quickly became subordinate in the Beatles. By the time his position changed in that regard, much about the group and the world they occupied would change as a result.

Still, Harrison's tenure as a Beatle seemed safe, if only because neither John nor Paul (or, for that matter, any other Merseyside musician) could match his finesse as an ensemble guitarist—that keen instinct for the right textures and fills that gave the Beatles' early performances such drive. As a result, a certain dynamic developed among the three initial key members: Lennon and McCartney were the band's center of attention and impetus, while Harrison initially saw himself as along for the fun and exploration. The group viewed its first notable tour—playing Scotland in May 1960—as a likely big break, but when they arrived back home and found that their best gig was backing a stripper, George was disheartened. "It was work," he later said, "but definitely not what any of us had in mind when we got together. As for me, I was just about convinced it was never going to happen, which gave me great reason for concern. After all, the only other reasonable alternative was to just go out and find a real job. Frankly, that was something all of us dreaded."

Later in 1960, the Beatles' forecast improved when they finally found a steady drummer, Pete Best. The Beatles discovered that Liverpool's female fans thought Best was the group's sexiest member, plus Pete's mother, Mona, owned a local club that the band could play at any time. Best, however, was a bit aloof from the others—he didn't share in their easy camaraderie—and like Stu, he was regarded as a limited musician. Even so, a drummer was essential to a Beat band having a palpable and sensual pulse, and with Best in the lineup, the Beatles were ready to seek management. In the late summer, a Liverpool entrepreneur, Allan Williams, booked the group into a season-long stint of club shows in Hamburg, Germany. Hamburg was an excitable and diverse scene—full of thugs, prostitutes and drug dealers on one hand and a budding intellectual movement on the other. With their Liverpool street and art backgrounds, the Beatles managed to find acceptance among both factions: The tougher sorts supplied them with sex and drugs (the Beatles were playing eight-hour sets daily at clubs like the Indra and the Kaiserkeller, and they became fond of mixing Preludin—a form of speed—with German beer to fuel their increasingly hectic live shows). Also, the art and existentialist crowd found something daring about the band, and adopted them as a sensation. In particular, artist Klaus Voorman (who later designed some of the Beatles' graphics and eventually played bass on various members' solo projects) and photographer Astrid Kirchherr took the group under their wing. Harrison formed a crush on Astrid, and although Astrid thought George was maybe the sweetest-tempered member of the group, she entered into an affair with Sutcliffe. Astrid also was the person who introduced the Beatles to a new, longer hairstyle, first adopted by Stu and George.

Harrison once called the Beatles' Hamburg tenure the only "higher education" of his younger life. In addition to the drugs and sex (both of which were plentiful and reportedly diverse), the Beatles would soon grow accustomed to playing for enthusiastic—even brutal—audiences. There were fistfights in the audience nearly every night they played, and all the members related how they had witnessed bludgeonings and stabbings as they wisely kept the beat steady, grinding out their sets. On one occasion, Paul was assaulted with a table from the dance floor. Another time, they watched as one hapless audience member was skewered in the neck with a meat hook and thrown into the street. John wasn't always crazy about the German audiences he played to and sometimes mocked them as "Nazi bastards," to Harrison's delight.

While in Germany, they learned to play a vast repertoire of rock & roll but also grasped how to pace their sets with novelty songs like "Sheik of Araby" and standards like "September Song" and "Summertime." Two other important things happened to the Beatles in this initial Hamburg visit. For one, they understood that becoming a tighter band was the key to becoming more popular, and that meant recognizing that neither drummer Pete Best nor bassist Stu Sutcliffe would likely survive Lennon, McCartney and Harrison's ambitions. More important, the Beatles got thrown out of the country, ostensibly because of George. When the group accepted a position at Hamburg's hottest venue, the Top Ten, the Kaiserkeller's owner claimed they owed him an exclusive arrangement and retaliated by notifying local authorities that George Harrison was still under the age of eighteen and thereby was playing adult clubs illegally. Within twenty-four hours, the police raided the Beatles, "looking for the one called Harrison." Lennon replied: "What the fuck do you want him for? He hasn't done anything."

Harrison was deported, and only Astrid Kirchherr and Stu Sutcliffe accompanied him to the train station. "He looked so lost and pathetic standing there on the platform holding his battered guitar case," said Kirchherr. "Tears were welling up in his eyes. . . . Of course this was the worst possible way for someone as proud as George to have to go home. As a failure. With nothing to show for all those months of hard work."

Harrison arrived back in Liverpool in December 1960. The city looked bleak at that time of year, and Harrison later said he felt bleak. He wasn't confident that John Lennon and Paul McCartney—who were increasingly more ambitious—would keep a place for him in the group. He walked the streets of his hometown, feeling like a washout—a defeated Beatle. Despite everything that would happen in the years ahead, in some ways Harrison never shook the insecurity and depression that accompanied him back to Liverpool that Christmas season.

Soon enough, Lennon, McCartney, Sutcliffe and Best joined Harrison back in the Mersey, also as deportees. McCartney and Best, according to the German police, had set fire to the place where they'd bunked while playing the Kaiserkeller—perhaps as vengeance for George being thrown out of the country. Sutcliffe soon quit the band, to return to Hamburg and Astrid, which allowed Paul to move into place as the bassist. The Beatles were now a quartet. As George and the others looked about at the even more burgeoning Liverpool Beat scene, they realized their prospects might be better than ever. They were no longer a band of skiffle hopefuls, but as a result of their intense Hamburg performances had transformed into the Mersey scene's most soulful rock & roll band—even though rock & roll had undergone significant change in both the US and the UK. By the early 1960s, the music's unruly spirit had been seemingly tamed, or simply impeded by numerous misfortunes, including—in the States—Elvis Presley's film and army careers, and the death of Buddy Holly. In short, there had been a tilt: In 1960, the music of Frankie Avalon, Paul Anka, Connie Francis and Mitch Miller (an avowed enemy of rock & roll) ruled both American and British airwaves and the record charts, giving some observers the notion that decency and order had returned to the popular mainstream. "When rock & roll died," George Harrison said, according to Alan Clayson's biography, *The Quiet One,* "and ballads and folk music took over, we just carried on playing our type of music. When at last we succeeded in cutting a record, the people were ready for a change, and we clicked."

Once more the Beatles began playing Liverpool's clubs, but to notably different impact: The crowds—particularly the young females—were now ecstatic in their devotion to the group. The Beatles may have left Hamburg as failures, but they now ruled their home scene, and they placed first in local polls as the best Merseyside band. The group booked themselves into the Cavern: a jazz club in a dank and airless cellar, where they packed the place for both lunch hour and evening shows (eventually, the Beatles played more than two hundred shows at the Cavern). Liverpool's enthusiasm for them was unbounded and unmatched in the region's entertainment history. While on a brief return trip to Germany (after George had turned eighteen, and the arson charge against McCartney and Lennon was forgotten), the Beatles recorded some sessions with Tony Sheridan—a British pop star who had relocated to Hamburg—and cut a few tracks of their own.

According to legend, one Saturday morning in 1961, a young customer entered a record store called NEMS, "the Finest Record Store in Liverpool," on Whitechapel, a busy road in the heart of Liverpool's stately commercial district. The young man asked store manager Brian Epstein for a new single, "My Bonnie," by the Beatles (its flip side was a Harrison-McCartney instrumental, "Cry for a Shadow"). Epstein replied that he had never heard of the record—indeed, had never heard of the group, which he took to be an obscure, foreign pop group. The customer, Raymond Jones, pointed out the front window, across Whitechapel, where Stanley Street ran into a murky-looking alley area. Around that corner, he told Epstein, down a small lane known as Mathew Street, the Beatles—by then the most popular of Liverpudlian rock & roll groups—were performing afternoons at the Cavern. A few days later, prompted by more requests, Epstein made that journey around Stanley onto Mathew and down the clammy steps into the Cavern. At first Epstein—a neat man given to sharp suits and ties—was appalled by the rowdy appearance of the band: They wore jeans and leather jackets, smoked cigarettes onstage, swore—and he couldn't fathom the reaction of the young audience around him, their almost hysterical commotion. Then, something in Epstein clicked: This group, he told himself, was great. He saw a vision for his future and for theirs.

When Epstein made his way backstage to meet the band, George greeted him curtly: "What brings Mr. Epstein here?" They found out soon enough. A month later, even though the group had entertained other offers, the Beatles entered into a management agreement with Brian Epstein. With Epstein's small trek to the Cavern, modern pop culture turned its most eventful corner.

From that point on, a lot happened—and happened remarkably fast. Some of it wasn't pretty: Epstein eventually fired Pete Best, to the outrage of the group's Liverpool fans (in fact, the news was met with a genuine street riot). Best's replacement was Rory Storm's old drummer, Ringo Starr, who would tell the *New Musical Express* that "he was lucky to be on their wavelength. . . . I had to join them as people as well as a drummer." Some of what happened was tragic: Stu Sutcliffe died of a brain hemorrhage in Hamburg, leaving the group shaken. George and Paul had recently repaired their relationship with the former bassist and had invited him to appear with them onstage in Germany. And some of what happened was simply the stuff of extraordinary fortune and legend. In July 1962, after being turned down by many London labels, Epstein secured a recording contract with EMI's Parlophone producer George Martin. By October, the four-piece ensemble had broken into Britain's Top Twenty with a folkish rock song, "Love Me Do." The song began a momentum that would forever shatter the American grip on the UK pop charts. Indeed, when Brian Epstein first saw the Beatles, he saw not only a band who delivered their American obsessions with infectious verve, but that also reflected British youth's joyful sense of being cultural outsiders, ready to seize everything new, and everything that their surrounding society tried to prohibit them. What's more, Epstein figured that the British pop scene would recognize and seize on this kinship. As the group's manager, Epstein cleaned up the Beatles' punkness considerably, but he didn't deny the group its spirit or musical instincts, and in a markedly short time, his faith paid off.

A year after "Love Me Do," the Beatles had six singles active in the Top Twenty in the same week, including the top three positions—an unprecedented and still unduplicated feat. In the process, Lennon and McCartney had grown enormously as writers—in fact, they were already one of the best composing teams in pop history—and the group itself had upended the local pop scene, establishing a hierarchy of long-haired male ensembles, playing a popwise but hard-bashing update of 1950s-style rock & roll. But there was more to it than mere pop success: The Beatles were simply the biggest explosion England had witnessed in modern history, short of war. In less than a year, they had transformed British pop culture—had redefined not only its intensities and possibilities, but had turned it into a matter of nationalistic impetus.

Then, on February 9, 1964, TV variety-show kingpin Ed Sullivan presented the Beatles for the first time to a mass American audience, and it proved to be an epochal moment. On the flight over to the United States the

group was nervous, George Harrison in particular. "America's got everything," he said to the others. "Why should they want us?" When the group's
plane landed at New York City's Idlewild Airport (later renamed JFK),
there was such a large turnout of spectators that the band assumed that
President Lyndon Johnson must have been coincidentally arriving at the
airport at the same time. After a crazed and hilarious press conference (one
reporter asked, "Why don't you smile, George?"; "I'll hurt my lips," George
replied), the band's press officer rushed them to their hotel. Epstein and the
others were seriously concerned: Harrison had an intense flu, and it was
possible he might not be able to make their TV appearance or first few US
dates. His sister Louise, who now lived in the United States, moved into his
hotel suite and, with the help of a lot of tea and various medications,
nursed him enough so that the group could make their American debut.

    The Sullivan appearance drew over seventy million viewers—the largest
TV audience ever, at that time—an event that cut across divisions of style
and region, and drew new divisions of era and age; an event that, like
Presley, made rock & roll seem an irrefutable opportunity. Within days it
was apparent that not just pop style but a whole dimension of youth society had been recast, that a genuine upheaval was under way, offering a fre-
netic distraction to the dread that had set into America after the
assassination of President John F. Kennedy, and a renewal of the brutally
wounded ideal that youthfulness carried our national hope. Elvis Presley
had shown us how rebellion could be fashioned into eye-opening style; the
Beatles were showing us how style could take on the impact of cultural revelation—or at least how a pop vision might be forged into an unimpeach-
able consensus. Virtually overnight, the Beatles' arrival in the American
consciousness announced that not only the music and times were changing, but that *we* were changing as well. Everything about the band—its
look, sound, style and abandon—made plain that we were entering a different age, that young people were free to redefine themselves in completely
new terms.

That's one version of the Beatles' early story: the miracle, rags-to-riches version. It's hardly inaccurate, but it's also hardly the full story. Actually, perhaps
it isn't fair to call it the *Beatles'* story—perhaps it's more exact to call it the
public story, *our* version of the fairy tale. There was also the internal experience within that adventure, and over forty-five years later it remains surprising that there are key details—a psychic and emotional landscape—that only
an ever-dwindling number of people truly know well. As the Beatles them-

selves grew fond of saying, nobody understood their experience in the way they did and therefore all biographies and essays have been speculative at best. And yet none of the four men who lived within that matchless twentieth-century exploit ever wrote a full-scale revealing autobiography. Years later, when McCartney, Harrison and Starr coauthored their authorized narrative (with posthumous contributions culled from John Lennon interviews), *The Beatles Anthology*, the storytellers clearly cut some of the story's rougher corners a bit clean. Perhaps the single most striking hard truth to emerge from *Anthology* was that there a great deal of pain involved in being the Beatles, and that pain started much earlier than many of us might have realized. The most notoriously publicized aspect of the Beatles' anguish was, of course, the bitter rift between Lennon and McCartney at the group's end, but it is likely that while the group was intact, nobody within it may have suffered greater grievances than George Harrison.

What accounted for that hurt? In part, it stemmed from the subsidiary role that Harrison found himself in, in relation to Lennon and McCartney. Though Harrison contributed significantly to some of the most important and memorable aspects of the Beatles' music—for example, the backward-guitar effects on "I'm Only Sleeping" and the innovative use of controlled feedback in "I Feel Fine," as well as the sitar phrases that imbued "Norwegian Wood" with both a haunting and witty quality—Harrison remained perpetually in McCartney and Lennon's shadow, not only in that pair's view but in producer George Martin's as well. Martin sometimes criticized Harrison's tuning and timing in the studio, even in the presence of a reporter. Much of the problem owed to Harrison's slow growth as a songwriter. John and Paul not only wrote the group's essential catalogue, but—along with George and Ira Gershwin, Duke Ellington and Billy Strayhorn, and Richard Rodgers and his partners Lorenz Hart and Oscar Hammerstein—they were now among the greatest and most prolific pop songwriting teams of the century. Up until *Revolver*—the Beatles' seventh album—Harrison had composed only a handful of songs and sang lead on relatively few as well (Lennon, for one, didn't think much of Harrison's voice). Harrison later said that he was reluctant to present his songs to the band's primary writers. "The hangup of my playing my songs to John and Paul always used to hold me back," he told *New Musical Express* in 1969, "because I knew how it would sound finished, and I had to try to convince them in one play. For that reason, there are a lot of numbers of mine that I decided not to do anything about. It was a shyness, a withdrawal, and I always used to take the easy way out." Another time, Harrison justified his reluctance by saying: "My part in the Beatles was I never wanted to be the one in the front." Yet even Lennon admitted that Harrison would never have been granted that chance for more than a song or two. Lennon told *Rolling Stone* that George was "like a bloody kid, hanging around all the time. It took me years to start considering him as an equal."

Another factor that made Beatlemania so troubling for George Harrison was in fact the mania. More than any other Beatle, he came to despise the quality and fervor of attention that the band received. By the end of their first American tour, according to Geoffrey Giuliano's *Dark Horse: The Life and Art of George Harrison,* Harrison was disillusioned with the inanity of fame. On the flight back to England, after the Beatles conquered America, Giuliano writes that George told his bandmates: "How fuckin' stupid it all is. All that big hassle to make it, only to end up as performing fleas." This feeling never left Harrison. In *Anthology,* Harrison related how, during a tense appearance in Japan (where the band had been threatened with death), every time an unexpected loud sound occurred, the band members would look around to see which of them had been shot. Harrison also disclosed his anger about the Beatles not being able to control their own schedules or movements during their hectic tours, and how, in 1964, he finally balked and insisted that the Beatles not participate in a ticker tape parade planned for a San Francisco appearance. "It was only . . . a year," he says, "since they had assassinated Kennedy. . . . I could just imagine how mad it is in America." Years later, he told *Rolling Stone:* "I was getting very nervous. . . . I didn't like the idea of being too popular." Later, when Harrison started to date model Pattie Boyd, he had to deal with the resentments of female fans who physically attacked Boyd, calling her demeaning names. There was no question that the Beatles were at the eye of a tremendous storm of public feeling, and though in *Anthology* Harrison claimed they were the sanest people in that scenario, it's also clear that their fame had isolated them from some of the meaning and pleasure of their experience. In Harrison's mind, the group's audience became an enclosing and demanding reality, always wanting, often threatening, rarely kind enough. "They used us as an excuse to go mad, the world did," he said, "and then they blamed it on us."

By the time of the band's 1965 tours in the US and elsewhere, Harrison was starting to make a case for the band to stop traveling and playing live so much. He believed it was only a matter of time before something irreparable would happen. The 1966 world tour only underscored Harrison's claims. When the Beatles failed to show up for a command audience in the Philippines with President Ferdinand Marcos, the band felt lucky to leave the country without serious harm. "They were waiting for us to retaliate," George said of the guards who bullied them at the Manila airport, "so that they could finish us off. I was terrified." Later, at a press conference, George told reporters, "We're going to have a couple of weeks to recuperate before we go and get beaten up by the Americans." Near the outset of that US tour, some remarks John Lennon had made earlier in the year to a British reporter—that the Beatles were now "more popular than Jesus Christ"— became widely publicized in America, and public response was intense. Brian Epstein offered to refund all the ticket sales if the US tour could be canceled. It hardly helped secure their safety when Lennon and Harrison finally came out in interviews and spoke up against American involvement in Vietnam, but by then everybody involved in the Beatles agreed that the phenomenon of their public performances was coming to a necessary fast end. The band played their last concert on August 29, 1966, at San Francisco's Candlestick Park. On the flight back home to England, George settled into his seat and announced: "Well, that's it. I'm not a Beatle anymore." Not even the three men who knew him best could tell if he was happy or sad in the moment that he uttered that remark.

But Harrison, of course, was still a Beatle. In fact, for the next year or two, being a Beatle would not only become a more fulfilling experience for Harrison, but his influence on the Beatles' growth—and how they affected their audience in the late 1960s—owed as much to him as to McCartney and Lennon.

The first manifestation of this influence—albeit an inadvertent one— was George's role in introducing the Beatles to LSD. One night in 1965, Harrison and Pattie Boyd and John and Cynthia Lennon accepted the invitation of Harrison's dentist to join him and his wife for a small dinner party. After serving his guests drinks, the dentist informed them he had just slipped them some LSD. Harrison and Boyd and the Lennons grew angry and frightened, and fled. They ended up visiting nightclubs and driving around London for hours before settling into a safe enclosure. The acid had scared them, but it also beguiled Harrison and Lennon, and they began to take it more regularly. For both men, it was the start of an intense exploration that had philosophical and spiritual aspects to it, and that would provoke immense influence and controversy in the pop world and youth culture. "Up until LSD," Harrison told *Rolling Stone*, "I never realized that there was anything beyond this state of consciousness. . . . The first time I took it, it just blew everything away. I had such an overwhelming feeling of well-being, that there was a God and I could see him in every blade of grass. It was like gaining hundreds of years' experience in twelve hours." Harrison soon married Pattie Boyd, a development he believed was now possible in his life from how psychedelics had helped him develop.

Harrison's experience with LSD would dovetail influentially with two other quests he had undertaken and would help transform the Beatles' meaning and history. The first was musical: At the suggestion of the Byrds' David Crosby, Harrison sought out the recordings of Indian sitar master Ravi Shankar, a virtuoso who occasionally mixed elements of Western music (classical, blues and jazz) into the more ancient form of raga structures. Harrison was fascinated by what he heard, and in time met Shankar and asked to study the instrument with him. Shankar cautioned Harrison that the sitar was an extremely difficult and demanding instrument to master, and that to immerse himself in it properly he should spend time in India. Harrison agreed and paid a visit to Shankar in India. Not just the Beatles changed as a result, but so did modern popular music. Writing about Harrison's death in the *New York Times,* composer Philip Glass said: "George was among the first Western musicians to recognize the importance of music traditions millenniums old, which themselves had roots in indigenous music, both popular and classical. Using his considerable influence and popularity, he was one of those few who pushed open the door that, until then, had separated the music of much of the world from the West. . . . He played a major role in bringing several generations of young musicians out of the parched and dying desert of Eurocentric music into a new world."

The beginning of this lifelong friendship with Shankar also provided the foundation for a change in Harrison's worldview. Through Shankar and Indian music, George said, he discovered a new openness to spirituality—especially to ancient Hindu teachings. He began to study the mystical literature of legendary Yogi Paramahansa Yogananda, and would also later form a lifelong relationship with Swami Prabhupada and the Krishna Consciousness movement. In the hotbed of late-1960s hippie culture, George's spiritual interest spread like wildfire—to other musicians and groups (including the Beach Boys, Mick Jagger and Donovan) and to much of American and British youth as well. For most people, of course, sampling ancient scripture like the Bhagavad Gita or the Upanishads, or chanting "Hare Krishna," was simply a vogue of the season. For Harrison (and, in different ways, for Lennon too) this turn toward the spiritual became permanently transforming. "You got the feeling that most people were dabbling in spirituality . . . ," Mick Jagger told *Rolling Stone* after Harrison's death. "But he did follow through on the courage of his convictions. He stayed with it and never rejected it. And, of course, he made mistakes—anybody following this who was one of the first people of a generation to do that would make mistakes—but not any glaring ones. You've got to start somewhere."

The combination of all these discoveries—the possibility of finding a connection to a God in oneself and in the world and the rich, complex pleasures of Indian sounds—also bore musical fruit for Harrison. He featured Indian instrumentation on *Revolver*'s "Love You To," on *Sgt. Pepper's Lonely Hearts Club Band*'s longest track, the psalmlike "Within You Without You" ("Forget the Indian music and listen to the melody," Paul McCartney once said about this remarkable recording), and on "The Inner Light" (a devotional on the B-side of "Lady Madonna"). For some listeners, these experiments were unbearably pompous and exotic, and yet today they all hold up not merely as adventurous but as enduring musical pleasures. Also, Harrison's openness to new sounds and textures brought fresh possibilities for his rock & roll compositions. His use of dissonance on such tracks as *Revolver*'s "Taxman" and "I Want to Tell You" was revolutionary in popular music—and perhaps more originally creative than the avant-garde mannerisms that McCartney brought to the Beatles from the music of Stockhausen, Berio, Varèse and Stravinsky in this same period.

With psychedelia and hippie counterculture at its peak in both England and America in the summer of 1967, Harrison decided to visit the scene's apparent center, the Haight-Ashbury district in San Francisco. According to Geoffrey Giuliano's account, Harrison, Pattie Boyd and the Beatles press agent took LSD before wandering into the Haight—and though Harrison remained polite to the young people who surrounded him, he was aghast at what he found. "They are hypocrites," he told *Creem* of his experience of the Haight residents. "I don't mind anybody dropping out of anything, but it's the imposition on somebody else I don't like. I've just realized that it doesn't matter what you are, as long as you work. In fact, if you drop out, you put yourself further away from the goal of life than if you were to keep working."

For Harrison, that was the beginning of the end of acid. He felt he had seen firsthand the wonders of the drug's experience but also the havoc it might cause for an unready or a naïve community. Harrison now realized, he said, how vast the Beatles' effect was on youth, and that he wanted that influence to be more positive. His wife, Pattie, introduced him to the teachings of Maharishi Mahesh Yogi, who had formulated some philosophical (and economic) twists on Hindu teachings. Harrison liked the Maharishi's teachings about overcoming human weaknesses through meditation to achieve bliss, and he persuaded the other Beatles to accompany him to one of the teacher's lectures. The Beatles were impressed by what they heard and accepted Maharishi's invitation to attend a sabbatical in Bangor, Wales. Later, the Beatles joined Maharishi for an even more extended study retreat in Rishikesh, India, but their relationship with the teacher soured when they heard rumors that he had attempted unwelcome sexual advances on a female devotee. Lennon and Harrison confronted the yogi, pronounced their disdain and then left him, despite his pleadings that they reconsider their judgment on him. (Later in their lives, Harrison and McCartney reconciled with Maharishi, though Lennon never did.)

But something even more significant to the Beatles' future than their spiritual explorations took place during that first retreat in Bangor. Manager Brian Epstein had been scheduled to join them, but he never showed. Epstein had been a depressed and lonely man for some time, and according to some who knew him, he was afraid that his place in the Beatles' life might be slipping. He had been taking more pills, and drinking more, and had attempted to find cures for his depression, to no avail. On August 27, 1967, while the Beatles were with Maharishi in Wales, they received news that Epstein had been found dead in London of an overdose of sleeping pills and antidepressants—an accidental suicide, some believed. The Beatles were shell-shocked by the news. Speaking at a hastily assembled press conference in Bangor, Harrison said: "The Maharishi told us not to be too overshadowed by grief. . . . I feel my course on meditation here has helped me overcome my grief more easily than before." But the expressions on his and the other Beatles' faces didn't convey any sense of overcoming. As Harrison later admitted, "We didn't know what to do. We were lost."

It's true that the Beatles were lost without Brian Epstein. At first they tried to manage themselves. They financed and produced their own TV film special, *Magical Mystery Tour*. It made for some good music but also for a disastrous film, and it was the first time the Beatles were ridiculed by critics (the show was considered so bad that it never aired in the United States). They also set up their own recording label and multimedia corporation, Apple, and signed numerous new artists. But between trying to create their own music, overseeing Apple's business affairs and other artists' record productions, and trying to fund various experimental philanthropic enterprises (and not-so-philanthropic ambitions, such as a short-lived ambition to own, populate and reign over their own island off Greece), they had stretched themselves too thin, and they almost went bankrupt. Clearly, they needed new management, and Lennon suggested the name of the entertainment industrialist who had seemingly helped the Rolling Stones recover: Allen Klein. Again, this is a period in which much happened with dramatic speed and effectiveness in the Beatles' history—but this time little of it was fairy tale; rather, it was a nightmare, and the public and press's backlash against them was often unforgiving. In May 1968, John Lennon began an affair with a respected avant-garde artist, Yoko Ono. Soon after, he left and divorced his wife, Cynthia, and his resulting inseparable closeness with Ono was seen as causing much tension within the Beatles' world.

Also, as the group's members—including George and Ringo—began to grow musically, they also began to have little room for one another in their lives and music. The most brilliant yet foreboding example of how the group was splintering came as they were recording a double album, initially titled *A Doll's House*, later called *The Beatles* but better known as the White Album. By this point, the band's members were largely recording as separate individuals or as each other's sidemen. Harrison had written some of his best songs yet—including the lovely "Long Long Long," "All Things Must Pass," "Wah-Wah," "Isn't It a Pity," "Not Guilty," "Something" and "While My Guitar Gently Weeps," but once again he found himself facing the harsh judgments of Lennon, McCartney and producer George Martin. Martin at first thought "Something" sounded too weak and derivative. The one song Harrison expected to receive the most enthusiastic response, "While My Guitar Gently Weeps," left Paul and John cold when he played a demo for them (the same version that is now regarded as the best track on *Anthology* 3). Harrison was determined to get the song on the new album and laid plans to make it happen: He invited his good friend Eric Clapton to attend and play lead on the session. Clapton panicked at the request. "I can't come," he said. "Nobody's ever played on a Beatles record"—but he gave in to George's insistence. Clapton later said he could tell that things were bad within the group—Lennon never appeared for the session—but George's plan worked: The other Beatles didn't feel they could refuse a track with such a standout guitar solo. "Not Guilty," though, never made the cut, perhaps because it was apparent to everybody that Harrison had aimed the song at Lennon and McCartney.

The Beatles could no longer figure out how to survive each other.

McCartney tried to keep the band on course. He wanted them to return to touring, but George and John wouldn't consider the prospect. Instead, they agreed to rehearse for a one-time live show at some undisclosed location, and to film their rehearsals. A few days into these sessions—which resulted in the album and film *Let It Be*—Harrison had reached a breaking point with McCartney. Lennon had by then abdicated his leadership, and George felt Paul was trying to exert too much control over the band, in particular dictating Harrison's own guitar parts unnecessarily. After one argument between the two over whether the Beatles should play a live show in Tunisia, George told Paul—on camera—"You're so full of shit, man," and for a brief time Harrison quit the band. He was back shortly, and the band played their impromptu live show on Apple Corp's rooftop, but little magic made it to the album of *Let It Be*. There were other trying matters: John and Yoko were arrested for drug possession and so were George and Pattie, plus there was the arrival and bullying manner of new manager Allen Klein (now trusted by John, George and Ringo, despised by Paul, and eventually sued by all). The apparent decisive rift in the Beatles occurred in the relationship between McCartney and Lennon, in arguments over Klein and creative directions.

It was only a matter of time before somebody would bolt the group for good, and yet despite all the growing bad will, the Beatles agreed to set aside their squabbles and enter the studio for what would be the last time, to record one of their most ingenious and satisfying albums, *Abbey Road*. George had two songs on this final set. "Here Comes the Sun"—a song written in Eric Clapton's garden one morning, in reaction to the darkness that was clearly setting in on the Beatles—became Harrison's equivalent to "Let It Be" or "Imagine": a graceful anthem of hope amid difficult realities. Also, "Something" finally got a fair hearing. George Martin admitted that maybe he had underestimated George: "I think it's possible he'll emerge as a great musician and composer. . . . He's got tremendous drive and imagination, and also the ability to show himself as a great composer on the par with Lennon and McCartney." Lennon, though he agreed that "Something" was *Abbey Road*'s best song, was a bit more roundabout in later comments to David Sheff for *Playboy*: "He was working with two brilliant songwriters, and he learned a lot from us. I wouldn't have minded being George the invisible man."

"Something" would be George Harrison's first A-side on a Beatles single, and would quickly reach the Number One position on America's charts. It would also be Harrison's only prominent Beatles single. In April 1970,

Paul McCartney served suit to dissolve the band. The Beatles were no more. The group had been marked by the emerging cynicism of the era that was to follow. They were already regarding one another as creations of undeserved hype. For everything they had once been—lively, novel and uplifting—the Beatles ended as bitter, mutually unbelieving strangers.

It would be almost a quarter century later—and an excess of grief, anger, fear and blood—before they would release new music together under the name of the most famous and beloved band in popular music history.

Popular history has told us for years that it was the increasing rivalry between Paul McCartney and John Lennon that ended the Beatles: that Paul wanted to dominate the group, or that John estranged Paul and the others with his intense love for Yoko Ono, or that they had simply out-grown mutual artistic interests and their need for one another. John had walked from the group before Paul had, but McCartney and Allen Klein persuaded him to wait until the group's final product was released before making his announcement. John was furious, then, when Paul seemingly pulled a fast one: On the eve of the release of *Let It Be* (recorded prior to *Abbey Road*, but held back for remixing and for a final film edit), he issued a press release for his own first solo work, *McCartney*, in which he announced that the Beatles were finished, and that, no, he didn't think he would miss Ringo Starr on the drums. Lennon felt McCartney had betrayed them all—though he also wished he'd been the one to use the band's breakup to his own commercial advantage. Harrison felt McCartney had been ungracious, but he was relieved that the band's division was official. "The split-up of the Beatles satisfied me more than anything else in my career," he later said, according to biographer Geoffrey Giuliano.

It is possible, though, that if Lennon and McCartney's drama hadn't been so bitter and public, then what Harrison was about to do on his own may have been effectively enough to make the Beatles beside the point. Indeed, it was something far more enterprising than even John or Paul had ever envisioned for themselves. Harrison had been seen as a lucky tagalong by George Martin, as a bothersome but esteemed kid brother by Lennon and McCartney, and as the "quiet one" by a press that never seemed to grasp his dry, derisive wit, and that had little patience to understand the real meaning or appeal for his deepening interest in Eastern philosophy. In truth, all these miscalculations would benefit Harrison in the short run, though they also left deep and lasting wounds.

• • •

By the time the Beatles were in their breakup stage, Harrison was clearly aspiring to something extraordinary. He had already recorded two solo efforts for Apple's subsidiary label, Zapple: *Wonderwall Music,* a soundtrack to a rarely seen film, though Harrison's music was inventive and the album remains among his best works, and *Electronic Sounds*, haphazard recordings he made with the first Moog synthesizer imported into England—an album that he later called "rubbish." Harrison had also recorded an album's worth of duets, originals and covers with Bob Dylan (including a cover of Paul McCartney's "Yesterday" that seemed designed to finish the song for good). The sessions have never been released, though Harrison drew on some of the songs over the years.

More important, Harrison had a considerable backlog of songs that had been left off earlier Beatles albums, and he was writing more new ones on a regular basis. Harrison decided that it was time to see if these songs could stand on their own, especially outside the context of the Beatles. He recruited a stellar group of musicians, including drummers Ringo Starr, Jim Gordon and Alan White; bassists Klaus Voorman and Carl Radle; keyboardists Gary Wright, Bobby Whitlock, Billy Preston and Gary Brooker; guitarists Eric Clapton and Dave Mason; horn players Jim Price and Bobby Keys; and pedal steel player Pete Drake. He also persuaded famed, idiosyncratic producer Phil Spector (who had remixed *Let It Be*, and was also working with John Lennon on his first post-Beatles album) to help oversee the effort, along with orchestral arranger John Barham. George relished not having to submit his songs to Lennon, McCartney and Martin for approval. He had more than enough strong songs—forty, he claimed—to make a multirecord set, but he was also intent on letting some of the tracks stretch to a greater length and fuller band treatments (including a robust horn section) than would have been possible with the Beatles. Harrison appeared to be enjoying his best musical experience, and he was flattered and bolstered by his new musical accompanists. "Having played with other musicians," he would tell *Melody Maker* years later, "I don't think the Beatles were that good."

The album, however, would take longer to record than Harrison anticipated. Harrison's mother, Louise, had developed a brain tumor, and George was committed to helping her recovery. "The doctor was an idiot and was saying, 'There's nothing wrong with her, she's having some psychological trouble,'" he later told *Musician*. "When I went to see her, she didn't even know who I was. I had to punch the doctor out. . . . She recovered a little bit for about seven months. And during that period, my father, who'd taken care of her, had suddenly exploded with ulcers and was in the same hospital. I was running back and forth to do this record . . . I wrote the song ["Deep Blue"] . . . at home one exhausted morning. . . . It's filled with frustration and gloom of going to these hospitals, and the feeling of disease that permeated the atmosphere. Not being able to do anything for suffering family or loved ones is an awful experience." Louise Harrison died on July 7, 1970, with George at her bedside, reading passages to her from a text about the Bhagavad Gita, commenting on the sacred book's views of death as a changeover rather than a termination.

By late November, Harrison had finished his album, *All Things Must Pass*. It was an unprecedented feat—the first three-LP set in rock & roll (it was reissued in 2000 as a boxed two-CD package)—and it went to the Number One album position in both the US and England. It would remain on the charts for most of the following year, and it enjoyed better reviews than McCartney or Lennon's first solo efforts, which were seen as slight in Paul's case, and as acerbic and indulgent in John's case. "I remember John was really negative. . . . ," Harrison told *Crawdaddy*. "John just saw the album cover and said, 'He must be mad, putting three records out. And look at the picture on the front, he looks like an asthmatic Leon Russell.'" It is possible that the cover irritated Lennon because it depicted George seated on a landscape surrounded by four lazy gnomes, who served to represent the fallen Beatles. "There was a lot of negativity going down. . . . ," Harrison continued. "I just felt that whatever happened, whether it was a flop or success, I was gonna go on my own just to have a bit of peace of mind." *All Things Must Pass* was indeed a success, despite its extravagances. It was musically resourceful and thematically broad—featuring loving yet saddened sendoffs to the Beatles ("Wah-Wah" and "Isn't It a Pity"), evocative warnings about the dangers of false values ("Beware of Darkness") and surprisingly beautiful Dylan collaborations ("I'd Have You Anytime" and "If Not for You"). The album also produced Harrison's first solo Number One single, the irresistible devotional "My Sweet Lord," a song as pervasive on radio and in youth consciousness as anything the Beatles had produced—though the song would later contribute to Harrison's calamity and withdrawal.

In all, as Anthony DeCurtis wrote in 2000 in *Rolling Stone*, "George Harrison had the most to gain from the breakup of the Beatles"—and he gained it. George Harrison was now the most respected member of his former group. He offered a cautious yet optimistic and tender worldview that stood in stark contrast to the ugly dissolution of the Beatles and the defeated idealism that then characterized so much of rock & roll culture. Harrison told a British newspaper that he now believed "music should be used for the perception of God, not jitterbugging." It was a preachy and somewhat misplaced sentiment. "Jitterbugging" can bring one every bit as close to enlightenment as singing hymns, and Harrison would make more than his share of frivolous music in years to come. But in the darkness at the end of the 1960s and the beginning of the 1970s—after the hippie dream had turned into cynicism and exploitation—it was refreshing to hear a man who had once been viewed as a side talent rise to his moment and find a voice of liberation, willing to face the "hopelessness" he saw around him "in the dead of night," and for one majestic moment, beat back the fears that had long consumed him. George Harrison was out of the shadows—at least for the moment. No matter what else might be said about him in the years ahead, he made some of the finest solo work that any of the ex-Beatles ever produced. And what was more, he was about to top himself.

In March 1970 Harrison and Boyd bought Friar Park—a sprawling, eccentric nineteenth-century mansion and estate, on the outskirts of Henley, England. Harrison built a state-of-the-art recording studio in his new home, and he developed a fixation about the property, tending personally to its flower gardens and uncovering lost underground water grottos and secret passageways that had been hidden for the better part of a century.

In 1971 John Lennon (who now admitted that *All Things Must Pass* wasn't so bad, and that he preferred it to the music his former songwriting partner was recording) invited Harrison to participate in the sessions for his own second, more ambitious solo album, *Imagine.* By this time, the chasm between Lennon and McCartney had reached new depths, and John's vitriol knew few limits. Two of *Imagine's* most caustic songs—"Crippled Inside" and "How Do You Sleep?"—were aimed at Paul. Lennon and Harrison had some differences, but they still enjoyed working together, and they still shared a common front against McCartney. Harrison played on both of Lennon's anti-Paul diatribes, many years later telling *Musician:* "I enjoyed 'How Do You Sleep?' I liked being on that side of it, rather than on the receiving end."

In 1971 Harrison's old friend and master Ravi Shankar came to him with a request. In March of that year, East Pakistan—now an independent nation, Bangladesh—had been sundered by a cyclone, and a Pakistan Muslim military force took advantage of the disaster by mounting an attack on the Hindu population that opposed a Pakistani dictatorship. Between the war and the natural disaster, millions of Hindus were fleeing to India for sanctuary, but India couldn't afford them relief. Members of Shankar's own family had been among the casualties and refugees, and Shankar appealed to Harrison to help him find a way to raise both awareness and funds to help deal with the tragedy. Harrison had been loath to perform again in any high-profile manner, but he thought that the quickest and most effective way to bring money and attention to the problem was to stage a benefit concert and follow it with the release of a recording and film. Still, to achieve the kind of attention that both he and Shankar hoped for, it would have to be quite a concert—something akin to a Beatles reunion. Harrison set aside his misgivings and pursued that possibility but quickly realized it couldn't happen. Reportedly, Paul delayed on committing himself, and John wanted Yoko Ono to perform with the band, which Harrison didn't want. Only Ringo Starr was willing to commit his services. Harrison then turned to Allen Klein to book August performance dates at New York City's Madison Square Garden, and Harrison began to make calls to musician friends to contribute their time and talent to the event. Harrison's ideal was to present famous and respected artists, performing familiar and stirring songs with top-notch sound. He ended up assembling an orchestra as impressive as the one that had played on *All Things Must Pass*. In addition to Starr, Harrison elicited the support of Eric Clapton, Billy Preston, Leon Russell, Jim Keltner, Klaus Voorman, Badfinger and numerous other musicians and singers, plus producer Phil Spector. But Harrison's fondest hope was to win the involvement of rock & roll's most elusive and esteemed songwriter, Bob Dylan, who had played only one announced concert since his retirement from live performances in 1966. Dylan was interested but hesitant. He attended rehearsals but bristled when Harrison suggested that Dylan sing his earliest anthem, "Blowin' in the Wind." Dylan shot back: "Are you going to sing 'I Want to Hold Your Hand'?" Dylan implied that if he performed at all, he was more inclined to do recent material; like Harrison, he was reluctant to be defined by his past work.

At the first of two concerts on August 1, 1971, Harrison introduced Shankar at the show's opening for an introductory set of Indian music. Harrison and his orchestra then took the stage, opening with "Wah-Wah" and "My Sweet Lord." An hour later, after a lovely acoustic rendition of "Here Comes the Sun," Harrison looked to the stage wings. Dylan still hadn't committed himself to performing, and "right up until the moment he stepped onstage, I was not sure he was coming," Harrison said. Dylan strode out from the wings, wearing a denim jacket and harmonica rack, and carrying an acoustic guitar. "I'd like to introduce a friend of us all," Harrison said with obvious glee, and, with Harrison on guitar, Leon Russell on bass and Ringo Starr on tambourine, Dylan performed a stunning and confident set that included "A Hard Rain's a-Gonna Fall" and "Blowin' in the Wind." Harrison accomplished what nobody else had been able to: He convinced Dylan to perform his early folk songs in the city that had given him his greatest triumphs, and three years later when Dylan returned to stages with his own nationwide tour, he attempted to emulate the professionalism that had made the pacing and construction of Harrison's Bangladesh concert such an artistic triumph and historic landmark. There would be other, larger benefits in the years to come, including the Live Aid concerts, the Farm Aid series, the concerts to benefit the victims of the September 11th attacks.

It is likely that, sooner or later, another eminent pop music figure would have taken the step that Harrison did, but in this event, it was Harrison who set the model for how to stage a large-scale charitable pop music event that could also be a satisfying entertainment experience. Looking back, it seems an almost miraculous moment: a summation of the best hopes of 1960s rock, an enactment of the dream that many of us inferred from the Beatles' earlier ideals. It also seemed something of an endpoint. Certainly, rock & roll artists would aim for a grander scale of philanthropy in the years to come, but no single event would embody so much spiritual aspiration or, if you prefer, so much naïveté. The Concert for Bangladesh seemed like a work of joy and possibility—much like everything the Beatles had promised despite their own distrust of one another. Given all the doubt and loneliness Harrison himself had endured to reach a point where he could make such a giving and inspiring gesture, his work of charity also seemed like a work of courage.

Unfortunately, *The Concert for Bangladesh* immediately ran into problems that impeded Harrison's best intentions. Harrison grew irritated and wary when he felt that various parties were holding up the album's release to figure a way to profit on what would be another three-record set's distribution. (Capitol felt that the production costs on the album were enormous.) Also, both the American and British tax systems insisted on taking a good deal of the proceeds. It would be over a decade later and numerous legal and financial negotiations before Harrison was allowed to present the US Committee for UNICEF with a check that amounted to a much smaller portion of the concert's proceeds than Harrison had hoped to offer. Though he found the delay embarrassing and disheartening, Harrison said: "It's nice to know you can achieve these sorts of things, even though the concert was ten years ago and the public has forgotten about the problems of Bangladesh. The children still desperately need help and the money will have a significant impact." In the late 1980s, when Bob Geldof invited Harrison to take part in the London side of the Live Aid concerts, Harrison wasn't ready to revisit the concert stage, but he offered Geldof something he considered far more valuable: meticulous advice about how to finesse the legal and tax system so that the large funds raised from a charitable entertainment event could be dispersed effectively, without the benefactors having to overcome bureaucratic hindrances.

The financial quagmire that obstructed Harrison's best intentions for *The Concert for Bangladesh* turned out to be the first major discouragement in Harrison's post-Beatles career, but he was also facing other problems. His marriage with Pattie Boyd was in trouble. Harrison, according to Boyd, had adopted a religious view that sex should be used for procreation. Pattie felt lonely and more distant from her husband, and began a relationship with Eric Clapton that later resulted in one of Clapton's most forceful and agonized compositions, "Layla." According to some who saw Harrison in this time, he seemed lonely and adrift. It hardly helped matters when, during a dinner with Pattie at Ringo and Maureen Starr's house, Harrison boldly proclaimed that he was in love with Starr's wife. Pattie left the dinner in tears, and Ringo didn't know what to say. When Harrison and Maureen reportedly consummated George's proposition, the news enraged John Lennon, who reprimanded Harrison, accusing him of virtual incest.

Even so, Harrison and Starr kept their friendship. Harrison helped Ringo considerably with his most popular solo effort, *Ringo*, writing the hit single "Photograph" for the drummer and agreeing to contribute guitar parts to the only session that ever featured a reconvened form of the Beatles during the members' concurrent lifetimes (though the four members recorded their contributions separately). In fact, Harrison, Lennon and Starr worked jointly in the studio so effectively on *Ringo* that at one point George suggested that the three of them again form a permanent group. Lennon wouldn't deign to give the suggestion any response—even a refusal. Even so, Harrison would later say: "I'd join a band with John Lennon any day, but I couldn't join a band with Paul McCartney. That's not personal, but from a musical point of view." Harrison also kept his friendship with Clapton. Later, when his marriage had clearly dissolved, and Pattie's affections had shifted to Clapton, George, Pattie and Eric met to resolve the matter. With Pattie looking on, George said, "Well, I suppose I'd better divorce her." Eric replied, "Well, that means I've got to marry her." (Pattie and Eric were wed in 1979, with Paul, Ringo and George—who called himself Clapton's "husband-in-law"—in attendance. The couple later divorced, though Pattie attempted to retain a good friendship with both her former husbands.)

In 1973 Harrison released his second studio song collection, *Living in the Material World*. The album sold well and produced another Number One single, "Give Me Love (Give Me Peace on Earth)," but critics saw it as a lesser collection than *All Things Must Pass*, and many writers began to react against what they saw as the relentlessly pious nature of Harrison's musical pronouncements. Harrison was prepared for the reaction. He had already told *Melody Maker*: "They feel threatened when you talk about something that isn't be-bop-a-lula. And if you say the words 'God' . . . or 'Lord' it makes some people's hair curl." Through it all, though—sex or abstinence, misconstrued pride and equally misunderstood generosity—neither Harrison nor any of the other ex-Beatles could overcome their glorious and now mythic past, nor could they overcome themselves at times. John left Yoko for a time and went on a drinking holiday in Los Angeles. Ringo and George also found themselves drinking too much, as their marriages struggled. According to friends of the Beatles, the four men often asked others how their former bandmates were doing. Both Paul and John expressed guarded regret that the band had split so determinedly, and Paul floated the possibility that the two might write together again at some point.

It was in this time and context that George Harrison elected to become the first ex-Beatle to mount a major tour of America, in 1974. The prospect was met with strong hopes—despite his personal problems, Harrison still enjoyed considerable public and commercial favor—but that would all change with what became known as the Dark Horse tour. Things went badly before the tour even began. Harrison had been launching his own label, Dark Horse Records (distributed by A&M, since Harrison had grown disaffected with EMI after their handling of *The Concert for Bangladesh*), and he had overextended himself with production and business tasks. He was also trying hurriedly to finish an album for the tour and to assemble a band and rehearse, all in short order. "It is really a test," Harrison told *Melody Maker*. "I either finish the tour ecstatically happy, or I'll end up going back into my cave for another five years." By the first date in Vancouver, BC, Harrison's voice sounded strained and it never recovered. Also, some fans and reviewers were put off by the show's mix of pop, Indian music and jazz, and took offense at how Harrison had chosen to recast the few Beatles-era songs he performed, including his version of John Lennon's "In My Life" (with the new lyrical twist, "In my life / I've loved *God* more"). The press almost universally savaged the tour, with *Rolling Stone* providing some of the most disparaging commentary. "In defense of his tour . . . ," one reviewer wrote, "George Harrison has argued that 'If you don't expect anything, life is one big bonus. But when you expect anything, then you can be let down.' So expect nothing—is that the moral of a shriveled career?" Harrison went back and forth during the tour from being philosophical to being defensive. At one press conference he said: "I can see a time when I'd give up this sort of madness." On another occasion he said: "Gandhi says create and preserve the image of your choice. The image of my choice is *not* Beatle George. Why live in the past? *Be here now*, and now, whether you like me or not, is where I am. Fuck 'my life belongs to me.' It actually doesn't. It belongs to . . . the Lord Krishna. . . . That's how I feel. I've never been so humble in all my life, and I feel great."

In Washington D.C, in mid-December, Harrison was invited to the White House to meet with President Gerald Ford. It was a good-tempered visit, and during their conversation Harrison implored the president to consider the case of John Lennon, who had waged a long fight to avoid extradition from the US under the Nixon Administration. Two nights later, Lennon visited Harrison backstage at Long Island's Nassau Coliseum, where the two got into an argument, reportedly about the old days, though it was likely an expression of the severe strains Harrison was under at the time. It ended with Harrison yanking Lennon's eyeglasses from his face and throwing them to the floor. John later said that he "saw George going through pain, and I know what pain is, so I let him do it."

Dark Horse, the album, followed the tour, and received the worst reviews that any ex-Beatle had yet received. Interestingly, today it stands up as one of Harrison's most fascinating works—a record about change and loss, with a radical reworking of the Everly Brothers' "Bye Bye Love" that was Harrison's farewell to his marriage. Still, *Dark Horse* was an embarrassing commercial failure, and between the tour, the dissolution of his marriage and the album's collapse, Harrison withdrew to his home. He claimed that the cumulative disapproval and problems hadn't affected him, but others believe he in fact felt battered. In 1977, looking back on that time of trial, Harrison told *Crawdaddy,* "You either go crackers and commit suicide, or you try to realize something and attach yourself to an inner strength."

•   •   •

George Harrison continued to issue records from time to time and to make occasional public appearances, but the crises he faced in the mid-1970s changed him. Some of those changes were clearly for the better. While forming Dark Horse Records, Harrison met Olivia Arias, who shared some of his interests in spiritual studies. The two became constant companions, and later Olivia helped Harrison treat his depression, which had been exacerbated by heavy drinking and hepatitis. On August 1, 1978, Olivia gave birth to Harrison's only child, his son Dhani, and Olivia and George were married in a secret ceremony the following month, on September 2. "I stopped being as crazy as I used to be," Harrison later said, "because I want this child to have a father a bit longer." (George's own father, Harry, had died earlier that same year, in May.)

Harrison's next two albums—*Extra Texture (Read All About It)* (1975) and *Thirty-three & ⅓* (1976)—both had rewarding moments (especially *Texture*'s single "You"), but the context and apparent meanings of popular music were changing. Beatles-related releases now mattered only to the degree that they produced enjoyable sounds, rather than cultural sway. Paul McCartney had enjoyed a run of thriving releases—*Band on the Run, Venus and Mars, At the Speed of Sound*—and pulled off a massively profitable and acclaimed US tour with his post-Beatles band, Wings. For his part, John Lennon had gone into seeming retirement after he and Yoko Ono reconciled and Ono gave birth to their son, Sean. Meantime, the pop world had given up not just hope for a fabled Beatles reunion, but also, for a time, much active interest in the ongoing significance of their collective or singular works. Rock & roll was still seen as a force that could change individual lives and larger society, but by the late 1970s, the brand of hopefulness that the Beatles had exemplified—and the spiritual transcendence that Harrison's *All Things Must Pass* had apotheosized—was now seen as quaint or ineffectual. The two movements that changed pop the most during this time—punk and disco (both of which Harrison hated)—spoke for changing social realities and class conditions that the Beatles seemed unaware of, even though they had grown up in a time and place of similar deprivations and uncertainties.

Also, George had faced new and sizable legal troubles that discouraged his music activity. In 1976 he was sued by Bright Tunes, who owned the copyright for the Chiffons' "He's So Fine." The suit charged that Harrison had lifted verbatim the melody and arrangement of "He's So Fine" for "My Sweet Lord." To most sensible observers it seemed like a ludicrous nuisance suit. Pop tunesmiths had been lifting or emulating melodies and arrangements for decades—it was simply an accepted tradition of pop—but the court agreed that Harrison was guilty of "subconscious plagiarism," and ordered him to pay the plaintiff over half a million dollars. Part of what made this so galling was that the active force in bringing the case on Bright Tunes's behalf was the Beatles' former manager, Allen Klein, who was perhaps seeking a sly revenge after Lennon, Starr, and Harrison finally came around to McCartney's view that Klein was not a scrupulous caretaker of the Beatles' interests. Harrison said the ruling "made me so paranoid about writing that I didn't want to touch the guitar or piano in case I touched somebody's note. Somebody may own that note."

Despite their belated agreement about Klein, the former Beatles were now disconnected socially, except for occasional business meetings (with Ono appearing on Lennon's behalf). George found himself missing the old band. "If John, Paul and Ringo get together in a room, I just hope they invite me along," he said in 1976. Three years later, when no such gatherings had happened, George told one reporter he "was very interested to know whether John still writes tunes . . . or does he just forget all about music and not play guitar?" Shortly afterward, Harrison got his answer: John and Yoko were working on an album of all new songs, *Double Fantasy*, to be released in time for the Christmas season. And then there was worse news: On the evening of December 8, 1980, a young man emerged from the shadows of the entrance to Lennon's apartment building, New York City's Dakota, called the singer's name and then fired four shots into his body. A short time later, Olivia Harrison was awakened by a call in the morning darkness, giving her the news. She woke George and told him. "How bad is it?" he asked. "A flesh wound or something?" Olivia had to tell George the truth about what four bullets at close range will accomplish: John Lennon, George's childhood friend, was dead.

George canceled his work for a while. He had been recording a new album, *Somewhere in England*, and he had also written a song called "All Those Years Ago," for Ringo's next effort. With Ringo's agreement, George withdrew the song and rewrote its lyrics as a tribute to his dead friend's stature, and he recruited Ringo and Paul to add tracks to the revised tune. The song became an immediate hit in the US, but it was of little consolation to Harrison. "John's shooting definitely scared all of us—me, Paul and Ringo," George is quoted as saying in Alan Clayson's biography. "When a fan recognizes me and rushes over, it definitely makes me nervous." After

Lennon's murder, Harrison heightened the security around his home, Friar Park. He was determined that no unwelcome party would ever make their way past his estate's gates.

After *Somewhere in England* Harrison recorded two more studio solo albums, *Gone Troppo* (1982) and *Cloud Nine* (1988), though he was close to finishing another album shortly before his death. Jeff Lynne, the former leader of the heavily Beatles-influenced Electric Light Orchestra, worked on *Cloud Nine* with Harrison. The two realized they shared a passion for an obscure James Ray song "Got My Mind Set on You" and worked it up for a laugh. The result was another Number One single for Harrison. Shortly afterward, in the spring of 1988, a casual jam session attended by Harrison, Lynne, Tom Petty, Roy Orbison and Dylan in Dylan's garage in Malibu, California, flowered into a full-blown band—the only group that Harrison ever joined after the Beatles. The resulting album, *The Traveling Wilburys (Volume One)*—was perhaps the craftiest and most joyful cooperative musical effort George had participated in since *Rubber Soul* or *Revolver*. Harrison planned a series of Wilburys albums—perhaps even a movie— but then Roy Orbison died in December 1988. When Harrison, Dylan, Petty and Lynne gathered for an Orbison tribute to benefit Romanian orphans, they performed "Nobody's Child," a song that the Beatles used to play with Tony Sheridan in Hamburg, back in the early 1960s. The Wilburys made a second record in 1990, but it didn't resound the same without Orbison, and Harrison never regrouped the band.

In 1991 Harrison toured Japan with Eric Clapton and his band (documented on the 1992 *Live in Japan* album). Part of the reason he went, he said, was that he had finally quit a lifetime of smoking and wanted some distraction and fresh air. In an October 1995 tribute concert to Dylan at Madison Square Garden, Harrison rendered startling versions of Dylan's "If Not for You" and "Absolutely Sweet Marie." He also turned up on occasional radio interviews, performing Dylan's "Every Grain of Sand," as well as versions of the Everly Brothers' "Let It Be Me" and Pete Seeger's "The Bells of Rhymney." It was evident from these various performances that Harrison still had talent to burn whenever he chose to. But he rarely chose to. The consensus among some observers was that George was scared of something. In the transcript of a 1996 conversation between Harrison and Swami Prabhupada, published in Giuliano's biography, Harrison said: "I feel a little animosity from people. In some ways the more committed you are, and the stronger you are in what you do, the stronger the animosity. Sometimes I get the feeling there's one person to whom it means something. . . ."

· · ·

In the remainder of the 1990s, George Harrison's primary public activity was making a peace with the Beatles, as people and as history. In 1989, when asked again if the band might still get back together, George Harrison stated: "As far as I'm concerned, there won't be a Beatles reunion as long as John Lennon remains dead." But in some ways a larger barrier was the relationship that persisted between Harrison and McCartney. Paul had expressed interest in writing with George, but George expressed hurt that Paul had waited so many years to make such an overture. Plus, both men freely admitted, they could simply grate on each other's nerves. Still, McCartney, Harrison and Starr had been long committed to *The Beatles Anthology* project, as a way of telling their own version of their history, releasing some previously unavailable tracks and reactivating their still commercially powerful recording catalog. Yoko Ono gave the surviving Beatles two unfinished tracks by Lennon, "Free as a Bird" and "Real Love," to complete as they saw fit. Though George would later somewhat disdain the new tracks, the final results sounded as if everybody involved worked sincerely and meticulously, and with "Free as a Bird" in particular, they even created something rather moving. "Whatever happened to / The life we once knew," McCartney sang in the song's middle part. "Can we really live / Without each other?" The song wasn't a statement about nostalgia, but rather a commentary on all the chances and hopes, all the immeasurable possibilities, that are lost when people who once loved each other cut themselves off from that communion. Not a bad or imprecise coda for what the Beatles did to themselves, and to their own history (and to their audience), with their dissolution. And moments later, Harrison played a guitar solo that summed up a quarter century of yearning and pain.

But there was more pain to come. In 1997, after beginning work on a new solo project, Harrison underwent surgery for throat cancer. The treatment was considered successful. Then, at 3:00 a.m. December 30, 1999, Olivia Harrison was awakened by a loud crash at the Friar Park home. Her first thought was that a chandelier had fallen to the floor, but she couldn't be sure. She awoke her husband, who went downstairs to investigate. There, he felt a cold blast of air from a shattered window and smelled cigarette smoke. George ran back upstairs and told Olivia to contact the grounds staff and call the police. Then Harrison saw a young man moving on the floor beneath him, carrying a lance that he had taken from a statue in Harrison's home. George asked him, "Who are you?" The man replied, "You know. Get down here." Harrison tackled the man, and the two rolled on the ground. The intruder began to stab at Harrison. Olivia rushed to join her husband and smashed the man in the head with a heavy table lamp. After a few blows, the man attacked Olivia and cut her head, then returned to Harrison, who had been stabbed severely in the chest and was fast growing weak. He grabbed the attacker's knife by its blade, then local police rushed in and subdued the trespasser. Harrison had been stabbed severely in the chest twice. His lung was collapsed, and the blade had missed his heart by less than an inch. George's son, Dhani, awakened by the commotion, rushed to his father's side. Both Dhani and the police noticed that Harrison was drifting out of consciousness, and they believed he was close to dying. "Oh Dhan," George said to his son, "I'm going out." As Harrison was taken away to an ambulance, Dhan called to him: "Dad! Are you with me. . . . ? It's going to be okay." Harrison was moved off the serious list by the following afternoon.

The young man who invaded Harrison's home had a history of schizophrenia that had not been treated adequately. He told his lawyer, "The Beatles were witches," and that God had sent him to put Harrison to death. In the trial that followed, the jury found the attacker not guilty on the grounds of insanity, and the magistrate committed him to the psychiatric wing of a Merseyside hospital. He would be eligible for release if a mental health examiner board determined he was no longer a threat. Harrison and his family asked to be notified if he should be released, but the judge denied the request.

Harrison's attack was followed by more death threats, and he and his family considered leaving Friar Park. In the spring of 2001, Harrison underwent a second operation to remove a cancerous growth on his lung. His lawyer reported that Harrison was in good spirits and that his prognosis was good. Harrison himself said: "I had a little throat cancer. I had a piece of my lung removed. And then I was almost murdered. But I seem to feel stronger." But throughout 2001 there were various reports of Harrison visiting hospitals in England and America in an effort to fight back the cancer, which eventually took the form of a brain tumor. On Thursday, November 29, 2001, Harrison succumbed to the disease at 1:30 in the afternoon, at the Los Angeles home of Gavin De Becker, a friend of the family's and a security expert. Harrison had been in the city for two weeks, but his presence there had been a well-guarded secret. He spent his last days surrounded by family and a few visitors, and in the company of close friends from the Hare Krishna community who chanted a mantra to help Harrison in his migration to death. "He left this world as he lived in it, conscious of God, fearless of death, and at peace, surrounded by family and friends," the family announced, in a statement. "He often said, 'Everything else can wait, but the search for God cannot wait, and love one another.'"

After his cremation, Harrison's remains reportedly were flown to India and scattered along the Ganges River and various other holy places in the vicinity.

The Beatles' second feature film, *Help!,* never matched the reputation of their form-breaking first movie, *A Hard Day's Night,* but as other observers have noted, it contains a moment that is central to how the Beatles occupied the modern imagination. Near *Help!*'s beginning, a limousine arrives outside a row of London flats. The four Beatles disembark from the car, and George, John, Paul and Ringo each walk to separate doors of four flats, lined up in a row. The Beatles enter their seemingly independent residences, but once they're behind the doors we see that there are no walls between their apartments. They all live in one grand living-and-bed-room residence, outfitted with sunken beds, a Wurlitzer organ that rises from one corner of the floor, a strip of lawn in another quarter of the floor, a library (largely full of John Lennon's writings) and a series of vending machines. At night, the Beatles sleep in beds sprawled across the room's spacious interior. The message was: This is the Beatles' idealized home and playground—the dream dwelling where they lived as partners on common terms and in a shared quest, with no partitions dividing them.

It was an adroit and mocking insight into how countless fans viewed the Beatles in the 1960s: as the exemplars of a self-made family that might serve as a model of community for youth culture and popular music. In one way or another, this longing for community—the dream of self-willed equity and harmony in a world where familiar notions of family and accord were breaking down—would haunt rock's most meaningful moments in the 1960s. There's every indication that the Beatles themselves shared this dream—at least for a brief time. "We were tight," Harrison said in *The Beatles Anthology.* "I'll say that for us." In 1983, though, Harrison reportedly told Geoffrey Giuliano: "All this stuff about the Beatles being able to save the world was rubbish. I can't even save *myself.*" In a different conversation, with Swami Prabhupada, George once said that there came a point in his meditations "where I can't relate to anyone anymore . . . Not even. . . . my friends, my wife, *anybody!*" Interesting remarks for a man who genuinely believed in ideals of love and unity, and yet who seemed to spend much of the last twenty-five or so years of his life keeping a wary distance from the world.

There is no question that Harrison's devotion to Indian teachings and spiritual precepts was sincere, even if he did not always stay with the disciplines that Hindu beliefs demanded. But then, the most interesting spiritual seekers tend to be the ones who are wise enough (or simply human enough) to wander off course periodically, turning their searches into enduring struggles. For Harrison, Hinduism—and the teachings of Swami Prabhupada and Paramahansa Yogananda, who were truly keen and even droll philosophers—may have fulfilled some deeper void that he had moved through during his entire life, and that his experience with the Beatles only deepened, rather than resolved.

But there's another side to Harrison's development with roots that run deep into the history of the music that helped form rock & roll. Even though blues music figured surprisingly little into his own guitar and compositional style (his occasional dissonance wasn't so much bluesy as it was simply willful or angry, or a sign of pain and loneliness, though later his ear generally favored sweetened melodies and harmonies), in a sense Harrison was, like his close musical friends Eric Clapton and Bob Dylan, at heart a bluesman who didn't need formal blues scales to frame his passions or hurt. In short, despite a good home life in his youth, and even though he formed an intense extended family within the Beatles for a time, Harrison was a man who didn't feel at home in the world. He resented what he saw as the oppressive social order that he had witnessed in his Liverpool youth: "I hate being dictated to," he told Beatles biographer Hunter Davies. And later, when he finally found the fame, success and adventure that he had pursued with the Beatles, he almost instantly recoiled from it. "After a bit," he said in an interview for his 1988 album, *Cloud Nine,* "we realized that fame wasn't really what we were after at all. . . . After the initial excitement and thrill had worn off, I, for one, became depressed. Is this all we have to look forward to in life? Being chatted around by a crowd of hooting lunatics from one crappy hotel room to the next?"

Harrison was in a strange place—a place that Bob Dylan likely understood well: namely, that the expectations of the world, the demands of renown and a mass audience's expectations, could be an isolating experience—one that offered no escape. True, one could retire into seclusion, but that offered primarily the forecast of a lonely, constricted life. At the same time, staying actively in the public eye—carrying on with your creative celebrity life—also necessitated a remoteness, or else one might be subject to the constant demands and dangers of being the object of others' hopes and hunger. The two members of the Beatles who yearned the most to enrich the welfare of the world around them—George Harrison and John Lennon—were also the two who would do their best to enforce a distance from that world and what it might want from them. Their mix of idealism and guardedness was as instinctive as it was earnest—and it was horribly prescient as well: Both artists were attacked by crazed fans who felt some lethal obsession with the fact these men had done so much to affect modern times.

It's fitting to think of George Harrison as a man who sought enlightenment, but it's also possible to consider him as a modern bluesman. The bluesman, like the seeker, is a person who learns how to live alone in the world, not necessarily in a happy way, but with few illusions. Certain Hindu practitioners adhere to a similar course, finding worldly pleasures transitory, even untrustworthy. George Harrison, like the rest of the Beatles, had great and plentiful opportunities in his life at an early age: He could see any place in the world he wanted, own any car or most property that he fancied, find sex or love on any day. And yet there was something in him that remained lonely and in need, something that lived in shadows that even he didn't always find access to. His beliefs in Hindu precepts gave him a way to be in the world but to withdraw from it at the same time. A way to experience pain and yet contemplate it from a different angle. That is, Harrison's religious beliefs afforded him the means to survive the Beatles while he was still within their community, and to bear the knowledge that his tenure with the band would likely eclipse every work or performance he might subsequently offer.

These beliefs didn't necessarily make Harrison a "better" man—a man at peace or a man full of natural beneficence. He was well known for being gruff and impatient, and he made it apparent in many ways that he didn't particularly harbor a great love for the Beatles' audience. ("They gave their money and they gave their screams, but the Beatles kind of gave their nervous systems, which is a much more different thing to give," he said in *Anthology*.) Rather, Harrison's beliefs seemed to afford him a way to continue despite his conviction that too much of life was hellish and futile. According to some reports, he had planned to call his final album *Your World Is Doomed, Part One*, though it was eventually renamed *Brainwashed* (and is perhaps his best album). The original title might serve as a nice summation of Harrison and his manners and views: He could be downcast, funny and unsparing all in the same breath, as well as immensely dignified. He was also complex, even contradictory—capable of great compassion and generosity, but also capable of withholding himself from the world and perhaps from those close to him. On the inside of his Friar Park mansion, there are reportedly numerous pictures and statues, celebrating his dedication to the world's most beneficent teachers. Outside the house's main gate there was a grand, well-designed sign bearing the advice "Get Your Ass Outta Here."

In the end, like his famous former bandmates, Harrison was not only the object of intense love, but he believed that acting with a will and devotion to love was among the highest purposes of life. But he also understood that you need a lot more than love to make it through this world or redeem your pain. Sometimes the darkness is irrefutable. Nobody in the Beatles carried that knowledge with greater weight, yearning or honor than George Harrison. Whatever the mystery inside him was, he bore it with a grace that hasn't yet left this world.

SGT. PEPPER'S LONELY HEARTS CLUB BAND: WITHIN AND WITHOUT THE BEATLES

In the autumn of 1966, the Beatles wanted to call the Beatles quits; their fame had hemmed them in, surrounded them with trouble. Their music still managed to maintain a façade of effervescence in the sounds of records like *Beatles for Sale*, *Help* and even *Rubber Soul*, but the content of the songs had turned more troubled. It was as if the group had lost a certain mooring—Lennon was singing more frequently about alienation and apprehension, McCartney about the unreliability of love—and whereas their earlier music had fulfilled the familiar structures of 1950s rock & roll, their newer music was moving into unaccustomed areas and incorporating strange textures. Primarily, though, the band was growing fatigued from a relentless schedule of touring, writing and recording. Following the imbroglio that resulted from Lennon's assertion that the Beatles were more popular than Jesus, and after one last dispirited swing through America (in which they were unable to play their more adventurous new material), the Beatles called a formal quits to live performances, in August 1966. "We were fed up with being the Beatles," McCartney said years later to biographer Barry Miles. "We really hated that fucking four-little-moptop approach. We were not boys, we were men. It was all gone, all that boy shit, all that screaming, we didn't want anymore."

Little wonder. In the time since February 1964, when the Beatles first appeared in America on *The Ed Sullivan Show* to an unprecedented level of instantaneous mass fame, a remarkable amount had changed in both American and British manners and culture. Some of it began congenially enough—youth's personal fashion turned more flamboyant—but as the decade wore on, this same youth began to take on more active involvement in social and political matters. They campaigned for civil rights and racial and economic equality, and in growing numbers they protested and opposed the United States' brutal and fruitless role in Vietnam's civil war. (Young Americans also died in Southeast Asia in growing numbers: more than fifty-five thousand in the end.) Musical tastes of the young began to reflect this unrest, at first through the folk music resurgence that yielded Bob Dylan and Joan Baez, but increasingly through rock & roll's unruly style, which spoke for a new concord.

Through it all, the Beatles' influence had been unequivocal. Their popularity had fostered a myriad of rival bands throughout Britain and America in the mid-1960s, but the group soon felt the need to keep pace with a scene that was becoming lyrically and musically bolder by the season. In 1966 the Beatles made their most innovative work, *Revolver*. It was full of remarkable sounds—including non-Western harmonies and instrumentation, tape loops that helped shape intense electronic trances, disorienting guitar reveries that curled backward—unlike anything heard before from a massively successful pop group. But once outside the studio, things shortly turned horrible. After a frightening world tour that same year—during which they were attacked in the Philippines, and threatened in America due to John Lennon's controversial remarks about Christianity—the Beatles left live performing for good.

Rumors of tension within the group—as well as rumors that they were disbanding—soon spread as the Beatles produced no new music for months. Up to that point, the group's status had been unquestioned; now it seemed as if popular music might in fact bypass them. They understood that any new work of theirs would either reestablish their eminence or finish them—not just their future but also the purpose of their history. "It was great, actually," McCartney told *Rolling Stone* in 2007. "Because we were done touring, people in the media were starting to sense that there was too much of a lull, which created a vacuum, so they could bitch about us now. They could say, 'Oh, they've dried up.' But we knew we hadn't. It was kind of cool—behind the scenes, we knew what we were making, and we knew we were very far from drying up. Actually, the exact opposite was happening: we were having a huge explosion of creative forces."

McCartney was referring to the sessions that became *Sgt. Pepper's Lonely Hearts Club Band*, the work that came to symbolize—immediately—the ambitions and longings and fears of the twentieth century's most controversial generation in the midst of a vital, complex and risky epoch. What began in 1963 and 1964 as a consensus—with the Beatles at its center—had transformed into a worldview. It was a time of great promise, but also of great risk. No single work had yet epitomized these bold new senses of community, art and ideas. Nothing, that is, until *Sgt. Pepper.* This was the moment when the Beatles were renewed in the minds of everyone, when a generation would feel closer to them than ever before, would feel that the Beatles were speaking to and for them in an uplifting accord. The paradox in this was that the Beatles themselves had never felt more removed from that audience, and before much longer, would start staking their distances from one another as well. *Sgt. Pepper* was both the means and the reason for that transformation: It was the most celebrated moment in popular music's history, but it ended up costing the most celebrated band in popular music the fraternity they signified.

The Beatles had come far closer to disbanding after their 1966 tour than was generally known. George Harrison, who had come to see the group's popularity as a weight and a danger, told manager Brian Epstein point-blank that he was leaving the group, then retreated with his wife, Pattie Boyd, to Bombay for five weeks, where he studied Indian culture and practiced north Indian classical music with sitar master Ravi Shankar. Meantime, John Lennon—who had formed the Beatles in part to make his way through the world unalone—found himself feeling an unexpected grief over the band's current parting. He later said that he had dropped to his knees one night in abject prayer: "God, Jesus, or whoever the fuck you are—*wherever* you are—will you please, just once, just *tell* me what the hell I'm supposed to be doing?" After the 1966 tour the Beatles went on hiatus for the first and last time in their career. On November 24, 1966, they reconvened at EMI's Abbey Road studios in London to see what music they could now make. They wound up surprising themselves. "Strawberry Fields Forever" was spooky and full of odd, disjointed lyrical and structural associations, and it grabbed the others right away—it was a new direction. The Beatles worked on it for weeks, something they had never done before. In the end, Lennon gave Martin the task of joining two disparate versions of the song—one spare and doleful, the other orchestrated with cellos, horns and inverted propulsive rhythms—in different keys for the final haunting mix that resulted in the most abstract hit in popular music history. "We could not have produced a better prototype for the future," George Martin later wrote.

When Brian Epstein and EMI Records insisted on new material for a new Beatles double-A-sided single, Martin gave them "Strawberry Fields

Forever" and McCartney's sparkling "Penny Lane." Though the producer later regretted this—he felt the new album was losing two of its strongest tracks—the pairing couldn't have been smarter. The songs were flip-sided memories—one haunted, the other wistful—of a time and place left behind, and for years a myth persisted that the Beatles had intended this new album as an autobiographical exploration of their postwar Liverpool youth. McCartney later disavowed the rumor: "There wasn't any conscious we'll-sit-down-and-remember-our-childhood," he told *Mojo* in 1995.

Whether or not the Beatles had considered looking homeward, they were nonetheless searching for an ideal of sanctuary, in addition to a new paradigm. They wanted distance from their image, and McCartney hit on an idea that might solve these concerns: "I thought, let's not be ourselves." Instead, McCartney suggested, they could invent an identity and work from inside the conceit of an alter-ego band that was making an album. "Everything about the album," McCartney said, "will be imagined from the perspective of these people, so it doesn't have to be us, it doesn't have to be the kind of song *you* want to write, it could be the song *they* might want to write." Doing whatever the imagined band wanted to do meant, of course, that the real band, the Beatles, could also perform in any style they wanted, not just rock & roll. They could, McCartney told Barry Miles, "do a bit of Stockhausen, a bit of Albert Ayler, a bit of Ravi Shankar, a bit of *Pet Sounds*." To set up this notion, McCartney—who had been enamored of the fanciful names that were starting to grace American psychedelic bands such as Big Brother and the Holding Company and the West Coast Pop Art Experimental Band—proposed calling this stand-in group Sgt. Pepper's Lonely Hearts Club Band, and wrote a title song to introduce the fictional premise at the album's outset. Lennon and Harrison reportedly had doubts about this make-believe scenario, but neither had any alternate ideas for showcasing the group's new music.

For McCartney in particular, this tactic opened up real opportunities. Though John Lennon, due to his art school background and his later experimentalist collaborations with Yoko Ono (including "Revolution 9," on the 1968 White Album), eventually earned a reputation as the Beatles' primary avant-gardist, McCartney had been the original pioneer along these lines. For some time, McCartney had been pursuing an interest in the musical vanguard, studying and listening to modernist composers Karlheinz Stockhausen, Luciano Berio and John Cage, and attending performances by Pink Floyd and the Soft Machine in London's burgeoning Spontaneous Underground scene. Barry Miles later wrote that McCartney would tell Lennon of his extraordinary music ideas, and that Lennon would push him to do them; even if they seemed arty, they also seemed audacious. "But Paul," notes Miles, "was very conscious of bringing Beatles fans along with them slowly, rather than alienating them with too much weirdness. Paul did contemplate a solo album and even had a title for it, *Paul McCartney Goes Too Far*, but nothing came of it." McCartney was in effect setting out to challenge the division between the high arts (romantic and modern classical music, in this case) and the lower ones (rock & roll and other pop forms), and that ambition, as much as anything about *Sgt. Pepper,* had significant consequences.

McCartney's gambit gained him an upper hand in the Beatles. He had already brought avant-garde approaches into *Revolver*, and these methods helped deepen the album's songs of resentment, loneliness, futility, abandonment, alienation and death. But with *Sgt. Pepper,* engineer Geoff Emerick later wrote, McCartney was emerging as the band's "de facto producer." Lennon later concurred: "I was . . . in a real big depression in *Pepper,* and I know that Paul wasn't at the time. He was feeling full of confidence. I was going though murder." (George Martin also felt that Lennon might have been jealous of some of the attention the producer gave to McCartney's music and ideas.) Despite Lennon's personal crisis—he felt dissatisfied with his private life and confused about his artistic purpose—he remained enthusiastic, as eager to push conceptual boundaries as McCartney. Richard Lush, an Abbey Road engineer at the time, told *Mojo* in 2007 that what Lennon sought daily in the project was "nothing normal. . . . I want to sound different today, nothing like I sounded yesterday." Also, the Beatles insisted on closed sessions. They rarely allowed visitors; they didn't want anybody cribbing their ideas.

Paul McCartney was playing a considerable role in shaping what became the Beatles' best-known achievement. In some ways, the others never excused McCartney for his governance of 1967, even if it was their eminent moment. In later years, all the Beatles but McCartney would distance themselves from *Sgt. Pepper* in various ways. Harrison and Ringo Starr said they often felt unoccupied at the sessions, mainly waiting to play what they were needed to play (though Starr's work on the album in effect redefined the sound and art of rock drumming). Lennon, though, was especially vehement, once denouncing *Sgt. Pepper* in front of McCartney as "the biggest load of shit we've ever done." Within months after finishing the album, Lennon never wanted to create anything like it again. In 1968, while discussing *Sgt. Pepper*'s methods with George Martin, Lennon said:

"That's not rock & roll to me, George. Rock & roll is grooving to a good song." *Sgt. Pepper*'s grooves, he had decided, were dishonest.

These dynamics meant that *Sgt. Pepper* would have two immediate lives: its famous public life and a trickier inner reality that had an unforeseen outcome. There were other elements mingling with all this as well, chief among them an influence the Beatles had long kept hidden. "When [George Martin] was doing his TV program on *Pepper*," McCartney recalled to Barry Miles, "he asked me, 'Do you know what caused *Pepper*?' I said, 'In one word, George, drugs. Pot.' And George said, 'No, no. But you weren't on it all the time.' 'Yes, we were.' *Sgt. Pepper* was a drug album."

The Beatles had been introduced to marijuana by Bob Dylan in 1964, and had used the drug steadily since. But psychedelics—which they were now taking—proposed chancier, more intense possibilities. The first two band members to take LSD—George Harrison and John Lennon—ingested the drug unknowingly, at a dinner party in 1965. The acid had scared but also beguiled them. Lennon in particular felt his songwriting initially benefited from psychedelic experience; "She Said She Said" and "Tomorrow Never Knows," from *Revolver*, and "Strawberry Fields Forever" were all informed by LSD consciousness, sometimes disquietingly so. But by the time of the *Sgt. Pepper* sessions, according to several accounts, Lennon was taking the drug so frequently, and experiencing its ego-shattering effect so constantly, that he sometimes felt he was disappearing within his band and within himself. George Harrison later said: "In a way, like psychiatry, acid could undo a lot—it was *so* powerful you could just *see*. But I think we didn't realize the extent to which John was screwed up." Lennon himself later said of this period: "Psychedelic vision is reality to me and always was."

By contrast, McCartney had initially been wary of LSD. One evening, Lennon had a bad reaction to an LSD dose, and that ended the night's work. McCartney had a house nearby and took Lennon there, then took LSD himself to try to draw closer again to his songwriting partner. It was an intense night—both saw the bond of their mutual love, and both saw the divergences that would break them apart. "It was a very freaky experience," McCartney said years later, "and I was totally blown away."

The effect of psychedelics on *Sgt. Pepper* became a subject of argument as soon as the album was released. For some, the drug's sensations permeated everything about the record, from its illusory perspective and imagery to its sonic formations. This was most obvious in Lennon's "Lucy in the Sky with Diamonds," with its depiction—as musical as it was lyrical—of a journey through an ethereal vista to an impossible deliverance. For decades, everybody involved in the song insisted that the resemblance between the title's main words and the initials LSD was mere happenstance, but in 2004 McCartney admitted that it was "pretty obvious" that the song was an acid trip. In addition, drugs were also seen—frivolously or not—to inform "With a Little Help from My Friends" (drugs join the friends in the song, or are in fact the friends themselves), "Fixing a Hole" (taken by some outraged moralists as a reference to injecting heroin, an interpretation that was wildly off the mark), "Getting Better" (personal improvement brought about by the euphoric drug state), even "Lovely Rita" and "Being for the Benefit of Mr. Kite," the latter for their dazed-sounding musical parts. Despite these readings, none of these songs failed or succeeded merely for any imagined or real psychedelic allusions. In the end, the Beatles were aiming for invention. Hallucinogens may have been an influence, but so were ambitions of freedom and experimentalism—ideals that were central to the momentum of the 1960s. Producer George Martin—who was a key partner to the chimerical sounds the Beatles were creating—neither comprehended the band's drug use nor himself took any substances, but he understood that the nature of that moment was to push for new possibilities.

At the same time, there's no question that drugs might connect to how the Beatles now viewed meaning and social convention. These concerns had bearing on the album's most important songs, "She's Leaving Home," "Within You Without You" and "A Day in the Life," all of which reflected unorthodox standpoints. "She's Leaving Home," with its neoclassical string quartet weaving in and around McCartney and Lennon's dialogue-style vocals, was McCartney's sympathetic portrayal of a runaway girl and the parents she abandoned, the only track on the album that dealt straightforwardly with the existence of social collapse. The world the girl was running to had changed enough to draw her from the futility of her home, though for her parents that same new world defeated their own values and hopes: It took their child from them. "Within You Without You" was George Harrison's sole track on the album and demonstrated another influence on the Beatles. Harrison had been the odd man out in the group since its inception—his early songs were even deeper cries of estrangement than Lennon's—and he was the first in the group to turn against their fame by seeking meaning outside. But Harrison's ventures into Indian philosophy—especially the Bhagavad Gita's doctrine of rising above the ephemeral and Yogi Paramahansa Yogananda's instruction on seeing through social roles—had renewed him. Now *Sgt. Pepper* gave Harrison an opportunity:

Eastern thought's beliefs in transcendentalism seemed well-suited to an emerging counterculture suffering from disillusionment with modern Western principles. Over the years, "Within You Without You" has been derided by various critics for its dirgelike structure (Harrison and his sitar were accompanied by a north Indian ensemble—joined later by a Western string section—with none of the other Beatles playing on the track), and for its air of sermonizing. It is hard, though, to imagine *Sgt. Pepper* without "Within You Without You." In an album that is about moving beyond limits, Harrison's stately contribution came the closest to articulating that aspiration in any idealistic way.

"Within You Without You" and "She's Leaving Home" were essential to *Sgt. Pepper*'s meaning—they held out a sense of compassion, of hope—but "A Day in the Life" was more complex and disturbing; it almost deflated those prospects. The song was primarily John Lennon's composition—no matter his doubts about himself and *Sgt. Pepper*, he ended up providing the album's crowning moment (though another of his songs, "Good Morning Good Morning," dealt more directly with his critical state of personal repression). In Lennon's original draft, "A Day in the Life" was a lovely and forlorn soliloquy, but just as with "Strawberry Fields Forever," the other Beatles and producer Martin saw a chance to make something unparalleled. Lennon's account of a man so sick of modern life that he mourned for it was full of ambiguous images, but along with a lulling musical tow the lyrics built calmly to a sense of dread and epiphany. Lennon asked McCartney for a middle part to the song; it needed a diversion that would lead away from, then back to, the core theme of desolate yearning. McCartney offered a fragment he'd been playing with, but he also thought of a way to make the song's crucial shifts both mesmeric and disorienting: an orchestra playing a measured, ascending chaos. Lennon loved the idea, Martin thought it was excessive, but in the end the songwriters prevailed, resulting in what may be the finest recording in the Beatles' catalog. In their ultimate collaboration, Lennon wrote his most meaningful song and McCartney realized his best avant-garde ambitions.

Although recorded before most of the album's other tracks, "A Day in the Life" found its place at the album's end, after the imaginary band had come and gone. But the song wasn't a coda—rather it was a requiem for both *Sgt. Pepper* and for its vision of sanctuary. As the track opens, Lennon tells of a man who "blew his mind out in a car." It may be an act of suicide, maybe a drug-induced illumination, but either way the singer can't look away: It isn't a man who has died but an age that can't be abided and can't be walked away from. From there the music turns into an inchoate swirl, and another singer, McCartney, tries to deliver us from the news into a dream of bearing everyday life with narcotic insensibility, but Lennon's voice won't allow misleading hope. He insists on deciphering the modern farce, and then the orchestra drives the performance off the known map of the twentieth century. "A Day in the Life" exists in the space between unawareness and disenchantment—the space that those times moved in—and it closes with the most famous moment in 1960s music: a single chord played by John Lennon, Paul McCartney, Ringo Starr, George Martin and assistant Mal Evans across several pianos at once, reverberating on and on, like a possibility without resolution. As that eventful chord lingered and then decayed, it bound up an entire culture in its mysteries, its implications, its sense of providence found and lost. In some ways, it was the most stirring moment that culture would ever share, and the last gesture of genuine unity that we would ever hear from the Beatles.

When the Beatles finished *Sgt. Pepper* in late April 1967, they had spent four months and $75,000 on the project—unprecedented investments at that time. Brian Epstein threw a listening party at his London apartment in May. The Beatles were ebullient, and they knew that what they had created was something different from anything they had done before.

As it developed, nobody was prepared for what would happen with *Sgt. Pepper's Lonely Hearts Club Band*. The British music publications printed the first news of the album upon its completion; after that, public demand was so strong that EMI moved its British release date up by six days, to June 1 (it was released in the US on June 2). "It was like Christ coming into Jerusalem," *Life* magazine reporter Robin Richman recalled in Steven D. Stark's book, *Meet the Beatles*. Maybe even bigger: The record sold 250,000 copies in Britain in its first week (500,000 by the end of the month), and 2.5 million in the United States by late August. It topped the UK's charts for twenty-seven weeks, and held the same spot in America for fifteen weeks. This is to say that *Sgt. Pepper* hit a nerve in popular culture as nothing before had; it was era-defining and form-busting, and intentionally or not, it tapped perfectly the collective generational mood of the times. The album's opening clangor, with a strident guitar cutting across the pomp of an antiquated brass band, was a herald of change: old was giving way to new—and that sound, that value, was suddenly everywhere. "For a brief while," critic Langdon Winner famously wrote, "the irreparably fragmented consciousness of the West was unified, at least in the minds of the young."

Real or not, this was seen—and is largely still remembered—as an occurrence of, or a call to, community. In some ways, the Beatles had represented this ideal, fused with the value of generational change, all along: They had made plain since their arrival that we had entered a different age, that young people were now free to invent themselves in completely new terms. With the Beatles we witnessed the social and cultural power that a pop group and its audience could create and share, and because *Sgt. Pepper* was all about new heights, possibilities of all sorts felt boundless. Under the momentum of the Beatles and others, rock & roll became collusive with the social and political disruptions of the 1960s. John Lennon later said: "Changing the lifestyle and appearance of youth throughout the world didn't just happen—we set out to do it; we knew what we were doing."

As a result, *Sgt. Pepper* helped raise a countercultural ethic and a progressive aesthetic from the margins to worldwide possibility, and it did so in a way that unerringly manifested the sense of independence and iconoclasm that now seized youth culture. It did this through its sound as much as anything. It wasn't that the Beatles had invented the psychedelic or avant-garde aesthetic that their new music epitomized. Much of the album's spacey codes and florid textures and arrangements had been partly derived from the music of numerous innovative San Francisco, Los Angeles and British bands, though several of these other groups found their aesthetic through improvisation, which is one area the Beatles couldn't excel in. But with *Sgt. Pepper,* the Beatles managed to refine what these other groups had been groping for, and did so in a way that reasserted their centrality. Brian Wilson told *Rolling Stone* editor Jason Fine about hearing "Strawberry Fields Forever" for the first time while driving in Los Angeles. He pulled his car to the side of the road and cried, because the Beatles had beat him to the exemplar that he had been hoping to achieve with the Beach Boys' upcoming *Smile.* He didn't finish that album for thirty-seven years.

In addition, *Sgt. Pepper*'s unusual and rich aural constructions certified to many (including *Time* and *Newsweek* and various classical musicians and reviewers) that rock was now art and that art was, more than ever, a mass medium. Avant-garde forms could work in popular contexts, and rock style could be taken seriously. Contrary to what some critics claimed, though, McCartney's success wasn't in elevating pop to art but rather wiping away the conventional view of high culture's preeminence over low culture. It was a democratic move that decisively changed how popular culture is regarded. Perhaps most important, though, *Sgt. Pepper* was a measurement: of how far the Beatles themselves had come in a remarkably short time, and how far the culture they touched had come. Everything had redefined itself. This was a new territory.

Yet for others, *Sgt. Pepper* in fact failed its times. In *Magic Circles: The Beatles in Dream and History,* Devin McKinney describes the album as speaking to a "mostly white and middle-class" hippie audience, "not activists but passivists. . . . They sat in for love, not against Vietnam; held up flowers, not fists. . . . Insofar as the hippies had a program, it lay in changing the world by changing the individual consciousness—revolution from within." This is fair enough criticism. The Beatles had designed *Sgt. Pepper* from an insular vision, and even though the outside world wound up embracing that dream, that same world was in fact turning uglier. Generational and political divisions only grew deeper and more dangerous; the war destroyed more homes and futures; the psychedelic ideals of San Francisco's hippie community turned into a cataclysm—and *Sgt. Pepper* didn't speak to its political moment in any confrontational way. But the album, and the entire phenomenon of the Beatles' history, demonstrated another truth about rock & roll's social effect: namely, that it didn't have to articulate a political program or objective to have a political consequence. Since the 1950s, R&B and rock & roll had helped ignite a sense of collective spirit and purpose in its audience that went beyond mere fandom. This affected race relations in the era of Elvis Presley, and in the Beatles' years it extended into a generational transformation that had the nerve and vision to challenge Western moral and political standards, especially America's offenses in Vietnam. With the Beatles we witnessed the social and cultural power that a pop group and its audience could create and share, and because *Sgt. Pepper* was all about new heights, prospects of all sorts felt boundless.

To some, though, it all went too far; the album's arty style was off-putting, soulless. Within months a pointed withdrawal from *Sgt. Pepper's* aesthetic frontier was under way. At the year's end, Bob Dylan recorded and released *John Wesley Harding.* It was hermetic in its own way. Dylan, injured in a motorcycle accident, had withdrawn from public view even more than the Beatles had. But Dylan's new music was also deeply aware that the times were in trouble, and with its sparse, almost stoical three-piece Sun Studios–derived acoustic rock & roll sound, *John Wesley Harding* was also received as a critique of psychedelic rock. The record set in motion a reevaluation of rock & roll's forms, reaffirming the importance of the music's blues and country music sources, and the Band, the Rolling Stones, the Byrds and numerous other artists embraced this renewed aesthetic. Roots music was, almost overnight, rock & roll's new vanguard.

· · ·

Sgt. Pepper's moment couldn't carry on, nor could it keep and hold the Beatles. It only intensified the necessity for Lennon to break free. He had given in to and supported McCartney's desires for the album, but he also noted his growing differences with his partner: Lennon reasserted his devotion to rock & roll purism, whereas McCartney was equally at home with the music of English Romantic composer Sir Edward Elgar as he was with that of Little Richard. Lennon also thought they were writing more and more from different perspectives. McCartney was composing everyman narratives and celebratory calls; Lennon was writing from what he saw as a more authentic and troubled personal viewpoint. "Paul said, 'Come see the show,'" Lennon said later. "I said, 'I read the news today, oh boy.'"

Shortly after *Sgt. Pepper*, the year went bad on the Beatles. During a meditation seminar with Maharishi Mahesh Yogi in Bangor, Wales, in August 1967, the group learned that their manager, Brian Epstein, had been found dead in his London apartment at age thirty-two, of a drug overdose. Within days McCartney presented plans for a film and album, *Magical Mystery Tour*. More than ever, McCartney was now at the helm of the Beatles. The others once again went along with his idea, but they also saw where things were headed. Singer and songwriter Donovan Leitch once said the Beatles broke up because McCartney was too creative, too productive. Still, McCartney needed an editor, a governor, but like Lennon he was moving toward being his own sovereign, and he saw *Magical Mystery Tour* as his bid to top *Sgt. Pepper*. The Beatles would still record some remarkable music in 1967—"All You Need Is Love," "Baby You're a Rich Man," "I Am the Walrus" and two Harrison tunes, "It's All Too Much" and "Only a Northern Song" (the latter originally recorded for *Sgt. Pepper*)—but as a whole, *Magical Mystery Tour* proved unrealized and dispensable. The film itself was lambasted. McCartney still wanted to pursue the *Sgt. Pepper* direction, but his bandmates wouldn't have it. In 1968 the Beatles returned to regenerating essential rock & roll forms with "Lady Madonna" (another McCartney song). They were still a great band, but they no longer had concord. (McCartney referred to their 1968 album, known as the White Album— which, from its discontinuous musical personalities to its bare cover, was pretty much the anti-*Pepper*—as the Tension Album.) By the time of the Beatles' 1969 *Let It Be* sessions, the band's relationship had disintegrated into distrust and antipathy.

Over the years, *Sgt. Pepper*'s reputation has risen and fallen and risen again, partly because subsequent generations haven't wanted to be limited by the vanities of the 1960s. But it's also because, rightly or wrongly, *Sgt. Pepper* is now seen largely as Paul McCartney's feat, and in recent revisionist views of the Beatles, McCartney's genius has been relegated as less compelling than Lennon's. Still, McCartney got the last word: The closing half of their final studio work, *Abbey Road*, was an unspoiled suite—a rehabilitated version of *Sgt. Pepper*'s ambitions.

The Beatles' dissolution doesn't take away from their canon—their music remains enormously popular and valuable—though it certainly deepens the enigma at the heart of *Sgt. Pepper*. It was a beneficent work, though from an enclosed vantage. The Beatles wanted to turn us on, but they also wanted to keep us at a remove (which was probably the right instinct, given that one crazed fan murdered John Lennon in 1980 and another stabbed George Harrison at the end of 1999).

The Beatles couldn't help it: After all, they wanted the world to hear what they had done. Their greatest flair had always been for rising to the occasion of their own moment in history. They never did that more memorably or more meaningfully than with *Sgt. Pepper's Lonely Hearts Club Band*. The record wasn't simply about new possibilities—it was also about new impossibilities. *Sgt. Pepper* was part of a moment when the last century was opening up to reveal the potentiality of a new century within, then just as quickly closed off that promise. The album exemplifies that moment because *Sgt. Pepper* is also the story of the season in which the Beatles depicted a place they would not go beyond. Neither would anybody else. An age that was a moment was lost then, and it was never coming back.

THE MYSTERY
INSIDE JOHN LENNON

It has been nearly thirty years, and it can still stop your mind.

It had been a good night. John Lennon had just finished making music with his wife, Yoko Ono, which he regarded as some of the best music of his life, and his judgment wasn't off the mark. He had also learned, just a bit earlier, that his and Ono's new album, *Double Fantasy*—the first collection with new music from Lennon in six years, following a mysterious sabbatical—had gone gold that day. Now he and Ono were on their way back home from the studio, to see their son, Sean, the five-year-old that Lennon had devoted himself to more than to his career. Their car pulled up to the Manhattan apartment building where they lived, the Dakota, and Lennon got out. It was a balmy night, for December. He moved to the Dakota's entrance, then he heard a voice call his name.

It should never have gone that way. John Lennon was murdered, shot four times in the back, in the presence of his wife. It was a murder of madness.

A future was gone—he wouldn't make music again, he wouldn't get to kiss his son—but also, the past suddenly made no sense. A story that had started in hope, holding prospects for everybody who witnessed or took part in it, had ended in blood. It was an awful pay-off—the ending ruined the story. Lennon had constructed the Beatles—the group that in its time meant *everything*—and then in his work after he left the band, he had strived for an honesty and an idealism that was unlike anything that rock & roll had produced before. In doing so, he threatened not just cultural conventions but also unforgiving powers, because he had an unusual command: He had made music that moved the world. This violent ending spoiled the epic.

Nobody ever pushed the possibilities or tested the limits of rock & roll like John Lennon, and probably nobody in the music's history has really mattered as much. This isn't to say that Lennon was the primary reason for the greatness of the Beatles, though the Beatles are, of course, unimaginable without him. Nor is it to say that after he left that group he necessarily made better albums than the other former Beatles—though he clearly made more interesting and consequential ones, and he clearly took greater risks. And it isn't to say that he led a life of uprightness or sanctity, because—and this is the important one—he didn't. With songs like "Give Peace a Chance" and "Imagine," Lennon idealized optimism and compassion, but he realized those ideals in himself only fleetingly. He had a notorious, biting temper, he wasn't always fair to the people who loved and trusted him, and he sometimes lashed out viciously at an audience that simply believed in him.

What John Lennon did, above all else, was look after himself. He wanted love and he wanted validation, and he wanted those things on his own terms—the only terms he cared about, and after he had become so legendary, the only terms he needed to accept. Fortunately for us all—fortunately for history—Lennon's terms involved high standards. He was prideful enough that he wanted to improve his art, both in and beyond the Beatles, and that ambition raised his art. He was also self-important enough to believe that he could wrestle with the times he lived in and make a difference—and the difference he made was immense. Lennon was looking after himself when he made art and proclaimed hopes that would outlast his being. He was looking after himself when he made a family and nurtured and preserved it as his most meaningful legacy—when he looked into his son Sean's face, and wanted to be worthy of the veneration he saw in that face. He did it when, after all his fuckups and all his years of silence, he believed enough in the purpose of what he had to say that he was willing to start over.

Maybe it's surprising or simply incidental that all this self-interest affected our history in such wondrous and valuable ways. Or maybe it isn't incidental at all. The marvel of John Lennon's story is that all he really wanted was peace for his own interests—he hated feeling hurt, and he felt it his whole life—and in pursuing that end, he changed the times around him, and the possibilities of the times that followed him. Deep-running hurt drove him. It's what made his story.

"You're born in pain," John Lennon told *Rolling Stone* in 1970, " . . . and I think that the bigger the pain, the more gods we need."

Lennon's pain reached back to some of his earliest memories and cut through his entire life. Without it, his most memorable and lasting artistic creation—the Beatles—would likely never have happened, or at least would not have accomplished what they finally accomplished.

Lennon was born in Liverpool, in northern England, on October 9, 1940, during the days when Britain was the primary major democratic force willing to stand up against the advancing of fascism in Europe. Because Liverpool was England's leading port town—in fact, one of the greatest ports of Europe—it was the frequent target of Nazi bombing raids. On the night of Lennon's birth, air raid sirens announced an impending attack, and the city shut out its lights. John Lennon was born that night into darkness. Though the city was hit hard and often, Liverpudlians were resilient people. Many of them lived hard-bitten but resolved working-class lives, and they were known as a populace with rough manners, harsh humor and a spirit of proud individualism. They needed those qualities, since much of southern England—particularly London—regarded the city as a plebeian backwater. Lennon himself wasn't truly working class, but he sometimes saw himself that way, and he despised aristocratic arrogance and southern Englanders' condescension. "We were looked *down* upon by the Southerners as *animals*," he told *Rolling Stone* in 1970. "We were hicksville."

Whereas the other young men who eventually joined Lennon to form the Beatles—Paul McCartney, George Harrison and Ringo Starr—grew up in housing projects and tougher, poorer parts of Liverpool, Lennon was raised for the most part in relative comfort, in his aunt Mimi's home in the cozy suburb of Mendips. But that benefit didn't shield the young boy from other deprivations. His father, Alfred, was a ship steward, and liked to drink; his mother, Julia, was impulsive and rebellious—traits that Lennon inherited and carried through much of his life. Julia and Alfred married young, in a burst of passion in 1938, and John Winston Lennon was born two years later. Alfred, however, was often at sea, sometimes for a year or more, and in 1944 Julia became pregnant by another man. Alfred returned home in 1946, and when he couldn't put his family back together, he told the five-year-old John to choose between his father and mother. John at first chose his father, but when he saw the pain this was causing Julia, he relented, crying, begging his mother not to leave him. John would not see his father again until well into his fame in the Beatles, and in 1970, when he severed his relationship with Alfred, Lennon still felt rage over the neglect from years before. "Have you any idea what I've been through because of you?" he screamed at his father. "Day after day in therapy, screaming for my daddy, sobbing for you to come home. What did you care, away at sea all those years." As it turned out, neither of Lennon's parents raised him. Julia's family was enraged at her extramarital conduct, and Julia's sister Mimi took custody of the boy. Mimi was stern—nothing like Julia. She tried to give Lennon a steady home and firm direction, though she was often unwilling to accommodate his youthful enthusiasms, and she withheld love unless he pleased her judgments.

Julia's influence, on the other hand, was immense; in many ways, it set in motion the course of Lennon's life. Whether she meant to or not, Julia provided her son a model of social defiance; she didn't feel bound by proper conventions and easy morals, and neither would John. She also encouraged his fervor for the mid-1950s development that would soon lift his life and save his future: rock & roll. In the mid-1950s, Lennon and much of English youth were in the grip of a passion for skiffle—a rhythmic mix of the British music hall tradition and American folk music, epitomized by Lonnie Donegan's "Rock Island Line"—when a harder beat began emerging from America, led by artists like bluesmen Muddy Waters and Howlin' Wolf, soulful R&B singers Ray Charles and James Brown, and by fierce new stylists such as Gene Vincent, Elvis Presley and Chuck Berry. Lennon loved this music immediately—he sought it out nightly on Radio Luxembourg, an early form of British pirate radio, playing music the BBC wouldn't yet play. The class-conscious Mimi, though, saw rock & roll as entertainment for commoners, and she wouldn't let Lennon learn to play it in her house. When John purchased a guitar anyway, Julia allowed him to have it sent to her home, where she taught him some chord patterns and rhythms, and gave him room to practice the new music with friends. She liked the same sounds her son liked. Rock & roll was music that would in time help change American and British society in substantial ways. It was music that would also always be reviled by some for its ability to inspire an unruly sensibility, and for how it brought outsider traditions—like black music and country-western—into the popular mainstream. Lennon caught the meanings implicit in the new music right away, and he gave himself over to those possibilities. As critics Robert Christgau and John Piccarella once noted, Lennon "found his form (and how) in rock & roll. This was the language of John's generation, a language and a generation that his history destined him to blast open."

Julia was killed in 1958—hit by a car driven by a drunken, off-duty policeman—and Lennon was left with the sense of an unfinished relationship that forever haunted his memories and longings. "I lost her twice," Lennon told David Sheff, in a lengthy 1980 *Playboy* interview. "Once as a five-year-old when I was moved in with my auntie. And once again . . . when she actually, physically died. The underlying chip on my shoulder that I had as a youth got *really* big then. Being a teenager and a rock & roller *and* an art student *and* my mother being killed just when I was reestablishing a relationship with her . . . it was *very* traumatic for me."

The adventure of the Beatles was forged by John Lennon's temperament and needs. He formed the group to make his way through the world unalone, in a partnership that might lessen his sense of anxiety and separation. Later, he would end the group for the same reasons.

As a teenager, at Quarry Bank High School and later at Liverpool College of Art, Lennon was seen as unusually bright, imaginative, creative—and as an unusual amount of trouble. He wrote clever prose and drew skillful caricatures, but he had no patience for conventions of form and showed little respect to school authority for its own sake. He was famously disruptive and truculent at Quarry Bank, and was caned there (that is, beaten with a stick) time and again. When Cynthia Powell first saw him at Liverpool College of Art in 1957, she said in the film *Imagine,* "He walked around without his glasses and a guitar on his shoulder, and a look that said *kill.*" Though Lennon struck some as a nasty character, he was also in serious pursuit of the securities and union that could be afforded by love and family. He found a romantic form of that quest in Cynthia—who married him in 1962 and bore him a son, Julian, the following year—but Lennon's true effort at building a family came in the communion he formed with the Beatles, which years later would help inspire visions of shared aims in an emerging generation. Indeed, the Beatles proved the great love story of the 1960s—love was their main theme, first as a romantic ideal, then later as a social and political end—but in the end, love wouldn't save their family.

The group debuted in 1962 with "Love Me Do" (a song by Paul McCartney) and first hit Number One in the British chart in 1963, with "Please Please Me" (a song by Lennon that was also a clever plea about oral sex). Within a year the Beatles were the biggest event in British society since the Second World War, and for a time they gave their nation a new sense of innovative identity while mocking its staid class structures. Within a year, after the group's breakthrough in America on *The Ed Sullivan Show,* the Beatles were simply the biggest thing in the world, short of nuclear fear. Though their astounding popularity might be attributed to their shock-of-the-new quality—their hair, their dress, their language, their chord changes—they embodied a response that went far beyond mere trend. They represented a sea change—in music, in culture, in democracy itself. They weren't always comfortable with having that effect. "People said the

Beatles were the movement," Lennon later said, "but we were only part of the movement. We were influenced as much as we influenced." True, but the Beatles were a key part of that movement. They represented youthful hope, and they represented the new social power that rock & roll might achieve—a power not only to upset, but to transform. The world was changing—or at least it felt that way—and the Beatles served as emblems of that change.

As wonderful as all that may have seemed to the Beatles' audience, the group's internal reality was rather different. It's evident now that there was something in the band's experience that was painful for them. They all would give signs of that later, but none as clearly or vehemently as Lennon. He called life with the Beatles "a trap." In part, he meant the confinements and pressures that came with their fame, and the fears—such as the dread they felt traveling America in 1966, under constant death threats in the wake of Lennon's controversial statement that the Beatles "were more popular than Jesus now." Clearly, Lennon reveled in the money and fame, the hedonistic opportunities that spilled forth in each new city the Beatles visited, but early on he began to grow restless. He hated the touring. He resented making nice for private audiences with local privileged officials, and felt the concerts offered no chance for musical growth. He also lamented that all these obligations kept him from his family, from time with his son Julian, though according to Cynthia in her recent book *John,* her former husband's emotional investment in his son was often strained even in the best of circumstances. The truth is, Lennon had inherited more of his mother's spirit than he understood. He lived intensely in the moment: He threw himself into attachments with real ardor, but when those moments and the infatuation had passed, he liked to move on. Quickly. He didn't trust constancy; he wasn't convinced there were verities worth staying tied to; he wouldn't afford regrets. As early as 1965, Lennon was already looking for something that might transcend the Beatles, even as he continued to work within the opportunity and fraternity that they afforded.

Lennon's first diversion came in the way of drug experiences, a pursuit that he shared with the other Beatles, though perhaps not for the same purposes. In London in 1964, in the first meeting of the Beatles and Bob Dylan, Dylan was surprised to learn that none of the band's members got high. He introduced them to marijuana, and the Beatles took to the drug with such enthusiasm that their brilliant 1965 album *Rubber Soul,* both Lennon and McCartney later said, was deeply pot imbued. When Lennon first experimented with LSD, he was horrified by the dreamlike hallucinations and unfamiliar thought processes that the drug induced, but he was also fascinated. He went on to take the drug regularly—by his own account, on a daily basis, amounting to more than a thousand occasions—and while his devotion to psychedelics worried his wife and some friends, including Beatles producer George Martin and journalist Ray Coleman (later, the author of a definitive Lennon biography), the LSD experience transformed the Beatles at a critical moment. The band had quit touring, at the insistence of Lennon and Harrison, and for the first time since the Beatles' rise, a new creative movement—a psychedelic-inspired form of music, played by bands from San Francisco and London, and associated with experimental lifestyles and mystical experience—had seized the vanguard in rock & roll, largely expanding on musical and lyrical possibilities that the Beatles, the Rolling Stones and Bob Dylan had opened up in their earlier music.

The Beatles took nine months in 1966 and 1967 to refine their musical and artistic direction, and emerged with *Sgt. Pepper's Lonely Hearts Club Band*, a record that, producer George Martin later said, was "all acid." Lennon's writing had been steadily opening up, becoming more personal and unorthodox, beginning with "Norwegian Wood" and "In My Life" on *Rubber Soul*, and hitting new peaks with "She Said She Said" and "Tomorrow Never Knows" on 1966's *Revolver* and the 1967 single, "Strawberry Fields Forever" (which was the beginning of the *Sgt. Pepper* project). On *Sgt. Pepper*, Lennon owned the album's best and most famous moment, "A Day in the Life," a lovely and dark song about confusion, death, despair, alienation and wonder, and it demonstrated the singer's ability to view his experience while standing outside of it at the same time—a perspective Lennon had gathered from his LSD ventures.

Lennon was soon ready to move past drugs. In part, this was the nature of the times. Long-held ideals of society, politics, sex and religion were seemingly subject to bold challenges and rapid transformations, and it wasn't uncommon to traverse what felt like years in the matter of a season or two. Also, rock & roll itself had now become a major cultural and artistic medium—a change accomplished by the Beatles more than anybody else—and as such it could now contain or affect the major concerns or interests of its times. One of those interests in 1967 was Eastern mysticism—a once obscure (that is, to Westerners) practice that was being explored by some seeking a philosophical or spiritual analog to the psychedelic experience. In August 1967, the Beatles visited Maharishi Mahesh Yogi, a teacher of a technique known as Transcendental Meditation, at a seminar in Bangor, Wales. (Lennon would later bitterly reject the Maharishi, after the Beatles studied with him in Rishikesh, India.) During this meditation seminar at Bangor, the group learned that its manager, Brian Epstein, had been found dead in his London apartment at age thirty-two, of a drug overdose. Epstein was a complex man, and though Lennon sometimes later derided the manager's contributions, Epstein was vital to establishing the Beatles. But Epstein was also in his own pain. He was homosexual in a time and place where homosexuality was illegal, and he'd lived much of his life as an outsider. After the Beatles quit touring, Epstein succumbed deeper into a depression he'd known his whole life, and had attempted suicide on at least one occasion. Though the manager's death was ruled accidental, Lennon felt guilty for having introduced him to drug use. With Epstein gone, the Beatles were on their own, and for all their success and bravado, they weren't ready for that. "I knew we were in trouble then," Lennon said in 1970. "I didn't really have any misconceptions about our ability to do anything other than play music. And I was scared. I thought, 'We've fuckin' had it.'"

But another event that would figure just as much into the Beatles' fate had already transpired. In November 1966, prior to the recording of *Sgt. Pepper*, Lennon visited London's Indica Gallery, for a preview of an exhibition by Yoko Ono, a Japanese-born woman who had been a key player in New York City's influential Fluxus avant-garde art movement in the early 1960s (she had helped conceive performance art). Her works were unlike anything Lennon had seen before. They were playful and intellectual at the same time, and all of them offered the viewers conundrums, but also invited them to become a part of the art by addressing the conundrum. There was no such thing as a false answer to the riddles in Ono's art. The answer was in fact the willingness to answer, to engage in an exchange with the art itself or its artist. Lennon was puzzled, even annoyed by some of the challenges in Ono's art, but he also got it, and he was captivated. She represented possibilities to him—certainly romantically, but more important, the possibility of growth as an artist, and the prospect of a new kind of partnership. In May 1968, Lennon sent Cynthia away on a vacation to Greece, and the night before her return, he invited Ono over to his country home in Weybridge. He and Ono talked for hours, and made a remarkable experimental recording, *Unfinished Music No. 1: Two Virgins*. At dawn, they made love. When Cynthia returned home that afternoon, she found the two sitting together in robes, drinking tea, and she was startled by their quiet intimacy. She later said, "I knew immediately [when] I saw them together that they were right for each other. I knew I'd lost him." For his part, Lennon knew there were other losses to come. "That's when I started freeing myself from the Beatles," he said. "And that's when everybody started getting a bit upset. . . ."

Whatever happened between John Lennon and Yoko Ono in the formation of their relationship, it was genuine and it was powerful and it puzzled many people—not the least of them the Beatles. Ono came from another culture; she had made vanguard art in New York; she loved and studied the music of avant-garde classical composers Alban Berg and Anton Webern; and she knew nothing about the rock & roll world initially, and wasn't particularly impressed by the Beatles.

John's prior major partnership had been with Paul McCartney—more so, in fact, than with Cynthia. The two men had strikingly different temperaments, and different approaches to making music. McCartney was orderly and meticulous, and placed a high premium on craft; Lennon was unruly, less prone to lingering over a song, and despite his cocky front, he was less secure in his work than his writing partner. In fact, Lennon routinely used studio tricks to cover for what he saw as flaws in his voice (though he was, in fact, among the greatest singers rock & roll produced), and he at times doubted his compositional contributions to the Beatles (in the end, he was responsible for a larger share of the Lennon-McCartney songbook than his partner). But the greatest difference between the two men in 1969 was that McCartney still deeply valued and needed the Beatles; Lennon was already exhausted by the group and thinking of leaving it behind. After Epstein's death, McCartney had attempted to hold the band together, and kept coming up with projects to give them direction (such as the misbegotten *Magical Mystery Tour* film). But like the other Beatles— separately and collectively—McCartney couldn't manage their business. The group had started an idealistic company, Apple (Lennon once described it as a capitalist form of the communist principle), but the venture was losing money so rapidly that it threatened to bankrupt the group. In time, Lennon brought in a controversial manager, Allen Klein, to salvage the Beatles' fortunes, and McCartney brought in Lee Eastman, a respected entertainment lawyer and the father of Paul's wife, photographer Linda Eastman. These vying ideas about how to handle the group's business would lead to festering divisions between Lennon and McCartney.

But the truth is, Lennon wanted to move past the Beatles. His relationship with Ono was inspiring a new adventurism, yet he felt that the Beatles were stifling to that spirit. "What I did," he later admitted, "was *use*

Yoko . . . it was like now I have the strength to leave because I know there is another side to life." Lennon began bringing Ono into the group's recording sessions, during the making of the two-record set *The Beatles*, more popularly referred to as the White Album. Ono performed on some of Lennon's tracks on the album, and some saw this as a violation of the group's self-contained ethos. It's true that Lennon wasn't being entirely fair to the others. The Beatles had always been a closed unit in the studio, never letting anybody interfere with their recordings other than George Martin. But in truth, the Beatles were no longer an integral unit at this point. Each member was recording his own tracks with the other members as sidemen, and in the case of "While My Guitar Gently Weeps," George Harrison recruited Eric Clapton to play the song's guitar solo. Lennon felt that the Beatles and others at Apple actively disliked Ono because she was a strong-willed woman and Japanese, and that they judged her "like a jury." Ono said: "I sort of went to bed with this guy that I liked, and suddenly the next morning I see these three guys standing there with resentful eyes." The disparagement that Lennon perceived wounded and outraged him, and he continued to reflect on it even in his last days. He felt personally condemned by the group that had come together at his invitation. In 1969, during a meeting surrounding the Beatles' wayward film and album project, *Let It Be*—another venture essentially directed by McCartney— Paul was trying to persuade the group to return to live performances, perhaps a single major concert or touring small venues under assumed names. This suggestion had been coming around for some time, and Lennon and Harrison hated it. With McCartney's hopes running so high, Lennon felt he had to come clean. "I wasn't going to tell you," he said, "but I'm breaking the group up." A shocked McCartney and Lennon's manager Klein persuaded Lennon to hold off making any public announcements. They still had *Let It Be* to finish, and there were two other albums to promote, *Hey Jude* and *Abbey Road*. Lennon agreed to the delay. On April 10, 1970, close to the date the Beatles were set to release the *Let It Be* album (which producer Phil Spector tried to rescue by remixing the songs and adding some embellishments), Paul McCartney released his first solo album, *McCartney*, along with a press release, blasting the Beatles in sour terms and announcing that he had quit the group and wouldn't miss them. His move was headline news around the world. Lennon was dismayed and furious. He had held off on his own announcement at McCartney's request, and now Paul had gotten the jump on him.

The Beatles' end served as motivation for the most vehement declarations Lennon would ever make. In a famous lengthy 1970 interview with Jann S. Wenner in *Rolling Stone*, Lennon largely held McCartney's wiles to blame for the group's dissolution, but he also had plenty to say about the Beatles in general and the audience that claimed them. Among those statements: "We sold out. The music was dead before we even went on the theater tour of Britain.... The Beatles' music died then, as musicians." "I didn't become something when the Beatles made it or when you heard about me, I've been like this all me life. Genius is *pain* too. It's just pain." "The Beatles' tours were like Fellini's *Satyricon*.... Wherever we went, there was always a whole scene going.... They didn't call them groupies then, they called it something else. But if we couldn't have groupies, we'd have whores and everything, whatever. Whatever was going." "Fuckin' big bastards, that's what the Beatles were. You have to be a bastard to make it, man. That's a fact, and the Beatles were the biggest bastards on earth." "One has to humiliate oneself to be what the Beatles were, and *that's* what I resent. I *did* it, but I didn't know, I didn't foresee that, it just happened bit by bit 'til this complete craziness is surrounding you. And you're doing exactly what you don't want to do with people you can't *stand*—the people you *hated* when you were ten.... And these fuckin' bastards, they're just sucking us to death. About all we can do is do it like fuckin' circus animals. I resent being an artist in that respect, I resent performing for fucking idiots who won't know—who don't know—anything. 'Cause they can't feel—I'm the one that's feeling, 'cause I'm the one that's expressing what they are trying to. They live vicariously through me and other artists."

Lennon's commentary, while fascinating—in fact, shocking at the time—sought to deflate the Beatles' significance while assuming that significance for his own stature under a stratagem of hard honesty. It was hard to read those words without feeling that Lennon was indicting not just the band, but those who had placed a stake in the Beatles. No other major artist ever intentionally razed his own image so devastatingly.

However—not surprisingly—when Lennon applied his hurt and vitriol to his music, the result was transcendent. He had been active in Los Angeles in an experimental form of therapy, Primal Therapy, authored by psychologist Arthur Janov. The therapy's premise was that for one to heal oneself, you had to go into your deepest, repressed pains in a cathartic way, and when you hit the center of that pain, you would erupt in a cry—the primal scream—and you would know yourself better. It seemed tailormade for Lennon. "I was the male who never cried, you know," he told *Playboy* in 1980. "I would never have gone if there hadn't been this promise of this scream, this liberating scream." Lennon brought some of that practice to bear on his first solo album, *John Lennon/Plastic Ono Band*, released in December 1970. The singer recruited Phil Spector to produce the record. Spector had formulated the lush, orchestral-like Wall of Sound style for his famed recordings with the Crystals, the Ronettes, Ike and Tina Turner and the Righteous Brothers, and he had applied some of that sensibility to the Beatles' *Let It Be* and George Harrison's *All Things Must Pass*. Lennon, though, wanted an altogether different sound for his first album: minimalist instrumentation—just guitar, bass, drums, piano and voice. The result was startling: Lennon sang about the most painful memories and undercurrents of his life—the death of his mother, the failures of faith and fame, the betrayals in misplaced ideals—in such a way that there was nothing buffering his emotions from their expression, and nothing to shield a listener from the resulting raw anger and anguish. He later said that he decided, for this album, to "shave off all imagery, pretensions of poetry, illusions of grandeur. . . . Just say what it is, simple English, make it rhyme and put a backbeat on it and express yourself as simply [and] straightforwardly as possible."

The album's crowning moment was "God," a litany of all the systems of belief and mythology that Lennon was now turning his back on as he forged a new beginning, until at song's end, in a mesmerizing and heartaching voice he pronounced: "I don't believe in Beatles." A short time later he told Jann S. Wenner: "I don't believe in the Beatles myth. I don't believe in the Beatles—there's no other way of saying it, is there? I don't *believe* in them and whatever they were supposed to be in everybody's head, and including our own for a period." But Lennon was also taking the measure of more than his former band. The song brilliantly caught the wonderful and terrible sense of a generation in its time—romantic, shattered, reeling as hope dissolved all around it and now left on its own. "The dream is over . . . ," he sang at the song's end, in the loveliest voice he ever summoned. "You'll just have to carry on." Few songs have ever hurt so much while sounding so heartening.

John Lennon/Plastic Ono Band would be the best-sustained and most powerful work of Lennon's solo career—perhaps the one album by a former Beatle that can stand in its entirety alongside the best of the band's recordings. It didn't, however, sell as well as any of the Beatles' releases, nor as well as McCartney's and Harrison's solo debuts. With his next album, *Imagine,* Lennon tried to present his concerns more accessibly. Spector produced again, but this time brought his more familiar warm, lush style to the new songs. Lennon's lyrics still chased troubling themes—his hatred of deceitful political leaders, jealous insecurities in his marriage, a bitter disdain for his former songwriting partner (he loved beating up on McCartney)—but even his most challenging beliefs were wrapped with a savvy pop sensibility that invited a wide range of listeners, rather than disaffecting them. The album's title track, in particular, put forth some daring notions, conjuring the vision of a world without religion or property or borders, and it did so in a lovely and haunting way. The song was a prayer, the most radical prayer that ever played widely on radio. "'Imagine,' both the song and the album," Lennon said, "is the same thing as 'Working Class Hero' on the first disc. But the first record was too real for people, so nobody bought it.... 'Imagine' was the same message but sugarcoated.... 'Imagine' is a big hit almost everywhere—antireligious, antinationalistic, anticonventional, anticapitalistic, but because it is sugarcoated it is accepted. Now I know what you have to do. Put your political message across with a little honey."

Lennon's gambit worked. *Imagine* reached Number One on *Billboard*'s album chart, and it produced an unorthodox anthem that has never been equaled in popular music. It was also the last great album John Lennon would make until the last few weeks of his life.

In 1971 John Lennon and Yoko Ono moved to New York City. Lennon felt vitalized by its art and music and politics, and how all those activities interacted and flourished in the city's West Village neighborhood. He and Ono became friendly with some prominent radical activists, including Jerry Rubin and Abbie Hoffman of the Yippies. (Both had been convicted in the infamous Chicago Seven trial that sought to punish protest organizers of the explosive 1968 Chicago Democratic Convention; their convictions were later reversed.) Lennon had been politically concerned for some time. He had spoken out against the Vietnam War on the Beatles' 1966 US tour, and he insisted that the group release his song "Revolution"—which fretted over the political obligations that come with fame—on the flipside of "Hey Jude."

By the time Lennon and Ono were living in New York, his politics had grown more radical and outspoken. For years, starting before the end of the Beatles, Lennon and Ono had pursued a media-directed campaign for the cause of peace—which at that time meant in part promoting an end to the war in Vietnam, though they were also promoting the larger philosophy of nonviolence that had guided India's Mahatma Gandhi and the Reverend Martin Luther King Jr. In March 1969, following their marriage in Gibraltar, the couple flew to Amsterdam, where they staged a

Bed-In for Peace. For five days they sat in bed in their pajamas at the Amsterdam Hilton, and gave hundreds of interviews, discussing their views that true peace began as a personal pursuit, and talking about intersections between activism, popular culture, ideology and Eastern and Western religion. In May they staged a similar "Lie-In for Peace" in Montreal, where they recorded the enduringly popular "Give Peace a Chance" in a hotel room with several friends and visitors. Lennon later said that he was trying to change his own heart as much as anybody else's. "It's the most violent people who go for peace," he told *Playboy*. "But I sincerely believe in love and peace. I'm a violent man who has learned not to be violent and regrets his violence."

After arriving in New York, the couple played some political benefits on the East Coast and appeared at demonstrations for social justice and against the war, though they still refused to take part in anything that might result in a battle. "We are not going to draw children into a situation to cause violence," Lennon once told Rubin and Hoffman. "So you can overthrow *what?*—and replace it with *what?*" Lennon and Ono capped their political activity with a double album, *Some Time in New York City*, that addressed concerns like harsh drug laws, feminism, the Irish conflict and justice for black radical Angela Davis (a philosophy instructor, tried and acquitted in a death penalty case for the shooting death of a California judge). It was . . . well, it was a truly awful album—the worst work of Lennon's career. The problem wasn't his political stances, but instead how he expressed those concerns: The songs lacked any of the lyrical originality or effectiveness of Lennon's prior writing. He later said he was aiming for a journalistic style of immediacy in the album's songs, but other artists— most notably Bob Dylan—had done better with the same tack by humanizing their subjects, drawing portraits of people who embodied the pains of war and injustice. For the first and only time in his life, Lennon demeaned his material. There was nothing threatening or inspiring about *Some Time in New York City*. It worked only as a parody of itself.

Unfortunately, the US government, under the administration of President Richard Nixon, saw Lennon's politics as a serious hazard. In 1972 a Senate internal-security subcommittee of the Judiciary Committee sent a letter to Senator Strom Thurmond, noting Lennon's political activities. The letter suggested that Lennon intended to interfere with Nixon's renomination at the Republican Convention in San Diego. Thurmond then wrote Attorney General John Mitchell, hinting that Lennon should be deported. The Immigration and Naturalization Service (INS) informed Lennon he must leave the country within weeks, due to a guilty plea he had entered in a 1968 marijuana possession case in England. Lennon fought the order and managed to win an extension, but he had to continue fighting the matter for years. The government was willing to go to considerable lengths to eject him. In 1974 the Board of Immigration Appeals rejected Lennon's plea, and he was ordered again to leave the US, but won another extension. The INS then directed regional narcotics officers to keep Lennon under surveillance and, if possible, arrest him for possession of illegal drugs. Lennon sued the government, charging illegal surveillance, prejudice on the part of the INS, and the denial of his constitutional rights. In 1975 Lennon finally prevailed, and the government withdrew its case. Later, when the matter was all settled, and after Nixon and much of his administration had been forced out of power over their criminal actions in the Watergate matter, Lennon told journalist Pete Hamill, in a *Rolling Stone* interview, that he didn't want to talk about the president's fall. "I'm even nervous about commenting on politics. They've got me that jumpy these days."

But Lennon faced other trouble during this time. In October 1973 he and Ono separated after four years of marriage. Lennon claimed she threw him out. Ono said she was feeling lost as an artist. "What am I going to do?" she said. "My pride was being hurt all the time." Lennon moved to Los Angeles for a time, accompanied by his and Ono's secretary, May Pang, who became his lover. At first Lennon asserted a delight at leading a single person's life. He caroused and drank heavily with Harry Nilsson (a favorite songwriter of Lennon's, who died of heart failure in 1994), the Who's drummer Keith Moon (who died in 1978, of a medication he was taking to treat alcoholism) and Ringo Starr (whose alcohol addiction in this period sometimes resulted in blackouts). It became apparent that Lennon was miserable without Ono. He called her—often many times a day—begging her to allow him to return home, to their apartment at the Dakota, but she refused. She told him he wasn't ready. Lennon fell apart. He behaved horribly in public, and he smashed up a friend's house where he was staying. Nilsson later recalled Lennon crying while drunk at night, wondering what he had done wrong.

Lennon's depression and bravado ran alongside each other in his 1974 *Walls and Bridges*. The work was essentially an open plea to Ono—indeed, parts of it, such as "Nobody Loves You (When You're Down and Out)" and "Bless You" were heartbreaking. Interestingly, the album yielded Lennon his first and only Number One single as a solo artist, the spry "Whatever Gets You Thru the Night," which he recorded with Elton John. On Thanksgiving night that year, Lennon appeared at Elton's Madison Square Garden concert in New York. It was Lennon's first appearance before a large audience in years, and it was a triumph. Ono attended the concert and found her estranged husband backstage; she congratulated him on his performance. Lennon was touched and grateful to see her, and within a few weeks, Ono allowed him to return to the Dakota. Almost a year later, on October 7, 1975, Lennon finally won his deportation battle. A US Court of Appeals judge declared: "Lennon's four-year battle to remain in our country is a testimony to his faith in the American dream." Two days later, the forty-two-year-old Ono—who had suffered three miscarriages before with Lennon—gave birth to a son, Sean. The date was also Lennon's thirty-fifth birthday. The dreams that Lennon had long wanted finally came true. That was when he decided to quit the world.

John Lennon's infant son transformed his life as nothing else ever had. His wife had offered him a deal: "I am carrying the baby nine months and that is enough. You take care of it afterwards."

Lennon took his charge more seriously. This time, he had to. He had already once repeated the failures of his parents. Just as his father and mother had in effect abandoned him, Lennon had also forsaken his first son, Julian, during his years with the Beatles, and only spoke with or saw him sporadically over the years since his divorce from Cynthia. Only weeks before his death, Lennon told *Newsweek*: "I was not there for [Julian's] childhood at all. I don't know how the game works, but there's a price to pay for inattention to children. And if I don't give him attention from zero to five then I'm damn well gonna have to give it to him from sixteen to twenty, because it's owed, it's like the law of the universe."

Sean was, almost certainly, Lennon's purpose for a kind of redemption. John turned his business over to Ono—who attended to managing his fortunes as if she were undertaking a new art form. Lennon, though, now had no room in his days for art. He became Sean's primary nurturer, with the help of a domestic staff. He designed the boy's play routine, cultural education and diet, and when he learned to bake loaves of bread, Lennon viewed the accomplishment with the same sort of excitement that once greeted the release of the Beatles' albums. Lennon and Ono also became adherents of destiny systems like astrology and numerology, basing major decisions—including relationships and press contacts—on how the stars or the numbers looked. Elliott Mintz, a former ABC radio interviewer who became one of the Lennons' closest friends, saw much of the Lennons' private life firsthand. While he kept his humor about it all, Mintz was also persuaded that the family's belief systems and rituals helped transmogrify Lennon. He told *Rolling Stone's* Chet Flippo in 1981: "We sometimes joked about the paradox of [Lennon] singing 'God' and 'I don't believe in I Ching and I don't believe in magic and I don't believe in Buddha and I don't believe in Krishna'—but let me tell you, he believed in *all* of it." Lennon also studied feminist history and theory—which was his interest more than Ono's. "It's men who have come the long way from even contemplating the idea of equality," he told David Sheff. "I am the one who has come a long way. I was the real pig. And it is a relief not to be a pig. The pressures of being a pig were enormous. They were killing me. All those years of trying to be tough and the heavy rocker and heavy womanizer and heavy drinker were killing me. And it is a relief not to have to do it."

Lennon said he didn't listen to much popular music during these years—certainly little new music. Instead, he played Hank Williams and Bing Crosby records, watched a lot of television and did a lot of reading. He composed only sporadically in these years (though two of his rough demos, "Free as a Bird" and "Real Love," became the Beatles' final two singles, when Paul McCartney, George Harrison and Ringo Starr expanded on them for the *Beatles Anthology* project in 1995). One of the few musicians Lennon allowed himself contact with in this time was Paul McCartney, who sometimes dropped by unannounced with a guitar, to Lennon's minor annoyance. When the Beatles' legal matters were settled in 1976, Lennon and McCartney were able to reestablish a cautious but respectful relationship. Each sometimes praised the other's solo work, and in some of his last interviews, Lennon paid McCartney his highest compliment. "Throughout my career I've selected to work with . . . only two people: Paul McCartney and Yoko Ono. . . . That ain't bad picking." Overall, Lennon's feelings about the Beatles had turned warmer—he knew they were unrivaled—but he had never seriously considered any of the many demands or invitations for a reunion of the group. "Why should the Beatles give more?" he said. "Didn't they give everything on God's earth for ten years? Didn't they give *themselves*? Didn't they give all?"

In the summer of 1980, Lennon abruptly decided that he and Ono would resume recording. Ono had sent him on a sailboat trip to Bermuda, but a three-day storm had made the captain and the boat's two hands sick. Lennon was forced to steer the ship for a night, keeping it on course as waves lashed at him. He sang sea chanteys and Beatles songs as he held the wheel tight. "I arrived in Bermuda," he said. "Once I got there, I was so centered after the experience at sea . . . all these songs came to me." He called Ono back in New York. It was time, he said, for them to make a new pop record together. In August, Lennon and Ono entered Manhattan's Hit Factory and produced a duo album. The new work was, in a sense, the most shocking music Lennon ever made. In the Beatles he had written and recorded some of the most daring songs of the 1960s, and he had taken numerous risks in his solo and experimental work. But *Double Fantasy* was a departure in unexpected ways that disturbed and disappointed some fans and critics. It was a collection of songs about marriage, family, about domestic affirmation, and it featured the most polished musicianship and professional production of any of his works. To some, it sounded as if Lennon had made an easy peace, philosophically and aesthetically. But *Double Fantasy* ran deeper than that; it was, as Lennon saw it, a work about how modern capitalism aims to undermine the family. It was no less defiant, for him and Ono, than the music of the Clash or any of the other punk bands making brave music in that time. It was all music about a better world. "In one sense," critic Stephen Holden wrote, "*Double Fantasy* literally fulfills the dream of 'Imagine' by describing a real utopia." Or to put it in other terms, John Lennon was finally making good on an old claim: All you need is love.

In any event, *Double Fantasy* proved a hit. The night of December 8, David Geffen—the head of the label Lennon and Ono had signed with— visited the couple at the recording studio to tell them the album had just gone gold. Lennon and Ono finished that night's work on a track for Ono, "Walking on Thin Ice," a dark and brilliant dance track that Lennon regarded as the best song they had recorded in their reemergence. He left the studio that evening a happy man—probably as happy as he'd ever been. He had wrested a satisfaction and purpose from life that long eluded him: He had established a secure family and he was making music he believed in. On that night, as he and his wife arrived back at the Dakota, Lennon carrying the tape of Ono's "Walking on Thin Ice," anxious to see their five-year-old son, he had found a balance. Then, as the singer walked to the entrance of his apartment building, a man stepped from the shadows and spoke to his back. "Mr. Lennon," he said.

After his death, things changed around us. America entered the years of Ronald Reagan; Britain, the years of Margaret Thatcher. Modern history was reversing its hopes. Rock & roll, and later hip-hop, still pushed against that reversal, but it has never pushed as hard as it did in the years of John Lennon. That isn't simply because Lennon was killed. Rather, it's because he lived. The Beatles set something loose in their times: a sense of generational transformation that moved quickly from the blissful to the artistic to the political, and for a few remarkable years, seemed irrefutable. The story of our times since then has been the product of a determination to make sure that nothing like that could happen again. While "Imagine" can still be played on radio because its music sounds familiar and comforting, there's little—if anything—with that sort of nerve in today's mainstream pop. The free market of ideas just isn't that free right now. A pop star as popular as Lennon proclaiming similar ideals in our current environment would run the risk of being judged a heretic.

So we got something when we had John Lennon, and we lost something when his voice was killed. We lost somebody as fucked up as us, who worked his whole life to overcome himself and in doing so, his creativity would help us overcome the madness of our times—at least for a while. Through it all, he told us to keep faith, to keep courage, to defy our hurt, our fear, to find love and hope and to fight for their meaning.

I remember that for about two years after Lennon's murder, I couldn't listen to "Imagine." That blighted message was just too heartbreaking. Instead, I was drawn to Lennon's valiant performance of a song he hadn't written, Ben E. King's "Stand by Me," from Lennon's *Rock 'n' Roll* album; the song held forth that the hardest prospects of life would be bearable if the person in the lyrics—the listener as much as Lennon—could just keep the company of somebody he loved and trusted.

The mountain crumbled, and of course we shed tears. We were on our own. We had been for a long time. The dream was over.

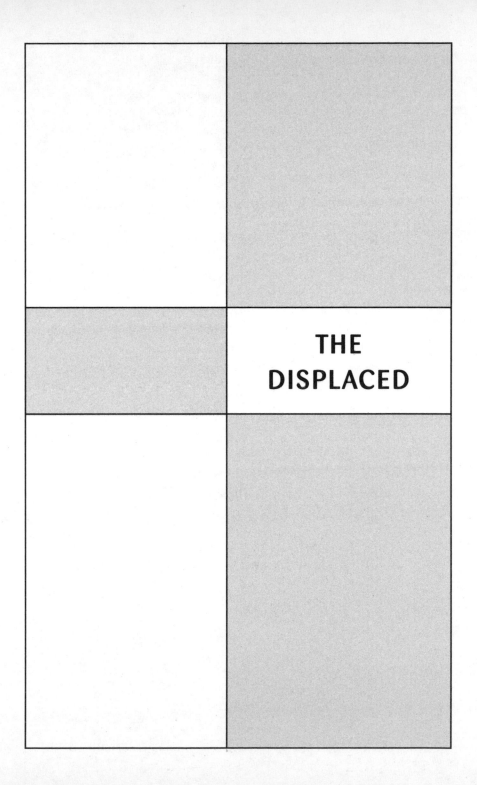

THE
DISPLACED

JOHNNY CASH:
SEPTEMBER WHEN IT COMES

When Johnny Cash died on September 12, 2003, it came as a grief to American music. It wasn't just that we had lost a towering giant of an earlier era—the most influential figure in country music since Hank Williams transformed the heart and soul of honky-tonk folk music in the 1950s—that made this loss so affecting. Rather, it was that, at age seventy-one, Cash was still a vital contemporary artist. For the last several years he had been making some of the most consistent, daring and probing music made by any major contemporary artist, in any genre or idiom of popular music. He did this even though he had been brought dangerously low, time and again, by a mysterious illness that altered everything recognizable about him but the intensity of his art and dignity, and his unmistakable sonorous voice. He continued in those efforts even after the unanticipated death, in May 2003, of the woman he had loved for over forty years, country and folk legend June Carter. Cash kept singing until his end days because singing was his way of living the examined life, and of keeping faith with what that life taught him. Keeping faith mattered to him.

Indeed, his first great hit, the 1955 Sun single "I Walk the Line," was a vow—a pledge to stay true to his family, his love, his belief and his standards—as well as a brooding performance and a brilliant one. The song's strange, modulating chord sequence—and the mesmerizing way those shifts played out the tricky balance the singer was trying to maintain—was unlike anything else in popular or country music at the time, even in that heyday of unprecedented rock & roll invention. But the song also claimed an impossible ideal for Cash. He was not an unswerving man. He strayed a lot, in fact—into rebellion, into abject addictions, into faithlessness of many sorts. It was the ways, though, that Cash fell—not only down, but also into hard truths—that gave him and his music their uncommon depths, though those depths came at considerable costs.

"Johnny Cash was out of line all his life," Merle Haggard said during the last years of Cash's life. "'I Walk the Line' was kind of ludicrous for him to sing, 'I walk the line.' He never walked *any* line.'" Which is true. But Cash was good for one promise he made in that first hit: He kept a close watch on his heart. He had to. After all, he knew what it was capable of.

Johnny Cash sounded and looked and moved like a man who had come up through hard times. He was from a people who carried the fear of God in their blood, and who also carried hard-won dreams of deliverance that their history told them might not always be redeemed in this life. The family traced its lineage back to the family of Caesche, related to early royalty in Scotland; the clan's motto, borne through the generations, was "Better Times Will Come." Cash's first American ancestor was a captain who brought pilgrims to the new land, then settled in Massachusetts himself. His descendants eventually migrated to Arkansas, where William Henry Cash became a farmer and a preacher who traveled his circuit with a gun. William's youngest son, Ray, was Johnny Cash's father; William died when Ray was fifteen, and Ray supported his mother until she died, a few years later. Ray married Carrie Rivers in 1920, and they settled into cotton farming. There was preacher blood on Carrie's side as well. Her father, John L. Rivers, was a skilled music teacher and singer; he led the music in his church; and people would come from miles around to hear his voice. Ray and Carrie would have seven children. Johnny Cash was their fourth. He was born in Kingsland, Arkansas, on February 26, 1932, with no name. His parents simply called him JR. Years later, they decided *J* stood for John; they never did figure out what *R* stood for.

By the time Cash was born, the Depression of the 1930s had overcome much of America. Few people were hit as hard as Southern farmers. Cash noted in his second memoir, *Cash: The Autobiography*, that cotton farmers like his parents had already been making meager livings in the best of times, near the bottom of Southern economy and class, and the Depression devastated them. Ray took work where he could, sometimes clearing land for railroads. When there was no work, he would hop a train to find work elsewhere. The family's home was next to railroad tracks, and Cash later said one of his first memories was the sight of his father jumping from a moving boxcar and landing in front of the house. That image, and the meanings of that sort of subsistence, stayed with Cash and figured into his music for the rest of his life. The first song he claimed to remember was "I Am Bound for the Promised Land," sung by his mother on a winter night in late 1934, as the family was loaded in a flatbed truck, headed for a new home in a new community, called Dyess, Arkansas. Dyess was an experiment in President Franklin D. Roosevelt's New Deal remedy to the Depression: It was a limited community where families of farmers chosen by the government formed a colony as a form of cooperative economic recovery. Cash sometimes later said, "I grew up under socialism," and in fact, these colonies were controversial with some landowners, who saw a place like Dyess as a menace to the ways of Southern agriculture. Still, Dyess succeeded in its early years. The Cashes grew cotton, and every member of the family, from the parents to the youngest, participated in the drudgery of that work.

Carrie taught her children to sing in the fields, and in the evenings afterward, at home and on the porch, as a way of enduring the work and as an act of family and faith. On Sundays, the Cashes attended the community's Baptist chapel; though Carrie was a Methodist, she served as the church's pianist. Cash wasn't enamored of church at first. The preacher's shouting, the congregants' writhing and crying—it all terrified him. "I could see no joy in what they were doing," he said. Rather, it was the songs that moved him, and through them he began to find his way to an understanding of the preacher's visions of fear and redemption. He began to use songs as his way to pray, and his mother encouraged him to keep singing; she heard something of her own family in his voice. When Cash was thirteen, a nearby friend taught him some guitar, showing him how to play rhythm and lead with his thumb, which remained Cash's signature style. Later, his mother took on extra work doing laundry to pay for vocal lessons for her son. But when the teacher heard Cash sing Hank Williams's "Long Gone Lonesome Blues," she told him: "Don't ever take voice lessons again. Don't let me or anyone else change the way you sing." Cash's father, though, was hardly as encouraging. "You're wasting your time . . . ," Ray told his son. "That's going to keep you from making a living. You'll never do any good as long as you've got that music on the mind."

In interviews throughout most of his career, and in his earlier autobiography, *Man in Black*, Cash spoke of his father in ideal terms as a good man, and as a staunch family head. Sometimes, though, he told his own children different accounts, and in his second, 1997 autobiography, he shared a much more blunt perspective with his collaborator, journalist and historian Patrick Carr. His father, Cash said, never imparted encouragement or expressed pride in his son until after Cash was already successful at recording. "He never once told me he loved me," Cash recalled, "and he never had a loving hand to lay on any of his children." Sometimes, Ray would come home drunk and rage at his wife. One time he attempted to beat her, but

Cash's older brother Jack intervened. Also, when Cash was five, his father killed his dog. There were too many dogs around, Ray said, and besides, the family had another one, also named Ray, that he preferred. "I thought my life had ended that morning," Cash wrote, "that nothing was safe, that life wasn't safe. It was a frightening thing, and it took me a long time to get over it. It was a cut that went deep and stayed there."

As a result of his father's cruelty, Cash turned ever closer to his older brother Jack, who was more nurturing. Jack was planning to be a minister, and it was his devotion to his younger brother's spiritual well-being that led Cash to declare himself as a Christian at a young age. Many nights, Cash said, he and Jack would stay up late at the kitchen table, Jack studying the Bible and Cash listening to the family's mail-order Sears Roebuck radio, catching channels from New Orleans, Chicago, Fort Worth and other far-away places. He found a lot of music he liked: the honky-tonk and country balladeering of Hank Williams, Roy Acuff, Eddy Arnold and Ernest Tubb; the gospel-blues of Sister Rosetta Tharpe and the bluegrass gospel of the Louvin Brothers; and the swinging popular music of Bing Crosby and the Andrews Sisters. But what compelled him the most was the music playing from the Grand Ole Opry in Nashville, and the haunting songs of country music's most important early voices, the Carter Family and Jimmie Rodgers, both of whom had helped expand and popularize Appalachian and Southern folk traditions. "Nothing in the world was as important to me as hearing those songs on the radio," Cash wrote in *Man in Black*. "The music carried me up above the mud, the work and the hot sun." Cash would pull his ear closer to the radio, trying to comprehend the stories and lives and places these voices sang about, until his father yelled: "Turn that radio off! You're wasting your time listening to them old records."

One afternoon when he was twelve, Cash was walking home from fishing when his father and the church pastor drove up and told him to drop his pole and get in the car. Cash knew, from his father's manner, that it was serious. Jack had been working at an agricultural shop, earning a few extra dollars for the family. He was cutting wood on a table saw, and he had fallen across the saw; he was cut through his ribs and stomach, down to his groin. Jack was unconscious when Cash reached the hospital, but came around a few days later—lively, laughing, talking about the future. But he soon lapsed, and three days later the family stood by his bedside as he called to his mother in delirium, describing the beautiful angels he was seeing, then died. Cash's oldest daughter, singer Rosanne Cash, later said about her father: "He can't be read or understood out of the context of losing his brother. After that, he was driven by his grief." Cash himself said, "There's no way around grief and loss . . . sooner or later you just have to go into it. . . . The world you find there will never be the same as the world you left."

The death of his brother, the heartlessness of his father, the confinement he felt in Dyess—it all began to breed restlessness in Cash and an itch for rebellion. He took to walking down the dark night roads around Dyess, humming songs to himself, thinking about those voices he'd heard on the radio, and their descriptions of sadness, which were also a means to tales of a hard-earned hope. "The long walk home at night was scary," he wrote in the liner notes to his album *American Recordings*. "It was pitch dark on the gravel road, or if the moon was shining, the shadows were even scarier. . . . But I sang all the way home . . . I sang through the dark, and I decided that that kind of music was going to be my magic to take me through all the dark places."

During his years at Dyess High School in the late 1940s, Cash had his first formative glimpses of a musical life. When he was eighteen, his senior class took a field trip to the Grand Ole Opry. That night he got to see the second-generation lineup of his favorite vocal group, the Carter Family, led by original member Mother Maybelle, singing now with her three daughters. Cash particularly like the youngest Carter, June. She was a funny and resourceful comedienne, she had a wail that was both plaintive and impish, and she was pretty. Another time, while listening to the *High Noon Roundup*—a popular country show from Memphis—Cash heard that the Louvin Brothers, his favorite country duo, would be appearing at the Dyess High School auditorium. He was at the school hours early that night, and got a chance to speak with Charlie Louvin. (More to the point, Charlie asked the teenager where the bathroom was). During the show, the Louvins sang a song at Cash's request, "The Kneeling Drunkard's Plea," written by June Carter. Cash said later that the Louvins' show at his high school was a turning point for him. "Nobody would believe what I wanted to say . . . : 'I'll be up there someday. That's what I'm gonna be.' I had no doubt."

After graduating from high school, Cash hitchhiked north to Pontiac, Michigan, to take a factory job at an automobile construction plant. He hated the job, he hated the crowded housing, and he hated the manners of the men he worked with, who swore, drank and chased women in ways that ran against his Southern religious ethic. A few weeks later, he hitchhiked back home, but there was no future there, even if he'd wanted to stay in farming. The land was losing its yield, and in time, the rest of Cash's family—like so many others in the fading community—would pack up and leave Dyess, about the time they were finishing paying the government back for their homes. With no other immediate options, Cash enlisted in the United States Air Force for four years, as the Korean War was under way and the Cold War was hitting its stride. He was stationed at Landsberg, Germany, where he found that he had a knack for quickly decrypting Morse code and intercepting Soviet radio transmissions. In fact, it was Cash who located the signal of the first Soviet jet bomber on its maiden flight from Moscow, and he was also the first Westerner to decipher the news that the Soviet leader Josef Stalin had died on March 5, 1953, of a brain hemorrhage.

His German tour of duty also proved a portent of Cash's future in some important ways. At first, he did a good job of living by his back-home standards; he stayed away from the rowdier men and didn't join them in their three-day drunks. Instead, he formed a guitar and string band, the Landsberg Barbarians, with a few other enlisted men. They stuck around the barracks, playing country and gospel songs—like "The Wild Side of Life" and "The Great Speckled Bird"—and Cash became more serious about learning guitar in that period, concentrating on playing rhythm with his thumb, which later became his signature style. It wasn't long, however, before Cash learned those things that most other enlisted men learn: "how to cuss, how to look for women, how to drink and fight." It started off with beer: Everybody in Germany drank it; it seemed harmless enough. Then some German cognac; he liked that. Then he stopped attending church services at the base chapel and stopped writing to his family. By his third year in Germany, he was joining the other men for their three-day benders. He got into fights and into trouble with local police. He picked up a crooked nose from a fight with a paratrooper (and also acquired a deep scar on his cheek from a drunken German doctor searching for a cyst). One time, Cash knocked out two security guards when they tried to stop him while he was on his way to sell cigarettes on the local black market. On another occasion, he was sitting at his typewriter, working on some song lyrics, when he suddenly started crying and threw his typewriter out the window. An officer sent him to the dispensary to take some aspirin.

The problem, he said later, was that he was feeling wayward from his life and values. But at the same time, he was learning that he had a capacity for thoughts and impulses and actions that fascinated him and also scared him. He started writing songs seriously while in Germany, and remarkably enough, one of his earliest compositions was "Folsom Prison Blues." He wrote the song after watching a film about the reality of life at Folsom

Prison, one of the oldest penitentiaries in California. He decided, he said in *Cash*, to write it "from the perspective of a convicted, unrepentant killer. . . . [The] line. . . . that still gets the biggest rise out of my audiences. . . . —'I shot a man in Reno just to watch him die'—is imaginative, not autobiographical. I sat with my pen in my hand, trying to think of the worst reason a person could have for killing another person, and that's what came to mind. It did come to mind quite easily, though." Perhaps Cash was starting to recognize some of the dark notions in his own heart, and where those urges might land him.

Just prior to shipping out to Germany, Cash was skating at a roller rink in San Antonio, Texas, and crashed into an attractive dark-haired woman named Vivian Liberto. The two wrote each other almost daily, carrying on a romance by mail while Cash was in the air force. When he arrived back in the States in July 1954, he said, the couple knew two things: He and Vivian were going to marry, and he would be a singer. At first, Cash's wife supported his ambition. She even agreed to move to Memphis, Tennessee—in part so that Cash could be close to his older brother Roy, who worked at the Automobile Sales Company—but also because Memphis was then the most vital music city in the South. It had always been an important blues town and for a time was a Western Swing center. By the mid-1950s, when Cash and Vivian moved there, the city was undergoing waves of inspired creativity that would have far-reaching and world-changing effects. Cash took a job as a door-to-door salesman, peddling home appliances, but his heart wasn't in it. Sometimes he seemed so distracted and impertinent to customers that they shut the door on him or threatened to call the police. As often as not, he'd just stay in his car, listening to the rhythm & blues and country and gospel stations that characterized Memphis in those years. Cash also spent a lot of time in black neighborhoods, listening to spirituals and blues, picking up guitar tips and money at the Home of the Blues—a superb record store where he discovered Alan Lomax's influential folk and blues collections.

By the time Cash and his wife moved to Memphis, producer Sam Phillips and his label Sun Records were already important forces in the local music scene. Phillips had been producing an exceptional array of black blues and R&B singers, including Howlin' Wolf, Junior Parker, B.B. King, Bobby "Blue" Bland, Little Milton and Rufus Thomas, but he had dreamed for some time of finding a white singer who could carry urban blues over to a larger pop audience with uncompromised spirit and authority. Phillips fulfilled that dream, of course, in the nineteen-year-old prodigy Elvis Presley, who helped fuse blues and country into an innovative blend called rockabilly and who would spearhead the national explosion of rock & roll. Cash never saw himself as a rockabilly singer, though he liked the music enough and later wrote a couple of songs in the style. In fact, he and Vivian had seen Presley at one of his first flatbed truck performances in Memphis and struck up a friendly acquaintance with him. Cash, though, already knew that his own strength was with more somber songs, backed by strong but meditative rhythms, and he thought that Phillips might be interested in the spare, rhythmic kind of gospel he had been working up. For better and worse, he was wrong.

There is a legend—almost certainly apocryphal—that when Philips first heard Cash's aspiration to sing gospel, the producer said: "Go back home and sin, and then come back with something I can sell." According to most accounts what Phillips actually told Cash was that while he liked gospel, he could never sell enough of it to justify its production and promotion costs—and besides, he was too busy with Presley to take on anything new. Cash tried a couple of other approaches that also met with rejection, and so one morning he sat himself down on the front stoop of Sun Records, holding his guitar, waiting for Phillips. He caught the producer in a good mood that day. Phillips said, "You don't give up, do you?" Minutes later Cash was inside the Sun studio, regaling the producer with his versions of Jimmie Rodgers, Carter Family and Hank Snow songs. What Phillips noticed immediately—what he couldn't miss, he said later—was Cash's voice: It was low, sepulchral, full of loneliness in a way that had never been heard in pop or country, and it had a riveting presence. Phillips knew he wanted that voice; he could do something with it if it was put together with the right song and arrangement. He asked Cash to play something original. Cash sang what he regarded as his best song at the time, "Belshazzar," but even though it was an upbeat kicker, it was still a spiritual. "What else you got?" Phillips asked. Cash reluctantly played "Hey Porter," an anthem to the South that he had written in Germany but that he didn't like. Phillips decided that was the one. He told Cash to come back the next day with a band, and they would record that song.

Cash had been playing with some likeminded musicians—bassist Marshall Grant and guitarists Luther Perkins and Red Kernodle—whom he met through his brother Roy, at the Automobile Sales Company. Roy himself had been in a string band called the Dixie Rhythm Ramblers back in Arkansas; when the band's other members were killed in World War II, Roy lost interest in a musical career, but he had always encouraged his younger brother. Cash called Grant, Perkins and Kernodle the Tennessee Three, and they started playing gospel and country at church socials and on Memphis radio, to good responses. That next day, though, when Cash brought the trio to Sun, he felt chagrined about their abilities—he saw them all as basic players. Kernodle, who was playing steel guitar on the session, got so nervous that he quit on the spot, and the Tennessee Three became the Tennessee Two. Since the band had no drummer, Cash and Phillips threaded a piece of paper between the strings of his guitar and its fret board and Cash played the instrument high on its neck, for a strong rhythmic effect. Phillips added some snap-back echo to heighten the band's dynamics. At the end of the day, the producer told Cash he was going to put out their recording of "Hey Porter" as a single but first they needed another song for the flip side. Phillips wanted a weeper, as a contrast. Cash came back the next day with "Cry, Cry, Cry"; it was uptempo and a little mean-spirited, but it fit well with "Hey Porter." Phillips issued the single in June 1955. It went to Number One on the Memphis country chart and peaked at Number Fourteen on *Billboard*'s national country chart.

In their first few Sun sessions, Johnny Cash and the Tennessee Two—aided by Sam Phillips's brilliant instincts—created Cash's core style for more or less the rest of his life. It was a steady rhythmic sound with spare instrumentation—often called *boom-chicka-boom* for its simple picking patterns and the cadence of its backbeat—and it placed Cash's voice in an uncommonly forward position in the mix. In 1960 Cash added session drummer W. S. "Fluke" Holland to the touring lineup, and his band was once more the Tennessee Three. Over the years, many critics—including Cash himself—have wondered how such lasting greatness came from such limited accompaniment. In *Cash*, the singer noted that Grant and Perkins often restricted the range of material he could perform, and yet the truth is that those limitations were an indispensable element in helping Cash to invent the power and durability of his best 1950s and 1960s recordings. The spare music framed the isolation in Cash's voice—a voice that, even at age twenty-three, conveyed a sense of haunted experience and regret with rare credibility. It would have been a mistake to allow any ornamentation or flourish to distract the listener from the presence of that voice and the stories it was telling. (That's why Cash shunned steel guitars and fiddles in so much of his work.) In time, Cash's straightforward approach would transform country music as surely and radically as Presley's Sun music had renovated popular music. For several years and in various hurtful ways, much of the country world would not forgive Cash for his originality.

•   •   •

In August 1955 Cash played the first big show of his career, opening for Elvis Presley. Cash later traced the roots of his marriage's dissolution to that concert. Vivian saw the passionate reactions that Presley was now getting from young women, and she realized her husband might meet with something similar. After that, she took a less supportive view of his music career. Later, to allay his wife's concerns—and likely his own as well—he started writing a song called "Because You're Mine." He'd been carrying the tune for it ever since Germany, when an accidentally twisted tape of some music he recorded with the Landsberg Barbarians played a chord progression backward, resulting in an unusual, unintentionally evocative sound. One night Cash was playing the new song for guitarist Carl Perkins, who joined the Sun fold around the same time as Cash. "I keep a close watch on this heart of mine . . . ," Cash sang. "Because you're mine, I walk the line." Cash asked Perkins what he thought. "Y'know, 'I Walk the Line' would be a better title," Perkins said. Cash put the song out as a declaration of his fidelity and the ideal man he wanted to be, and yet the song's massive success had the effect of only taking him further from his wife and his new daughter, Rosanne.

As it turned out, Cash was trying to walk more than one line at this point. Was it possible, he wondered, to maintain a Christian life in the popular music world, playing in honky-tonks where he found himself drinking more, as he watched men pull knives on each other and chase women who weren't their wives? Could he withstand those temptations himself? He didn't have time to sort out his answers. He was on the road more and more, and more and more he was enjoying the excitement of the shows—especially the reactions he was getting to his second single, "Folsom Prison Blues." When Jerry Lee Lewis came into the Sun fold a short time later, he had some of the same questions Cash had earlier, except Lewis—who had left Bible school just before joining Sun—already *knew* the answer: "I'm out here doing what God don't want me to do, and I'm leading the people to hell," he'd tell Cash. There was no way a Christian life could be reconciled with a rock & roll or honky-tonk life, Lewis insisted. Cash found himself growing weary of the sermons. Because of his touring schedule, he was now missing church regularly. That bothered him, but it couldn't be helped. Walking the line was becoming something a bit different for him: It was now a matter of being able to stay the course for what his music and touring life were demanding of him.

In 1955 Sam Phillips sold Elvis Presley's contract to RCA Records for

$35,000. He then took the money and invested it into promoting Cash's "I Walk the Line"—which turned out to be Cash's biggest hit at Sun, climbing to Number One on *Billboard*'s country chart. Despite that success, though, Cash had doubts about his future with Sun. When a trailblazing Columbia Records producer, Don Law (who had documented the music of Robert Johnson and Bob Wills and had recently been working with Marty Robbins and Lefty Frizzell), approached Cash after a *Town Hall Party* TV appearance in Los Angeles, and asked him if he might be interested in changing labels after his Sun contract ended, Cash was immediately curious. He wanted to know if Columbia would let him record an album of spirituals, an ambition of his that Phillips still resisted. Law said yes, that would be no problem. Cash then went on to tell Law about some other, more ambitious projects—concept albums that he knew would be impossible, given Sun's limited resources—and Law was interested. Cash signed an option right away. When Phillips caught wind of the deal, he confronted Cash, and Cash lied: He'd signed no options, he said. Phillips was deeply hurt, and Cash must have realized that in deceiving Phillips he was acting out of accord with his own ethics.

At the same time, Cash didn't feel Phillips had been fair with him. Sun wouldn't let him record much of the material that he wanted to record and started to saddle Cash with some unsuitable pop arrangements. Also, Phillips wouldn't pay his artists the standard industry royalty rate. But the main issue, Cash said later, came down to a perceived slight. "[Phillips] never gave me a Cadillac," he wrote in *Cash*. "He gave Carl Perkins one when Carl sold a million copies of 'Blue Suede Shoes,' but I never got one when 'I Walk the Line' became such a huge hit. . . . I still think I should have that Cadillac." Cash also pointed out that by encouraging his artists to think in such uncompromisingly independent terms, Phillips may have unintentionally imbued them with the very nerve that they would later need to move past Sun Records: Cash had learned to think for himself, and in doing so he had outgrown Sun and what Phillips could offer him. Cash and Phillips later mended their friendship; they had too much respect for each other's creativity and historical standing to bear grudges, though the business about the Cadillac still rubbed Cash the wrong way.

Cash moved to Columbia in 1958, and at the same time moved his family—Vivian and daughters Rosanne, Kathy and Cindy—to Los Angeles, to a San Fernando Valley home he purchased from TV host Johnny Carson. Cash was now free to record the songs he had envisioned—including the spirituals that had been his original inspiration for pursuing Sun. But by the time Cash settled into the recording sessions for *Hymns by Johnny Cash*, he was already on his way down a course that would place both his soul and his life at risk. In the years that lay ahead, he would find himself in a dark place, where neither music nor prayers would stave off the horror of the depths that he steadily descended into.

Johnny Cash started his Columbia years in terrific form. His first album with Don Law, *The Fabulous Johnny Cash*, showcased a confident and original stylist with an unusually adept feel for mixing country, folk and pop sensibilities. His second single for his new label, "Don't Take Your Guns to Town," was a spare and riveting portrait of pointless death in the fatalistic old American West; its start-and-stop tempo, and the way it exacted mounting suspense from subtle shifts in tone and beat, was utterly unlike anything else on the radio at the time. The single's flip side, "I Still Miss Someone," was probably the loveliest—and most enduring—song of romantic despair that Cash would ever write. There was no question: Johnny Cash had fully arrived as a young artist with uncommon new visions for old forms, and he had talent to burn.

But as Cash's creativity soared, problems were already setting in. In fact, they had started before the end of his Sun career. Though he denied it through much of his life, Cash had a depressive nature. The years of hardship in Arkansas, the pain he felt over his father's hardness and his brother's death, left him brooding, tense and wary. More immediately, the exhaustion from touring and the increasing strain on his marriage were taking a toll. He had gone rather quickly from struggling ambition to fame, and there were drawbacks to such a blazing transition. The elation he felt onstage while performing and the downturn that came afterward were only increasing his edginess. Writing about Cash in 1974 in *The Great American Popular Singers*, critic Henry Pleasants said: "It seems almost to be a curse . . . that life begins, day after day and night after night, when the curtain goes up and is suspended when it comes down. . . . It was the occasional night off that was regularly and predictably his undoing." One night in 1957, Cash thought he found a remedy for his fatigue and dejection. He was on a tour with Faron Young, Ferlin Husky and several other Grand Ole Opry artists, and he had become friendly with musician Gordon Terry, from Young's band. During an all-night drive, Terry noticed that Luther Perkins, who was driving one of the cars, was getting sleepy, and he offered him a white pill to stay awake. Cash asked what the pill was. Terry said it was "Bennies"—a common term for benzedrine, Dexedrine and other amphetamines that were popular and readily available at the time. Cash wanted to know if they would hurt him. "They've never hurt me," Terry reportedly said. "Here, have one." Cash still hadn't slept by the next town, so he took another pill before going onstage. He didn't like the comedown from the pills—he felt even more tired and depressed—but he liked how he felt when the pills took him up. He thought they enhanced his performing ability, he wrote in *Man in Black*. "My energy was multiplied, my timing was superb, I enjoyed every song in every concert and could perform with a driving, relentless intensity. They made me think faster and talk more." He later told Christopher Wren—the author of an early Cash biography, *Winners Got Scars Too*—that as much as anything, he was perhaps looking for a spiritual satisfaction in drugs.

By the early 1960s, Cash was fully hooked on amphetamines, and he had started mixing them with alcohol and barbiturates (a potentially deadly combination), so that he could ease off the speed into sleep. Also, the drugs were now affecting his live performances. His timing wasn't as sharp as he had felt before, and after days of speed, his voice would turn dry, and he would develop laryngitis. Other times, his manner was simply inexplicable. All those problems combined in May 1962, when Cash finally received a chance to bring his music to Carnegie Hall. When he arrived in New York, after days on speed, his nerves were shot, and so was his judgment. Cash had an obsession at the time with the brilliant music and tragic fate of Jimmie Rodgers—who was called the "Singing Brakeman" because he worked on the rails from his childhood through his early career; his ill health and early death from tuberculosis traced back to the early conditions of those years. That night at Carnegie Hall, Cash went onstage dressed in Rodgers's brakeman outfit (he'd obtained it from Rodgers's widow) and carrying Rodgers's railway lamp; he intended to surprise the audience by singing only Jimmie Rodgers songs. The audience, though, didn't make the connection, nor did a mystified Don Law, who had planned on recording the show for an already announced live album. The audience yelled instead for "Folsom Prison Blues," and when Cash tried to sing the song, he found he'd lost his voice. He croaked his way through the show, but the night was a debacle.

Despite what the drugs were doing to him—maybe even because of what they were doing to him—Cash made some of his most daring and groundbreaking recordings in these years, in an unprecedented series of ambitious folk and country concept albums that included *Songs of Our Soil* (1959), *Ride This Train* (1960), *Blood Sweat & Tears* (1963), *Bitter Tears (Ballads of the American Indian)* (1964), *Orange Blossom Special* (1965) and

The Ballads of the True West (1965). These were works that spoke about hidden truths, as opposed to received myths, in American history. The albums also spoke to and about remarkably diverse populations, including the poor and the violent, exploited laborers and Native Americans, and jingoists and the dispossessed. In some ways, the series owed something to the folk resurgence that was then burgeoning in New York's Greenwich Village and on numerous US college campuses and that was having an increasingly liberal-minded effect on American politics. Cash had always heeded folk music—he understood that the Carters and Jimmie Rodgers had emerged from it—and in the early 1960s he formed friendships and alliances with some of the movement's key postwar figures, including Ramblin' Jack Elliott, Pete Seeger and Peter LaFarge (a Hopi Indian who was an exceptional and fearless songwriter). In particular, though, he was smitten with young Minnesota-born singer and songwriter Bob Dylan, whom Cash regarded as the best hillbilly singer and most original songsmith he had ever heard. While working a series of clubs in downtown Las Vegas, Cash would stay up through the late hours to the dawn, playing *The Freewheelin' Bob Dylan* and *The Times They Are a-Changin'*. He could hear that Dylan was trying to break new ground and create new freedoms, just as Cash had been attempting in his own music.

Cash's most controversial (and probably best) album in this period was *Bitter Tears*, his spirited and angry essay about the suffering, betrayals, violence and indifference visited upon the American Indian. Peter LaFarge (who had drug problems of his own during this time and would shortly die from them) helped Cash with his research for the album and wrote five of the songs for the collection, including the album's single, "The Ballad of Ira Hayes": the story of a Pima Indian who was among the US Marine heroes who helped raise the flag after the bloody World War II battle at Iwo Jima, and who later died of neglect and alcoholism, drowning in a two-inch ditch of water. The song was more heartbroken than rabble-rousing, but country music radio wouldn't touch it, while Cash regarded it as one of his best recordings. Cash responded with a full-page open-letter ad in *Billboard*, in which he wrote: "D.J.'s—station managers—owners, etc., where are your *guts?*. . . . 'Ballad of Ira Hayes' *is* strong medicine. So is Rochester—Harlem—Birmingham and Vietnam. . . . I had to fight back when I realized that so many stations are afraid of 'Ira Hayes.'" Some country and Nashville forces were livid. The editor of one magazine, in a subsequent open letter, wrote: "You and your crowd are just too intelligent to associate with plain country folks, country artists and country deejays," and he demanded that

Cash resign from the Country Music Association. Country music never did touch "The Ballad of Ira Hayes," but it hardly mattered. The song went on to become one of Cash's most successful singles of the mid-1960s.

June Carter joined Johnny Cash's stage show in late 1961. Cash first met her backstage at the Opry in 1956. He walked over to her and introduced himself. "I know who you are," she said. Years earlier, Carter had toured with Elvis Presley and had a close relationship with him. Sometimes, when she and Presley were together, he would play Johnny Cash's music for her. He was enamored of the singing and told Carter that Cash was going to be a big star. That night at the Opry, Cash took her by the hand and said: "I've always wanted to meet you. You and I are going to get married someday." Carter looked back and said: "I can't wait." Both were already married—she to honky-tonk singer Carl Smith, with whom she had a daughter, Carlene. After her marriage with Smith ended, Carter married Rip Nix and had a second daughter, Rosey (who died shortly after Cash's death in 2003).

In the meantime, Cash's drug intake was starting to wear him down in these years—and he responded by taking even greater quantities. He began carrying guns and firing them off for little or no reason. (He got thrown out of a hotel in Australia when he and Sammy Davis Jr. staged a fast-draw duel in the lobby, firing off blanks and sending other guests fleeing.) He even carted a cannon around and occasionally fired it off in his dressing room. He chopped through locked doors in hotels with a hatchet just to wake his band members. After a night of dope and booze, he sometimes pissed on the radiator in his hotel room, creating an unbelievable smell when it came on. Other nights, he sawed the legs off the room's furniture, so that "small people" might have a place to sit. He dumped a huge load of horse manure in one hotel lobby. He also wrecked every car he owned and was lucky to walk away alive from some of the smashups. His most destructive act in that time wasn't committed under the influence of drugs, but it was a product of the neglect and contempt that his drug use was fostering in him. He was driving a camper, which he knew had a cracked bearing, in the Los Padres National Wildlife Refugee, near Ventura, when oil dripped from the crack onto sun-hot grass and sparked a fire. A wind stirred up, and the blaze went out of control. Before emergency crews subdued it, the fire had destroyed three mountains of forestry in the refuge area and drove out almost all the fifty-three protected wild condors living in the area. The government filed suit, and Cash went into the depositions high on amphetamines. When an attorney asked him if he felt bad about what he had done,

Cash replied, "Well, I feel pretty good right now." When he was asked if he felt bad about driving the condors from their refuge, Cash said: "I don't give a damn about your yellow buzzards. Why should I care?" Cash ended up as the first US citizen the government ever successfully sued for setting fire to a national forest, and he paid $125,000 in damages.

Cash did care, though, about what happened to him at the Grand Ole Opry in 1965. He went onstage, his nerves raw as the result of drugs, and when he attempted to take his microphone from its stand, it wouldn't come loose. "Such a minor complication in my mental state," he wrote in *Man in Black,* "was enough to make me explode in a fit of anger. I took the mike stand, threw it down, then dragged it along the edge of the stage, popping fifty or sixty headlights. The broken glass shattered all over the stage and into the audience." He stopped the show and left the stage. The Grand Ole Opry manager met him and said, "You don't have to come back anymore. We can't use you." Cash would later say that he always held mixed feelings about the Opry. When he first performed there, in the mid-1950s, he knew he was branded by his association with the Memphis scene, and some country music figures weren't that happy to see a rockabilly associate being invited into their more formalist stronghold. In a 1992 *Rolling Stone* interview, Cash told Steve Pond: "A lot of people supported me coming to Nashville: Ernest Tubb, Hank Snow, Minnie Pearl. . . . And then there were some who would make it a point to let me hear the remarks they were saying as I walked by. It was the same thing they were calling Elvis: 'white nigger.' And you know . . . I said: 'I don't want to go back to this place anymore. I don't have to put up with this crap.'"

When Cash left the Opry that night after the light-smashing incident, he was angry, hurt and humiliated. He started driving. He was crying, there was rain and a thunderstorm, and he ran into a utility pole, breaking his nose. He ended up in the hospital, where he was given morphine.

The new Cadillac he had been driving was totaled, and the woman who owned it was June Carter—the singer he had seen years before with the Carter Family, onstage at the same building Cash been dismissed from the night before. June was pissed as hell at Cash. So was her husband, Rip Nix, the policeman who investigated the accident.

Carter had developed complicated and troubling feelings about Cash. For one thing, she had fallen in love with him, and long before either of them would leave the people they were then married to, Cash and Carter's love affair was more or less an open secret in the country music world. Also,

Carter had known Hank Williams—she was the godmother of Hank Williams Jr.—and she didn't want to see Cash wind up the same way as Williams did, a brilliant artist who destroyed himself young. The combination of their love and Cash's self-destructiveness made for a volatile relationship. Carter interceded at every point she could, sometimes telling doctors whom Cash invited backstage not to write him prescriptions. She also learned the places he would hide his drugs and then she would uncover them and destroy the pills. She and Cash would get into arguments, and he would throw her possessions and say horrible, hurtful things to her. One time he told her, "If you weren't a woman, I'd break your neck." She shot back: "You'd miss me." Years later, writing in the liner notes for Cash's *Love God Murder* collection, Carter said of her early relationship with Cash: "I knew from first looking at him that his hurt was as great as mine, and from the depths of my despair I stepped up to feel the fire and there is no way to be in that kind of hell, no way to extinguish a flame that burns, burns, burns." Thoughts like these, during an all-night aimless drive, Carter said, inspired her to write "Ring of Fire." When Cash first heard the song, he knew it was about his and Carter's relationship, but he didn't say as much. He did tell her, though, that he'd had a dream about the song. In the dream, he heard "Ring of Fire" played by Mexican horns, and he was singing along with it. After he realized that dream in 1963, the song reigned on *Billboard*'s country chart for seven weeks, rising to Number One.

Vivian tried to pull Cash back into their family in California, and also tried to convince him to stop taking uppers and downers. Cash would spend the occasional few hours, maybe a day, at home with his wife and children, but then he was off—on a tour or looking for more drugs. Once or twice, he admitted later, he even broke into pharmacies. During a stopover in El Paso in 1965, Cash decided to cross the border to Juarez, Mexico. He had heard he could readily acquire a large supply of drugs there, and with the help of a taxi driver, he came back to the US with bags of pills. As he sat in his plane on the airstrip in El Paso, police officers arrested him. They found 688 Dexedrines and 475 capsules of Equanil (an antianxiety agent) stuffed inside a cheap Mexican guitar and the lining of his suitcase, and arrested Cash for illegally obtaining amphetamines and barbiturates. Speaking to a reporter after the arrest, Cash said, "I don't pretend to be anything I'm not. . . . I am guilty of as many sins as the average person, but I don't say that I am guilty of any more than the average person. I may have a few different ones, but certainly no more."

Vivian came to El Paso to stand by Cash's side when he was released from jail. Later, some white supremacists saw her photo and didn't like her dark skin tone. The Ku Klux Klan started picketing Cash's shows, branding him a "degenerate" who had mongrel children. ("If there's a mongrel in the crowd, it's me," Cash fired back at the Klan. "Because I'm Irish and one quarter Cherokee"—though if there in fact was any Cherokee blood in Cash, it was considerably less than that.) When the illegal possession case went to trial, Cash received a thirty-day suspended sentence and a fine of $1,000. Don Law paid the fine for him.

In October 1967, Cash finally hit his end. He had lost an alarming amount of weight, and no amount of drugs could any longer calm his jitters or fears. If he had once thought he could find a spiritual state in drugs, that thought was long gone. He had cut himself off from God, he felt, and in some ways that estrangement hurt even more than being separated from his wife and four daughters. He decided to crawl into Nickajack Cave on the Tennessee River, and let himself die there. The place was full of the bones of Civil War soldiers, Indians, cave explorers and others who had become lost in its dark maze. He crawled for hours until his flashlight gave out, and he lay down, feeling empty of everything good that he had once known or been. But an unexpected feeling came over him, he later said. He realized he wouldn't die there, and he also realized he would no longer continue his descent into drugs and madness. With no light to guide him, he found his way out of the cave. When he emerged, June Carter was standing there, and so was Cash's mother. Johnny Cash would go through withdrawal over the next month, and he would recommit himself to his life and his music and his faith, with more devotion and insight than before. Vivian would grant him the divorce he sought, and on March 1, 1968, after several months clean and sober, he married June Carter. The couple settled into Cash's sprawling, eccentric countrified mansion in Hendersonville, twenty miles north of Nashville. Johnny Cash's most famous moment in music lay just ahead of him, and when he arrived at the moment, he brought with him everything he had learned from the lower depths about how sometimes people's lives went wrong, and they would find themselves in dark places, cut off from hope and forgiveness.

In the late 1960s, Don Law—who had overseen most of Cash's brilliant earlier Columbia work and who had stood by the singer despite his failings—resigned from Columbia, and Cash hooked up with another maverick mind, Bob Johnston. Johnston had worked with Marty Robbins and Patti Page (he produced the latter's haunting "Hush, Hush, Sweet Charlotte"), and had recently hit an amazing stride, producing Simon and Garfunkel's *Sounds of Silence* and *Parsley, Sage, Rosemary & Thyme*, and Bob Dylan's *Blonde on Blonde* and *John Wesley Harding*. (Johnston would later produce Dylan's *Nashville Skyline, New Morning* and *Self Portrait*, as well as Leonard Cohen's *Songs From a Room* and *Songs of Love and Hate*.) Cash, feeling renewed after his recovery, wanted to pursue a project that he had been after for years but that Columbia had flatly refused: He wanted to record a live album in a prison. In particular, he wanted to sing "Folsom Prison Blues" for the men in Folsom Prison, and he wanted America to hear how the men there responded to a sympathetic voice. When Cash told Bob Johnston that he had always found prisoners the most responsive and enthusiastic audience, Johnston said: "That's what we've got to do, first thing."

Cash had been playing prisons for over a decade, since performing at Huntsville, Texas, in 1957. As he told the London *Daily Telegraph* near the end of his life, "I have a feeling for human nature in difficult situations. Don't know why, but I always have." Indeed, while other entertainers, including numerous country artists, had performed for prisons over the years, nobody had a better feel for playing in such desolate and perilous places, and certainly nobody had a keener sense of cultural timing, than Cash. This was the late 1960s, and in the face of rising fears about violent crime, civil rights protests and youthful unrest, two of 1968's presidential candidates, George Wallace and Richard Nixon, were wielding the easy slogan of "law and order" as a corrective measure and as code for suppressing activism and for branding the disenfranchised. Maybe none of this was in Cash's mind at the time. Maybe he simply saw playing for incarcerated men as his Christian obligation. But it was in this context that the singer finally stepped onto the stage at Folsom on January 13, 1968, and announced, "Hello, I'm Johnny Cash," then bolted into "Folsom Prison Blues," the prisoners roaring in recognition at the song's depictions of violence, remorse and defiance. The moment had tremendous resonance throughout American popular culture. Alongside "Folsom Prison Blues," even inflammatory songs like the Rolling Stones' "Street Fighting Man" or Jefferson Airplane's "Volunteers" seemed affected. Cash was singing from inside the place where American law and order and American hell met and fused, and nobody else in popular music could match him for radical nerve or compassion.

At Folsom Prison, though, wasn't Cash's last word on the matter. On February 24, 1969, he recorded a second prison album (and filmed a documentary special for British television), *At San Quentin*, which produced the biggest single of his career, a rendition of Shel Silverstein's novelty song, "A Boy Named Sue." (In the time between the two prison appearances, Cash's longtime guitarist Luther Perkins suffered fatal burns. He was replaced by Bob Wootton by the time of the San Quentin date.) Though the *Folsom Prison* album was more groundbreaking, and generally featured better performances, all participants regarded the concert for San Quentin as the riskier affair. San Quentin was a notoriously bleak penitentiary. Cash had played there on previous occasions (including a 1958 performance which Merle Haggard, an inmate at the time, later described as "the first ray of sunlight in my life"), but for some reason, things were especially tense on the 1969 date. Cash prowled the stage restlessly that night. He taunted the guards. He ridiculed the prison system and its authorities. He commiserated with criminals and violent men and sang prayers for them, while guards paced on catwalks above the crowd, cradling loaded machine guns.

In her liner notes for the reissued version of *At San Quentin,* June Carter wrote: "Some kind of internal energy for those men, the prisoners, the guards, even the warden, gave way to anger, to love, to laughter. . . . A reaction like I'd never seen before. [I was enraged inside, a feeling of fire, dangerously tense. And John sung quietly, 'San Quentin, you're livin' hell to me. . . . ' 'Sing it, Cash! You know it, man, we're all in hell here!' 'So you give us the word, Cash, and we'll beat the hell out of them, just for the hell of it.' It took awhile, maybe ten minutes, before he got to repeat the first and second line of his first-time-ever-heard-of song, 'San Quentin. . . . '] John held these men in suspense, they were mesmerized, hypnotized and spellbound and so were we. . . . He held them by a thread, and we were saved by that thread." Cash later told journalist and author Bill Flanagan: "The guards were scared to death. All the convicts were standing up on the dining tables. They were out of control, really. During the second rendition of that song all I would have had to do was say 'Break!' and they were gone, man. . . . Those guards knew it, too. I was tempted."

Cash sometimes took heat for identifying himself with prisoners and prison reform. In a 1973 interview in *Country Music,* he said: "People say, 'Well, what about the victims, the people that suffer—you're always talking about the prisoners; what about the victims?' Well, the point I want to make is that's what I've always been concerned about—the victims. If we make better men out of the men in prison, then we've got less crime on the streets, and my family and yours is safer when they come out."

Years later, on Christmas Day 1982, Cash found his ideals put to a hard test. He was spending the holiday with family members and friends at a home he owned in Jamaica. As the group was sitting down to dinner, three young men wearing nylon stockings over their heads—one brandishing a pistol, another a knife, the third a hatchet—burst in. They roughed up the women, put a gun to the head of Cash's son, and demanded a million dollars. For the next few hours, Cash spoke to the men calmly, with measured respect. He convinced them there was no way he could get them that much money right then. He had a few thousand dollars in the house, though, and they could have it. They could also take all the valuables that were at hand. The men eventually assembled their loot and left, locking Cash and the others in the cellar. Before they left, the robbers gave the captives the Christmas dinner that had been disrupted earlier. That night, the Jamaican police captured the gunman and killed him on the spot. Weeks later the other robbers were caught, and killed when they tried to escape prison. In his 1997 autobiography, Cash wrote that he had spent a good deal of time trying to come to terms with the knowledge that "desperate junkie boys" who had menaced him and his family "were executed for their act—or murdered or shot down like dogs . . ." Cash wrote: "I'm out of answers. My only certainties are that I grieve for desperate young men and the societies that produce and suffer so many of them, and I felt that I knew those boys. We had a kinship, they and I: I knew how they thought, I knew how they needed. They were like me." And that comprehension, Cash believed, was what helped him and his family and friends to avoid murder when it walked in their door that Christmas Day.

In February 1969 Johnny Cash and Bob Dylan recorded several tracks together in Nashville, with Bob Johnston producing. The two singers had been friends since the early part of the decade, when Cash wrote Dylan, telling him how much he liked his music. Since that time, Cash had served as a passionate advocate of Dylan. In 1964, when *Sing Out!*—the magazine of the folk movement—published an open letter to Dylan, taking him to task for writing fewer protest songs, Cash wrote the magazine, saying: "Shut up and let him sing!" A year later, at the Newport Folk Festival, when outraged folk purists tried to cut off the power as Dylan played a loud set of electric rock & roll, Cash was among those who blocked their efforts. "I don't think anyone around today has so much to offer as him," he told one reporter at the time. And yet in mid-1969, when Dylan released his and Cash's lovely duet performance of "Girl From the North Country" on *Nashville Skyline*, the moment came as something of a shock to both the country and rock & roll worlds. Observers on both sides wondered what the teaming signified. Why was Cash singing with the man regarded as rock's most revolutionary voice? Why would Dylan record in the country idiom, which at that time was seen as music of conservative values and prejudice? There is a wonderful moment in Robert Elfstrom's 1969 documentary, *Johnny Cash: The Man, His World, His Music*, during a duet on Dylan's "One Too Many Mornings" (a song about people who are alienated from one another), when Cash sings to Dylan, "You are right from your side, Bob / And I am right from mine," and Dylan grins back and says, "I know it." In that exchange, the two men were acknowledging that there was room for more than one complex perspective among reasonable people in difficult times.

Of course, singers who speak to and for people's ideals and experiences always run the risk of having their art misread or misappropriated. In 1970 Cash received a call from President Richard Nixon's office, inviting him to perform for an Evening at the White House. Nixon's chief of staff, Bob Haldeman (who would later resign his position and spend eighteen months in prison for his involvement in the Watergate scandal) had put together a list of requests. Among them were "Okie from Muskogee," a Merle Haggard hit that took a dim view of youthful drug users and war protesters (Haggard later claimed the song to be a misunderstood jest), and "Welfare Cadillac," a Guy Drake song that derided the integrity of welfare recipients. Cash respected the office that Nixon held and also supported the US troops in Vietnam (though after the US assault on Cambodia, Cash talked about the war as a terrible waste of life). He could not, though, bring himself to sing the songs that Nixon requested. For one thing, they weren't his songs; also, having grown up poor himself, he wasn't about to sing a song like "Welfare Cadillac," which he later described as a "lightning rod . . . for antiblack sentiment." Though Cash accepted Nixon's invitation, he insisted on picking his own material. "The show is already planned," he had his secretary tell Haldeman; he would perform for the president the same sort of show he performed for prisoners and everybody else. Later, introducing Cash to the audience at the White House, even Nixon got the point. "One thing I've learned about Johnny Cash," he said, "is that you *don't* tell him what to sing."

To be sure, Johnny Cash was a complicated patriot, and those complications—like the contradictions of the nation itself—never ceased. Moreover, as Henry Pleasants wrote, Cash's "concern is people rather than ideas." In the early 1970s, Cash performed for a progressive student body at Nashville's Vanderbilt University, and at the peak of the Vietnam War, debuted the song that became seen as his testimonial, "Man in Black": "I wear the black in mournin' for the lives that could have been / Each week we lose a hundred fine young men." Some fifteen years or so later, he stood before a much more conservative audience at Nassau Coliseum, in Uniondale, New York, and said: "I thank God for all the freedoms we've got in this country. I cherish them and I treasure them—even the rights to burn the flag. I'm proud of those rights. But I tell you what, we've also got . . ." He paused, because the crowd had started booing loudly enough to drown him out, then he confidently hushed them. "Let me tell you something—*shhh*—we also got the right to bear arms, and if you burn my flag, I'll shoot you. But I'll shoot you with a lot of love, like a good American." It was a statement full of extraordinary twists and turns, genuine pride and dark-humored irony—and only Cash could get away with weaving such disparate stances and affectionate sarcasm together. When all was said and done, Johnny Cash looked at America the same way he looked at himself: with forthright regrets and unrelenting hope.

In 1969 Johnny Cash was at the peak of his popularity. He began hosting a summer series for ABC-TV, *The Johnny Cash Show,* which would feature such guests as Bob Dylan, Joni Mitchell, Ray Charles, Merle Haggard, Waylon Jennings, Louis Armstrong, James Taylor and Neil Young. The show—which was broadcast from Nashville's Ryman Auditorium, the residence of the Grand Ole Opry since 1943—immediately enjoyed high ratings, and ABC renewed it as an ongoing series. By the year's end, according to Clive Davis (who was president of Columbia Records at the time), Cash had sold more than 6.5 million records and had placed seven albums on the *Billboard* chart—more than any other recording artist in 1969. The next year, June Carter Cash gave birth to the couple's only child—and Cash's only son—John Carter Cash. A short time later, though, en route to visit and play for American troops in Vietnam, Cash lapsed back into drug abuse. It was a short but hard tumble ("I had been the most negative and evil man I could ever remember being," he wrote in *Man in Black*), and it wouldn't be his last one. He missed drugs, he admitted later in his life, and it sometimes took all his faith and will to carry that hunger without succumbing to it.

Then, in the early 1970s, everything shifted—and the shift lasted for a long time. Weighed down by the demands of a weekly TV show, Cash's music began to slip. His albums seemed tamer, more perfunctory, and the big hits stopped coming. After "Flesh and Blood" and "Sunday Morning Coming Down"—both from 1970—Cash had only one major single in the ensuing decade, the 1976 song "One Piece at a Time." Also, he was growing tired of the TV show; he felt that ABC executives were forcing too many artists on him who didn't fit his aims, and they were denying him other guests. "I want them . . . to tell me why Pete Seeger can't be on my show," he said angrily to the show's director, according to a *New York Times Magazine* article. "Pete Seeger is a great American; he's sold the Appalachian Mountains in Asia. Why can't I have my friends on this show?" (Seeger had been severely criticized for his politics by the House Committee on Un-American Activities—was even declared in contempt of Congress by the committee—and as a result of his ongoing opposition to the Vietnam War, network television refused to book him on any shows.) In 1971 ABC declined to renew Cash's contract, and he was relieved. "I got to feeling that not only was Johnny Cash of secondary importance," he told *Rolling Stone* in 1973, "but his artistry was of no importance. . . . I resented all the dehumanizing things that television does to you, the way it has of just sterilizing your head."

As the 1970s progressed, Cash found that his once innovative brand of insurgent country was proving less provocative. The Outlaw movement—made up of Willie Nelson, Waylon Jennings and Tompall Glaser, among others—was making its own hard-edged brand of country that mixed a storytelling sensibility with honky-tonk ethics, cowboy defiance and touches of rock & roll rhythm and tonality. The results riled Nashville's more conventionalist ethics but also influenced numerous other country and rock artists. Cash didn't begrudge the movement—after all, he had once helped displace Nashville's weary standards himself, and Waylon Jennings was a longtime friend and onetime roommate. But he also knew that he was no longer at the center of the country music world, after more than a decade in which he had held sway as its most liberating and successful artist. A few years later, he would find his music eclipsed by that of the New Traditionalist movement—which included George Strait and Randy Travis—and by the successes of members from his own family: His stepdaughter Carlene Carter, his oldest daughter, Rosanne Cash, and Rosanne's husband at the time, Rodney Crowell, all made vital and attention-grabbing progressive country music in the late 1970s and early 1980s. (Cash and his wife were fortunate enough—if that's the right term—to be present when Carlene Carter told a New York audience that she wanted to "put the 'cunt' back into country.")

In the mid-1980s, Cash joined the two main leaders of the Outlaw movement, Willie Nelson and Waylon Jennings, along with singer-songwriter Kris Kristofferson (who had worked as the janitor in the Nashville

Columbia studios where Cash recorded in the 1960s), for an all-star makeshift troupe called the Highwaymen. The group's recorded output was hit and miss (though *The Highwayman* and *The Road Goes On Forever* featured some terrific moments), but their live shows were solid, and the four men's partnership met with good record and ticket sales. Even so, Columbia Records had little faith in Cash's ongoing creativity, and various executives and producers pressured him to accommodate new styles that might appeal to contemporary country audiences, which were now viewed as liking their music with fewer rough edges. Cash was tired of trying to adjust to Columbia's demographics-driven concerns, and in 1986 he gave them a new song called "Chicken in Black," accompanied by a video in which Cash dressed as a chicken. His message was that if the label was being cowardly, and if they wanted a chicken for an artist, then there was no point in making any bones about it. The song was also, Cash said, intentionally awful. Columbia dropped Cash. He wasn't selling, and they weren't interested in an album of just him and his guitar, which had been a pet project he'd pushed for years. He signed to Mercury. They didn't want the guitar-and-voice project either, though he did record two decent albums—*Johnny Cash Is Coming to Town* and *Boom Chicka Boom*—that the label took little interest in. Cash later said that he felt he had once again hit a low point. Life was turning hard again. He'd fallen into another addiction in the early 1980s—again involving pills and alcohol—until his family sent him to the Betty Ford Clinic. In 1989 he underwent double-bypass surgery and came close to dying. By the early 1990s, his album sales had more or less dried up, and Columbia let all but a few of his albums disappear from print. Cash had given up wanting to deal with record companies, he said. He was resigned to playing places like Branson, Missouri—an entertainment center that is also sort of a hell's waiting room for aging pop and country performers, where they play their glory-days hits for people looking for music that reassures their nostalgia. Cash had been a giant, but to the modern music business he was already a figure from finished history.

What Cash didn't anticipate—what nobody anticipated—was that he was about to embark on his most surprising and fate-obsessed artistic growth period since the 1960s. More than that, he was about to pass through the most extraordinary winter phase of any major artist in popular music history.

Johnny Cash was perplexed when Rick Rubin first approached him in 1993. Rubin was a producer with his own label, American Recordings, and he was known for his pivotal support of hardcore hip-hop and rock & roll acts like the Beastie Boys, Danzig, Slayer, the Red Hot Chili Peppers and Public Enemy. Cash knew some of the music, or at least music akin to it. In the 1980s, when his son John developed a passion for Metallica, Cash attended some of the band's shows with his son and learned to hear and enjoy some hard thrash music. Still, Cash couldn't fathom what interest Rubin might have in him or how they would work together. "[Rubin] was the ultimate hippie," Cash wrote in his second memoir, "bald on top but with hair down over his shoulders, a beard that looked like it had never been trimmed (it hadn't), and clothes that would have done a wino proud. . . . Besides, I was through auditioning for producers, and I wasn't at all interested in being remodeled into some kind of rock act." Rubin didn't see Cash as needing to fit a rock mold, or any other mold. In fact, Rubin understood something about the singer that no other music executive or producer seemed able to grasp at the time: namely, that Cash ran deeper than any one tradition—he was an archetype of the outsider, the lonely figure with a dark side, who changed everything for the better for everybody else, and he still had the power to make music that would embolden some people while disturbing others. What Cash needed to do, Rubin knew, was figure out the songs he wanted to sing, and then sing them—just him and his guitar. Nothing else should come between him, his spellbinding voice and the listener that he sang to. "You'll come to my house . . . ," Rubin told Cash, "take a guitar and start singing. You'll sing every song you love, and somewhere in there we'll find a trigger song that will tell us we're headed in the right direction. I'm not very familiar with a lot of the music you love, but I want to hear it all." It sounded to Cash a lot like the philosophy that Sam Phillips brought to bear on their early sessions. Also, it sounded like an opportunity to make the record he had always wanted to make.

Maybe it was simply the way his worldview had taken on as much gravity and depth as his voice. Or maybe it was just a demonstration of how life adds up—how it gives and takes, then takes and gives. In any event, Cash's first work with Rubin, 1994's *American Recordings*—which was also his first true solo work—had an effect like no other album Cash had ever made. It was a collection of songs (by writers like Tom Waits, Glenn Danzig, Kris Kristofferson, Leonard Cohen, Loudon Wainwright and Cash himself) about betrayal, murder, love, death, fear of self, faith, more death, rootlessness, deliverance, death again and life and vengeance after death. The trigger song—in this case literally—that Rubin had been looking for turned out to be "Delia's Gone," Cash's vicious and heartbroken rewrite of a folk blues song that went at least as far back as Southern blues singer Blind Willie McTell, in the 1920s. Cash had taken three earlier, lyrically identical passes at the song in the 1960s, yet the *American Recordings* version was so unadorned and plaintive that its matter-of-factly brutal first-person narrative about a man killing the woman he loves shocked some listeners, especially in the moments that Cash sang: "I found her in her parlor and I tied her to her chair . . . / First time I shot her, I shot her in the side / Hard to watch her suffer but with a second shot she died." It even shocked MTV, who refused to air the song's video, in which Cash heaped dirt on Delia (played by model Kate Moss). Cash told author Nick Tosches that the more traditional historical version of the song "was not quite as bloody and criminal-minded a song. I just decided I'd make this man who kills Delia a little bit meaner than he already was. Tie her to the chair before he shoots her. Have a little more fun with her." In the end, Delia had the last word. In jail, the cell door locked, the night comes down, the killer lies awake, listening to Delia pacing around his bed. "Delia's Gone" may have been unnerving, but it was an effective reminder that folk music—the wellspring for blues, country and rock & roll—was at heart a weird and scary music, full of dark American secrets that would never stop revealing themselves yet could never be fully uncovered.

American Recordings sold more copies than any other Cash work in years, ranked high in numerous year-end 1994 critics' lists and appealed to a whole new younger audience that was unafraid of bleak musings, and that also saw Cash as a rare exemplar of integrity and authenticity. In the years that followed, this newfound audience—which included fans of alternative music of all sorts—proved as loyal to Cash and his recordings as his rural and working-class audiences had in decades before. Meantime, *American Recordings* enjoyed little or no country radio airplay and received no Country Music Association Awards nominations. In fact, the only time Cash received any CMA recognition (before a belated, sentimentally driven outpouring at the organization's 2003 Awards Show) was in 1969. Though many in the country world had continually appreciated Cash, plenty others had always been uncomfortable with his renegade spirit and his freethinking social concern, and radio programmers in particular were decidedly not enamored of the spare style and the disquieting outlook of his new music. So in the 1990s, they treated him as an artist who no longer made music that mattered. In 1998, when his *Unchained* album won a Grammy for Best Country Album, Cash took out another of his full-page *Billboard* ads. It read: "*American Recordings* and Johnny Cash would like to acknowledge the Nashville music establishment and country radio for your support." The words appeared alongside a famous 1969 photo of Cash flipping a "fuck you" middle-finger directly into a camera's lens, with a fierce scowl on his face.

Cash, though, couldn't appear at the Grammys to accept his award for *Unchained,* the second in his series of albums with Rubin. The singer had been walking down Madison Avenue in New York in October 1997 when he found himself walking backward. He saw a doctor and was told to go home to Nashville immediately and get into a hospital. He contracted blood poisoning and double pneumonia and almost died, and he stayed near death for ten days. He recovered to learn he'd been diagnosed with Shy-Drager syndrome, a neurological disorder that is a worse variation of Parkinson's disease. He improved enough to return to performing. But then, one night onstage in Flint, Michigan, his guitar pick slipped from his fingers. He leaned over to retrieve it but almost fell. The audience was unsure of what was going on. A few people laughed—and then Cash told them he had Parkinson's. "It ain't funny," he said. "It's alright. I refuse to give it some ground in my life." The Shy-Drager and Parkinson's diagnoses would turn out to be incorrect—Cash in fact had autonomic neuropathy, a disorder of the nervous system. But by the time he received the 1998 Grammy, he could no longer make public appearances and had quit touring, after forty-two years on the road. In addition, any more recordings seemed unlikely. Some doctors didn't think he could live another year. But Cash and Rubin recorded new sessions whenever possible. The work was fitful, brought to several halts by bouts of pneumonia, onsets of diabetes and a ten-day coma that nobody thought he would come out of.

Against all reasonable odds, Cash's last two albums during his lifetime, *American III: Solitary Man* (2000) and *American IV: The Man Comes Around* (2003), are damn near the best music he ever made—and certainly his bravest and most chilling. Cash's voice showed more age and vulnerability, though it rarely sounded frail. Indeed, his singing on parts of *Solitary Man* is astonishing. In his versions of Will Oldham's "I See a Darkness" and Nick Cave's "The Mercy Seat," he sings like a man in his worst hour of desperate prayer, discovering a voice he never knew he had before as a show of strength, though his heart and mind are plunging into despair and chaos (in the case of "The Mercy Seat," Cash sang in a voice narrating the singer's entry into death and hell's deliverance). But in all of Cash's American recordings, there is nothing as revealing as his version of Nine Inch Nails's "Hurt," from *The Man Comes Around.* "Hurt" is the story of a man who suffers more for all the ways he makes others suffer. In fact, it is a song about an addict who looks unblinkingly at the worst truth he has ever encountered: the abyss of his own heart. "What have I become, my sweetest friend . . . / I will let you down, I will make you hurt." Cash knew this territory well. He had mapped it, ransacked it and even tried to crawl off and die inside its caves, and now he was describing unsparingly what he had learned of himself in his darkest recesses.

In the end, Cash's *American Recordings* series stands alongside his best music for Sun in the 1950s and for Columbia in the 1960s. It is resourceful music that details how a man grows and deteriorates at the same time, as he bears witness to all that he finds painful and promising in the world that he is living and dying in. It is all the more remarkable given that, as he made this music, everything was slipping away from Cash—everything except his integrity and the love of the woman who kept faith in him even when he could not stand his own heart, who did everything she knew to keep him alive. "She's . . . certainly made me forget the pain for a long time, many times," he once wrote. "When it gets dark, and everybody's gone home and the lights are turned out, it's just me and her."

Then, it was just him.

For years, June Carter Cash was seen as the necessary balance in her husband's life—the woman who fought for his intrinsic worth, who stood by him, onstage and in their personal life, offsetting his grave image with down-to-earth sass. She also brought a blistering sexuality to his music. Her famous song about their love affair, "Ring of Fire," was infused with an uncommon mix of Biblical language and metaphors of lust. And when she and Cash would perform their live duet of "Jackson," they turned the song's story of romantic ennui into an enactment of mutually overpowering erotic need.

June Carter never objected to her image as her husband's steadfast helpmate. "I chose to be Mrs. Johnny Cash," she said in 1999. "I decided I'd allow him to be Moses, and I'd be Moses' brother, Aaron, picking his arms up and padding along behind him." Yet June Carter Cash was a formidable American music figure in her own right—not only an inheritor of the Carter Family tradition, but an artist who might have extended it. "The Kneeling Drunkard's Prayer," which she cowrote, served as a key model for the sort of keenly observed songs of compassion that her husband himself would aim to write throughout his career. As Cash once noted: "She started at the age of nine and has spent more years on the road than even Bill Monroe had

when he died. Sadly, I think her contribution to country music will probably go underrecognized simply because she's my wife; it certainly has been
up to now. That's regrettable—my only regret, in fact, about marrying her."

On *Press On*, the 1999 album that was Carter's first solo release in
decades, there is a fascinating track called "I Used to Be Somebody," in
which Carter talks about her friendships with James Dean, Tennessee
Williams and Hank Williams, and her rumored affair with Elvis Presley. As
the song unfolds, she seems to come to an understanding of all that she left
behind in her life to become the wife to a man as overwhelming as Cash.
"Well, I used to be somebody, Lord," she sang, "I used to have a friend . . .
/ I used to be somebody, dear Lord, where have I been / I ain't ever gonna
see Elvis again." No doubt Carter was resolved and fulfilled in the choices
she made, though being married to Johnny Cash could not have always
been an easy thing. In 2000 she wrote: "I'm still searching deeper into the
soul of this man for the light that shines somewhere within him"—but
maybe there had to be a bit of darkness in Carter herself in order to attract
and withstand Cash. Theirs was no doubt a real marriage: passionate,
volatile, full of secret hurts and private fervor and an unending prayer that
they would stay in the presence of each other until they died.

On May 7, 2003, June Carter Cash underwent a heart valve replacement
at Nashville's Baptist Hospital. Severe complications set in after surgery, and
on May 15, she died, at age seventy-three. So many of us had grown accustomed to keeping a watchful eye on Cash's health that it never seemed likely
that June would be the first who left. The closest anybody came to suggesting as much was Carter herself, in a recording session for her 2003 album,
Wildwood Flower. In her version of the Carter Family's "Will You Miss Me
When I'm Gone?" she sang: "When death shall close these eyelids / And this
heart shall cease to beat . . . / Will you miss me—miss me when I'm gone?"
It was a lovely and blue rumination about one of the most heartbreaking
prospects the dying can face, and there could be no doubt of the answer
that the song's question raised.

At Carter's funeral, Cash had to be helped from his wheelchair to view
his wife's face one last time. At a family gathering, he said, "I don't know
hardly what to say tonight about being up here without her. The pain is so
severe there is no way of describing it." A few days after Carter's burial, Cash
called Rick Rubin and told him that he wanted to get back to recording
songs as soon as possible. "I don't want to do anything of this world,"
Cash said. "I want to make music and do the best work that I can. That's

what she would want me to do, and that's what I want to do." In the next few months, Cash recorded more than fifty new tracks, including some original material and versions of black gospel songs, such as Blind Willie Johnson's "John the Revelator."

Despite his determination and hard work, Cash reportedly could not recover from the loss of his wife. Guitarist and singer Marty Stuart— Cash's close friend and former son-in-law (Stuart had once been married to Cash's daughter Cindy)—told *Time* that in his last months Cash would sometimes break down into deep sobs, saying, "Man, I miss her so much." Stuart also told *USA Today* that in Cash's last months, a pair of vultures had started sitting outside the window of the singer's Hendersonville office, staring at Cash as Cash stared back. In late August, Cash planned to attend the MTV Video Music Awards in New York, where "Hurt" had been nominated for six awards including Video of the Year, but his health made the trip impossible. When the evening's major prize went to Justin Timberlake for "Cry Me a River," Timberlake told the audience, "This is a travesty. . . . My grandfather raised me on Johnny Cash, and I think he deserves this more than any of us tonight." Several days later, Cash suffered some respiratory problems and was admitted into Baptist Hospital. On September 12, 2003, after a nearly fifty-year career, John R. Cash breathed his last breath, at age seventy-one, due to respiratory failure brought on by diabetes. Three of his surviving siblings and three of his five children were at his beside. One of the last recordings he made was a duet with his daughter Rosanne.

I never met Johnny Cash, but I did speak with him once, on the worst day of my life.

I grew up in a family that agreed on very little—especially when it came to whether to respect or hate one another—but one thing we managed to share was a love for Johnny Cash and his music. My mother had grown up with country music, my older brothers came of age to early rock & roll, my father sequestered himself with opera and I had my own passions for Bob Dylan, the Beatles and Miles Davis—yet something in Cash's voice and stories spoke to us across our differences. I'm sure it had to do with his image as country music's angry man, and the fact that he stood up for underdogs.

I had a brother named Gary—ten years older than I. He had been in and out of jails since he was fourteen, and spent all but a few months of his adult life in prison for armed robbery. I didn't always feel close to Gary. Sometimes he scared me. Sometimes I hated him. And worse, sometimes I loved him. But when Cash put out *At Folsom Prison* in 1968, it couldn't help but make me think of my brother and how he loved Cash even more than the rest of us. It also made me think about what his daily life must really be like, behind bars. I tried sending him a copy of *At Folsom Prison* for Christmas that year, but the authorities wouldn't allow him to have it.

In 1976, following Gary's parole from prison, on consecutive summer nights in Utah, my brother murdered two innocent men during armed robberies, in a mix of drugs, alcohol and cold, pain-filled rage. He was arrested, tried, convicted and sentenced to death, and he demanded that the state carry out the sentence that it handed him. Nobody had been executed in America in almost ten years. That meant that if Gary's demand were to be granted, America would be back in the business of putting select criminals to death. Johnny Cash was opposed to the death penalty. He didn't make a big point of it, but he also didn't pretend otherwise. When he heard that my brother was a fan of his music, he issued a dignified plea to Gary, asking him to reconsider his decision. He also sent him a copy of his autobiography, *Man in Black*, along with a letter, in which he restated his plea. "They've already killed too damn many us," he wrote, describing his view of the prison system and executions. Gary appreciated Cash's attention, but he was determined to die. On the final night of his life, my brother received a phone call from his favorite singer. Later that night, in my last conversation with Gary, I asked him what Cash had said. Gary said: "When I picked up the phone I said, 'Is this the *real* Johnny Cash?' And he said: 'Yes it is.' And I said: 'Well, this is the real Gary Gilmore.'"

The next day, in the hours after Gary's execution, I sat around my house trying to understand how I would be able to live with the horrible things my brother had done and the horrible way he had died. I had already written some articles for *Rolling Stone* at that time, and my editor, Ben Fong-Torres, called me that afternoon and said, "Johnny Cash would be willing to talk to you." I called the number Fong-Torres gave me; it was for a recording studio in Nashville. In moments Cash was on the phone, talking to me in that familiar low voice. I told him: "I just wanted to thank you, on behalf of my mother and myself, for the help and comfort you offered my brother. I know it helped him at the end. I just wanted to—" And then I couldn't talk anymore. I was just feeling too awful, too awkward, too afraid of falling apart. "That's alright, son," said the low voice at the other end. "I know you and your mother tried. We all tried. I'm sorry for what has happened. I know how much this must hurt right now, but I hope in time you can find some peace. Our prayers are with you."

I don't know that I ever found the peace that Cash wished me that day, but I know that in those moments that he took the time to speak with me, I found something that made as much difference as anything might on that impossible day: I heard a voice—from a man who had always represented courage and dignity in my family's mind—offer a stranger understanding and kindness, without any judgments. That was more grace than I expected or perhaps deserved from somebody who wasn't a friend in those hours, and I have always been grateful for it.

Cash didn't have to talk to me that day. He didn't have to talk to any of us in America about those forces or impulses that hurt and bewildered us. But he chose to anyway, and he did it not because doing so made him a better person, but rather because he *wasn't* always a better person, and he knew he had to understand the meaning of that truth at least as much as the meanings of faith or piety. For something good to come from all the times he had fallen, all the times he had risked his health and sanity and spirit, the times he had let down those who loved or trusted or needed him, he had to comprehend his own history and heart. In 1994 he said, "I think anybody would be making a mistake if they didn't recognize that they have a dark side or a side that isn't really good." By recognizing his own dark side, Cash also came to recognize how others who were lost or angry, or who were feeling just plain fucked up, might arrive at the worst choices in their lives. He did this in part to find ways to control his own darkness, but he also did it to find ways to speak to or about other people, with a voice that might make a difference.

Johnny Cash doesn't have to try to manage darkness anymore—he is in it now, whatever its nature might be, whether it is of God or of nothing. He's out there with a lot of other good and bad men and women, with the ghosts of poets and fugitives and all those somewhere between. He had a way of speaking to them all.

We won't get another like him, and we know it. We are likely too far down the line from the histories and conditions and experiences that shaped him and others like him. That old America has truly melted away into fable. But we do get to hold on to Cash's voice—that revealingly imperfect voice that ran so deep, in so many ways. It will continue to sing to us, to help us along from time to time, as we make our way through the dark places in our own hearts, and through those uneasy American nights still to come.

BOB MARLEY'S
HELL ON EARTH

Bob Marley was already dying when he stood onstage before the audience in Pittsburgh that night, in September 1980. The world's leading reggae star had developed a malignant form of melanoma—an incurable cancer by this time—that he had let progress unchecked, for reasons that he probably could not fathom at this hour. He was a man with no time, with a mission that nobody in popular music had ever attempted before. In the last few years, he had managed to popularize reggae—a music that had once sounded strange and foreign to many ears—and he had managed to convey the truths of his troubled homeland, Jamaica, for a mass audience. Now he wanted to find ways to put across truths about people outside of Jamaica and America, England and Europe. He wanted to speak for the dark world outside familiar borders, a world that his audience didn't yet know enough about.

He wouldn't see that dream fulfilled. He would be dead within a year, his body sealed in a mausoleum, back in that troubled homeland of his.

But something fairly fascinating has happened since Bob Marley died twenty-eight years ago: He has continued. It isn't simply that his records still sell in substantial numbers (though they do), it's that his mission might still have a chance. It isn't a simple mission. Marley wasn't singing about how peace could come easily to the world, but rather about how hell on earth comes too easily to too many. He knew the conditions he was singing about. His songs weren't about theory or conjecture, or an easy distant compassion: His songs were his memories; he had lived with the wretched, he had seen the downpressors and those who they pressed down, he had been shot at, and probably would have been again. It was his ability to describe all this in palpable and authentic ways that invited our attention and that sustains his body of music unlike any other we've ever known.

Bob Marley made hell tuneful, like nobody before or since. That's what has kept him alive.

.   .   .

Marley's history begins in many other histories; some of them horrible, some remarkable. The real triumph that emerges from his journey—past his death, to the possibilities of the present—is just how much he managed to transform his dire origins into a creation that reached outward, touching a sprawled community of the earth's dispossessed, and how he did it despite hard odds and limited time.

Robert Nesta Marley was born in a small rural Jamaican village called Nine Miles. His father was a white man, Captain Norval Marley, a superintendent of lands for the British government, which had colonized Jamaica since the 1660s. Marley's mother, Cedella, was a young black woman, descended from the Cromantee tribe, who as slaves had staged the bloodiest uprisings in the island's plantation era. Captain Marley seduced Cedella, promising her marriage, as he reenacted an age-old scenario of white privilege over black service. When Cedella became pregnant, the captain kept his promise—and he left her the next day. His family demanded as much or else he would face certain disinheritance.

The couple's only child was born in the early part of 1945, as World War II neared its end. Nobody is sure of the exact date—it was listed on Marley's passport as April 6, but Cedella was sure it was two months earlier. It took her a long time to record the birth with the registrar; she was afraid, she later said, she'd get in trouble for having a child with a white man. While mixed-race couplings weren't rare, they also weren't welcome, and generally it was the child of these unions who bore the scorn. Bunny Wailer, who was Marley's childhood friend and was among the original Wailers, remembered that Marley's birth was considered "reproachful," since children born of blacks and whites were children who should not be seen; the society didn't want them. But Marley's mixed inheritance gave him a valuable perspective. Though he became increasingly devoted in his life to the cause of speaking to the black diaspora—that population throughout the world who had been scattered or colonized as the result of slave trade and imperialism—he never expressed hatred for white people, but rather hatred for one people's undeserved power to subjugate another people. Marley understood that the necessary struggles for justice and power might result in bloodshed, but he also maintained that if humankind failed to stand together, it would fail to stand at all.

In the 1950s Cedella moved to Kingston—the only place in Jamaica where any future of consequence could be realized—and she later brought her son to join her. They made their home in a government tenant yard, a crowded area where poor people lived, virtually all of them black. The yard they settled in, Trenchtown, was made up of row upon row of cheap corrugated metal and tarpaper one-room shacks, generally with no plumbing. It was a place where your dreams might raise you or kill you, but you would have to live and act hard in either case. To Cedella's dismay, her son began to come into his own there—to find a sense of community and purpose amid rough conditions and rough company, including the local gangs of street youths. These gangs evolved soon enough into a faction called Rude Boys, teenagers and young adults who dressed sharp, acted insolent and knew how to fight. Kingston hated the Rude Boys, and police and politicians had vowed to eradicate the city of them.

It was in this setting of grim delimitation that Marley first found what would raise his life and give it purpose: Kingston's flourishing and eccentric rhythm & blues scene. In the late 1940s, Jamaican youth had started to catch the fever of America's urban popular music—in particular, they fancied the earthy and polyrhythmic dance and blues sounds pouring out of New Orleans. By the 1960s, Kingston was producing its own form of R&B: a taut, tricky and intense music in which rhythms shifted their accents to the off-beat—almost an inversion of what one heard in American rock & roll and funk. This new Jamaican pop music was, like American R&B, the long-term result of how black music survived and evolved as a means of maintaining community in uncaring lands. It was music that gave a displaced population a way to tell truths about their lives, losses, passions, dreams, hopes and their suffering. Sometimes they would make their expressions of suffering sound exultant; it was a way of claiming victory over daily misery, or at least a way of finding a respite.

In Jamaica's case, its popular music forms of the last century—from calypso to mento—had always served as means to spread stories, about neighbors' moral failures or the overlord society's duplicity. The commentary could be clever and merciless, and the music that Marley first began to play had the tempo to carry such sharp purposes. It was called ska (after its scratchboard like rhythms), and just as R&B and rock & roll had been viewed in America as disruptive and immoral, Jamaica's politicians, ministers and newspapers looked upon ska as trash: a dangerous and debased music from the ghetto that was helping to fuel the Rude Boys' violence. But the Rude Boys would soon receive an unexpected jolt of validation.

•   •   •

Cedella Marley was worried that her son had grown too comfortable with ghetto life and was too close to the Rude Boys. It was all too risky—there were frequent fights, even stabbings, in the Trenchtown streets and at ska dances.

Marley, though small and slight, was known as a force in Trenchtown. He even had a street name: Tuff Gong. But he had no aspiration for a criminal life. "Don't worry," he told his mother. "I don't work for them." The truth was, Marley found qualities of ruthless honesty, courage and rough beauty in tenement yard community, and he didn't necessarily want to transcend or escape it. Instead, he wanted to describe its reality and to speak for its populace, which was subject not only to destitution, but to easy condemnation as well. Marley also didn't like to see poor people killing other poor people as an effect of surviving in society's margins. He had already written a song about cheap moralism, "Judge Not," recorded it with one of Kingston's leading producers, Leslie Kong, and released it in 1963—the same year that the Beatles and Bob Dylan were first making their music felt. That year Marley formed a vocal group with some friends, Neville Livingston (who was the son of Cedella's boyfriend and who later became known as Bunny Wailer) and Peter McIntosh, a tall guitar player who would shorten his name to Peter Tosh. The group spent considerable time working on vocal harmonies with singer Joe Higgs. Higgs had done some work for Clement "Coxsone" Dodd, Kingston's dominant record producer, who also ran the scene's most successful recording house, Studio One. In addition, Dodd presided over the island's most popular sound system—a sort of DJ booth on wheels that played the new American and Jamaican sounds at makeshift dance halls, until the police would bust them up, breaking heads and looking for Rude Boys who might be carrying knives or marijuana (the latter grew prolifically in Jamaica).

Marley and the others auditioned several original songs for Dodd in 1963, including one that he had written out of deference to his mother's concerns, called "Simmer Down." It was a plea to the local gangs to back off from violence before meaner ruling powers stepped into the situation, and it was set to the sort of aggressive beat that might well excite the sort of frenzy that the song's words disavowed. Dodd recorded the tune the next day with his best studio musicians, the Skatalites, and that same night he played the record at one of his sound-system affairs. The audience called for it to be played again, over and over. It was an immediate sensation, and for good reason: For the first time in this emerging scene, a voice from the ghetto was speaking to others who lived in the same straits, acknowledging their existence and giving voice to their troubles. That breakthrough had a transformative effect, on both the scene and Marley and his group, who would call themselves the Wailing Wailers and, finally, the Wailers. The name was meant to describe somebody who called out from the ghetto—a sufferer and witness—and several of the group's early singles continued to talk about those concerns. Marley had already found one of the major themes that would characterize his songwriting through the entirety of his career.

Dodd was so impressed with Marley's musical discipline and work ethic that he entrusted him with rehearsing several of Studio One's other vocal groups, including the Soulettes—a female vocal trio that featured a teenage single mother and nursing student named Rita Anderson, who had a dream of becoming known as Jamaica's Diana Ross. Marley had eyes for other women during this time—he would always have eyes for other women—but he was drawn to Anderson for her devotion as a mother. In turn, she felt a need to protect Marley, who now lived alone in the back of Dodd's studio, since his mother had finally tired of the Kingston life and moved to Delaware. Rita and Marley married in 1966, just days before he gave in to his mother's tireless insistence that he come visit her and try to establish a home in America. The Wailers continued to record without him—with Rita sometimes contributing vocals—but the group floundered without his songwriting and his nervous, urgent-sounding lead vocals.

Marley didn't stay long in America. He didn't like the pace of life there, nor the circumscribed job opportunities available to black men. For that matter, he didn't fancy any higher career goals either; he couldn't imagine becoming a doctor or some other well-paid professional, he said later. He wanted to make music; also he missed his wife and home. While he'd been gone, though, something significant happened in Jamaica that would utterly transfigure Marley's life and destiny: A living God had visited Marley's homeland and walked on its soil.

The living God's name was Haile Selassie, the Emperor of Ethiopia, and the product of yet another complicated strand of history that marked the lives of Marley and Jamaica. Selassie's importance for Jamaicans began in the life of another man, Marcus Garvey, an early-twentieth-century activist who encouraged blacks to look to their African heritage and to create their own destinies apart from the ones imposed on them by America and by European colonialism. According to a persistent myth, Garvey instructed his followers in 1927 to look to Africa for the crowning of a black king, as a sign that a messiah was at hand. In point of fact, Garvey never uttered such a prophecy, but the claim remains attributed to him to this day. In 1930, when a young man named Ras Tafari maneuvered his way onto the throne of Ethiopia, the prophecy that Garvey never proclaimed took on the power of the word made flesh for many. Selassie was the living God, the reinstatement of the rightful Jehovah to the earth and a beacon of hope for the world's long-suffering of the black diaspora.

In Jamaica, a cult called Ras Tafari sprang up around this belief in the 1930s. Rastafarianism developed as a mystical Judeo-Christian faith with a vision of Africa, in particular Ethiopia, as the true Zion. Beyond that the Rastafarians never developed true doctrine, but rather a set of folk wisdoms and a worldview. One of their beliefs was that marijuana—which the Rastas called ganja—was a sacramental herb that brought its users into a deeper knowledge of themselves. More important, Rastas had an apocalyptic vision. They saw Western society as the modern kingdom of Babylon, corrupt and murderous and built on the suffering of the world's oppressed. Accordingly, Rastas believed in social justice and that Babylon must fall—though they would not themselves raise up arms to bring its end; violence belonged rightfully to God. Until Babylon fell, according to one legend, the Rastas would not cut their hair. They grew it long in a fearsome appearance called dreadlocks. The Rastas lived as a peaceful people who would not work in Babylon's economic system and would not vote for its politicians. Jamaican society, though, believed it saw a glimmer of revolt in the Rastas, and for decades they had been treated as the island's most despised population.

In 1966, while Marley was visiting his mother in Delaware, Selassie made an official state visit to Jamaica. A crowd of one hundred thousand met him at the Kingston Airport. Rita Marley saw Selassie as his motorcade made its way through Kingston's streets, and when he passed by her, she believed she saw the mark of a stigmata in his palm, signifying that he was God come to earth. After that, she adhered to the Rastafarians' belief system and ways of life, and she let her hair grow. When Marley next saw his wife, he said, "What happened to your hair?" He was put off by her sudden change and by the degree of her belief. Indeed, one of the more interesting questions about Marley's life is just when exactly he too became a Rastafarian. According to some accounts, he adopted the religion soon after his return to Jamaica, as early as 1967 or 1968. But according to Timothy White's meticulous biography, *Catch a Fire*, Marley's conversion wasn't complete until around the time of *Natty Dread*, in 1974.

This much, though, is certain: In the years that followed Selassie's visit to Kingston, Marley would not only grow into Rastafarianism but would also come to exemplify it as nobody before or since. In turn, his faith would help Marley find new depths in his music and it would help coalesce his best ideals. Rastafarianism—and especially its beliefs in social justice, and its critique of the West's political, economic and class systems as the equivalent of a modern-day Babylon—would play a key part in Bob Marley rising to meet his moment and to address the world he lived in.

The timing could not have been better. In 1966 and 1967, as Marley and the Wailers began recording again, the Jamaican music scene was undergoing another critical change. Ska had slowed its beat—as much for social reasons as anything else. Life in Kingston was growing grimmer, and there was less interest in dancing to music as exuberant as ska. The resulting new trend was called, for a time, rocksteady; it was music that didn't jump but throbbed. By 1968, though, ska and rocksteady had given way altogether to a music that was fluid and resilient enough to incorporate both faster and slower rhythms. This new style was called reggae, for its ragged cadence. It ran deeper than any Jamaican form that had preceded it, and its lilting and mesmeric quality seemed especially suited for new dimensions of storytelling and social commentary. Most important, reggae was allowing room for other previously precluded voices. Rasta viewpoints had been exerting an increasing influence on Jamaican arts, somewhat akin to how hippies' ideals were entering American popular culture. Though no Kingston radio stations would play reggae, it immediately made itself felt as a vital cultural form. It was inventive and irresistibly danceable, and it came to function as an alternative form of social reportage among the island's population, as it spread narratives and views that Jamaica's newspapers would never have allowed to be voiced.

Marley took to reggae. It gave him new vision and ambition: He wanted to make music that would satisfy and represent his homeland but that would also reach outward and prove accessible to a larger world outside. After a series of breakthroughs (in particular the recording of some of the band's best music with the innovative producer Lee Perry in the early 1970s) and a setback or two (including the making of a misbegotten album for Jamaican release and a floundering artist deal at CBS), Marley and the Wailers approached Jamaican-born Chris Blackwell, the head of Island Records, in England. It was a bold move, in more ways than one. At the time, Island was probably the most respected rock & roll label in the world, with a roster that included Roxy Music, Traffic, King Crimson, Jethro Tull, Emerson, Lake and Palmer, Fairport Convention, Richard and Linda Thompson, Cat Stevens and Nick Drake, but Blackwell foremost loved

Jamaican music. He had helped distribute reggae in the UK for years through the Trojan label, and he had invested in the film *The Harder They Come*, about a Rude Boy singer turned outlaw. When the Wailers approached Island, Blackwell said, "The attitude they gave off was like real rebels." Blackwell, though, had been advised against the group; they had a reputation for bad attitude. Even Lee Perry had described them as "so stink, so rude." Still, Blackwell elected to take a chance. He gave the band a modest advance and told them to go make a record of their own vision.

The resulting work, *Catch a Fire,* was a landmark: It was the first wholly formed, cohesive reggae album, and it immediately cast Marley into the artistic big leagues for many critics. The record, however, sold marginally. Though Blackwell had dubbed some rock touches (lead guitar and soulful keyboards), reggae's off-kilter pulse and Marley's heavily accented vocals were still too foreign to be palatable to either a rock or black music audience. It wasn't until Eric Clapton's massive 1974 hit version of "I Shot the Sheriff" that a larger audience would begin to notice and seek out Bob Marley and his music.

The rock world's gradual acceptance of Marley, however, really did nothing to enable his artistry; by 1973 he was already a fully formed, astonishing songwriter and bandleader in his own right. Even so, this new acceptance nicely coincided with the Wailers' most satisfying recording period. *Catch a Fire*, 1973's *Burnin'* (the last album to feature original Wailers Peter Tosh and Bunny Livingston, who left after the group was rechristened Bob Marley and the Wailers), *Natty Dread* (1974), *Live!* (1975) and *Rastaman Vibration* (1976) are as essential as any body of work that popular music has ever produced. Like the milestone albums of the Beatles, Bob Dylan, Jimi Hendrix, the Rolling Stones, Marvin Gaye, Sly Stone, Stevie Wonder or Bruce Springsteen, these were records that created new sonic ground and that changed how we would hear music. They were also albums that announced Marley as a preeminent musical figure: Though his music in this time didn't sell millions, he was quickly seen to possess a creative brilliance and fearless integrity. In short, Bob Marley became a considerable and widely recognized musical force, and numerous other artists during the 1970s, from Paul McCartney and Stevie Wonder to Elvis Costello and the Police, would reflect his influence by following through on some of the possibilities that his music was creating.

But Marley's early- to mid-1970s Island recordings are also something a good deal more than pioneering entertainment: They put forth an uncompromising and startling vision of a society kept in hell and ready to storm its gates. Songs like "Burnin' and Lootin'," "Small Axe," "Concrete Jungle," "Revolution," "Them Belly Full" and "War"—especially "War," with its proclamation of worldwide conflict—brandish unsettling images and incendiary pronouncements that are probably the most authentic in modern music.

This sort of work didn't come without risk—risk far greater than any prospect of censorship. The Jamaican hell that Marley was describing so vividly in his songs was an active and deadly place, and some of its most powerful people didn't want to see the sort of social and economic change that Marley implied was necessary. Much of the violence in Kingston that had been attributed to ghetto malcontents and criminals was in fact a violence sustained by the island's government and police forces. Since Jamaica's independence in 1962, its black population had never been allowed any consequential political power. Instead, the two dominant political parties, the People's National Party (PNP) and the Jamaican Labor Party (JLP), were run by largely white structures, fiercely invested in holding their own power. The PNP was headed by a bright socialist, Michael Manley, who some feared was too leftist to govern. The conservative JLP was more ruthless. The party's head, Boston-born Edward Seaga (once a music producer on the Kingston scene), was seen as favored by the United States, who was believed to play a heavy hand in the region's political affairs.

By 1976, Bob Marley was recognized by both parties as a force to contend with. He had been friendly with Manley over the years, though as new elections approached in December, Marley professed neutrality about the race. Politicians, he said, were of the devil. Each party, though, believed it could be helped or hurt by Marley. His growing fame—not only among music fans the world over but also among human-rights campaigners, political activists and even freedom fighters in Africa—had now established Marley as the most admired Jamaican the world over, and in his homeland he was seen as one of the island's true moral leaders, much to the disgust of those who reviled his radical ghetto and Rasta identity. As the election neared, violence was out of control; Kingston had become so tense that people were staying home from work and off the streets. Some members of the PNP visited Marley at his Kingston home on Hope Road, where he lived and rehearsed his band, and they pressed him to play a free outdoor Smile Jamaica concert on December 5 to help keep the city subdued until the election.

Marley consented to play, and even wrote a song for the event called "Smile Jamaica"; he agreed that the city was too tightly wound and could turn explosive. But while he professed no favorite in the race, there was a widespread perception that Marley was sympathetic to Manley and wanted to see him become the next prime minister. According to various accounts, Marley received several threats as the concert approached—including a supposed warning from America's CIA. Some people close to Marley left the city—even left the country. A group of vigilantes volunteered to guard Marley's home, but early in the evening of Friday, December 3, that guard disappeared. At about 8:30 p.m., Marley and his group of musicians took a break from rehearsals. A short time later, two small white cars pulled in the driveway and several men with rifles scrambled out. Some of them surrounded the property, while others headed for the house and opened fire. When the gunfire was over, something like eighty-three bullets had been expended. Rita Marley had been hit in the head as she tried to flee, and the bullet lodged between her scalp and her skull; Marley's manager at the time, Don Taylor, took five shots, including a bullet near the base of his spine; and Marley ended up with a bullet grazing his chest and burrowing into his arm as a shooter aimed to center his heart.

Nobody died that night, but Jamaica's tensions understandably grew worse. Marley fled to a secluded property of Chris Blackwell's, guarded by machete-bearing Rastas. Two nights later, he decided not to bow to any feared dangers and went ahead and played the Smile Jamaica show, to keep the peace. At the end of his set, Marley lifted his shirt and displayed his wounds. He struck a mock pose, as if he were a pistol-bearing badman, tossed his head back and laughed—and then he was gone. He left the island for a long time, heartsick that fellow countrymen had taken up guns against him, and in some ways Jamaica was never again his home. For a time, nobody knew where he was; he would never say. He later spent time visiting American relatives in Delaware and Miami and then traveled to England, where Lee Perry introduced him to British punk bands, most notably the Clash. In early 1978, he would return to play another show intended to keep Kingston from exploding into war. On April 22, at the One Love One Peace Concert, Marley managed to coax both Michael Manley and Edward Seaga onstage with him and held their hands together with his in a gesture of peaceful coexistence. Both men looked horribly uncomfortable. Nothing much, though, changed in Jamaica. Manley had won the election, while political violence still roared from time to time, hurting some, killing others, frightening everybody. Meantime, the poor were kept in hell, the gates closed tight.

There were never any arrests made for the attempt on Marley's life. There was also never any explanation for what happened and why. There were rumors that the JLP may have had a hand in it, and several journalists and documentary filmmakers have put forth intriguing arguments about possible CIA involvement, supported in part by a former agent at the time. The police never named any suspects, the case went nowhere. There was never any justice reached in the matter—at least there was never any official justice.

Bob Marley later said that he believed that Haile Selassie had protected him that night. Selassie was now dead—he had been driven from his throne during a 1974 rebellion and died in August 1975 while confined to his palace. For Marley and most Rastafarians, though, Selassie remained the living God, somehow transfigured. Selassie had shielded him, Marley believed, because Marley still had work to do, and it would be God alone, and never man, that would take him from the world. Even so, Marley would have to work steadily. He told his friends that he didn't expect to live past thirty-six.

There was, to be sure, something urgent and possessed about Marley in his last few years. He wrote songs whenever he had the time; he recorded continuously; he toured exhaustively; he made love to the women he desired and could trust, and he often didn't sleep before morning's light. "Sleep is an escape for fools," he said. There was also, in all this, a reckless mix of bravado and fear. In 1975, during a soccer match with friends (he had played soccer since a child in Trenchtown), Marley's foot was badly smashed and his right toe injured. Doctors told him he would have to stay off the foot, but he ignored them. He wouldn't stop prancing onstage or playing soccer; he didn't believe a foot should be serious enough to halt his momentum. In Paris, while on tour in May 1977, he injured his right toe again—this time, far worse. The toenail tore off and the laceration wouldn't heal. A few months later, when he was limping painfully, he saw a doctor in London who said the damage had turned so bad that the toe could turn cancerous and should be amputated. Marley wouldn't hear of it. He thought the doctors were lying. "Rasta no abide amputation," he told them. Instead, he saw an orthopedic surgeon in Miami who performed a skin graft and told him the treatment had been successful. According to Rita Marley, in her 2004 autobiography, *No Woman No Cry: My Life with Bob Marley*, her husband's demurral had less to do with religious misgivings than with his sense of how he might appear to others. "How could I go onstage?" he said to her. "They won't stay looking at a crippled man." Rita tried to persuade him to deal with his health, but she also feared debilitating him during this time of relentless creativity. Cindy Breakspeare, Jamaica's former Miss World and one of

Marley's main lovers in his last years, also urged him to take the problem seriously, but he bristled whenever the suggestion came up: "Do you want me to have cancer?" he would reply. Some saw Marley's refusal as courage or blind faith; just as likely, there was real fear at work. Marley didn't want to learn that death might be growing inside him. Instead, he concentrated on doing what made life most meaningful to him: He set out to make music that might help improve the world that he would leave behind.

Marley's later series of albums, like his earlier groundbreaking recordings, forms a progressively related body of work, though of a fairly different sort. Those earlier records featured lovely music bearing tales of unbearable realities. By contrast, the later studio albums—*Exodus* (1977), *Kaya* (1978), *Survival* (1979), *Uprising* (1980) and the posthumous *Confrontation* (1983)—wore much of their resistance in the albums' titles, whereas their contents were only occasionally about conflict and upheaval; rather, these were largely albums about sustaining hopes, small pleasures and the solace of love. In their moment, these recordings were more commercially successful than Marley's world-altering albums, but the newer stuff struck many critics as too unfocused, too full of popwise moves. Some of these albums received devastating reviews—especially in *Rolling Stone*. In that period, when punk bands who were informed by reggae, such as the Clash, were making music that intended to turn everything upside down, those reviews seemed to make sense. Today, though, the latter records sound lovely; their melodies are endless gifts, and there's a deep sorrow about them that offsets their prettiness. Reviewing *Kaya* in the *Village Voice*, critic Robert Christgau wrote: "[Marley] hasn't abandoned his apocalyptic vision—just found a day-to-day context for it, that's all."

By the time Marley finished recording the tracks for *Uprising* and *Confrontation* in 1979, day-to-day was all he had left, though nobody seemed to know it. In 1980, Marley began a lengthy tour, ostensibly to promote *Uprising*, though the real objective was to reach the American black audience that had proved so elusive to him. At New York's Madison Square Garden on Saturday, September 20, 1980, Marley's exhaustion seemed to catch up with him, and he almost passed out onstage. He woke up the next day feeling confused, unable to remember clearly what had happened the night before. That morning he was jogging in Central Park with a friend, when his body froze up on him and he fell forward, unable to help himself. Later, he saw a doctor who told him the devastating news he had long been afraid to hear: His blackout had been due to a brain tumor. Later tests revealed that the cancer had spread through his lungs, liver and brain, and would continue on; it was certainly now untreatable. He probably had another ten weeks to live.

Nobody had informed Rita Marley about her husband's fall in Central Park or about the diagnosis of his tumor. She was touring with Marley in her customary role as the leader of his harmony group, the I-Threes, but she was traveling separately. She didn't see him until two days later, before the next scheduled show in Pittsburgh; he looked astonishingly older and thinner than a few nights earlier. When Marley gave her the news, Rita insisted that the tour be canceled immediately, but, according to Timothy White's account, one handler told her that since Marley was going to die anyway, they should simply continue with the tour. Marley went onstage in Pittsburgh and played his full show, but that was as far as he could go. His live performances ended that night. He visited cancer clinics in New York, Miami and Mexico, then traveled to Bavaria, Germany, to submit to the care of Dr. Josef Issels, who practiced controversial approaches to cancer therapy. Marley would live another eight months—much longer than anybody had predicted.

Rita Marley stayed close to her husband throughout this time. Their marriage had been neither simple nor painless for her. Marley had grown distant from his wife just as his career began to ascend in the early 1970s. He saw numerous other women and he fathered at least seven children outside his marriage. (Marley and Rita had four children of their own.) Even so, he could be intensely possessive of his wife, and on one occasion, wrote Rita in *No Woman No Cry,* her husband almost raped her when she tried to refuse him sex. She thought about divorcing him, but she believed the bond of their partnership ran too deep and that Marley still needed her protection. As Marley's life was closing, the disease had drained him so much that he cried out: "God, take me, please." Rita writes that she held him and sang to him, until she began to cry. Marley looked up at her, and with what voice he had left, he said: "Don't cry. Keep singing."

Bob Marley died in Miami, Florida, on May 11, 1981. He was thirty-six. His body was flown to Jamaica, where Prime Minister Edward Seaga—who had bestowed Jamaica's Order of Merit, the country's highest honor, on Marley a month before his death—ordered a state funeral. It was a belated respectful gesture from a government that had never really respected the man or his concerns, and that had never liked his music. But anything less would have been unthinkable.

On May 20, a national day of mourning, twelve thousand people viewed

Marley's body as it lay in state at the Kingston National Arena, and another ten thousand waited outside. The next day the arena was filled to capacity for his funeral. As a pickup truck bore his coffin back to his birthplace, Nine Miles, hundreds of cars followed. Thousands of Jamaicans—not just Rastas—lined the roads all the way to glimpse the cortege. According to a 1982 account by Isaac Fergusson in the *Village Voice,* Marley's coffin was placed inside a mausoleum atop a hill at Nine Miles, and a sacred seal was affixed. A wire grill and boards and wet cement were applied to the front of the burial place to protect the body's sanctity. Ten thousand voices cried: "Hail him! Praise him!" They cried it over and over. Darkness fell and a sound blared through a speaker, ringing off the surrounding hills to the valley below. It was the sound of Marley singing "Redemption Song," and it played as a tribute to the land and people that Marley had tried to speak for.

In the years since Bob Marley's death, his legacy has only grown, though it's also been the object of numerous troubles. In the last twenty-seven years, it has seemed at one point or another that everybody who was ever close to him has sued one another or said unkind things. In her book, Rita Marley tells her side of an incident in which former Wailers Peter Tosh and Bunny Wailer—who didn't reach out to her husband as he was dying, nor did they attend his funeral—refused her offer to participate in their late partner's legacy, telling her that Marley's sins had brought on his own death. (In 1987 Tosh was murdered during a robbery at his home. Tosh was forty-two.)

The various legal suits now seem largely settled. The Marley family controls the rights to Marley's songwriting, and Island Def Jam has been doing a splendid job of reissuing Marley and the Wailers' 1970s and 1980s Island albums as expanded double CDs. But controversy continues around the reggae legend: In early 2005, Rita Marley announced her intention to have her husband's remains exhumed and taken to Ethiopia. That decision set off a firestorm of hostility in Jamaica, and it raised an interesting question: Whom does Bob Marley's legacy belong to?

Some remains, of course, have their own way of seeking out inheritors. Marley's message of resistance, of spirit as a means to defeat oppression and claim one's inherent rights, has clearly emerged as his most powerful and important legacy. It's true that many others in popular music have spoken to these same concerns, including Bob Dylan, John Lennon, Marvin Gaye, Bruce Springsteen and Tupac Shakur. But with the exception of Tupac, these voices addressed injustice, intolerance, deprivation and oppression from outside the living heart of that experience. Marley risked his life to say the things he believed, and as a result both his art and his example managed to uplift or embolden others—particularly members of the African diaspora—in cultures and conditions that no other Western pop star has entered with such authenticity. In the years since, only hip-hop has had the same international impact.

Of course, part of what has made Marley's message so effective and enduring is how he framed it. He was a superb melody writer—he wrote some of the most adept and insinuating pop hooks of the last thirty years—and those hooks serve to pull the listener into the songs and into the realities Marley was describing. It's a wonderful yet subversive device: Marley sang about tyranny and anger, about brutality and apocalypse, in enticing tones, not dissonant ones. His melodies take up a resonance in our minds, in our lives, and that can provide admission to the songs' meanings. "One Love," the Marley song that England's BBC named as the Song of the Millennium, is a good example of his methods. On the surface it might sound like a feel-good chant-along about the simple power of love to bring unity, but you enter that song and you'll find something else: It is about war, it is about damnation and a vengeful God's Armageddon, and it is about those who have been so wicked in their efforts to oppress the souls of mankind that they can't possibly escape the fire that is going to rain down on them. The "one love" refrain is really just the part of the song that pulls you in. Once you're there, you realize what it's really about: one hell. And still you hum it, you sing it when you're by yourself. You can't help it. Your children will do the same; trust me. I doubt if anybody has ever pulled off feats like this better than Marley. He was the master of mellifluent insurgency.

I can think of song after song that fits this way of hearing Marley, but the one that most recently took me by surprise is "I Shot the Sheriff," the song that Eric Clapton made into a Number One hit in 1974. The song is a great tale of injustice and its results. It's almost like a Western movie: A lawman is hounding another man who represents something—perhaps it's race, perhaps it's class—that he just can't abide. The sheriff sets out to kill that man and his progeny, until the downtrodden person who is telling the story strikes back. He kills the sheriff—it's all he can do—but he doesn't kill the deputy; he knows the guilt doesn't spread that far. That's how I've always heard "I Shot the Sheriff," as a parable of justice and compassion, until recently, when I realized the singer might mean something entirely different. He didn't shoot the deputy because there simply wasn't time. But that time will come. Make no mistake.

Starting this article, I had to wonder if Bob Marley's visions could stand the test of our times. Much has changed these last few years—there are fresh raging and deadly arguments about just who is the oppressed and who the oppressor in the world today, and there are not going to be any easy ways out of the costs of that disagreement. How could Marley's music count in the knowledge of all this? Then I let "One Love" pull me into its comforting-on-one-hand, terrifying-on-the-other context, and I realized that its scariness and its sorrow are perfect for now. The song really may be a prophecy, and it's hard to say which would be worse: fulfilling the prophecy or averting it. Either way, the song can still find us—it can still disrupt easy notions of what's right and wrong; it can still be a threat. And it can still stand for how Bob Marley continues to resonate for us.

Music is what saved Marley. He knew it. It preceded his faith and his worldview and in time it became as one with both of those elements. It also gave Marley the means to do the best he could with his life, and finally it became his way of enduring past his own death.

One of the last things Marley wrote was "Redemption Song." It was also the last song he sang in public, as he perched on a stool onstage that night in Pittsburgh, September 22, 1980, and accompanied himself alone on his acoustic guitar. Weary, knowing his death was inside him, the house lights bearing down on him, sweat pouring from his face, Marley raised his voice in the loveliest tone he could muster, and sang a personal prayer that invited us all in: "Won't you help to sing, these songs of freedom / 'Cause all I ever had, redemption songs."

He must have known he was singing his epitaph. You see the pain drawing his face, you hear the yearning, the resignation, the pained love in his voice, and you want to say to him: Don't cry. Keep singing.

But nobody had to tell him that. He did it his whole life, up to the last note.

GENIUS, INTOXICATION, DOWNFALLS AND HARD RECLAMATIONS

PHIL OCHS'S
TALE OF AMERICAN RUIN

Sometimes I feel that the world isn't mine,
It feeds on my hunger and tears on my time,
And I'm tired, yes I'm tired.
                    —Phil Ochs, "I'm Tired"

In 1997 Rhino Records released *Farewells & Fantasies*, a much overdue
though also much welcome tribute to one of America's greatest lost voices.
Phil Ochs—a folksinger who had served as both an early champion and a
contemporary of Bob Dylan   spent the better part of his career writing
songs of angry hope and fierce humor, songs that seethed with idiosyncratic
dreams of a better and more ethical culture. At the same time, some of
Ochs's most memorable work also radiated with moving, firsthand images
of anguish and madness, until by the mid-1970s—after his vocal cords had
been severely damaged by a mugging attack in Africa and his career had all
but collapsed in disillusion—the agony became insufferable. In April 1976,
Phil Ochs hanged himself at his sister's home in Far Rockaway, New York,
and popular music lost one of its most conscientious and compassionate
voices.

  Farewells & Fantasies—a three-CD set—covers Ochs's difficult migration
from a man who dreamed of hope to a man who finally dreamed only of
death. The majority of the set's first two discs could almost serve as an historical sketch of the trajectories of the horrid explosion of the Vietnam War
and the struggle for black civil rights, and how these disruptions transformed America's dreams and destinies and revealed both a great ugliness
and a great bravery at the nation's heart. With the notable exception of Bob
Dylan, few 1960s songwriters wrote more affectingly or intelligently about
this period of upheaval than Ochs. Though Dylan's best topical songs may
have been more tuneful or visionary, Ochs might have had a deeper grasp of
both the historical and the emotional forces that brought the nation to

that awful time, and he also spoke in his songs—unflinchingly—of what would come of it all. Songs like "Power and the Glory," "Love Me, I'm a Liberal," "Here's to the State of Mississippi," "I Ain't Marching Anymore" and "There But for Fortune" still work as rousing and deep-felt statements of conscience, but they are hardly Ochs's deepest political works. Instead, with such later songs as "When in Rome" and "Pretty Smart on My Part," Ochs addressed something far more formidable and frightening than a cause: He, in fact, looked at what America was making of itself. These are among the most harrowing folk and rock & roll songs of the last forty years or so— songs that tell their tales from inside the heart and mind of American murder and American ruin—and with these tales, Ochs made plain that the awful and bloody place that this land was about to become was being shaped in the ferment and betrayals of the late 1960s.

According to this set's historical text (by former *Rolling Stone* music editor Mark Kemp), Ochs became disillusioned and deeply depressed by the brutal confrontations between youthful protesters and police forces during 1968's Chicago Democratic Convention (along with Jerry Rubin and Abbie Hoffman, Ochs had helped organize the event's protest coalition). But by this time, Ochs had already started exploring different styles in his writing and recordings. He had grown enamored of the inventive textures in the music of the Beatles and was also impressed by the complex orchestrations in the arrangements of American classical composer Charles Ives and the Beach Boys' Brian Wilson, and he incorporated some of these interests into his epic 1967 album, *Pleasures of the Harbor*. To my mind, this is the beginning of Ochs's most interesting and complicated period: On *Harbor* (and on the subsequent *Tape from California* and *Rehearsals for Retirement*), Ochs mixed beauty with dissonance, hope with terror, fervor with despair, and life with death. And yet this is the period that *Farewells & Fantasies* has the greatest difficulty with. On some occasions, the set's compilers have opted for live or demo versions of songs that were better served in their original recordings ("Tape from California" and "Cross My Heart"), and in one instance, this practice of substitution proves almost tragic. "Crucifixion" (from *Harbor*) is perhaps Ochs's most startling and unforgettable song—a transfixing account of the John F. Kennedy assassination and how that event began the end of one set of American possibilities and the beginning of another. In its original form, "Crucifixion" was not an easy song to hear or withstand (grotesque electronic sounds swirled throughout the composition's terror-tale—but in that cacophony, one hears America's blessings and history pull apart), and so the anthologists here have opted for a simpler live acoustic performance, thus dismissing one of Ochs's most brilliant achievements. It's as if, in the end, they had grown afraid to follow Ochs too closely into the darkness that he saw so clearly.

Maybe that's how it should be. Certainly, Ochs's decline into alcoholism, depression, paranoia and solitude was a painful trek, and in some ways it remains one of popular music's sadder mysteries: how a man so full of hope grew so lost. The conventional view is that there was a part of Ochs that grew sad and manic and that enabled him to take his life. However, listening to this music, one also hears the inspiring expression of a man who wanted to live—very, very much—and who wanted his country to realize its grandest promises. Perhaps as Ochs saw all that became lost, both in his own reality and in the nation's, he could not sanely withstand such pain. He almost said as much at one point: "Basically, me and the country were deteriorating simultaneously . . ."

Phil Ochs is gone now, never to return—and so is that American moment that he documented so incomparably. But we still have the sounds and memories of what once was. *Farewells & Fantasies* is a fine reminder of all that is now forsaken, though Ochs's albums from 1967 until his end are still better cases in point. Long may that loss haunt our dreams.

HUNTER S. THOMPSON: THE LAST OUTLAW

Hunter S. Thompson was sixty-seven when he sat down before his typewriter for the last time, on February 20, 2005, in Woody Creek, Colorado. It was almost evening. He had been in a black mood that afternoon, his wife Anita later said. The two had argued and Thompson ordered her out of the kitchen, his workspace. "He'd never asked me to leave the room before," she later said, adding that he had a strange look on his face. He wanted her to join his son, Juan Thompson, elsewhere in the house, but she didn't want to. She got her gym bag and told him she was leaving. "I don't want you to leave the house," Thompson told her. But she left.

Juan was nearby, in the house's office. Thompson's daughter-in-law, Winkel, was in an adjacent living room, playing with her six-year-old son.

Thompson had a glass of Chivas Regal close by. There was also a .45-caliber handgun resting next to his typewriter. At 5:16 p.m., Anita called her husband from the gym. She wanted to make up. The couple talked for about ten minutes, and she would claim it was a good talk. Thompson asked her to come home when she was done at the gym. She said he wanted her to help him with his weekly column for the ESPN website. Then she heard a clicking sound. She thought maybe he had set the handset down or turned on the television. Maybe he was typing. She waited for a minute. He never came back on the line.

At 5:42, Juan and his wife heard a loud noise. Both thought it was the sound of a book falling. In a way, they were right. What Thompson's son and daughter-in-law heard was the sound made by the collapse of a life that long before had become the stuff of literature.

Probably no other twentieth-century author seemed so inseparable from his own stories as Hunter S. Thompson. His best-known work, *Fear and Loathing in Las Vegas*, is a landmark, defining work. Like Herman Melville's *Moby-Dick*, Mark Twain's *The Adventures of Huckleberry Finn* or F. Scott Fitzgerald's *The Great Gatsby*, it peers into the best and worst mysteries of the

American heart. But *Fear and Loathing* is also the story of the sort of life Hunter Thompson lived. The drugs and drink should have killed him, the anger should have worn him down, and maybe in the end, it all contributed to how he died that night in February. But Thompson never regretted how he lived. It was essential to how he did the work that he did. In a dark time, he sought to understand how the American dream had turned a gun on itself. Nobody in modern literature has come closer to answering that question, and in the end, perhaps Thompson came closer than anybody should. He would have had it no other way. He never flinched, even in his last moments.

Hunter Stockton Thompson was born in Louisville, Kentucky, on July 18, 1937. He was the first of three sons. His father, Jack R. Thompson, was an insurance salesman, and his mother, Virginia Ray, was a librarian. It was a middle-class family, not affluent like the families of the friends Hunter often chose.

Thompson never said much about his parents—in fact, when an *Esquire* interviewer once inquired about the journalist's father, Thompson just sat in silence, staring. What little is known comes from one of Thompson's brothers, Davidson, and a few childhood and adolescent friends. His father, they told biographers, was a quiet man who cared about baseball and politics, and Thompson respected him deeply. His mother, meantime, was sensitive to her son's volatility and insecurities—his apparent need to test limits, as well as to make his mark in some way that would win him respect. Those needs came naturally, but Thompson often seemed to work against his own desires. Early on, he liked provoking trouble and resented being censured. When he was eight, police filed a report on him for waging a vicious spitball fight and vandalizing a local park. A pattern started to set in: He would draw people in with his bearing and charisma, but then he'd push their limits and sometimes repel them.

By the eighth grade, Thompson was seen as unusually literate, though he was also suspected of being a chief member of a petty-crime group that called themselves the Wreckers and specialized in breaking into schools and churches and doing serious damage. By the time he was a sophomore in high school, according to biographer Paul Perry, he had discovered the euphoria of drink—and he never turned back. He got into the habit of taking Mondays off from school to recover from weekend hangovers. After police arrested him once for alcohol possession, he showed his resentment by getting drunk with some friends for twenty-six nights in a row. But during this same time, he also became an active and respected member of Louisville's prestigious Athenaeum Literary Society—a noteworthy feat in Thompson's case, since almost all the group's other members came from powerful and wealthy local families. At the society's long weekend meetings, Thompson felt free to profess his deep liking of Ernest Hemingway, who had toughened up twentieth-century American literature, and F. Scott Fitzgerald. He felt that Fitzgerald's best characters exemplified something vital in the American spirit: They were people fundamentally on the outside of society, even if they worked within it—it was their dark willfulness, their vision of social doom, that placed them apart. It was in the *Athenaeum Literary Journal* that Thompson published his first essays—mocking the values of a placid and conformist life—and it was also in service of the journal that he learned the merit of drinking through the night, writing and working to make a deadline.

Things took a bad turn toward the end of Thompson's senior year, in June 1955. His father had died, leaving the family without money, and Thompson—already known for being temperamental—now appeared angrier to friends. One night just before graduation, he and two wealthy friends were arrested on an armed robbery charge. His friends enjoyed enough privilege to escape punishment, but due to his earlier reputation, Thompson was sentenced to sixty days in the Children's Home, despite his mother's pleadings. He would not be allowed to attend his high school graduation. His friends felt he had been scapegoated—one of the other boys arrested said Thompson was the innocent one in the group that night—but the hurt had been done. Thompson stayed in jail, frightened and resentful, for thirty days, and by the time he was released, his peers were preparing for college life and distancing themselves from him. In *Fear and Loathing: The Strange and Terrible Saga of Hunter S. Thompson*, writer Paul Perry quoted one of the students who now resented Thompson and wanted him ejected from the Athenaeum Literary Society: "Everything he did was outside convention. Among writers, that attitude is saluted. But for us he had gone over the edge. . . . We didn't want to be outside convention. We wanted to belong."

After his release, Thompson bought a case of beer and visited the home of one of those who had turned against him: the local school superintendent. Thompson hurled each beer bottle, one after another, through the superintendent's windows. "That'll teach the bastard for suspending me from school," he pronounced.

•   •   •

Thompson's sentence also required that he move to reform school after his release from the Children's Home or join the military. He chose the latter, and a few weeks later he was on his way to Kelly Air Force Base, in San Antonio, Texas. When he debarked from the plane and was met by two drill sergeants, Thompson was so drunk he began vomiting on the runway, then passed out. He was soon assigned to Eglin Air Force Base in Florida.

It was in the air force, in 1957, that Thompson's journalism career began, and it's also where he learned to make his exaggerations work for him. At first, he didn't like being in the military. In fact, he never liked it; he didn't like being told what to do. But when the base newspaper needed a new sports editor, Thompson decided to get the job. He had never studied journalism, but after a couple of nights at the library reviewing the subject—learning how to fashion headlines and how to build and stagger news story paragraphs—he convinced the necessary people at the base to give him the position. But Thompson couldn't help himself: He also began writing a sports column for a nearby citizen newspaper, something strictly forbidden by the military. There were other signature traits beginning to take form as well: He didn't always wear a regulation uniform to work, he sometimes left the base without permission, and he was creating his own rules of journalism. One night, he remade the camp's newspaper at the last minute, inserting a front-page story that exposed an improper discharge the base had granted a star football player to help his professional career. His commanders were livid. One officer noted: "[This] airman, although talented, will not be guided by policy or personal advice and guidance. Sometimes his rebel and superior attitude seems to rub off on other airmen staff members. He has little consideration for military bearing or dress and seems to dislike the service and want out as soon as possible." The newspaper's editor, a master sergeant, arranged for Thompson's honorable discharge in the fall of 1957. Even so, Thompson wouldn't leave without an event: Hunter filed a final story, describing a fictional drunken nighttime riot at Eglin Base, resulting in the explosions of airplanes and the rape of female cadets—none of which ever happened. He also wrote a press release, describing his military departure as more of an escape than a discharge, with Thompson barreling his car out the gates, hurling a Molotov cocktail. He closed the release by quoting a nonexistent captain, declaring Thompson as "one of the most savage and unnatural airmen I've ever come up against."

Thompson took a job at a small paper in Pennsylvania, but not for long. He fled after wrecking an editor's car. He ran as far as New York City, where he landed a job as a copyboy at *Time* magazine. In his off time, he was reading the Beat authors and poets, Jack Kerouac, William Burroughs, Allen Ginsberg and Gregory Corso. Above all, he revered Kerouac, who had produced work that was changing not only the way things could be said in American literature, but in fact what was now allowed to be said. The writer's best-known work, *On the Road,* was all about freedom of the self in a convention-bound society, and it helped fuel Thompson's own aspirations. The one time, though, that he saw Kerouac reading his work at a New York venue with Gregory Corso, the author was so drunk and nearly incoherent that Thompson felt embarrassed for him. Minutes later, when Corso got up to read, Thompson—who might have been a bit drunk himself—took out some of his disappointment on the short poet, kicking beer cans noisily across the floor, until Corso stomped off, refusing to read more, and pointing at Thompson and declaring, "You—*you* are a fucking creep!"

Thompson began to chafe at his *Time* job; he felt it was beneath his abilities. He asked the editors to make him a reporter, maybe a foreign correspondent, but things weren't done that easily at *Time*. Thompson sulked. He grew resentful. He slowed down at taking copy from writers or delivering it to editors—which was unacceptable. *Time* fired him. Thompson began pushing his limits more, staying up nights drinking and writing a novel, *Prince Jellyfish*. He finished a first draft in early 1959, but he knew it wasn't working. That same year, he met Sandy Dawn—his first serious girlfriend. He took a job at a sports magazine in Puerto Rico, brought Sandy down there with him, but wrote for the magazine as little as possible when he found out he was mainly covering bowlers. For the next few years, he moved around a lot—sometimes with Sandy (he would marry her in 1963, succumbing to his mother's pressure), sometimes without her, frequently taking his frustration out on her in unkind ways and seeing other women when the desire and opportunity meshed. He grew angry at not getting published. He started getting into guns. He wasn't a hunter—he apparently wasn't good at killing things—but he got a hell of a kick from shooting at bottles, dead cars and other big and noisy items. It became one of his life's favorite pastimes. Then, in 1961, he saw how awful the consolation of a gun could be when the news broke that American literary giant Ernest Hemingway—one of Thompson's heroes—killed himself with a shotgun at age sixty-one, in Ketchum, Idaho. Thompson was shocked. "I think he killed himself because he couldn't write anymore," he later said. "He just didn't have it anymore, so he decided to end it."

Hemingway's death had a strong impact on Thompson. He realized he had only so much time to do his work and make his mark. In 1962, he started writing for New York's *National Observer*—then the most adventurous newspaper in America. He filed several stories from South America. Some of them seemed so strange as to have been made up (the editors could never verify the articles' accuracy), though others—stories of poverty and abuses of life and justice in places like Brazil—felt frighteningly accurate. He didn't stay all that long in South America—he became one of the *Observer*'s main roaming reporters—but something vital to Thompson's development as a writer happened while he was there: He began taking drugs. He'd developed dysentery, which meant he couldn't drink alcohol as much as he liked, and so he started to ingest various stimulants, including coca leaves and amphetamines. He used the stuff so much, his hair fell out during his time there. The drugs sapped him of strength—especially when he came off them—but paradoxically they also give him energy. Thompson eventually determined that the right drugs, in balance with the right amounts of alcohol, would help him churn out an increasingly prodigious—and for a time, an amazingly inspired—amount of writing.

As Thompson's writing began to take off, he became more fearless, but also less patient. He left the *National Observer* in 1964 after the paper refused to run his admiring review of Tom Wolfe's *The Kandy-Kolored Tangerine-Flake Streamline Baby* (New Journalism was on the rise, and established journalism was reticent to honor the movement). In 1964, Thompson and Sandy moved to San Francisco's Haight-Ashbury district, where a young community—drawn together in part by the city's burgeoning and inventive local rock & roll scene—was coalescing around daring new sets of ideals regarding drug use, sexual relationships and opposition to America's increasingly deadly involvement in Vietnam. Thompson sympathized, but he thought the idealism was too naïve and vulnerable to all manner of dangers and disenchantment. In 1965, he wrote an article for *The Nation* about the Bay Area's other outside-the-law community, the Hell's Angels, who were notorious for the loud, frightening-looking Harley-Davidson motorcycles they rode and for their mythic capricious violence. Thompson produced a singular piece of writing, told from the inside of the Hell's Angels experience, putting their outlawry in a human context: These were lost men, fuckups who had no hopes and who found a meaning in their hardbitten solidarity—but they were also a new breed of dangerous subculture. Thompson later found out just how dangerous when he expanded the article's premise into a full-length book for Random House. He grew worried as some Angels made noises about what they might do to his attractive young wife and their new infant son, Juan Fitzgerald, if the book misrepresented them. At the tail end of his yearlong association with the biker gang, at an outdoor rally, Thompson made the mistake of telling an Angel that he, the author, had a faster bike than the Angel. The Angels beat the shit out of him, breaking his nose, coming close to crushing his skull when a senior Angel called them off. Frightening but riveting, *Hell's Angels* was Thompson's first major work. "His language is brilliant," said *The New York Times Book Review*, "his eye is remarkable, and his point of view is reminiscent of Huck Finn's. He'll look at anything; he won't compromise his integrity. Somehow his exuberance and innocence are unaffected by what he sees."

Thompson's innocence, though, would be shattered soon enough. He and Sandy and their son left the Haight in 1967 and bought a home in Woody Creek, Colorado, five miles northwest of Aspen. He loved the isolation, and the fact that he could stand on his front porch in the middle of the night, enjoying the drugs he had taken and listening to Bob Dylan at peak volume. The following year, Thompson visited Chicago, to write about the Democratic National Convention. It was going to be a high-stakes and historic event—everybody in America knew it, though they would still end up shocked. It had already been a convulsive and deadly year—one of the worst in the nation's history. Months earlier, as opposition to the Vietnam War began to spread beyond vulnerable youth into America's mainstream, President Lyndon Johnson's credibility was so damaged that he was forced to announce he would not seek reelection. For a short time, there was a glimmer that the country might make an urgent turn—Senator Robert F. Kennedy, committed to ending the war, would likely be the party's new nominee. But nearing the convention, Kennedy was assassinated. Johnson's vice president, Hubert Humphrey—a yes man to the war—was suddenly set to take the nomination; nothing, it seemed, would get better. That was the backdrop, as brutal power holders and enraged protesters gathered in Chicago. Entering the convention on its first night, Thompson saw a crowd of demonstrators confronting the Chicago police—the proxy bully force for the prowar powers. Thompson got close to the scene just as a vicious battle suddenly broke out, the cops clubbing and teargassing young people mercilessly, seriously hurting many. Though Thompson had press credentials—and was therefore hands-off to the police—an officer rushed him, punching him hard in the stomach with a riot club, sending him through a plate glass window. Lying in the broken glass, he watched as many others received worse treatment.

Thompson once claimed he'd become political-minded in 1960, during the race between John F. Kennedy and Richard Nixon, but there was no clear political obsession in his earlier writing. It was that night in Chicago, when American hope was devastated in ways that would never be redeemed, that Hunter Thompson—the great American writer—was born. He had seen something horrible up close—he knew that the brutes who held the nation's real power would rather beat America's children than accede to their hopes. Thompson returned home to Woody Creek, and for weeks he couldn't talk about that night without crying. "For me," he later wrote in *Rolling Stone*, "that week in Chicago was far worse than the worst bad acid trip I'd even heard rumors about. It permanently altered my brain chemistry, and my first new idea—when I finally calmed down—was an absolute conviction that there was no possibility for any personal truce, for me, in a nation that could hatch and be proud of a malignant monster like Chicago. Suddenly, it seemed imperative to get a grip on those who had somehow slipped into power and caused the thing to happen."

As a result, Thompson now saw Aspen and its own power holders—who wanted to make the town a vacation resort for rich tourists and also wanted longhaired youth to feel unwelcome—with new sharp eyes. He organized a local political contingency, the Freak Party, and he fielded a mayoral candidate and would later himself run for sheriff. He made some interesting promises: He vowed to change Aspen's name to Fat City; he swore to eat psychedelics in the sheriff's office; he guaranteed to keep drug dealers honest. "The die is already cast in my race," he wrote. "And the only remaining question is how many Freaks, heads, criminals, anarchists, beatniks, poachers, Wobblies, bikers, and Persons of Weird Persuasion will come out of their holes and vote for me." He didn't expect to win—didn't *want* to win, he insisted—but he wanted to scare the arrogance of the local plutocracy: He wanted to show them that democracy is numbers, and that with the right numbers, the tables could turn. He drew a fair amount of national coverage—most of it contemptuous and disdainful, yet astonished when Thompson came damn close to winning.

In 1970 Thompson asked an obscure magazine named *Scanlan's Monthly* for an assignment to cover that year's Kentucky Derby horse race, held in the writer's hometown, Louisville. The magazine wanted to assign a photographer to accompany Thompson, but he insisted instead on a largely unknown but brilliant British illustrator, Ralph Steadman. The resulting article was thoroughly unexpected—even by Thompson himself. Thompson and Steadman spent days running around Hunter's old Louisville stomping ground, drinking and inadvertently offending people as Thompson took copious notes. Then, *Scanlan's*'s editors flew Thompson to New York to write his article. He sat in front of a typewriter in his hotel room for days, looking at blank pages. He took drugs. He drank whiskey. Nothing came. His editors were frantic. Desperate, Thompson tore some pages from his notebook, sent them to the magazine and waited to get fired. In the end, that's all the article was, raw notes, stitched together. Thompson felt ashamed, but when the article was printed, editors around the country raved about it as an absolute breakthrough in modern writing. "I was convinced I was finished," Thompson told an interviewer in 1974. "I'd blown my mind, couldn't work. . . . Then when it came out . . . I thought, 'Holy shit, if I can write like this and get away with it, why should I keep trying to write like the *New York Times*?' It was like falling down an elevator and landing in a pool of mermaids." It's a great story, mythic—and no doubt true. But while the resulting article, "The Kentucky Derby Is Decadent and Depraved," feels freewheeling when you read it, it doesn't feel accidental. The writing is *right there*, on the page—startling, unprecedented and brilliantly crafted.

Thompson had hit on not just a style, but a voice: He was inside his story—documenting his own reactions, state of mind, following loopy digressions until they landed in unanticipated wells of revelation—but he was also, on another level, outside the scenes he wrote about; that is, he was a misfit, chronicling systems of accepted values that really had no value at all. "Forget all this shit you've been writing," one editor wrote to him, "this is it; this is pure Gonzo. If this is a start, keep rolling." Thompson liked that term—*gonzo journalism*—and he seized its calling. He had already chronicled his battle for Aspen's political soul in *Rolling Stone*, in 1970, and had written another major piece about the LA police shooting of a Hispanic newsman. He now had an assignment from the magazine to cover a police convention in Las Vegas. Coincidentally, *Sports Illustrated* hired him to visit the same town and write a few hundred words for photo captions of the Mint 400 motorcycle race. Thompson took along his friend Oscar Zeta Acosta, an East LA lawyer and activist he'd met the previous year while reporting for *Rolling Stone* about the murder by police of Hispanic LA newsman Ruben Salazar. Thompson and Acosta ran crazy through Las Vegas, taking massive amounts of speed and LSD and running up huge hotel bills. Acosta sobered up and took off, leaving Thompson alone in a hotel room with the bills, trying to make sense once more of his pages upon pages of notes. His idea, he later wrote, was that "the eye & mind would be functioning as a camera. The writing would be selective & necessarily interpretive—but once the image was written the words would be final . . .." At the same time, he was trying to write all this while drinking and taking amphetamines, which tended to have its own impact on the method. Thompson was producing wild and hallucinatory stuff, and *Sports Illustrated* wanted no part of it—which left only *Rolling Stone*. The article was coming in fits—rushes of pages followed by frozen anxiety—when the magazine sent him back to Las Vegas to cover the National District Attorneys Association's Third Annual Institute on Narcotics and Dangerous Drugs. Thompson returned, again with Acosta, and this time the two outdid themselves, wrecking rental cars, calling room service for guns, annoying and frightening one fuck of a lot of people, then carousing at a law and order convention while full of a phenomenal array of drugs.

The resulting story, "Fear and Loathing in Las Vegas: A Savage Journey to the Heart of the American Dream"—which ran in two parts in consecutive November 1971 issues of *Rolling Stone,* and was collected in book form the following year—didn't come quickly. Thompson worked on it for more than six months, carefully crafting its craziness, in the end producing a work with more immediacy, vitality, hilarity and meaning than perhaps anything else published in that decade. "We were somewhere around Barstow on the edge of the desert when the drugs began to take hold . . . ," the story began. "And suddenly there was a terrible roar all around us and the sky was full of what looked like huge bats, all swooping and screeching and diving around the car, which was going about a hundred miles an hour with the top down to Las Vegas. And a voice was screaming: 'Holy Jesus! What are these God-damn animals?'"

That screaming voice, of course, was the writer's own.

Much has been made about how Thompson injected his own character into the article, so that the narrator, the story's momentum and its real-life author were all one and the same—which is true, up to a point. However, the fear and loathing Thompson was writing about—a dread of both interior demons and the psychic landscape of the nation around him—wasn't merely his own. He was also giving voice to the mind-set of a generation that had held high ideals and was now crashing hard against the walls of American reality. "Fear and Loathing in Las Vegas" was a requiem—crazed, angry and funny, and not at all pretty. "[What] is sane?" Thompson wrote near the story's end. "Especially here 'in our own country'—in the doomstruck era of Nixon. We are all wired into a survival trip now. No more of the speed that fueled the Sixties. Uppers are going out of style. . . . All those pathetically eager acid freaks who thought they could buy Peace and Understanding for three bucks a hit. But their loss and failure is ours, too . . . a generation of permanent cripples, failed seekers, who never understood the essential old-mystic fallacy of the Acid Culture: the desperate assumption that some-body—or at least some force—is tending that Light at the end of the tunnel. . . . Whatever sells today is whatever Fucks You Up—whatever short-circuits your brain and grounds it out for the longest possible time." Thompson's fear and loathing was about disillusion—the feelings that gnawed at you after the comedown from a dream that proved only a hallucination. It was also about the terror of losing that illusion and having no refuge. Thompson later told Paul Perry: "It was a kind of weird celebration for an era that I figured was ending. I kind of assumed that this was sort of a last fling; that Nixon and Mitchell and all those people would make it very soon impossible for anybody to behave that way and get away with it. It wouldn't be a matter of a small fine. Your head would be cut off."

"Fear and Loathing in Las Vegas" was a jolting piece of writing—it still is—but it was a fringe tale. Thompson's next *Rolling Stone* assignment was about the biggest story around at the time, the US presidential campaign of 1972, which would come down to a race between Republican president Richard Nixon and Democratic senator George McGovern. The risks were bigger than before. Vietnam had become a sinkhole of death for young soldiers and Marines; thousands upon thousands of Americans were marching to stop the war; and college students had been beaten, even shot to death, for their protests. Thompson went into the campaign as an unknown force in US media; most of those few political reporters and campaign managers who knew who he was didn't like, respect, or trust him, and *Rolling Stone*—a rock & roll / counterculture magazine—had established no record for covering electoral politics. Indeed, in 1972 political matters were widely covered by media in much the same way as they are today: with undeserved seriousness and deference. But that wasn't Thompson's approach. "When I went to Washington," he later said, "I went with the same attitude I take anywhere as a journalist: hammer and tongs—and God's mercy on anybody who gets in the way." Thompson's coverage of the election—later collected into *Fear and Loathing: On the Campaign Trail '72*—was startlingly hilarious and irreverent. He was as hard on Democrats—especially former vice president Hubert Humphrey (who had lost the 1968 election) and Senator Edmund Muskie—as he was on Nixon, whose power craze was deadly, insatiable and criminally mean. Also, Thompson saw what almost nobody else in the political press recognized: that Senator

George McGovern was the man who would win the Democratic nomination, despite his innate decency. The election, Thompson believed, would be like no other in modern times: a clear encapsulation of good versus evil, and in the end, the dark forces won. The nation chose Nixon, in a devastating landslide that cleared the way for the fearful destiny that America might still be hurtling toward. "The tragedy of all this," Thompson wrote, "is that George McGovern . . . is one of the few men who've run for President of the United States in this century who really understands what a fantastic monument to all the best instincts of the human race this country might have been, if we could have kept it out of the hands of greedy little hustlers like Richard Nixon."

By the end of the campaign, Thompson was widely regarded as having written some of the most iconoclastic and effective political coverage and commentary that American journalism had ever produced. His name was made—he was now a superstar groundbreaking literary legend, and in his partnership with *Rolling Stone*, both the magazine and the writer had reached new heights. But his pioneering achievements came at real cost. In "Fear and Loathing in Las Vegas," he had looked deep into the heart of what had been lost in the American dream; in *Campaign Trail '72*, he looked into the abyss of the future—certainly the nation's, and perhaps his own as well. Behind it all, Thompson was a man of pitiless morals and case-hardened ideals. He had believed that America could be led to reaffirm its best principles and truths. Following 1972, he was disabused of that notion, and almost everything he did and wrote—or just as important, *didn't* write— afterward was his way of coping with that awful verity.

Following his 1972 election coverage, Thompson briefly considered moving to Washington, DC, to become a full-time correspondent. The media and political enclaves that had once disdained him now welcomed him. Incredibly, even some of the people around Richard Nixon tried coaxing Thompson into helping rehabilitate the president's image with America's youth. Instead, Thompson edited and assembled his campaign coverage into book form and then seemed to be casting about for direction. Several of those around him at this point thought he seemed confused, even lost, likely burned out. He had long been fueling himself with prodigious combinations of drugs and alcohol—the former to keep him going, the latter to loosen his thoughts—and he kept doing so impressively, outstripping anybody else in his company. But his excesses appeared to be catching up with him. He started covering the Watergate hearings that investigated

Nixon's criminal activities, but his new dispatches were less inspired. In late summer 1974, when it was apparent Nixon would resign, *Rolling Stone* assigned him to cover the president's fall. It was a natural for Thompson—writing about the deadly and deceitful man's self-ruin—but he couldn't do it. He sat in front of a typewriter and not a word came to him. Concerned friends suggested that he take some time to rest and rejuvenate his talents. One editor advised him to try setting aside the Gonzo style and recuperate, before he ended up trapping himself in his own mannerisms. Thompson's reply: He produced a dose of LSD from his wallet and swallowed it in front of the editor, then walked out on the conversation.

In the years that followed, Thompson would take coveted assignments—chronicling the fall of South Vietnam, visiting Zaire, Africa, to cover the historic 1974 Muhammad Ali–George Foreman heavyweight title boxing match—yet would produce nothing but ludicrous expense ledgers. He became a highly paid speaker on the lecture circuit, then would show up late at the engagements, with bottles of whiskey and not much to say; sometimes the bottle ended up tossed (out a window, at least once), and Thompson would be asked to leave the stage. His dissolute exploits only enhanced his myth and sometimes became his primary art. His demons, though, stayed busy, and in 1979, his wife, Sandy, had enough of them and his bad temper and his infidelity. She divorced him, and for a time, he was reportedly wrecked.

Whatever his failings, though, Thompson never lacked nerve or a certain obstinate integrity. He wouldn't turn against his bad habits, he wouldn't abstain from them or apologize for them. "I like drugs," he told *Playboy* in 1974, and even though the culture around him had grown intolerant of any such sentiment, even though the government and workplaces and schools now enforced strict bans on nonprescription drug use, and even though few politicians or even entertainers would dare admit any other perspectives, Thompson was never cowed. It was hard to tell how much of his stance was the product of self-determined principle and how much might have been a reasoning born from addiction—or how much might simply have been a guise. It didn't really help that his character sometimes seemed cartoonish—literally, in the case of Garry Trudeau's characterization of Thompson as Raoul Duke in the *Doonesbury* comic strip—or that the two films made about him, *Where the Buffalo Roam* and *Fear and Loathing in Las Vegas,* only caught his comic overindulgence and not his anguished depths. Nor did it help much when, in 1990, a former adult film producer, Gail Palmer-Slater, filed a complaint against him for sexual assault. Thompson vehemently denied the charges, but the Aspen district attorney determined that Thompson had long been a man out of control and ordered a police search of the journalist's home. After eleven hours of ransacking, officers found a gram of cocaine, some marijuana, numerous LSD doses, and dynamite and blasting caps, and the DA filed charges of sexual assault and possession of explosive devices. (According to Paul Perry's book, local police had also cited Thompson for shooting at a porcupine with a machine gun and for trying to shoot golf balls with a shotgun at the Aspen driving range, though in the latter case, Thompson said he was trying to create a new sports form.) The DA's office dropped the sex assault charges and offered Thompson a probation plea on the drug charge—but Thompson wouldn't hear of it. He instructed his attorney to treat the matter as a Fourth Amendment case—that is, illegal search and seizure by law enforcement—and he ended up prevailing. The DA's office dropped all charges and was severely castigated by the presiding judge.

Despite the traps of Thompson's persona—what one writer has called his "sacred monster" image—he still wrote periodically over the last many years; brief columns mostly (for the *San Francisco Examiner* in the 1980s and the ESPN website in his final years), and he published two prodigiously entertaining collections of letters, covering the years 1955–1976 (*The Proud Highway* and *Fear and Loathing in America*). In addition, Thompson proved capable, from time to time, of the sort of masterful long-form journalism that virtually nobody else could match. In particular, some readers consider "A Dog Took My Place," Thompson's *Rolling Stone* account of a notorious 1980s divorce trial in Palm Beach, Florida, and a pair of fantasias he wrote for the magazine in the 1990s—"Fear and Loathing in Elko" (a fiercely funny blast at an imaginary Judge Clarence Thomas on a wild tear with whores in Nevada) and "Polo Is My Life" (about the writer's brief obsession with, of all things, the art and inanity of the affluent polo class)—among the best writing he ever did. Even so, his later writings were always inevitably compared to his earlier renowned work and found wanting. The newer pieces lacked the sort of sustained rage-in-the-face-of-the-world spirit of Thompson's best earlier stuff, and more crucially, critics noted, Thompson himself no longer aimed to depict the zeitgeist of his times. The comparisons, though, weren't entirely fair. The *Fear and Loathing* texts were stylistic and thematic tours de force. It would have been hard for Thompson to top them: The effort would have run the risk of self-parody at best, or mental collapse. Perhaps it seemed better not to try to top himself.

Yet there remained moments when Thompson could tack down hard truths with a fitting ruthlessness that nobody has dared match. When Richard Nixon died in 1994, much of the press and even his old foes paid him respectful tributes. Not Thompson, though. "[Nixon] was a cheap crook," he wrote, "and a merciless war criminal who bombed more people to death in Laos and Cambodia than the US Army lost in all of World War II, and he denied it to the day of his death. When students at Kent State University, in Ohio, protested the bombing, he connived to have them attacked and slain by troops from the National Guard. Some people will say that words like *scum* and *rotten* are wrong for Objective Journalism—which is true, but they miss the point. It was the built-in blind spots of the Objective rules and dogma that allowed Nixon to slither into the White House in the first place."

In addition, perhaps nobody wrote as perceptively or prophetically about the horrors of 9/11 in the immediacy of the event as Thompson did the following day, in his column on the ESPN website. "The towers are gone now, reduced to bloody rubble, along with all hopes for Peace in Our Time, in the United States or any other country. Make no mistake about it: We are At War now—with somebody—and we will stay At War with that mysterious Enemy for the rest of our lives. It will be a Religious War, a sort of Christian Jihad, fueled by religious hatred and led by merciless fanatics on both sides. It will be guerrilla warfare on a global scale, with no front lines and no identifiable enemy. . . . We are going to punish somebody for this attack, but just who or what will be blown to smithereens for it is hard to say. Maybe Afghanistan, maybe Pakistan or Iraq, or possibly all three at once. . . . Victory is not guaranteed—for anyone, and certainly not for anyone as baffled as George W. Bush. . . . He will declare a National Security Emergency and clamp down Hard on Everybody, no matter where they live or why. If the guilty won't hold up their hands and confess, he and the Generals will ferret them out by force. . . . He is in for a profoundly difficult job—armed as he is with no credible Military Intelligence, no witnesses and only the ghost of Bin Laden to blame for the tragedy."

The invaluable voice that gave us that is gone now. There aren't that many in today's national media that are willing to tell us the hard stuff, and just about none who are willing to name swine as swine. We have managed to recover the decorum that Hunter Thompson once savaged, and we are the worse for it.

The most common sentiment voiced in the days after Thompson's death was how so many who knew him were surprised he hadn't died long before. For their part, his family—the son who found his body, Juan Thompson, and his second wife, Anita—said that the writer had made it plain for some time that he would likely take his own life, but they didn't expect it so soon. "He feels at the peak of his life right now," Anita told a reporter who noted she was still speaking of her late husband in the present tense. "[He] has a very successful career. If he quit now, he would feel he was a champion."

According to other reports, though, Thompson certainly felt worse than that toward the end. In his last two years he had undergone major spinal surgery, and he had also broken his hip and a leg. He was now often wheel-chair-bound and in intense pain that none of the drugs could alleviate. Also, some claimed that writing was again coming hard for him. He had a lengthy assignment for a major magazine, and he couldn't make the words happen. He was back to looking at blank pages, and there isn't anything that makes writers feel worse—not even bad reviews. That blank page is an indictment of your mind and imagination, and after looking at it so many times over the years, it becomes horribly scary and depressing.

In the end, there was probably little left for Thompson to say in written words. He'd already documented the abyss as had few other writers. More important, he'd stared it down, and reported about that too—about how to maintain your spirit as the dreams around you are choked until they breathe their last. He had no more to say about it, and no more to say about himself. On that cold February night in 2005, as Hunter Thompson stared at his typewriter, he picked up his .45, put it in his mouth and finished his story.

JIM MORRISON AND THE DOORS: THE VIRTUES OF WASTE

In that strange, wondrous year that was 1967, in the middle of a season in which rock & roll was seeking to define itself as the unifying force of a new youth community, Jim Morrison of the Doors proclaimed to anybody willing to listen: "Can you picture what will be / So limitless and free . . . / And all the children are insane. . . ." You heard that assertion—midway through "The End," the long, startling track that closed the band's debut album—and either you took those words as confirmation of your worst fears, or you were emboldened by their promise. If you were worried about where youth culture was headed, "all the children are insane" likely came across as a threat. But if you were one of those children that Morrison was singing about at that time (me, I was sixteen in those days), then you were hearing a voice that recognized and embraced you, that gave implicit support to your "insanity." This, in its own offbeat and mystifying way, was also a kind of affirmation of love—though not in quite the same good-tempered way that, say, the Beatles or Jefferson Airplane were attempting to extend ideals of hope and community to their audiences. In effect, the Doors were asserting themselves as the archetypal band for an American apocalypse that we didn't even know was creeping up on us. While the band has enjoyed a lasting renown for their prescience in that regard, in their time—in the heady and chancy swirl of the late 1960s and early 1970s—the extremes of how far that vision would extend seemed to cost them everything, including their reputation and their commercial and critical viability. It would even cost one of them his life.

Over thirty-seven years have passed since Jim Morrison died in Paris, France, on July 3, 1971, at age twenty-seven, the apparent victim of heart failure and of personal and artistic disappointments that manifested themselves in severe and sustained alcoholism. Jimi Hendrix and Janis Joplin died less than a year before Morrison—both also only twenty-seven. Despite the fact that Hendrix and Joplin died of drug overdoses—and were well known for their indulgences—their deaths nonetheless came as shocks to the rock & roll world; both were artists who seemed full of life and rich creative possibility. By contrast, Morrison's sad end did not come with such mind-stopping unexpectedness. He had long been viewed—by the media, by his fans, even by some close friends—as a man who had devoured his own dreams of excess with such a rapacious appetite that there probably wasn't much growth, experience or time left to him. And yet here we are once again, trying to assess Morrison's life and loss, and his enduring legacy. Was he a visionary, as many of his devotees and comrades have claimed, or was he instead "a drunken clown in a leather suit," as one of his detractors contended? Were Morrison's notorious acts of dissipation and his impulses to jeopardize his life and his band's reputation worth what they cost—to him and to those who cared for and worked with him? Could his death have been avoided—could he have been helped to recover from his dissolution? Or were all his excesses in fact the perfect extension—the logical end—of his unflinching and intoxicated vision?

The truth is, we can't solve these questions—just as we apparently can't resist them. On one hand, there is something about Morrison's story that makes no sense: Where did such a perplexing combination of extraordinary talent and unwavering self-destructiveness truly come from? At the same time, there is also a certain logic to his rise and flameout. Some people live relatively short lives but create intense bodies of work, and when they have gone as far as they can go, they go no farther. In this sense, death proved to be Morrison's most rewarding friend: It halted the singer's decline before he might have gone on to even worse behavior or art, and to a large degree it also helped absolve him for the failures of his last few years. But the real question isn't so much whether we can find the virtue in Jim Morrison's art despite the waste of his life. Rather, the question finally is: Can we separate the two? And if not, what do we make of that?

It's unlikely that anybody who knew James Douglas Morrison in his earlier years might have predicted that he would be both a titanic rock & roll star and a major debauched poet with such lasting effect, for good or ill.

He was born in the middle of World War II, in Melbourne, Florida, on December 8, 1943, the first of three children to Steve and Clara Morrison. His father was a career US Navy officer and would eventually rise to the rank of admiral. Consequently, the family moved many times and over great distances—from Florida to Washington, DC, from New Mexico to

Southern California, then to Virginia—during Jim's childhood. By all accounts, Morrison's parents were never physically abusive to their children though they could be verbally fierce, and the father tried to bring a military-style sense of discipline to the home life. Jim, in particular, resented these attempts. He began acting out a rebellion against his father's authoritarian bearing, and that dynamic became one of the driving patterns of his life. Some of Morrison's biographers conjecture that the boy also begrudged his father's long absences from the family, when Steve was commanding navy forces at sea. In any event, Morrison was unusually intelligent—he scored in the "genius" range in his school IQ tests—and he was a voracious reader. In the sixth grade he wrote his first poem, "The Pony Express," and in high school he wrote the words to "Horse Latitudes" (which would eventually appear on the Doors' second album). "I always wanted to write," he told journalist Jerry Hopkins, in a 1969 *Rolling Stone* interview, "but I always figured it would be no good unless somehow the hand just took the pen and started moving without me really having anything to do with it."

There is much that isn't known about Morrison's childhood and family life. As a result, there has been speculation that some rift may have taken place in the family. Apparently, Morrison's parents disapproved when, in 1963, he announced he wanted to attend the UCLA film school in Los Angeles. When Morrison decided to make the move anyway, he did so without his family's knowledge and support. Reportedly, his father disowned Jim at that point. In the Doors' early publicity statements and interviews, he would claim that his parents had been killed in a horrific automobile accident. (Morrison had in fact witnessed a fatal car accident as a child, while traveling with his family in New Mexico, and the incident left a lasting impression on his imagination.) Later, he told Jerry Hopkins, "I just didn't want to involve them." When Morrison's mother showed up without warning at a 1967 Washington, DC, show, he wouldn't see her and apparently never spoke with her again.

Whatever the reasons for the rupture with his family, the estrangement was never explained or documented by Morrison. This is simply one of those key areas in Jim Morrison's biography that, even after all these years, figures as a fundamental mystery. Still, Morrison clearly fixated on certain impressions and experiences of childhood in his work. Many passages in his lyrics and poetry make reference to abandoned houses and destinies either found or lost on the seas. His most infamous commentary about family appeared in the song "The End," on the 1967 album *The Doors*, when Morrison described walking down a hallway in the last hours of a night to a long-coming moment of murder and release. Morrison himself later said that he intended the passage as a metaphor for bidding good-bye to childhood and creating your own lot in life. That's hardly an uninteresting or improbable reading—especially given how many young people shared a similar sense in the 1960s—though the recitation also seems to depict both a lethal rage and psychic damage that possibly even Morrison himself didn't want to explore much once they had been given voice.

Morrison didn't particularly stand out among his peers at UCLA. He made an experimental film about sexual neurosis and mass hysteria (now lost) that received scorn from other film students, though Morrison went on to graduate from UCLA with a bachelor's degree in cinematography. In addition to his interest in film, Morrison remained a devoted student of philosophy, literature, poetry and history. He had a particular ken for Friedrich Nietzsche's controversial writings on aesthetics and morals, for the visionary art and verse of William Blake, for the fatalistic writings of Franz Kafka, and for the form-changing poetry of Arthur Rimbaud, among others, and he developed a deep knowledge of Greek tragedy. In addition, Morrison regarded Norman Mailer's powerful existential murder novel, *An American Dream*, as an exemplary work of modern American fiction. For the duration of Morrison's life—even when he was heavily drunk (which eventually was much of the time)—Morrison relished the times when he could talk with friends or strangers late at night about poets and philosophers. You sense some of his fondness for the world of ideas occasionally in the language he brought to his press interviews and certainly in his poetry—though you also get the sense that he was most confident at his own versions of ethics and metaphysics in his disquieting songs and their performances, and in the even more disquieting manner in which he lived his life.

When Morrison graduated UCLA in 1965, he told friends that he planned leaving for New York City. He believed there was a creative explosion taking place there, and he had hopes of establishing himself as a poet or playwright on the thriving scene—or even as a sociologist-philosopher. Instead, Morrison ended up spending the summer living on the rooftop of a forsaken office building in the LA-area beach town of Venice. There, he experimented with whether it was possible to stay high on the hallucinogenic drug LSD for days and nights in a row as he began writing new poetry in earnest. This was at the height of the mid-1960s transformation of rock & roll: The Beatles were turning from exuberant pop anthems to writing more complex works; the Rolling Stones were mixing blues and libido to terrific effect; Bob Dylan was rapidly changing all the possibilities of what could be done with language and metaphors in twentieth-century songwriting; and a vibrant youth culture—replete with bands like the Byrds, the Buffalo Springfield and Love—was blooming on LA's Sunset Strip, in dance clubs and coffeehouses. Also, jazz innovators like John Coltrane, Ornette Coleman and Miles Davis were creating new prospects in American and international music. As a smart, intensively media-aware young adult, Morrison followed these trends to one degree or another, but he always insisted that he had never been especially drawn to the dream of performing rock & roll. Nevertheless, as he spent nights on that Venice rooftop and worked hard on forming words from the impressions that now came continually to him, Morrison found that he was beginning to write poems that had definite melodies and cadences. In other words, he had unintentionally become a songwriter. He later said: "I was just taking notes at a fantastic rock concert that was going on inside my head. And once I had written the songs, I had to sing them."

One afternoon that summer, Jim Morrison came down from his rooftop for a stroll on Venice Beach, where he ran into Ray Manzarek, a film school acquaintance. Manzarek was a classically trained keyboardist with a zeal for blues piano and the progressive jazz of pianists Bill Evans and Lennie Tristano, and yet like countless other young musicians of the time, he was caught up in the protopsychedelic style of garage rock that was sweeping much of American and British pop music. He was even leading his own combo, Ray Daniels and the Ravens. Morrison told Manzarek that he had been writing his own songs and proceeded to sing an a cappella version of onc of them, "Moonlight Drive." Manzarek was taken with the song's odd moodiness and thought he heard a natural dramatic—even spooky— quality in Morrison's unpolished baritone. The two agreed to start playing music together and see what developed. In the next several weeks, Manzarek recruited John Densmore—a drummer who aspired to play like jazz trendsetters Art Blakey and Elvin Jones—and a classical- and blues-steeped guitarist named Robby Krieger. By March 1966, the band—named the Doors by Morrison, after a line by English poet William Blake ("If the doors of perception were cleansed every thing would appear as it is, infinite")— was regularly playing a dive beer bar on the Sunset Strip.

Initially, Morrison was a painfully introverted performer. He would often sing with his back to the audience, or when he turned to face the small crowds, he shut his eyes tight. Morrison's own ideal was to emulate the intimate colloquial style of his favorite singer, Frank Sinatra, while Manzarek kept pushing him toward a rawer blues intonation. In time, Morrison found that the regular use of drugs, combined with the musical impetus of his bandmates, helped open up his confidence—in fact, helped him find an astonishing boldness that soon earned the Doors the reputation as the essential new band to see in LAs club scene.

Soon the Doors secured a position as the house band at the Sunset Strip's hottest club, the Whisky a Go Go. This was the period in which Morrison and the Doors began forging their singular sound—based on tense and tough rock & roll song structures, mixed with freestyle jazz inventiveness and Morrison's own increasing penchant for improvisatory word flights. One night, reputedly while on a massive dose of LSD, Morrison began a story riff during "The End"—an atonal dirge that he had been working on about a failed romance. Manzarek, Densmore and Krieger sensed that Morrison was headed someplace different—and interesting. The music began to stretch and give up its predictable rhythmic sway, and as Morrison moved into progressively stranger lyrical territory, the legend goes, the club's audience and employees became transfixed by the spell that the singer and band were building. When Morrison got to the passage about the killer and his Oedipal quest, the singer teased the audience's interest with well-timed pauses in his narrative part, and then he held nothing back: "Mother?" he said calmly, then shouted: "I want to *fuck you*." He repeated the last phrase with increasing fervor as the band played frenziedly behind him. The Whisky's management fired the Doors on the spot. It was Morrison's first real adventure in meeting resistance to what he wanted to do as a performer onstage—and the first time he would be reproached for uttering obscenity to an American audience. Similar conflicts had, of course, taken place in America's literary subcultures and other quarters for some time. In the late 1950s, San Francisco had prosecuted Lawrence Ferlinghetti for publishing Allen Ginsberg's epic poem *Howl*, and even in the 1960s several of Henry Miller's best-known books were still hard to find in the United States, though they had been written a generation or more before. Only a few years earlier, the University of California at Berkeley had erupted in historic demonstrations over the issue of free speech on American campuses. In that same era, in New York's East Village, a raunchy folk and jug band called the Fugs were singing songs about sex and politics, as one of the band's singers occasionally played with his dick hanging from his pants (a practice that didn't seem to disturb East Village clubgoers to any notable degree).

But on that 1966 night at the Whisky, Morrison crossed a decisive line on the ongoing cultural battlefield of rock & roll. Whereas in the 1950s Elvis

Presley had provoked outrage with his suggestive gyrations (and his mix of black and white musical styles) on nationwide TV, and while in more recent years Bob Dylan's political songs and drug references and the Rolling Stones' sexual innuendo stirred expected complaints, Jim Morrison simply pulled out all the stops in one motion. He blew a hole through the walls of that time, and today there are still many people climbing through that hole, to the revulsion of various social critics.

Morrison's insistence on pushing limits and on exercising his most immoderate impulses would, in shorter time than anybody imagined, begin to contribute to his own devastation. "All the children are insane," Morrison intoned, only moments before launching into his deliberative rant about killing Dad and fucking Mom. Perhaps in those moments Jim Morrison decided not to help foment and celebrate such generational insanity, but to find his own place in the promises and hazards made possible by such an ambition. It was a liberating moment, but the force it liberated would not come without a considerable price.

In the mid-1960s, Elektra, an independent folk-based label, was trying to expand its roster with rock & roll bands. The company had already signed the Butterfield Blues Band and another LA Sunset Strip group, Love, who enjoyed substantial hits with "Little Red Book" and "7 & 7 Is." Despite Elektra president Jac Holzman's initial reservations, in 1966 he signed the Doors to a multialbum contract and assigned Paul Rothchild to produce the group. (Rothchild had helped Bob Dylan assemble his electric band for the Newport Folk Festival and was also producing the Butterfield Blues Band, Love and Tim Buckley for Elektra, and would later produce Janis Joplin.) Rothchild wanted to capture the Doors' sound in a straightforward, minimalist production style, without utilizing any of the gimmicky recording effects that other psychedelic groups were relying on. Rothchild believed that this was the best way for the band's recordings to stand the test of time. Rothchild's challenge, however, was to convince Morrison that he simply could not use words like *fuck* on a record release or make overt references to drug experiences.

Rothchild also realized that, despite the impressive musical prowess of the band's three musicians (who could, in their own way, rival other adventurous improvising groups of the time, such as the Bay Area's Jefferson Airplane, Grateful Dead and Quicksilver Messenger Service), the Doors' crucial magic depended largely on Morrison—that is, on those occasions when the "muse," as Rothchild put it, would visit the studio. In those days,

Morrison's muse visited regularly—and powerfully. Recalling the night the band recorded "The End" in the studio, Rothchild later said: "We were about six minutes into it when I turned to Bruce Botnick [the Doors' career-long sound engineer] and said, 'Do you understand what's happening here? This is one of the most important moments in rock & roll. . . .' Jim . . . said come with me and I did. And it was almost a shock when the song was over. . . . It felt like, yes, it's the end, that's the end, that's the statement, it cannot go any further." After everybody had left, Morrison went back and hosed down the studio with a fire extinguisher. He was drunk, he later admitted, and felt that unless he extinguished the fire he'd set loose earlier that night, he wouldn't be able to find any rest.

The Doors' self-titled debut album was released in January 1967—at the outset of one of the most epochal years in popular music history. The first single, "Break On Through (to the Other Side)," enjoyed only moderate radio acceptance. But then, in the spring, FM disc jockeys began playing the full-length jazz-inflected version of "Light My Fire." Elektra edited out the track's improvised parts and turned the song into a wildly popular single. Indeed, "Light My Fire" was the dominant song of the summer of 1967, and its urgent—even desperate—vision of desires, pleasures and a heedless, fiery temper transformed it into one of those songs that defines a generation in its time. On July 29, 1967, "Light My Fire" became the Number One song on America's national pop charts, and its success buoyed the album, which climbed to Number Two, just behind the Beatles' *Sgt. Pepper's Lonely Hearts Club Band* on *Billboard*'s album chart.

In short, *The Doors*' impact on 1967 was enormous—and singular. Bands like the Beatles, like many of the artists from the Bay Area scene, were touting a fusion of music, drugs and idealism that they hoped would reform and redeem a troubled age—and benign as those intentions may have been, they were still troubling enough to many observers. By contrast, the Doors were fashioning music that looked at prospects of hedonism and violence, of revolt and chaos, and embraced those prospects fearlessly. Clearly, Jim Morrison understood a truth that many other pop artists did not understand: namely, that these were dangerous times—and dangerous not only because youth culture was under fire for breaking away from established conventions and aspirations. On some level, Morrison realized that the danger was also internal—that the "love generation" was hardly without its own dark impulses. In fact, Morrison seemed to understand that any generation so bound on giving itself permission to go as far as it could was also giving itself permission for destruction, and he seemed to gain both delight and license—and, of course, fate—from that understanding.

Consequently, in those moments in "The End," when Morrison sang about wanting to destroy his father and violate his mother, he made the moment sound not only convincing, but also somehow *fair*. Even more than the songs of Bob Dylan or the Rolling Stones, Jim Morrison's lyrics were a recognition that an older generation had betrayed its children, and that this betrayal called for a bitter payback. After all, if your parents and the commanding and powerful adult society around you were increasingly seeing fit to treat a daring part of its youth as an alien, hostile force within the larger nation, then why *not* kill those "parents"—even if only in a metaphorical outburst? It's hardly surprising that the Doors' music (in particular, "The End") became such a meaningful favorite among the American youth fighting in Vietnam, in a war where children had been sent to kill or die for an older generation's ruinous ideals. Other groups were trying to prepare their audience for a world of hope and peace; the Doors, meanwhile, were making music for a ravenous and murderous time, and at the group's best, the effect was thoroughly scary, and thoroughly exhilarating.

The band's second album, *Strange Days* (released in September 1967) was less musically propulsive, but its moods ran, if anything, deeper. Several of its best songs were meditations on dread, loss and aberration, and even some of the tracks' titles—such as "I Can't See Your Face in My Mind," "You're Lost Little Girl," "People Are Strange" and "Unhappy Girl"—conveyed alienation and uncertainty. It was now the end of 1967. The summer had gone, and the blithe hopes it had seemingly offered couldn't forever hold. Within the coming seasons—during the tumultuous year of 1968—the war in Vietnam would become deadlier abroad and more divisive at home. Civil rights leader Dr. Martin Luther King Jr. would be shot to death in Memphis, triggering massive rioting across America. Democratic presidential candidate Robert F. Kennedy would be gunned down in Los Angeles, on his way to his party's possible presidential nomination; subsequently, the broken hopes of millions of people would erupt in violence at the Chicago Democratic National Convention, at which police brutally bludgeoned American youth. And Richard Nixon's dismayingly canny political resurrection would result in his election to the American presidency. Throughout all of this, rock & roll—like so much else in America—was becoming a field of hard options and opposing arguments.

Certainly the Doors weren't the only band offering harder music for more merciless times. The Velvet Underground, Iggy Pop and the Stooges, and the MC5 were also making plain that underneath the veneer of altruism and idealism, the '60s youth scene was riddled with some restless and shadowy realities. Increasingly the best late-'60s music was music about fear, doubt and the possibility of apocalypse. Consequently, when Jim Morrison paused near the end of *Strange Days'* ambitious closing track, "When the Music's Over" and announced: "We want the world and we want it, now / Now? / *Now*," the moment emboldened its audience. Make no mistake: The Doors were not foremost a political band. The Beatles, Rolling Stones and Jefferson Airplane would all make more overt and complex statements about the necessity or wisdom of revolution and resistance. But in the late 1960s, nobody seemed to embody threat more palpably than the Doors—or at least Jim Morrison. A friend of Morrison's, Robert Gover, later wrote: "His charisma was such that your ordinary upholder of the established order could be infuriated merely by the sight of Morrison strolling down the street—innocent to all outward appearances but . . . well, there was that invisible something about him that silently suggested revolution, disorder, chaos."

That's where a certain part of the Doors' story seems to end: They recorded two remarkably imaginative and successful albums, and by late 1967 they were America's biggest rock & roll band. Plus, they had a reputation for delivering brilliant live performances. Even though part of their new larger audience attended shows mainly to see Jim Morrison, the volatile sex symbol, the musicians continued to extend their sound. It's worth remembering that the Doors were jazz fans and had come of age when many modern innovators had made their most significant strides. Manzarek, Densmore and Krieger could lay legitimate claim to playing their own amalgam of jazz and rock & roll.

Then the Doors slipped into a bewildering, even cataclysmic decline. And this is where an equally important, though more troubling, part of the band's story begins: in the particulars of how and why that deterioration took place, and the effect it had on the band's standing and on the group members themselves—in particular, Jim Morrison.

With their first two albums, the Doors had recorded much of the backlog of polished material they had been developing since their formation. When the time came to record their third album, *Waiting for the Sun*, they had used up their best reserve and now felt pressure to produce a third masterwork that, as it turned out, wasn't ready to materialize. Indeed, a large-scale musical poem they had planned, "The Celebration of the Lizard," wasn't cohering in the studio. Morrison gradually lost interest in completing the project with the sort of concentration and passion that had made "The End" and "When the Music's Over" into such unified performances, despite their sprawling lengths. When *Waiting for the Sun* was finally released, in July 1968, it struck most critics as hit-and-miss and lacking focus. Also, the band was severely criticized for the transparent commercial appeal of the new hit single, "Hello, I Love You," which struck many listeners as a blatant take-off on the Kinks' "All Day and All of the Night" (though today, "Hello, I Love You" plays as a refreshing blast of pop verve). The album's best track was "Five to One"; a violent song about both a failed love affair and a disintegrating and dangerous nation, it was *Waiting for the Sun*'s clearest statement of menace.

But greater problems were starting to pile up. Morrison had exhausted whatever inspiration he felt he could draw from hallucinogens and had quickly adopted a new drug of choice: alcohol, long favored by many writers and poets. Morrison, in fact, was drinking pretty much on a regular basis and was becoming notorious for his inebriated antics—such as clinging to or walking the ledges of high buildings when drunk beyond the point at which most other heavy drinkers could even stand up. He had also taken to trying to record his vocals while drunk, which resulted in tension with the other Doors and in much wasted time. (Paul Rothchild later said that after the first two albums, Morrison's vocals were so erratic that they had to splice together words and phrases from various takes to create acceptable final tracks.) Indeed, Morrison was rapidly becoming embroiled in the patterns of alcohol abuse and public misconduct that eventually proved so disastrous to him and those who depended on him. To some degree, this sort of behavior was simply expected of the new breed of rock hero: In the context of the late 1960s and its generational schisms, youth stars often made a point of flaunting their drug use or of flouting mainstream morality. "I obey the impulses everyone else has but won't admit to," Morrison told *Creem* magazine. In Morrison's case, this impudence was sometimes merely ostentatious, or naïve, though on certain other occasions—such as a December 1967 incident at a New Haven concert—these gestures helped bolster (and justify) the rock audience's emerging spirit of defiance. In New Haven, Morrison had been sprayed in the face backstage by a police officer after he got in an argument. During the show when Morrison told the audience what had just happened, he was promptly surrounded by policemen and forced from the stage (as a result, Morrison became the first rock performer arrested onstage). Afterwards, outside of the range of the audience, several officers punched and kicked Morrison.

As often as not, though, many observers began to suspect that Morrison's unruliness wasn't so much a show of countercultural daring as it was a sign of the singer's own appetite for disruption. In March 1969, at a notorious performance in Miami, this cheerless fact came across with catastrophic results. The concert had been delayed nearly an hour due to a quarrel with the show's promoters. By the time the group arrived onstage, Morrison was already intoxicated. After the music started, Morrison halted one song and started to berate the audience. "You're all a bunch of fuckin' idiots," he declared. "Let people tell you what you're gonna do. Let people push you around. How long do you think it's gonna last? How long are you gonna let it go on . . . ? Maybe you love getting your face stuck in the shit . . . You're all a bunch of slaves . . . letting everybody push you around. What are you gonna do about it?" Then, he and the band vaulted into "Five to One." Later, Morrison said: "I wanna see some action out there. I wanna see you people come up here and have some fun. . . . No limits. No laws. . . . I'm not talking about guns and riots, I'm talking about love. . . . Take your clothes off and love each other." And then, critically, Morrison pulled on the front of his weatherworn leather jeans and barked: "Do you want to see my cock?" Oddly enough, though nearly forty years have passed, and more than ten thousand people witnessed Morrison's performance—including band members and police officers onstage—it has never been clear whether Morrison actually exposed himself that night. Finally, toward the end of the show, Morrison persuaded audience members into swarming onstage. The platform began to collapse, and fights broke out between security, police and fans.

Most people involved with the band saw the episode as an embarrassment—and as further proof that when Morrison took to a stage drunk, the results could be too volatile. (In 1968 Morrison showed up drunk at a club where Jimi Hendrix was playing. In the middle of one of Hendrix's solos, Morrison crept onstage, wrapped himself around Hendrix's legs and announced, "I want to suck your cock." The scene culminated when Janis Joplin appeared onstage and clubbed Morrison with a bottle of liquor, and all three artists wound up rolling on the floor, fighting. Later that same year, in Amsterdam, Morrison showed up in the middle of a Jefferson Airplane performance, dancing and spinning until he crashed to the floor, passed out drunk, leaving singers Grace Slick and Marty Balin convulsing in disgusted laughter.) About Miami, Morrison would later claim that in part his behavior that night was a reaction to what he saw becoming of the Doors' live shows. During its club days, the band had found room for a more intellectualized brand of experimentation that invoked the audience's participation. The Doors now found themselves playing arenas, surrounded onstage by policemen who weren't there to protect the band so much as to contain it. Morrison admitted that he saw these performances as invitations to provocation—though he also saw them as rituals in creative futility. Morrison later told *Rolling Stone:* "I think that was the culmination, in a way, of our mass performing career. Subconsciously, I think I was trying to get that across in concert—I was trying to reduce it to absurdity, and it worked too well."

It would be difficult to overstate how important the Miami event proved to the Doors' history—and to Morrison's own state of mind. Within days of the show, the *Miami Herald* and some politically minded city and legal officials had inflated the sad fiasco into a serious affront on Miami and the nation's moral welfare; in addition, Morrison himself was designated as a foul embodiment of youth's arrogant indecency. The Doors' touring schedule ground to an immediate halt, and it appeared the band's performing days could be over. Interestingly, amid all the controversy that would follow, almost nobody saw the unfortunate truth of that evening: The Doors' lead singer—who only two years before had been one of rock's smartest, scariest and sexiest heroes—was now a heartrending alcoholic, with little control over his problem and little memory of its worst effects (Morrison himself had no idea of whether he'd really displayed his penis that night). Morrison needed help; he did not merit the horrid, moralistic-minded brand of jailhouse punishment that the State of Florida hoped to impose on him.

And the punishment Florida intended was significant. Morrison was eventually charged with lewd conduct, open profanity, indecent exposure and public drunkenness, and he faced as much as three and a half years' imprisonment at Raiford State Penitentiary, one of the South's toughest prisons. Morrison told various friends that he viewed the possible incarceration as a virtual death sentence. During the six-week trial (from August to September 1970), Judge Murray Goodman admitted to Morrison's attorneys (out of range of the jury) that they had "proven that Mr. Morrison didn't expose himself." Still, the judge declined to instruct the jury on this point, and Morrison was convicted of lewd and lascivious behavior and profanity. An appeals court would almost certainly have thrown out the verdict, according to legal observers—and so in a sense Morrison won his case, though the damage was lasting.

While the Doors would yet go on to deliver some of their most inspired performances (as evidenced by some of the recordings on 1997's *The Doors Box Set*, and in a series of live albums released by the band's internet label,

Bright Midnight Records, in conjunction with Rhino Handmade), the group never escaped the expectation that they were now a vehicle for shock theater, and the strains of the ordeal certainly contributed to the confused nature of the band's 1969 effort, *The Soft Parade* (though it's also a work that has gained force over the years). More disturbingly, Morrison received surprisingly little support from others in the rock community or from the rock press itself. The Miami trial, by and large, wasn't seen as an argument about free speech (though clearly that was among the pivotal issues at stake), nor was Morrison viewed as somebody who had been targeted by legal moralists, in much the same way that comedian Lenny Bruce had been hounded only a few years before. It seems Morrison had simply alienated too many people with his drunken misadventures and with the band's recent bungled albums. Also, around this time Morrison was gaining weight from his daily alcohol consumption and had grown a full beard. He now more closely resembled a lumberjack or truck driver than the gaunt and mysterious rock star he'd personified in 1967. To some degree, this transformation seemed to be what Morrison wanted—or at least what he convinced himself he wanted. Near the end of his 1969 interview with Jerry Hopkins, Morrison suggested discussing the virtues of his submission to alcohol. "Getting drunk . . . you're in complete control up to a point," he said. "It's your choice, every time you take a sip. You have a lot of small choices. It's like . . . I guess it's the difference between suicide and slow capitulation . . ." In one of his poems he wrote: "I drink so I / can talk to assholes. / This includes me."

It is all the more noteworthy, then, that the Doors' final recordings as a quartet were unqualified triumphs. In February 1970, the band rebounded artistically with *Morrison Hotel*—a blues-indebted work that purportedly had been composed largely by Jim Morrison. In the album's opening moments ("Roadhouse Blues"), Morrison describes waking up, grabbing a beer, then awaiting death's nearness. The band's following April 1971 album, *L.A. Woman,* was even stronger: as dark and imaginative as the band's first albums, but showing new musical strengths that few critics expected the band could now muster. It's also a fascinating portrayal of dissolution. Whereas *The Doors* and *Strange Days* were largely albums about fear and loss, *L.A. Woman* actually seemed to live within those states of mind. And yet like much of the best blues music, it expressed its terrors with the sort of fervor that might also chase dread away. In songs like the title track, you hear Morrison's voice push and fray and gain a new credibility as it actually struggles not to fall apart. Morrison had always claimed that his biggest vocal influence was Frank Sinatra, and *L.A. Woman*, for once, demonstrated that influence, in Morrison's determination to sing as if it were the latest hours of the night and he was sharing a few final words with sympathetic friends. In Sinatra's case, it took decades to achieve that brandytone world weariness. Morrison, though, had acquired it in four short years that must have felt like a lifetime.

The pressures and excesses of those last few years had taken a toll on Morrison. According to his friends, the Miami experience had knocked much of the spirit out of him, and he was drinking more than ever. By this time, he had already published some of his poetry (his greatest dream, he had often stated, was to be regarded as a serious poet), and he had been recording a solo spoken-word album (parts of which were released years later on *An American Prayer*). Also, Morrison was growing disillusioned with his life in Los Angeles—and in America. He now wanted to pursue his writing more attentively, and he also had some hope of turning his life around. As the other Doors were mixing *L.A. Woman*, Morrison announced that he was taking an extended leave from the band and that he didn't know when or if he might return. In spring 1971, accompanied by his longtime lover, Pamela Courson, Morrison moved to Paris, France—the home of some of the most respected authors, poets, philosophers and musicians in Romantic and modern history, as well as the favored haven of many early-twentieth-century American literary expatriates. Morrison was clear on this much: He was going to take time away from the demands of rock & roll and remake his life, one way or another.

Jim Morrison's brief time in Paris comprises the final mystery period of his life. In many ways, its truths are as elusive as those of his childhood years. According to some who knew him, Morrison was writing new inspired works in the flat he now shared with Pamela Courson on Paris's Right Bank, and he was attempting to come to terms with his alcoholism. According to others, his drinking in fact only got worse—he was worried that there may be no way out of it—and his writing was not progressing as he had hoped. The best information indicates that Morrison lapsed into severe depression over his inability to reinvoke his poetic muse, and had taken instead to writing desperate notes. In one notebook he simply scrawled for page after page: "God help me."

There are also diverging accounts of his last hours. According to Pamela Courson, Morrison had been ill with a respiratory problem—possibly caused by a fall he had taken before leaving Los Angeles. Courson said that on the night of July 2, 1971, Morrison went to see a Robert Mitchum movie, *Pursued*, came home late and went to sleep. At 4:00 a.m., he awoke, vomited some blood, complained of pains and went to take a bath. But according to accounts that appear in James Riordan and Jerry Prochnicky's *Break On Through: The Life and Death of Jim Morrison*, Morrison may have started to take heroin around this time. (Morrison never used opiates heavily and had never taken drugs intravenously, though Courson did.) One rumor claims that Morrison ended up in a late-hours Paris club that night—that he snorted some heroin there and immediately overdosed. This version of events has Courson and others somehow taking Morrison secretly back to his flat, where Courson placed him in a tub of ice, hoping to revive him. In recent years, author Stephen Davis has constructed an account of Morrison's last hours, in *Jim Morrison: Life, Death, Legend*. According to Davis, Morrison and Courson had snorted heroin in the postmidnight hours at their apartment. Courson nodded out, but Morrison became alarmingly sick, vomiting blood. Courson managed to place Morrison in a bathtub of water, perhaps with the help of somebody else. When she and her sometime boyfriend, drug dealer Jean de Breteuil, broke through into the locked bathroom at 7:30 a.m., Morrison had bled out into the water and was dead. Through various maneuvers and the vagary of French law, Courson managed to convince Parisian authorities to declare that Morrison died of a heart attack. The examining doctor that morning was shocked to learn that Morrison was only twenty-seven. "I was going to write fifty-seven," he said.

Rumor and myth may always attend Morrison's death. It has often been claimed, for example, that the only person to have seen Morrison's corpse was Courson herself, though it's clear that policemen and a doctor also examined his body. Also, a mortician packed Morrison's body in ice repeatedly over the next couple of days, due to a heat wave (the body remained at the flat until just before the burial). In any event, there was never an autopsy. Courson declined the need for one (she certainly feared the discovery of the couple's heroin usage), and Morrison's parents never requested one. Initially, Courson denied rumors that Morrison was dead. Her aim, apparently, was to have Morrison buried at Paris's Père-Lachaise Cemetery with absolutely no media attention or public spectacle. After that, the news officially broke: James Douglas Morrison was dead.

In the years after Morrison's burial, Courson's grief never ended—it only deepened. So did her drug problems. She eventually returned to Los Angeles, and on April 25, 1974, she died in her Hollywood apartment, of a suspected heroin overdose, also at age twenty-seven. It is possible that Courson took some secret about the final phase of Morrison's life to her own grave, but it is undeniable that her consuming anguish in the intervening years only attested to the inescapable truth: Jim Morrison died of heart failure at age twenty-seven, on July 3, 1971, in Paris, France, smiling into the face of a slow-coming void that, long before, he had decided was the most reassuring certainty of his life. The day after his death, Pamela Courson reportedly found among Morrison's final writing a poem. Its end read: "Last words, last words / out."

In listening to and reading about the Doors again at length, I repeatedly came across those inevitable statements of tribute and disdain that pertained to Jim Morrison through his life and his death. I even came across my own, from an article I wrote for *Rolling Stone* in 1991, upon the occasion of Oliver Stone's film *The Doors*. At the time, I wrote: "It's almost as if, somewhere, somehow, a macabre deal were struck: If Morrison would simply have the good grace to die, then we would remember him as a young, fit, handsome poet; we would forgive him his acts of disregard and cruelty and drunkenness, and recall him less as a stumblebum sociopath and more as a probing mystic-visionary."

Well, time can change various things—but it certainly hasn't reduced the Doors' stature in rock & roll history. From time to time—first, aided by Francis Ford Coppola's incendiary use of their music in his film *Apocalypse Now,* then by the late-1970s LA punk scene embracing the band as their rightful local antecedent—the Doors have undergone interesting bouts of cultural resurgence. Plus, various ploys on behalf of the band's label and former members and associates have aimed to reaffirm and lengthen their durability in both rock & roll history and the pop marketplace. More important, many of the issues that characterized the band's history are still vital concerns in popular and media culture—for example, a continuing apprehension on the part of many parents and adults that the children just *might* be insane after all. Some social critics claim that there are not really any comparable conditions between the youth culture of the 1960s and that of today—that today's dangers have different contexts and causes. But part of what is different is that we now live in a time when the media and society have infantilized adolescents; that is, youth are now regarded more as susceptible children than as near-adults. This tactic may not be designed to protect the children so much as it aims to protect the adults. It is unlikely that American society will ever be eager again to allow adolescents the kind of dominion that they briefly enjoyed in the 1960s and 1970s. Instead, youth's power today is largely confined to a marketing power—though that power is worrying as well to many people. When the young applaud hip-hop artists whose work is deemed vulgar or violent-minded, or when they popularize disturbing video games, alarms go off in media and politics about what is becoming of our children. Have they become dangerous? Are they going . . . *insane*?

This much, though, *has* changed: These days the culture would never tol-erate the idealization of a famous drug user or drinker like Jim Morrison. Recovery (or abstinence), not indulgence, is today's standard of living—which, of course, many of us regard as a healthy turn of affairs. As some-body who has had to discover for himself the ruin that comes from unbridled alcohol abuse, I can't help but have compassion and hope for those people who struggle to live in ways that are healthier both for them-selves and for those who care about them.

But there's an old saying worth invoking at this point: Hindsight is a motherfucker. In other words, modern-day concerns and ideals aside, things clearly didn't work out that way for Jim Morrison. He didn't recover. He didn't pull back from the abyss in the same way that, say, Bob Dylan or Eric Clapton did. Morrison succumbed to that void—he agreed to it—and that truth is inseparable from any meaningful examination of his life's work and worth, no matter what our final judgments may be. Clearly, Morrison found something in his acquiescence to alcoholism—something other than just his own death (though that may have been part of what he was seeking). Anybody who drinks regularly and heavily does so for any number of reasons. Perhaps they have a genetic bent, or perhaps they're fucked up emotionally and the drinking seems to give them a quick respite from their troubles. But there are other reasons: Drinking—like drugs—can seem to offer illumination in measured doses. Also, drinking—like drugs—can feel like a wild or brave adventure. It can give you permission for all manner of behavior—some of it fun or silly, and some of it horrible beyond belief. The trouble is, these advantages have a short lifespan. That is, they have a diminishing lifespan night after night, and as the nights add up, the drinker himself has a diminishing lifespan. Like Jim Morrison said, "It's the difference between suicide and slow capitulation."

Naturally, I can't help but wish Morrison had found a way out of that slow capitulation. For all his bravado and his awful behavior, I think that not just a fierce heart beat inside the man, but also a fiercely loving and compassionate one. Morrison had some of the same sort of improbable humanity that you find in the work of Louis-Ferdinand Celine or Jean Genet: Their writing may seem nihilistic, but behind it lies a recognition that bringing the unmentionable to the surface might help free us of some of our fears or cruelties. In any event, Morrison had a great capacity to sing for those who felt wayward and deserted and angry—indeed, he was a bit intrepid in how far he would go in that regard.

Fearless, and also a bit foolish, because in the end Morrison failed to draw any saving distinctions between the temper of his art and the intensity of his life. As a result, his visions ultimately helped destroy him. He must have understood that he was headed that way; he certainly told enough people he didn't expect a long life. In Morrison's work with the Doors you hear promises being born and possibilities being lost—sometimes in the same breath. But even when the alcohol and other excesses were wreaking their consequences, Morrison still knew well the meanings of the experiences he was describing, and there was a courage and dignity in his best efforts at those disclosures.

It's true, Morrison might have had a longer life, but that's not the way he chose it. He defied everything that might have contained his nerve, and he decided to grow by negating himself. Some people, as many of us learn, simply cannot be saved or forced to recover themselves. Their decline becomes part of the object of their life. Just the same, Jim Morrison had the determination to overcome his self-negation through a body of dark and beautiful work that, some thirty-five-years-plus past his death, endures— and still heartens—with good reason. Let's give him that due, even as we hope for our own kinder ends. After all, he had the grace to sing to young people in this land, in times when they were treated as insane children, desperately in need of some stranger's hand.

THE ALLMAN BROTHERS BAND: BONDS OF MUSIC AND ELEGY

Some say there was a ghost. Some unkind spirit, the rumor went, had clambered up out of a dark legacy of death and bad news, and had attached itself to the Allman Brothers Band, like a mean dog trailing its quarry, until it had dragged the band down into the dust of its own dreams.

Maybe the group had attracted the spirit on one of those late nights more than a generation before, when various band members would gather in the Rose Hill Cemetery, not far from where the Allman Brothers lived in Macon, Georgia. The story is, they drank wine and whiskey there, smoked dope, took psychedelics, played and wrote dark, obsessive blues songs, and laid their Southern girlfriends across sleek tombstones on humid, heat-thick Southern nights. Maybe on one of those occasions, sex and hallucinations and blues all mixed and formed an unwitting invocation, an insatiable specter was raised, one that decided to stay close to the troubled and vulnerable souls that had summoned it. Or maybe it was something even older and meaner that trailed the Allmans—something as old as the hellions and hellhounds that were said to haunt Southern rural crossroads on moonless nights.

Yes, some say there was a ghost. Some even say they witnessed that ghost—or at least, witnessed how palpable it was for those who had to live with the effects of its haunts. There are stories about late-night reveries in the early 1970s, when the band's most famous member would sit in darkened hotel rooms, watching early-morning TV, brooding. By this time, the Allman Brothers Band was the most successful pop group in America—in fact, the band had played for the largest audience ever assembled in the nation's history. But perhaps that success was never enough to stave off fears that there was yet more that this band was destined to lose.

In those postmidnight funks, the blond blues singer sat and watched TV, sometimes horror movies with the sound down. An empty chair was sometimes close by. To at least one visitor, the singer insisted that a spirit sat in that chair—and that he knew that spirit well. In fact, he said, he and the ghost were brothers.

Walk into a room to meet the surviving members of the original Allman Brothers Band, and you walk into the midst of a complex shared history. It is a spooky, gothic story of family ties—of both blood brotherhood and chosen brotherhood—and it is also a story of amazing prodigies, dogged by amazingly bad fortune. Indeed, the four men seated in this room—keyboardist Gregg Allman, guitarist Dickey Betts and drummers Jai Jaimoe and Butch Trucks—are people who helped *make* history: They once personified what rock & roll and blues could achieve in those forms' grandest moments of musical imagination, and they also once played a significant role in the American South's social and political history. But like anybody who has made history that matters, the members of the Allman Brothers were also bruised by that history. They do not seem like men who are unduly arrogant or proud; rather, they seem like men who have learned that proud moments can later form the heart of indelibly painful memories.

It had been several years since these musicians had recorded together, but on this sultry afternoon in midspring, as they gather in the lounge at Miami's Criteria Recording Studios, they are beginning the final work on *Seven Turns*—a record that they boldly claim is their most important and accomplished work since 1973's *Brothers and Sisters*. In many ways, this is an adventure they never thought they would share. In 1982, after a restive fourteen-year history, the Allman Brothers dissolved into the caprices of pop history. The band had broken up before—in the mid-1970s, on rancorous terms—but this time they quit because the pop world no longer wanted them. "We had been credited as being a flagship band," says Dickey Betts, pulling nervously at his mustache, his eyes taking a darting scan of the other faces in the room. "All of a sudden managers and record company people were telling us that we should no longer use terms like 'Southern rock,' or that we couldn't wear hats or boots onstage, that it was embarrassing to a modern audience. We finally decided we couldn't meet the current trends—that if we tried, we were going to make fools out of ourselves and ruin any integrity we had left. Looking back, splitting up was the best thing we could have done. We would have ruined whatever pleasant images people had of us by trudging along."

The band members went separate ways. Allman and Betts toured with their own bands off and on, playing mainly clubs and small venues, and even teamed up for a tour or two. Butch Trucks went back to school, opened a recording studio in Tallahassee, raised his family and involved himself in the difficult fight to stop record labeling in Florida. Jai Jaimoe packed a set of drums in his Toyota and spent years traveling around the South, playing in numerous jazz, R&B and pop bands. Occasionally, the various ex-Allmans would come together for the odd jam or gig, but nobody talked much about the collective dreams they had once shared. Clearly, the glory days were behind them, and there wasn't much point in talking them to death.

Then, toward the late 1980s, pop music began going through one of its periodic revisionist phases. Neo-blues artists like Stevie Ray Vaughan and Robert Cray began attracting a mass audience; plucky country singers like Lyle Lovett and K. D. Lang had started attracting a broad spectrum of alternative and mainstream fans; and the long-suffering, brandy-voiced Bonnie Raitt enjoyed a major comeback with her surprisingly straightforward renditions of blues and R&B music. As a result, Dickey Betts received a call from Epic Records: Was he interested in making a Southern rock LP? Betts thought Epic was joking, but nope—the label even wanted him to assemble a band with a twin-guitar frontline, and yes, if he really wanted, he could wear his cowboy hat onstage. Betts put together a solo act, and eventually he and Trucks received calls from Epic that led to an invitation to reform the Allman Brothers. At first, Jaimoe and Trucks were wary; Gregg Allman's drug and alcohol problems remained legendary, and they weren't sure about touring or playing with him under those circumstances. But Betts, who had seen Allman often in recent years, said that Gregg was in good shape and better voice than ever, and that like the rest of them, he had missed the music they had made together. So Betts called Epic back and asked: For a Southern rock band, how would the label like to have *the* Southern rock group, the Allman Brothers Band? Epic was thrilled—until it was learned that the band planned to tour before recording.

"They were afraid we would *break up* again before we ever finished the tour," says Betts, laughing, at a 1990 recording session. Actually, touring was reportedly part of the deal the band members had struck among themselves concerning Gregg Allman: Before entering a studio to work on new material, they wanted to see how Gregg would handle the road; in fact, they wanted to see how *everybody* would handle working together again. Mainly, they wanted to see if they could still play like the Allman Brothers, rather than as a once-removed imitation.

"It would have been pitiful to have put this band back together, just to be an embarrassment," says Betts. "I don't think we could have dealt with that. The trouble is, we'd already been compared to ourselves a lot, and not always in a good way."

As it turned out, the timing was good: Numerous other older acts—including the Rolling Stones, the Who, the Jefferson Airplane, Ringo Starr and Paul McCartney—were hitting the road in 1989 with largely retrospective tours, and PolyGram was also preparing a multidisc historical overview of the Allmans for imminent release. For the first time in nearly a decade, the Allmans had a context to work in. Betts and Allman recruited some new members—guitarist Warren Haynes, bassist Allen Woody and keyboardist Johnny Neel—and the Allman Brothers Band was reborn. More important, they were once again a forceful live band, playing their hard-hitting brand of improvisational blues with the sort of vitality the band had not evinced since the early 1970s. "Once more, we were getting compared to ourselves," says Betts, "but this time in a positive way. The ideal, of course, would be to have all the original members of the band still alive and with us, but that can't be. But I'll say this: This is the first lineup we've had since Duane Allman and Berry Oakley were in the band that has the same spirit that we had in those days."

Butch Trucks—who can be the most paternal and also the saltiest-talking member of the band—puts it differently. "It feels like the Allman Brothers again," he says, "and it hasn't felt that way in a long, long time. I like it. It makes my sticker peck out."

Periodically, as Betts and Trucks talk, Gregg Allman tries to seem interested in the conversation. He will lean forward, clasp his hands together, look like he has something to say . . . but he never voluntarily fields a single question. After a bit, he settles back into the sofa and simply looks as if he's in his own world. He seems to spend a lot of time inside himself, staring into some private, inviolable space. In the entire conversation, he will say only one complete sentence: "It's hard to live those ten or twenty years, and then try to start all over again with another band."

Abruptly, Gregg is on his feet, excusing himself. He is scheduled to begin final vocals today, and he is restless to get started. When asked if it's okay to watch him record at some point, he visibly freezes. "Um, Gregg won't let *anybody* in there when he's singing," says Betts, coming to Allman's rescue. "Vocals are real personal, you know. You're just standing there naked."

"Yeah, with your dick hanging out," says Trucks. After Gregg leaves, Trucks adds: "I've never seen anybody so nervous about letting others listen."

There had been some concern about Gregg's vocals. Tom Dowd—the producer of the band's early classics, *At Fillmore East* and *Eat a Peach*, who is producing *Seven Turns*—was worried that he might not get workable performances from Allman and would have to paste the final vocals together from earlier rough tracks. Nobody knows at the moment whether Gregg can sing as well as they are hoping he will—indeed, any Allmans reunion effort would fall flat without Gregg's trademark growly vocals—and nobody's sure how Gregg's current unease bodes for the band's upcoming summer tour.

"It's hard to be sober again after all these years," says Trucks, who went through a drying-out period of his own. "At a time like this, Gregg probably doesn't even know if he can talk to people, much less sing. But the thing is, he did it for too many years *not* to go for it now."

Around midnight, a warm spring storm is dropping heavy sheets of rain all over North Miami. Drummer Jai Jaimoe (who was once known as Jai Johnny Johanson, but now prefers to be called simply Jaimoe) stands in the main hallway at Criteria Studios, unpacking a crate of new cymbals, caressing their nickel-plated gleam with obvious affection. He is wearing a pink-blue-and-green knitted African cap, bright green baggy pants and a knee-length black T-shirt bearing the statement, "The objects under this shirt are smaller than they appear."

Down the hall, Gregg Allman is taking passes at his vocal on "Good Clean Fun," and from what one can hear, he is sounding more confident, more vibrant, by the moment. A few feet away, Dickey Betts is strumming an acoustic guitar for some friends, singing "Seven Turns"—a haunting song he has written about the Allman Brothers' hard losses and renewed hopes. In the main lounge, Butch Trucks sits watching a golf tournament, trying to explain the Zen principle of the sport to his wife. Various Allman wives and girlfriends—including Gregg's new wife, Danielle—sit around talking or reading true-crime books, and Dickey's and Gregg's dogs wander in and out of the action, sniffing empty food cartons and looking perplexedly at the downpour outside. Also drifting in and out are producer Tom Dowd—who wears a perpetually rumpled professorial manner—and the legendary Allmans roadie Red Dog, a notorious but charming womanizer, a terrific dirty-joke teller and plainly the band's most devoted fan. It must seem a bit like old times here, only considerably more easygoing. "I missed playing with these people," Jaimoe will say at one point. "We had something together that I could never find with other bands."

Between storm bouts, Jaimoe suggests taking a walk across the parking lot to a nearby studio, where it will be possible to talk with less distraction. People in and around the Allmans will often joke about Jaimoe: They say that for over a generation, he has been perpetually reclusive, inscrutable, even spacey. But they also make awed references to the drummer's near-encyclopedic knowledge of jazz and rhythm & blues artists and styles, and certainly nobody can imagine attempting a reunion at this time without his involvement. In fact, it is often joked that Jaimoe was *the* original member of the Allman Brothers—or at least that he was the one who had always been waiting for a band like the Allmans to come along. "All my life I had wanted to play in a jazz band," says Jaimoe, settling into a sofa in an empty, dimly lighted studio control booth. "Then I played with Duane Allman."

Like Allman, Jaimoe had harbored a special passion for Southern-based musical styles. By the mid-1960s, he had served as a regular session drum-mer at the Fame Studio in Muscle Shoals, Alabama—where some of the most renowned Southern soul music of the period was recorded—and he had performed with numerous R&B and blues artists, including Percy Sledge, Otis Redding, Joe Tex and Clifton Chenier. "I think I had been preparing to play in this band without really knowing *what* I was preparing for," says Jaimoe, shifting his weight on the sofa. "I think it was from play-ing with all those other musicians that I got all that fiery stuff that people hear in my playing."

In the course of his studio work, Jaimoe met the two people who would become among the principal driving forces behind the Allman Brothers Band: Duane Allman and a fledgling entrepreneur named Phil Walden. Walden was born and raised in Macon, Georgia, a middle-sized town that still relied on agriculture for much of its economy and that still maintained much of its pre–Civil War architecture (General Sherman had considered the town too insignificant to plunder or ravage). In the 1950s, Walden had grown enamored of Memphis-style rock & roll and, in particular, the black R&B of singers like Hank Ballard and the Midnighters and the "5" Royales, and by the mid-1960s he was managing numerous black stars, including Sam and Dave, Percy Sledge, Al Green, Johnny Taylor, Joe Tex, Arthur Conley and, most famously, Otis Redding.

Walden's affection for black music was anathema to many of Macon's leading businessmen and church officials. Walden didn't present himself as a civil rights activist, but he *did* bristle at provincial racism, and he refused to kowtow to local pressures. The South, he often told his critics, would have to change its attitudes, and what's more, the popularity of the new Southern soul was a harbinger of that change. "I think rhythm & blues had a hell of a lot to do with turning the region around on race relations," he would later tell an interviewer. "When people get together and listen to the same music, it makes hating kind of harder."

But Walden's involvement in R&B was cut suddenly and brutally short. In December 1967, Otis Redding—a few months after his triumphant appearance at the Monterey International Pop Festival, and on the verge of a long-anticipated mass breakthrough—was flying a small twin-engine plane from Cleveland to Madison, Wisconsin, when the plane went down in a Wisconsin lake, killing Redding and four members of his backup band, the Bar-Kays. Walden was known as a proud, ambitious and clever man—even indomitable—but for him, Redding's death was more than the loss of a prize client, and more than the termination of one of the most brilliantly promising artistic careers of the period. It was also a devastating personal loss, and according to many of the people who knew him, Walden thereafter kept a greater emotional distance from his clients.

Duane Allman had also had his life transformed by sudden death. In 1949, when Duane was three and his little brother Gregory was two, the Allman family was living in Nashville, Tennessee. That Christmas, the boys' father, an army lieutenant, was on holiday leave from the Korean War. The day following Christmas, he picked up a hitchhiker, who robbed and murdered Duane and Gregg's father. The Allmans' mother, Geraldine, eventually enrolled her young children in a military academy in Lebanon, Tennessee, and then in 1958 relocated the family in Daytona Beach, Florida. As young teens, the Allman brothers rarely talked about their father's death—they were too young to know him well—and in many ways, they were like other boys their age: Duane hated school and quit it in a hot temper several times, then spent his free time attending to his favorite possession, a Harley-Davidson 165. Gregg, meantime, stuck through school and was reportedly a fair student and athlete, though he regarded it as a thankless ordeal.

Early on, both Duane and Gregg found themselves drawn to music of loss and longing—particularly the high-lonesome wail of country music and the haunted passions of urban and country blues. Gregg had been the first to leap in: He had listened to a neighbor playing old-timey country songs on an acoustic guitar, and at thirteen, he worked a paper route and saved money to buy a guitar at the local Sears and Roebuck. While Gregg was slogging his way through school, Duane started playing his brother's guitar—and to his surprise and Gregg's initial annoyance, discovered that he had a gift for the instrument. Soon, Duane and Gregg each owned electric guitars, and Duane would hole up with his instrument for days, learning the music of blues archetype Robert Johnson and jazz guitarist Kenny Burrell. Around that time, Duane and Gregg saw a B.B. King show during a visit to Nashville, and Duane's mind was made up: He and his brother were going to form a blues band of their own; in fact, they were going to make music their life. Duane continued studying numerous guitarists, including King, Muddy Waters, Howlin' Wolf's Hubert Sumlin, Elmore James and French jazz prodigy Django Reinhardt, as well as the emerging British rock guitarists—especially a young firebrand, Eric Clapton—and the guitarists who were playing for soul artists like James Brown and Jackie Wilson. Duane also began paying attention to saxophonists like John Coltrane, to hear how a soloist could build a melodic momentum that worked within a complex harmonic and rhythmic structure. Meantime, Gregg was listening to jazz organists like Jimmy Smith and Johnny Hammond, and developed a special passion for sophisticated blues and R&B vocalists like Bobby "Blue" Bland, Ray Charles and Roy Milton.

But there was more to the brothers' quest than a mere attraction for music that took painful feelings and turned them into a joyful release. The Allmans—in particular, Duane—seemed intent on forming bands as an extension of family ideals, and they often invested these bands with the same qualities of love and anger, loyalty and rivalry, that they had practiced at home. In a way, this family idealism was simply a trend of the era: The 1960s were a time when rock bands were often viewed as metaphors for a self-willed brand of consonant community. But in the Allmans' case, the sources of this dream may have run especially deep. Their real-life family had been shattered, and forming a band was a way of creating a fraternity they had never really known.

But the Allmans were also forming musical bonds in a time when the South was being forced to reexamine some of its cultural and racial traditions, and Duane and Gregg were unusually open to ideals of interaction and equality. To their mother's initial displeasure, the brothers preferred the music being played by local black talents, and in 1963, they helped form one of the area's first integrated bands, the House Rockers. It was a period of fierce feelings, but the Allmans, like Phil Walden, would not back off from a belief that their culture was starting to undergo radical and deeply needed social change.

In any event, Duane and Gregg went through a rapid succession of blues-oriented rock bands, including the Allman Joys, who toured the Southern teen circuit and recorded two albums' worth of material (including several Yardbirds and Cream covers). By 1967 the group had been overhauled into the Hour Glass and had relocated in Los Angeles, where they recorded two LPs for Liberty. Both were better-than-average cover bands, and they gave Duane a chance to hone his flair for accompaniment and improvisation and also helped Gregg develop as a sultry organist and an unusually inventive modern blues composer. But none of these groups matched Duane's boundless ambitions, and in 1968, after the Hour Glass split up, Duane accepted an invitation from Rick Hall, the owner of Fame Studios, to work as a sideman on a Wilson Pickett session. Duane left Gregg in LA to fulfill the Liberty contract, and in Muscle Shoals, Alabama, he played sessions with Pickett, Clarence Carter, King Curtis, Arthur Conley and Ronnie Hawkins; in New York, he played with Aretha Franklin. By 1969 Duane Allman had gained a reputation as one of the most musically eloquent and soul-sensitive session guitarists in contemporary music.

It was in this time that Jai Johanny Johanson met Allman. "I had a friend who was doing session work with Wilson Pickett and Aretha Franklin," says Jaimoe. "He came home to Macon one day and told me, 'Jai, they got a white boy down in Alabama by the name of Duane "Skydog" Allman. He's a hippie with long, stringy hair,' he said, 'but you've *got* to hear him play.' I remember listening to the radio late one night in Macon—there wasn't anything else to do there; everything was closed up—and this Aretha Franklin thing, 'The Weight,' came on the radio, with this standout guitar solo, and I thought, 'That's got to be "Skydog" Allman, man.' I thought he was a cool guitarist, but he wasn't any Barney Kessel or Tal Farlow, and those were the only Caucasian cats that I heard who could really play the instrument."

A bit later, Jaimoe visited Muscle Shoals during a King Curtis session and sought out Allman. The two musicians became close friends, and between sessions they would hang out in one of Fame's vacant studios, jamming for hours head-on. Then one day, another skinny longhaired white boy—a bassist named Berry Oakley, whom Duane had met in Jacksonville, Florida—started joining in on the jams. "Man," says Jaimoe, "when Berry joined us, that was some incredible shit. I remember that people like [bassist] David Hood, [pianist] Barry Beckett and [drummer] Roger Hawkins [all among Muscle Shoals' most respected session players] would come into the room when we were playing, and we were trying to get them to join in. But *none* of them would pick up an instrument. We scared the shit out of them guys."

Somewhere around this time Allman attracted the attention of Phil Walden, who was in the process of forming his own label, Capricorn

Records, to be distributed by Atlantic. One day Rick Hall played for Walden a new album he had just recorded with Wilson Pickett, including a cover of the Beatles' "Hey Jude." Walden was transfixed by the work of the guitarist on the session, and after traveling to Muscle Shoals, he eventually made a deal to manage Duane Allman. Walden thought he had found his Elvis Presley: a white musician who could play black, blues-based forms in a way that would connect with an entire new mass audience.

There had been talk of Allman, Jaimoe and Oakley forming a trio based on the sparse but furious improvisational dynamics of the Jimi Hendrix Experience or Cream, but Walden encouraged Allman to seek his own mix of style and texture. Allman knew he wanted to work with Jaimoe and Oakley, but he had also been drawn to a few other musicians, including lead guitarist Dickey Betts (who had played with Oakley in a band called the Second Coming, and with whom Allman had played several twin-lead jams), and drummer Butch Trucks (with whom Gregg and Duane had played in Jacksonville). One day these five musicians gathered at Trucks's home in Jacksonville and began playing. It turned into a relentless jam that stretched for four hours and left everybody involved feeling electrified, even thunderstruck. When it was over, Duane stepped to the entrance of the room and spanned his arms across the doorway, forming a human block-ade. "Anybody who isn't playing in my band is going to have to *fight* their way out of this room," he said.

Duane told Walden and Atlantic vice president Jerry Wexler that he wanted to bring his brother Gregg back from LA to sing in the newly formed group, but the company heads initially balked. Says Jaimoe: "I remember Duane saying, 'Man, Jerry and them, they . . . don't want no two brothers in the band. It's always been trouble. I mean, me and my brother, we don't get along that much—I don't like him. You know how it is: broth-ers don't like each other.' And then Duane would say, 'But Jaimoe, . . . I can't think of another motherfucker who can sing in this band *except* my brother. That's who I really want.'"

In the end, Duane Allman got his way—and it proved to be a brilliant choice. Gregg Allman had been lonely in Southern California, had endured a troubled love affair and had even, he would later report, contemplated suicide. When Duane called him to join his new band, Gregg saw the invi-tation as deliverance from a grim reality. And what he brought with him would amount to one of the band's signature attractions: a powerfully erotic, poignant and authoritative blues voice. When Gregg Allman sang a song like "Whipping Post," he did so in a voice that made you believe that the song's fear and pain and anger were the personal possessions of the singer—and that he had to reveal those dark emotions in order to get past the bitter truths he was singing about.

Phil Walden moved the band to Macon, and then put it on the road year-round. He and Duane didn't always see eye to eye on matters, weren't always close, but they agreed on one thing: The Allman Brothers Band was going to be both the best and the biggest band in the country.

Another day into the new 1990 sessions, Dickey Betts is seated on a worn sofa in the foyer at Criteria Studios. Down the hall, Gregg Allman is still working on his vocals, and it is apparent from his and Tom Dowd's improved moods that the work is going well.

Betts had stayed up late the night before, listening to a cassette of an Allman Brothers show from 1970 at Ludlow Garage in Cincinnati. Poly-Gram's Bill Levenson (who compiled the 1989 Allmans retrospective, *Dreams*) recently remastered the session for commercial release, and last night was the first time Betts had heard the performance in twenty years. "I knew if the quality was anywhere above being embarrassing, that it would be good," he says with a fast smile. Betts seems edgy—he gets up and moves around while he talks, and he is wary about how he phrases things—but behind that manner, he is amiable and honest, and he clearly possesses a remarkable breadth of intelligence. For many years now, he has been regarded as the real heart of the Allman Brothers Band, though he often tends to downplay his leadership role. Right now he seems to enjoy talking about the revolutionary music the band began making in its early days. "If I recall," he says, "Ludlow was like a dungeon: a cement floor, with a low ceiling, kind of like a warehouse garage. Real funky. As I remember, it was recorded around the time of our first album, way before we started getting anywhere. We were still underground at that point. We had a private, almost cultlike following."

The Allman Brothers may have been relatively "underground" in 1970, but they had already developed their mix of bedrock aggression and high-flown invention that would become their hallmark fusion. Like many bands of the time, the group was trying to summarize a wide range of rock, blues and jazz traditions and at the same time extend those traditions in new unanticipated directions. In contrast, though, to the Grateful Dead or Miles Davis (who both often played improvisatory blues in modal formats and freewheeling structure), the Allmans built tremendously sophisticated melodic formations that never lost sight of momentum or palpable eroticism. For one thing, the band was genuinely attuned to the emotional meanings of blues and the stylistic patterns of rock & roll—that is, group members not only found inspiration in the music of Muddy Waters, Howlin' Wolf and Robert Johnson, they also understood how that music's spirit had been extended and transmogrified in the later music of Chuck Berry, James Brown and other rock and soul pioneers. At the same time, the Allmans loved jazz and had spent many hours marveling not only at the prowess of musicians like Davis, Coltrane, Charlie Parker, Eric Dolphy and Roland Kirk, but also at how these visionaries had taken the same primitive blues impulses that had thrilled and terrified Robert Johnson and Louis Armstrong and turned them into an elaborate art form, capable of the most intricate, spontaneous inventions. Plus, there was an exceptional confluence that resulted from the Allmans' collective talents. In its straight-ahead blues mode, the band could barnstorm and burn with a fervor that even such white blues trendsetters as John Mayall's Bluesbreakers, Cream and the Rolling Stones were hard-pressed to match. And when the Allmans stretched their blues into full-scale, labyrinthine improvisations—in the largely instrumental "In Memory of Elizabeth Reed," "Whipping Post" and "Mountain Jam"—the band was simply matchless.

"Duane and Gregg were students of the urban blues," says Betts. "Their thing was like a real honest, truthful, chilling delivery of that music, whereas Oakley and I may have been influenced by the blues and were students of it, but we were more innovative. We would try to take a blues tune and, instead of respecting the sacredness of it, we would go *sideways* with it. But on our own, Berry and I were always missing something—a certain foundation—while Duane and Gregg didn't quite have the adventurous kind of thing. So when we all came together, we gave each other a new foundation."

It proved to be a unique amalgam, with Allman's and Betts's twin-lead guitars often locking into frenzied and intricate melodic flights, and Jaimoe's and Butch Trucks's double drumming forming a webwork of rhythm that both floated and pushed the drama of the guitars. "I was always real fond of the twin guitars that Roy Clark and Dave Lyle played in Wanda Jackson's band," says Betts. "But it wasn't that we consciously copied any of these sources. It was just that later we realized that people like Clark and Lyle, and Coltrane and Pharoah Sanders, had been pursuing the same idea many years before. For a rock & roll band, though, it was a pretty new adventure. I mean, one of the good things about the Allman Brothers, we listened to jazz and were influenced by it without ever pretending we were jazz players.

"But make no mistake: It was a matter of Duane being hip enough to see that potential and responding to it. He was absolutely in charge of that band. Had he missed that possibility or that chemistry, there would have been no Allman Brothers Band."

Betts also cites Berry Oakley as a key shaper of the Allmans' early sound. Certainly, Oakley was a singular bassist. Like such jazz hero–bassists as Oscar Pettiford, Jimmy Blanton, Ray Brown and Scott LaFaro, Oakley had a profound melodic sense that combined fluently with a pulsing percussive touch; and like the Dead's Phil Lesh or Jefferson Airplane's Jack Casady, he knew how to get under a band's action and lift and push its motions. "There were times," says Betts, "when Berry would be playing a line or phrase, and Duane would catch it, then jump on it and start playing harmony. Then maybe I'd lock into the melodic line that Duane was playing, and we would all three be off. That kind of thing was absolutely unheard of from a rock bassist. I mean, Berry would take over and *give us* the melody."

In fact, says Betts, it was Oakley who came up with the arrangement for "Whipping Post," the Allmans' most famous jam vehicle. "Oakley heard something in it that none of the rest of us heard—this *frightening* kind of thing. He sat up all night messing around and come back in the next day with a new opening in eleven/four time, and after that, ideas started flying from every direction. That sort of thing always happened with him."

By the end of 1970, the Allman Brothers had acquired a formidable reputation. They had recorded two critically praised LPs of blues rock, interlaced with classical- and country-derived elements, and Duane had gained pop renown for his contributions to Eric Clapton's Derek and the Dominos project, *Layla and Other Assorted Love Songs*. But it was as a live unit that the band enjoyed its greatest repute, and in the year or so ahead, they would play somewhere around two hundred concerts. In part to sustain their energy during the incessant and exhausting touring, and in part as a by-product of a time-old blues and jazz tradition (and a by-product of rock culture), various band members used an increasingly wide range of drugs—at first, primarily marijuana and occasional psychedelics and, in time, cocaine and heroin. It was a habit that bought the band some short-term potency, maybe even inspiration, but it would also eventually cost them their fraternity. Looking back, Betts has misgivings about the whole experience and its legacy. "The drugs that were being done back in the '60s and '70s," he says, "were a lot easier to have fun with and be open about, and to find acceptable, because they were drugs to enhance your awareness, instead of an escape into some blackness. I'm not saying those drugs had any redeeming qualities, but at least that was the idea that people had at the time: It was an effort to open the mind up and go even further.

"Today, though, the drugs are so damn deadly, so absolutely dangerous. There's nothing about them that's trying to enhance your awareness at all. The whole idea is to *kill* your awareness, to escape. It's just a perverted thing, and that's why I think that nowadays it's absolutely irresponsible and ignorant to sing in a positive way about doing drugs."

It was in this period that the Allman Brothers single-handedly pioneered a style and demeanor that would become popularly known as Southern rock: music that was aggressive yet could swing gracefully, played by musicians who were proud of their region and its musical legacies. Though later bands would reduce Southern rock to a reactionary posture and a crude parody of machismo, the Allmans began the movement as a blast of musical and cultural innovation. In fact, their outlooks and music were emblematic of the American South's ongoing struggle for redefinition, and of its mounting desire to move away from its violently earned image as a region of fierce racism and intolerance. But while the South of the early 1970s was less like the land of fear and murder that had destroyed the lives of so many blacks and civil rights activists, Betts acknowledges that the territory could still live up to its vulgar notoriety. "There were times," he says, "when you would go out for breakfast after you finish playing a club and just have to accept the chances of getting in a damn fistfight with somebody. But what are you gonna do: sneak home? I mean, you'd just go out and somebody starts calling you some kind of faggot or something about your long hair. I guess we *were* shocking in those days, and some of those damn cowboys are pretty quick to show their feelings. Now half of them have hair as long as mine. Also, there were a few times in some real ignorant little towns where we'd have trouble going into a restaurant with Jaimoe." Betts pauses and shakes his head with remembered exasperation. "Those were isolated incidents, but they stick out in my mind. I was horrified at that kind of thing.

"But you know, things just changed tremendously in the '70s, at least in Florida, Georgia, North Carolina and the other Southeastern states. The South just got new attitudes."

By the early 1970s, Macon—which had once been troubled by Phil Walden's championing of R&B music—regarded the Allmans as home-grown commercial and regional heroes. For that matter, nearly all the acts that Walden signed to Capricorn had strong Southern identities, and some observers believed it was Walden's aspiration to build a personal and political empire, based on the ideal that "the South will rise again." Betts, though, disavows this ambition. "We had *nothing* to do with that whole ideal, 'the South will rise again,'" he says. "That was somebody else's idea. The thing is, we *did* appreciate our culture, and a lot of people in the South were proud of the Allman Brothers, because we were typically and obviously Southern. That was part of our aura. But beyond that, I don't think we were part of what was changing the South. It was people like Jimmy Carter and Martin Luther King Jr. and John Kennedy who helped affect Southern attitudes. We were just a good thing for some people to identify with, and obviously, we influenced the music from the South a great deal. A lot of musicians thought, 'Hey, they're speaking for or representing the way *I* feel'—and that was a cool thing."

It was a heady time. In 1971 the Allmans toured the country relentlessly, and in March they recorded two of their three performances at Bill Graham's Fillmore East in New York, for a two-record set, *At Fillmore East*— still widely regarded as the finest live recording that rock & roll has ever produced. In its August 1971 review of the album, *Rolling Stone* described the Allmans as "one of the nicest things that ever happened to any of us," and as the band's popularity grew, the rock mainstream seemed finally ready to share this estimation. In concert, the Allmans earned every inch of their adulation. Night after night, Duane Allman would stand center stage, and bouncing lightly on his heels, he would begin constructing meditative, rhapsodic solos that ended up going places that rock had never gone before. An unschooled musician, Allman thought in perfectly formed complete lines that had all the grace and dynamics of a carefully considered composition. He was perhaps the most melodically inventive and expressive instrumentalist that rock would ever witness.

But on October 29, 1971, as the band was at its creative peak and was recording a new work that promised to be both a commercial and a creative leap forward, bad news made its first fateful visit to the Allmans. That afternoon, Duane had visited the band's "Big House" in Macon to wish Berry Oakley's wife a happy birthday, then mounted his motorcycle to head back to his own home. Some have speculated that Duane was overtired from relentless touring and was less attentive to his driving than usual. In any event, in the early evening darkness of a Southern night, Duane swerved his bike to avoid a truck that had turned in front of him. His cycle skidded, pinning Allman underneath and dragging him fifty feet. Duane's girlfriend and Oakley's sister had been following in a car and stayed with Duane until an ambulance arrived. After three hours of emergency surgery, he died at Macon Medical Center. He was twenty-four years old. Like the young deaths of Charlie Parker, Hank Williams, Patsy Cline, Buddy Holly, Sam Cooke, John Coltrane, Otis Redding, Jimi Hendrix and Janis Joplin, the loss of Duane Allman was the loss of a tremendous musical promise. There would be bright days to come for the Allmans, but the band had been stripped of its creative center and emotional driving force.

"We *knew* what we had lost," says Betts. "We even thought seriously about not going out and playing anymore. Then we thought, 'Well, what can we do better? We'll just do it with the five of us.' We had already risen to great heights by that point. But Duane didn't experience the highest point—he didn't experience being accepted across the board." Betts pauses for a long moment, and his intense eyes seem to be reading distant memories. It's as if, after all these years, he can still sense deeply all the potential joy and invention that were obliterated on that day.

A few minutes later, Gregg Allman walks in, smiling. "We got it," he tells Betts, with obvious pleasure. Betts rushes off to the control booth, where Dowd plays back the finished vocal. After a few bars of Gregg singing with an uncommon ferocity about a man who just wants to feel some hard-earned pleasures before life cheats him again, Betts's face lights up in a proud and relieved grin. Later, in a private moment, Betts corners Allman in the hallway and slugs him affectionately in the shoulder. "That was some good work," he says. Gregg blushes and the two trade a look that speaks volumes. For all the disappointments they have shared, and all the anger that has passed between them, Dickey Betts and Gregg Allman are still brothers of the closest sort.

Early in the evening, as another storm seems to be closing in, Butch Trucks is conducting an impromptu tour of Criteria Studios. He is looking for some of Tom Dowd's most prized trophies—the gold records he earned for engineering and producing countless legendary acts, including Wilson Pickett and Aretha Franklin—when, in one of the older studios, he stumbles across an ebony-colored grand piano. "That's the 'Layla' piano," he says, referring to the instrument on which Jim Gordon played pop's most famous and rapturous coda. It is impossible to resist touching its still-shining white and black keys. It is not unlike touching something sacrosanct. Clearly, this is a room where essential modern cultural history was made—where American and British rock & roll met for its finest and most enduring collaboration.

Trucks settles into a nearby chair and begins to recount the story of the *Layla* sessions. Clapton had come to Miami to record with the Dominos (pianist Bobby Whitlock, drummer Jim Gordon and bassist Carl Radle). Producer Tom Dowd, who had worked with the Allmans on *Idlewild South* and *At Fillmore East,* mentioned the visit to Duane Allman, a longtime Clapton fan, who asked if he could come by some night and watch the recording. During one of the Dominos rehearsals, Dowd relayed the request to Clapton, who replied, "Man, if you *ever* know where Duane Allman is playing, let me know." A couple of days later, the Allmans were performing in Miami Beach, and Dowd took the Dominos to the show. Later that night, back at Criteria, the bands started jamming, and Clapton invited Allman to play twin lead on the sessions. Together, Clapton and Allman found an empathy they had never experienced with any other players and that they would never match. They played probing, deeply felt interweaving melodic lines like two strangers earnestly striving to discover and match each other's depths—which turned out to be an ideal musical metaphor for the sense of romantic torment that Clapton wished to convey with *Layla.*

On another night, Trucks says, Clapton invited the Allmans in for an all-night jam with the Dominos. "I don't remember how good we were," says Trucks, "but it was fun. It sure would be great to hear that music again.

"After we finished that jam," he continues, "Eric and Duane were playing the song 'Layla' back for us, and all of a sudden Duane said, 'Let me try something.' And he put on his guitar and came up with that five-note pattern that actually announces the song (a rephrasing of an Albert King riff)—that signature phrase that just kind of set that song on fire." Trucks pauses and shakes his head. Perhaps he realizes that he is sharing a remarkable disclosure: The most revelatory riff of Eric Clapton's career was actually one of Duane Allman's inspired throwaway lines.

Trucks is surprised to learn that archivist Bill Levenson has recently dug up the Dominos-Allmans session and plans to edit and master it for release in a *Layla* retrospective package. Trucks seems intrigued at the prospects, but he also admits that perhaps some experiences are better left to memory. "I remember one night that was the epitome of this band," he says. "It was during the closing of Fillmore East, but it wasn't the closing night, which was the one we recorded for *Eat a Peach.* Instead, it was the night *before.* We went on for the late show, about one a.m., and played a normal three-and-a-half-hour set, and when we came back for the encore, the feeling we got from the crowd . . . it was something I'll never forget. I remember sitting there with tears, just really emotional, and then we started jamming, about four in the morning, and we quit about eight o'clock. It was just one jam that went on and on, one thing leading to another, and it was magic.

"All together, we ended up playing seven or eight hours, and when we finished playing, there was no applause. The place was packed, nobody had left, but not even one person clapped. They didn't need to. Somebody got up and opened the doors and the sun came in, and this New York crowd, they just got up and quietly walked out while we were all sitting up there onstage. My mouth's hanging open, and I remember Duane walking in front of me, just dragging his guitar behind him, his head down, shaking it, and he says, 'Goddamn, it's like leaving church.' To me, that's what music is all about. You *try* to reach that level. If you're lucky, you might get there once or twice. That night—maybe the greatest night of our life—*wasn't* recorded, and in an odd way, I'm glad."

Like Betts, Trucks says the loss of Duane Allman was insurmountable. "On just about any level you can think of, it was devastating. What kept us going was the bond that forms when you have to deal with that kind of grief. Also, we did it for his sake as much as ours. We had just gone too far, and hit so many new plateaus in what we were doing, to simply quit.

"The funny thing is, when Duane came back from King Curtis's funeral [the R&B saxophonist—one of Allman's favorite musicians—had been stabbed to death in New York in August 1971], he was thinking a lot about death, and he said many times, 'If anything ever happens to me, you guys better keep it going. Put me in a pine box, throw me in the river and jam for two or three days.' We tried taking six months off after his death, but we were all just getting too crazy from it. There wasn't any other way to deal with it but to play again. But the hardest thing was just that he wasn't there, you know? This guy was *always* right there in front of me—all I did was look over and there he was—and he wasn't there anymore."

But the band paid hard costs for its determination. Gregg Allman would later say he began his long bouts of drug and alcohol addiction in the months after Duane's death. In addition, bassist Berry Oakley began having serious difficulties. In some ways, the mantle of leadership passed to Oakley, but according to many observers, he was too grief-stricken over Duane's death to accommodate the demands. Then, in November 1972, Oakley was riding his motorcycle through Macon when he lost control and slammed into a city bus. The accident occurred just three blocks from where Duane had been fatally injured a year and two weeks earlier. Like Allman, Oakley was twenty-four. And like Allman, he was buried in Macon's Rose Hill Cemetery.

"As much as Duane, Berry was responsible for what this band had become," says Trucks. "But in some ways, you could see Berry's death coming. With Duane, man, it was just a shot out of the blue. But Berry . . . he just couldn't cope with Duane being gone, and he got very self-destructive. There were nights when you wouldn't even know if he would be capable of playing. More than once, he would just fall off the stage. By the time Berry died, it was almost a relief just to see the suffering end. It was devastating, but it was expected. We could see it coming.

"That might sound cold or whatever, but by then another direction was coming."

In some ways, it was a more fruitful direction. The Allmans had recruited a second keyboardist, Chuck Leavell, and after Oakley's death, they added a new bassist, Lamar Williams, who had played around Macon with Jaimoe years before. In 1973 the band released its long-anticipated fifth album, *Brothers and Sisters*; within weeks it went to Number One and spawned the group's first Top Ten single, Dickey Betts's countrified "Ramblin' Man." At long last, the Allman Brothers Band had become the dominant success that Duane Allman and Phil Walden had dreamed it would become; indeed, as much as any other act, the Allmans defined the American mainstream in the decade's early years. At the same time, no central guiding vision or consensus had emerged to replace Duane's sensibility. In time, there were reports that Chuck Leavell wanted to lead the band on a more progressive, fusion-jazz-oriented course, but that Betts felt the group was drifting too far afield from its original blues and rock & roll roots. Also, a somewhat uneasy spirit of competition was developing between Betts and Gregg Allman. Both had released solo LPs and had formed their own bands (Allman's included Jaimoe, Williams and Leavell), and gradually, Gregg was becoming the most identifiable celebrity in the group. In part, this was due to his stellar romance with (and turbulent marriage to) superstar Cher, as well as his widely rumored drug appetites. But Gregg's fame was also based on something more morbid: He was a survivor in a band that seemed both brilliant and damned, and many watched him with a certain fatalistic curiosity.

"By this time, the initial spark was gone," says Trucks. Outside, the flash storm is hitting hard. A raging rain slashes against the windows around the room. "We were getting a lot more predictable and were cashing in, and we did more and more of that as the years went on—to the point where it just finally got ridiculous, where even *we* could see it through our drunken stupor."

Even the band's biggest moment—when the Allmans appeared at

Watkins Glen, New York, with the Grateful Dead and the Band, for an audience of six hundred thousand, the largest crowd ever assembled in America—was a hollow and somewhat bitter experience. "We just gave the people what they expected," says Betts. "Also, it was not a time for making friends. I remember that Jerry Garcia came out onstage with us and took over. There was no *doubt* he was going to dominate: He'd step right on top of Dickey's playing. Then he made the mistake of playing 'Johnny B. Goode,' and Dickey just *fried* his ass, and we left." Trucks laughs at the memory, then looks saddened. "They never seemed to like us, the Grateful Dead, and they had been gods to us at one time. But everything was so on edge in those days, and like us, they were really in a certain eye of the storm. They were playing for huge audiences and were trying to sell lots of records and they had also lost a couple members of their band, so they were probably feeling a lot of the same doubts."

Trucks pauses and watches the rain for a moment. "The lifestyle we were going through," he says with open distaste. "It was just insane, fucking rockstar ridiculousness. Also, we had quit living together, which I think really had a lot to do with our demise. Everybody would get their own limousines and their own suites, and we'd see each other onstage, and that was it. And, God, the cocaine was *pouring*. You would go backstage and there would be a line of thirty dealers waiting outside. We were drifting further and further apart, until the last couple of years were just pure bullshit. Actually, to me they were just a blank. I was drunk twenty-four hours a day."

Then, almost simultaneously, the Allmans achieved their proudest success and their greatest downfall. By 1975 Phil Walden was taking a hand in Georgia politics. He had met and struck up a friendship with Governor Jimmy Carter a couple years before, and Walden was among the first to know of Carter's plan to seek the presidency. In the fall of 1975, when Carter's campaign was almost bankrupt, Walden began organizing benefit concerts featuring numerous Capricorn acts, including the Allman Brothers—Carter's favorite American band. In the end, with Walden's help and federal matching funds, Carter had raised over $800,000; without Walden's and the Allmans' support, it is unlikely that Carter would have survived the expensive primary campaigns long enough to win the Democratic Party's 1976 nomination.

But at the same time, the Allmans' cavalier attitude toward drug use caught up with the band. In early 1976 a federal narcotics force began investigating drug activities in Macon. In a short time, Gregg Allman found himself threatened with a grand jury indictment unless he testified against his personal bodyguard, John "Scooter" Herring, who had been charged with dealing drugs. Allman complied, and Herring was sentenced to seventy-five years in prison. The band members were furious. They felt that Gregg had dishonored the group's sense of fraternity. "There is no way we can work with Gregg again ever," said Betts at the time—and his sentiment was reportedly shared by every other member of the band. In effect, Gregg Allman had killed off the Allman Brothers Band. The various members went on to other projects. Betts formed Great Southern; Leavell, Williams and Jaimoe played in Sea Level; and Gregg moved to Los Angeles, where he recorded with Cher and suffered a difficult marriage in exile.

It took a couple of years, but the wounds healed. Betts now says: "Six months later I read the court transcripts and said, 'Goddamn, this guy had his ass between a rock and a hard place.' Actually, I think we had all been set up by a Republican administration that was trying to discredit Jimmy Carter through his connection with Phil Walden and us."

In the interim, the band members found they had missed playing together—that they couldn't achieve with other bands what they had found together and couldn't win the success separately they had enjoyed collectively. In 1978 they regrouped; Leavell and Williams opted out for Sea Level, and the band added guitarist Dan Toler and bassist Rook Goldflies. The band made one successful record, *Enlightened Rogues,* but then quit Capricorn, filing suit against Walden for unpaid royalties. Shortly, Capricorn went bankrupt; Phil Walden's great Southern rock empire had collapsed.

The Allmans moved to Arista and made two misconceived records, *Reach for the Sky* and *Brothers of the Road,* but at decade's end, the great pop wars of disco and punk were raging, and there was no longer an embracing receptivity for Southern rock. "If we had found an audience that was ready to listen," says Trucks, "we would have kept going. But the yuppies wanted to get as far away from sex, drugs and rock & roll as they could get. Wanted to raise their families and pretend like it never happened. Our generation was denying its history. Well, all good things come to an end."

In 1982 the Allmans disbanded a second time. The group members occasionally toured in pairings or collected for a jam, but they were playing music that seemed to have outlived its historical moment. And there were further bad ends: In 1979 Twiggs Lyndon—who was the Allmans' first road manager and favorite roadie; who had once stabbed to death a club manager because he tried to cheat the band; who had gone to prison and undergone tremendous remorse—was skydiving over a New York town named Duanesburg and failed to pull his rip cord; he was dead before he hit the ground. In 1983 Lamar Williams died of cancer. The greatest American band of the 1970s was no more; it was itself merely another ghost in a memory-skein of ghosts, knitted together by the bonds of dark remembrances and lost dreams.

There remains one subject that people in the Allman camp aren't always anxious to speak about, and that is the matter of Gregg Allman—the troubled singer who still bears the band's deepest debts and highest expectations. "It's almost unfair that we're called the Allman Brothers Band," says Trucks, "because people just zone in on that blond singer: the last Allman. It puts a lot more pressure on him than needs to be there. At the same time, he puts the pressure on himself. He's messed up plenty, and he knows it. He's doing everything he can to rectify it, but it's a heavy burden. And like anybody that has his problems, it's a day-to-day procedure, but we're all here with him.

"Anyway, one thing's for sure: You couldn't do the Allman Brothers without him. We've lost too many of us already."

Indeed, Gregg is at once the most problematic and essential member of the band. His drug, alcohol and temperament problems have caused both him and the band famous grief, and he has suffered lapses recent enough to have made some people in and around the band wonder if this reunion can truly last. And yet, as Trucks notes, the group cannot do without him: Gregg Allman is more than the band's most visible namesake; he also has the band's voice. Dickey Betts, Johnny Neel and Warren Haynes can write the blues, and along with Trucks and Jaimoe, they can still play it better than any other rock band in the world. But Gregg genuinely *sings* the blues. It is not an easy talent, nor can it be faked. Unfortunately, it is also a talent that, to be rendered at its most effective, has too often involved the physical, moral, emotional and spiritual ruin of those who practice it. Living the blues may sound like the hoariest cliché in the rock world, but it is also true that really *living* the blues can cost you everything—and Gregg Allman has lived the blues, as much as any singer alive.

The trick is getting Gregg to *talk* about the blues he has lived. Actually, the trick is getting Gregg to talk about much of anything. He doesn't open up much to outsiders, and he even seems reticent with the friends and musicians who have known him for a generation or more. In particular, though, he is wary with members of the press—and for fair reason: It must not have been much fun to find his marital and drug problems plastered across the front pages of sensationalist tabloids for years on end. Also, he has gone on record at length about his brother's death (it almost drove him crazy), the Scooter Herring incident (it terrified and humiliated him) and his troubles with Cher (which confused and angered him), and chances are, he may not yet truly understand just *why* he has had so many recurring drug and alcohol problems. Or perhaps he understands perfectly well and wouldn't dream of explaining it.

What *would* be interesting to know, however, is how Allman's relationship to music has sustained him—and whether its siren's call has hurt him more than it ever healed him. But in Miami, he isn't of a mind to talk. He stays busy finishing the vocals for *Seven Turns*, and he doesn't spend his voice on gratuitous conversation with anybody. And late at night—a time when, it has been suggested, Gregg may be more inclined to talk—Gregg is nowhere to be found.

One weekend a few weeks later, though, Gregg is playing a blues festival and civil rights benefit in Jackson, Mississippi. *Seven Turns* is now finished, and reportedly Gregg is as ready as he will ever be for an interview. Also, Gregg's personal manager, Dave Lorry, wants the singer to get used to playing some live shows before the Allmans' summer tour begins. Apparently, Gregg can still be nervous about performing live, and this anxiety is part of what has contributed to his difficulties with drugs and alcohol in the past. For his part, Gregg is playing the festival because two of his old blues friends, B.B. King and Bobby "Blue" Bland, are on the bill; in addition, Little Milton is scheduled to appear. Little Milton is Gregg Allman's favorite singer—a model for his own passionate style—but in a quarter century of following blues, Allman has never seen Milton sing live, nor has he met him. He says he is looking forward to the chance and is especially anxious to play a late-night jam that will feature himself, King, Bland and Milton.

The blues festival is being held in a big open-air metallic structure at a fairgrounds on the edge of town. Like Miami, Jackson is subject to sudden storms, and just before Gregg's van arrives at the site, a late-spring torrent has turned the surrounding area to mud. Looking for a dry place for the interview, Dave Lorry talks Bobby Bland into accommodating some visitors on his homelike bus.

Seated in the bus's central room, with his wife Danielle nearby, Gregg isn't much more talkative than he was in Miami. It isn't that he's unfriendly, nor is he unintelligent; it's more like he's shy or wary or simply exhausted from twenty years of inquiries. He doesn't really have much to say about *Seven Turns* ("It's a good record; I'm proud of it") or even about working with the

Allmans again ("They're a fine band; I'm proud to work with them"). Even when he's talking, Gregg seems to be living someplace inside himself. He gets in and out of answers as quickly and simply as he can. Music is something he plays and sings rather than talks about, and his life, he makes plain, is off limits. "The private facts of my life are just as private and painful as anybody's," he says in his most direct moment. "I don't enjoy going over that stuff all the time."

After a few minutes, Bland comes back to visit with Allman. It is a heartening experience to meet Bobby Bland, to watch and hear him speak. He is probably blues music's finest living singer—a vocalist as sensual and pain-filled as Frank Sinatra. In addition, he has a transfixing face: big, open, warm, impossibly beautiful and animated. It is a gracious face and he is a gracious man. If there were any justice, Bobby Bland's image would be celebrated on postage stamps, his bus would be full of Grammys, and he would have the pop audience he has always deserved.

When Bland takes a seat across from Gregg, Allman's entire manner changes. He relaxes visibly, puts his feet up on a nearby bench, sinks back into the sofa and even allows himself a few unguarded smiles. Clearly, these two men like and respect each other. They start by talking about watching the Rolling Stones' recent live TV broadcast, but it is not Mick Jagger or Keith Richards or even guest guitarist Eric Clapton that they gossip about. What engaged their interest and humor was the appearance of quintessential boogie bluesman John Lee Hooker onstage with the Stones and Clapton.

Allman laughs as he recalls the times he has seen Hooker on the blues circuit. "He always has these two big white women with him, both of 'em taller than he is," says Allman, smiling.

"Yeah," says Bland, "John Lee is crazy about them white women." His face opens up into a gentle leer, and he and Allman share a knowing laugh.

Bland regards Gregg warmly for a moment, then says, "I just wanted to see you were okay. You know, taking care of yourself." He levels an inquiring look at Gregg.

Gregg Allman returns the look and then blushes. "Yeah, man," he says, "B.B. King gave me the same once-over last night."

Bland smiles without embarrassment. "Well, we're just checking on you," he says with paternal warmth. "Letting you know we care."

For whatever their differences in age, temperament or cultural and racial background, these two men are colleagues. Bland regards Allman as a fellow traveler on the inescapable blues road. He knows the life Allman has lived. He knows its hopes, and he knows its ends.

Bland also knows it's time to let his family come aboard the bus and get out of the pouring rain. This means, for the moment, the interview is over—after maybe ten minutes. Gregg can't help looking a bit relieved. "We'll talk later," he says. "Right now I'd like to stay and talk with Bobby a little while."

Actually, as it turns out, the interview is over for good. Later, Allman simply disappears again. One moment he and Danielle are seated at the side of the stage, watching Bland's elegant blues act, and then he is nowhere to be found. He will not be there when the evening's blues-superstar jam transpires, nor will he meet or hear his idol, Little Milton. When those events take place, Gregg is someplace else—maybe in a darkened motel room, watching TV, brooding.

But midway through the afternoon, he is true to his vocation and takes the stage in Jackson, with the rudimentary blues band that backs Wolfman Jack. This isn't the Allman Brothers, but Gregg remains that band's spirit, and as he sits behind a Hammond organ, he sings Blind Willie McTell's "Statesboro Blues," Muddy Waters's "Trouble No More" and Sonny Boy Williamson's "One Way Out," not as if they were tired songs that he has sung for a generation, but as if they were bitter facts that he was just facing in his life. *This* is not the man who seemed skittish back in Miami, nor is he the relaxed crony who shared ribald laughs with Bobby Bland earlier. No, it is a different man altogether who sits on this stage, before maybe five hundred people, and closing his eyes tight and tilting his head back until his blond hair grazes his shoulders, sings as if his soul depended on it. *This* man is a blues singer—he sings the music as if it were his birthright, and as if it offers the only moments in which he can work out the mysteries of his life and his confusion. Gregg Allman shuts his eyes very, very tight and sings like a man who understands that every time he sings, he is singing to ghosts. Maybe he's trying to make his peace with those ghosts, or maybe he's just trying to haunt them as much as they have haunted him.

THE LONG SHADOW
OF LED ZEPPELIN

And as we go on down the road,
Our shadows taller than our souls . . .
—Robert Plant,
"Stairway to Heaven"

There is no other story in rock & roll like the story of Led Zeppelin because the story is an argument—about music, who makes it, who hears it and who judges its meanings. Mainly, though, it's an argument about the work, merits and life of a band that has been both treasured and scorned now for nearly forty years. The arguments started as soon as the band did, rooted in a conviction that Led Zeppelin represented a new world, a new age—a rift between the hard-fought values of the 1960s and the real-life pleasures and recklessness of the 1970s. Either the band was taking us forward or taking us under, illuminating the times or darkening them. Part of what makes their story such an intrigue is that those in the band weren't always sure themselves where everything was headed; things moved big and moved fast, and nothing simple happened. When everything was done, good and bad, the music withstood it all. Led Zeppelin—talented, complex, grasping, beautiful and dangerous—made one of the most enduring bodies of composition and performance in twentieth-century music, despite everything they had to overpower, including themselves.

Hearing that music now, you have to wonder: How could anybody have missed this? How could Led Zeppelin have split opinions more than anybody else in popular music? You listen to the songs, the arrangements, the imperative riffs, the unforgiving humor, the solid momentum—not to mention the heart and mind underpinning the sound—and it's clear that this is music that had as much right to lay claim on its times as the music of the Beatles or Motown or Bob Dylan. But it's also true that the music of Led Zeppelin was in a way scarier, a herald of a different kind of severe change.

It was, in fact, genuinely radical. You listen to the live recordings on *How the West Was Won,* from 1972 performances, and that music races and breathes, changes shape, direction and mood, falls down and springs back up in constant cross-motions, forming something as abstract, uncompromising and visionary—and as much its own language—as the most farsighted music of John Coltrane from a few years before, or as abstruse and merciless as the electric music that Miles Davis was making at the same time.

Led Zeppelin was playing for new ears, and three and a half decades later, their music still plays the same way. Those sounds rushed through us and ahead of us, into territory that seemed to have no ending.

Led Zeppelin would come to epitomize the 1970s as nothing else ever has, but their ingenuity and ambition was deeply rooted in the changes of earlier decades. Jimmy Page was drawn to guitar in the 1950s by Lonnie Donegan's skiffle sounds and Elvis Presley's sexualized rockabilly, and by the 1960s he was a major player in the London pop scene. He made a reputation playing on sessions for the Kinks, the Who, Them, the Pretty Things, Herman's Hermits and Donovan, among many others. In 1966 Page joined Jeff Beck in the Yardbirds, an experimental, improvisation-based blues band that had a string of innovative pop hits including "Shapes of Things" and "Over Under Sideways Down" to their credit. But the band was already fraying from Beck's dark-cloud temperament, and by mid-1968 all the members had abandoned the group. Page, with the help of the group's manager at the time, Peter Grant, assumed the rights to the band's name and set out to find new members to continue with. When John Paul Jones, a respected arranger and bassist who had worked with Page on Donovan's "Sunshine Superman," heard about the new band, he called Page to say he was eager to join. Page told Jones he would be back in touch soon; first, there was a singer he had to see. Page was looking for a vocalist who was commanding, versatile and undaunted—who could interact spontaneously with guitar improvisations. He had thought about a couple of singers, Steve Marriott, formerly of Small Faces, and Terry Reid, but they weren't available. The day after Jones's call, Page and Grant went to hear Robert Plant, whom Terry Reid had recommended.

Plant was from an industrial area known as the Black Country, in England's Midlands. Like Page, he had been drawn to rock & roll by the popularity of Elvis Presley, though Plant had a special affinity for American country blues singers, such as Skip James, Bukka White and Memphis Minnie. He also had a thing about *Lord of the Rings,* which was reflected by the name of the band he was singing in, Hobbstweedle, when Page first heard him performing at a teacher's college in Birmingham. When he heard Plant sing a version of Jefferson Airplane's "Somebody to Love" on that occasion, in what Page later described as a "primeval wail," the guitarist said it unsettled him. It was exactly the voice he wanted. "I just could not understand why," Page said, "when he told me he'd been singing for a few years already, he hadn't become a big name yet." Page and Plant met at the guitarist's houseboat on the Thames and discussed their tastes. Page played a track recorded by Joan Baez, "Babe I'm Gonna Leave You," and explained that he wanted to find a way to play a song like that in a new context, one that would bring alive both the darkness and the lightness of the material and heighten those contrasts. Plant found the idea odd enough to win his involvement. "We were dealing from the same pack of cards," Plant said in 2005. "You can smell when people . . . had their doors opened a little wider than most, and you could feel that was the deal with Jimmy. His ability to absorb things and the way he carried himself was far more cerebral than anything I'd come across before, and I was so very impressed."

Plant recommended John Bonham, a drummer he had worked with in an earlier band. Bonham admired soul and Motown drummers and the innovations of jazz musician Gene Krupa. But it was Cream's Ginger Baker, Bonham thought, who changed modern possibilities. Baker, Bonham said, "was the first to come out with this 'new' attitude—that a drummer could be a forward musician in a rock band, and not something that was stuck in the background and forgotten about." Bonham was nobody to remain in the background. He had a crushing attack and had been tossed from clubs for playing too loud. A producer had once told him that his sound was just too big to be recorded. Page later said that when he first heard Bonham, he decided what his band would sound like. "This could be a breakthrough band," Page told Bonham. Jimmy Page, John Paul Jones, Robert Plant and John Bonham met together for the first time in a room below a record store in London. Page suggested that they try "Train Kept a-Rollin'," a rockabilly song popularized by Johnny Burnette that had been given new life by the Yardbirds. Everybody there that day told the same story every time they were asked about it: It was like an eruption—they had their sound and groove in that first song. "As soon as I heard John Bonham play," John Paul Jones told Bonham's biographer, Chris Welch, "I knew this was going to be great—somebody who knows what he's doing and swings like a bastard. We locked together as a team immediately." Robert Plant has said that was the moment that he found the potential of what he could do with his voice, and he has also claimed that it was the moment that defined the band: "Even though we were all steeped in blues and R&B, we found in that first hour and a half that we had our own identity."

Days after that first meeting, Page took the New Yardbirds to Copenhagen and Stockholm for some shows, playing cover songs and some of his new material. Page understood right away that working any longer with the Yardbirds moniker would prove a liability; that band had been seen as troubled and depleted by its end, and there was no life left to its image. Page settled on a new name, from a remark that the Who's drummer, Keith Moon, had made during a moment when Page, Beck, Moon and Who bassist John Entwistle had all flirted with the idea of forming a group. "It would probably go over like a lead zeppelin," Moon joked. The phrase stayed with Page; it afforded a further example of contrasts between hard and light things. Peter Grant, who would now be the manager of this new band, decided to remove the letter *a* from *lead*; he was worried that the word might be mispronounced as "leed."

When the band returned from their tour to London in October 1968, Page took Led Zeppelin into Olympic Studios with engineer Glyn Johns (who also worked with the Beatles, the Rolling Stones and the Who). Page simply wanted the sound forged in those early live shows; he didn't want anything that couldn't be reproduced live effectively with just the four of them. Even the aural effects that he brought into a track like "Dazed and Confused" were sounds that could be rendered live without excess gimmickry. Part of the astonishing presence and depth of those recordings— which had more resonance than anything else from that time and which still feel fresh—came from the way he placed speakers and amplifiers in the room, to get varying sounds of vibrancy and decay. "Distance is depth," Page told Johns. It was an idea as old as the sounds of the Sun and Chess blues and early rock & roll recordings, and yet in Page's hands it became something refreshingly extreme.

The group members spent roughly thirty hours of studio time making their first album. They knew they had something singular. The band played three nights at London's essential Marquee venue, to largely good reviews— and then the easy times stopped. In November Peter Grant visited New York, where he won the band a contract with New York–based Atlantic Records—the label of John Coltrane and Ornette Coleman, and the parent label of Atco, which brandished Cream, Vanilla Fudge and Iron Butterfly on its roster. Atlantic paid the band a $200,000 advance from Atlantic

Records—an unprecedented amount at that time for a new act whose first album nobody had yet heard. Even more important, though, was the contract terms that Grant secured: Essentially, Led Zeppelin held all the control. They alone would decide when they would release albums and tour, and they had final determination over the contents and design of each album. They also would decide how much they would do to promote each release (not that much beyond tours, though those would be extensive) and which tracks to select as singles (Grant and the band wanted none). It was a significant accomplishment: A major band would be working for itself, not for a company or for management (Led Zeppelin had no contract with Grant). It wasn't the same as seizing the means of production, but it did amount to control of what the production would be and how and when it would happen. Said Page: "I wanted artistic control in a vice grip, because I knew exactly what I wanted to do with these fellows."

However, the Atlantic deal created an image and a problem for Led Zeppelin that, in a real sense, the band never got past. The political sensibilities that had emerged in the mix of the counterculture, the active underground press and the new rock culture held a great deal of mistrust and contempt for power and wealth—especially in a flagrant display by those aligned with the counterculture. The band's large advance and the advantage of their contract cast them as mercenaries in the view of many critics. Even though they were an essentially unknown quantity, Led Zeppelin was being termed a "hype."

All of this took place before anybody had heard Led Zeppelin's first album. Once that changed, it was love or hate, and little in between.

The Atlantic deal had rubbed enough tastemakers in the British scene the wrong way that Peter Grant couldn't get the sort of venue bookings that he wanted in England. The band played a few dates at London's Marquee, but there were complaints they were too loud. Grant decided to send the band to America for some dates instead—though this was possibly his intent all along. "By the time I got Zeppelin," Grant said, "I knew America inside out." Grant told Richard Cole—who had been the Yardbirds tour manager in the United States—to guide the band through its American dates. Cole was a hard drinker and a hard guy, who had also been a road manager for the Who. Cole met the band in Los Angeles on December 23, 1968, booked them into the Chateau Marmont on the Sunset Strip and set about entertaining them in his fashion. Page was well prepared for the libertine Los Angeles rock scene—he knew groupies from his earlier tours with the

Yardbirds—but for Plant and Bonham this was a whole new world. They were startled to see policemen carrying guns in public places, and they had never seen so many limousines on one street before.

Led Zeppelin's first US tour was well timed. Midway through their trek, on January 12, the group's first album, *Led Zeppelin*, was released in America. It was pretty much unlike anything else. The song arrangements were more sculpted than those of Cream or Jimi Hendrix, and the musicianship wasn't cumbersome like Iron Butterfly or bombastic like Vanilla Fudge. The closest comparisons might be the MC5 or the Stooges—both from Michigan—yet neither had the polish or prowess of Led Zeppelin, nor did Led Zeppelin have the political, social or diehard sensibility of those landmark bands. What they did have, though, was the potential for a mass audience. Young record buyers loved the album, but there were others who did not. Some of this had to do with the hype claim—that this was an unproven band claiming a prodigy they did not possess and popularity they did not deserve. It also had to do with the notion that here was another white British band exploiting and colonizing American black musical forms.

But what bothered critics the most about Led Zeppelin was the *sound*: John Bonham's thundering drums, Robert Plant's lusty, high-pitched yowl, Jimmy Page's roaring guitar lines—it was all seen as a manifestation of anger and aggression. Critic Jon Landau described a Boston show as "loud . . . violent and often insane." This was about the music—not about anything that was being said in the songs or from the stage. These weren't, after all, declarations of revolution of the sort made by Jefferson Airplane or the MC5. This was just music that *felt* like a disruption or threat. It was also "cock rock," music that, theorists Simon Frith and Angela McRobbie once famously claimed, "was explicitly about male sexual performance" and held little concern, according to these critics, for love or the needs of the women in the band's audience. (Critic Charles Shaar Murray once described the band's famous version of "Whole Lotta Love" as akin to "thermonuclear gang rape.")

But there was a trickier element about the critical contempt for Led Zeppelin: Not everybody was comfortable with who seemed to be responding to the music. This was a younger audience than the one that had responded to the cultural and political epiphanies invoked by the Beatles, Bob Dylan or the San Francisco bands. In effect, it amounted to an unexpected generational divide within a generation. Jon Landau again: "Zeppelin forced a revival of the distinction between popularity and quality. As long as the bands most admired aesthetically were also the bands most successful commercially (Cream, for instance) the distinction was irrelevant. But Zeppelin's enormous commercial success, in spite of critical opposition, revealed the deep division in what was once thought to be a homogeneous audience. That division has now evolved into a clearly defined mass taste and a clearly defined elitist taste." The mass taste, though, is the one that counted here: This was largely a new audience, its members deciding for themselves what spoke to them, what represented them, what inspired or empowered them, and to dismiss that was to dismiss that popular music would always evolve with the culture and times around it.

None of these concerns impeded Led Zeppelin's early success, which as Landau indicated, proved phenomenal. Whereas the first album had formed in quick bursts in the studio, *Led Zeppelin II* was recorded piecemeal in various locales during the group's hectic 1969 touring schedule. Though Page had doubts about how it might all hold together, its impact, musically and culturally, was only bigger. Combined with the first album, *Led Zeppelin II* forged a new sensibility in rock & roll—or at least codified something that had been forming. Some called it hard rock or heavy rock, others dubbed it heavy metal (a term already used to denote bands like the MC5, Blue Cheer, Deep Purple and Iron Butterfly, though both the term and the music would have far different dimensions in the generations that followed). It wasn't quite plain yet, but Led Zeppelin was effecting—or representing—a sea change in popular music and popular culture. They were, as Steve Pond once noted in *Rolling Stone*, the last band of the 1960s and the first band of the 1970s. In 1969 and early 1970, *Led Zeppelin* had competed with the Beatles' *Abbey Road*, the Rolling Stones' *Let It Bleed* and Simon and Garfunkel's *Bridge over Troubled Water*. Those were all epochal works, in part because they were summarizing or finishing an epoch. Led Zeppelin's albums were also epochal, because they were starting one.

In 1969 Led Zeppelin played 139 shows, the vast majority of them in the United States (they played only thirty-three in the UK that year). Clearly, they had settled on America as the primary foundation for their fame and accomplishment. "It felt like a vacuum and we'd arrived to fill it," Page once told Cameron Crowe. "It was like a tornado and it went rolling across the country." Just as clearly, Led Zeppelin saw live performances as a means to growth and prominence every bit as vital as making records. In part, this owed to Peter Grant's vision of how Led Zeppelin would flourish: He wanted to see their acclaim built on the fame of their live shows rather than through the media.

A touring life that extensive could be exhausting, of course. These were men away from their wives and children for long periods (only Page wasn't married, though he later lived with a woman, Charlotte Martin, and would have a child with her). But touring offered considerable rewards as well. It built the following that Grant envisioned, made money and offered ample opportunities for immediate pleasure—including late-night drinking and drug taking, and all manner of sexual adventures. None of this sort of thing was new, of course; these practices traced back to the early decades of blues, jazz and country music. Led Zeppelin, though, was studying to make a fine—or wretched—art of a reputation for debauchery. The most notorious and oft-cited instance along these lines took place at a Seattle wharfside hotel, the Edgewater Inn, where road manager Richard Cole talked a young woman into letting him insert dead fish parts into her vagina and anus as the band members looked on. Another time, after playing a concert to benefit radiation survivors in Hiroshima, Japan, the band visited a geisha house where they drank so many geishas under the table that the establishment had to call in a new crew of women to take over the drinking.

Other times, though, things turned undeniably ugly. In 1969 *Life*—one of the biggest magazines in America at that time—assigned journalist Ellen Sanders to cover the band's US tour. "No matter how miserably the group managed to keep their behavior up to a basic human level," she later wrote, "they played well almost every night of the week. If they were only one of the many British rock groups touring at the time, they were also one of the finest. The stamina they found each night at curtain-time was amazing. . . ." At tour's end, she stopped by the band's dressing room to say good-bye. "Two members of the group," she wrote, "attacked me. Shrieking and grabbing at my clothes, totally over the edge. I fought them off until Peter Grant rescued me, but not before they managed to tear my dress down the back. . . . If you walk inside the cages at the zoo, you get to see the animals close up, stroke the captive pelts, and mingle with the energy behind the mystique. You also get to smell the shit firsthand."

Peter Grant later decided the band needed to improve its media relations and overall image. He hired publicists Lee Solters and Danny Goldberg, who told him forthrightly that Led Zeppelin was seen as "barbarians" by the US press. Goldberg worked with the band for years, doing the best he could. Grant also decided to produce a feature film about the band, showcasing Led Zeppelin's extraordinary performance strengths, among other things. The idea had been Joe Massot's, who had written *Wonderwall* (scored by George Harrison) and directed *Zachariah*, both well-received rock-related films.

Massot, though, didn't find the band or its entourage easy to work with, and he ended up filming Madison Square Garden concert dates at the end of the tiring 1973 tour, when the group was off peak. Just the same, he felt he had something to show the band in spring 1974. "They finally came to a preview theater," he said, "to see the 'Stairway to Heaven' segment and started to fight and yell when the film began. They thought it was my fault Robert Plant had such a big cock. It took them another year to recuperate."

Massot was fired and replaced by Peter Clifton, who found Led Zeppelin "crude and rude," plus uncooperative. "Peter Grant had created this incredible aura around them . . .," Clifton said, "which partially obscured the fact that they were all *assholes!*"

The final film, *The Song Remains the Same,* debuted in 1976, to generally terrible reviews, though it has proved profitable for the band in the years since.

In 1970 Jimmy Page decided that Led Zeppelin had earned enough credibility with their audience that the group could afford extending musical directions a bit. He and Plant retreated to a remote cottage in Wales and wrote a suite of acoustic-based songs that reflected the pair's affection for British folk forms (both were fans of Fairport Convention, and Page cited guitarist Bert Jansch, who played in Pentangle, as a major influence). Plus, they wanted to pay tribute to the sort of music that Crosby, Stills and Nash and Joni Mitchell were producing from California (the entire band regarded Mitchell as perhaps the best songwriter in contemporary music). The songs Page and Plant assembled—including "That's the Way" and "Gallows Poll"—appeared on the second half of *Led Zeppelin III,* with bounding electric tracks like "Immigrant Song," "Celebration Day" and "Out on the Tiles" on the first half. By far the most affecting of the songs was "That's the Way," which Page regarded as Plant's first major breakthrough as a lyric writer. Though it seemed to be about the gulf between two boyhood friends from different social backgrounds, it was in fact a song about the band's ambivalent relationship to America, the land that had become their home away from home. The group's members were sometimes frightened and confused by what they saw or experienced in the United States—they were spit on, had guns drawn on them and were heckled at airports and on planes—and they were deeply troubled over the violence that they had seen policemen visit upon youth who protested the war in Vietnam, as well as upon the fans at their shows. "We've been to America so much and seen so many things that we don't agree with," Plant said, "that our feelings of protest have to reflect in our music. When you have the justification, it must be done."

Led Zeppelin III sold well initially but quickly lost ground. Neither fans nor critics knew what to make of a record with such sharp electric and acoustic contrasts, though the album yielded a collection of resilient songs that remained more or less constant in the band's repertoire. With the next album—an album with no title, generally referred to as *Led Zeppelin IV*—the group did a stronger job of melding sounds and interests. There isn't a missed step anywhere—indeed, it is an extraordinary statement of prowess and dreams, unbelievably complex yet straightforward at one extreme ("Black Dog," with its staggering range of time signature changes), and an alluring tale of scorn turned to transcendence at the other ("Stairway to Heaven"). Over the years, Led Zeppelin's fourth album has emerged as the group's best- (and most consistently) selling album and is now regarded as one of rock & roll's unadulterated masterpieces. Alone, the album goes a long way to validating Led Zeppelin's renown and durability.

Something else, though, resulted from the album: It expanded the band's use of myth, both as subject matter and as a characteristic of the band's iconic status. In *Led Zeppelin III*, Plant and Page had begun to mix images of legend with the band's self-image in "Immigrant Song," casting Led Zeppelin (in a consciously hilarious though not inaccurate way) as gods, conquering and plundering the lands they visit. Now, on the fourth album, they deepened the conceits just enough, evoking the resonance of history and horror (and a bit of *Lord of the Rings*) in "The Battle of Evermore," and suggesting a shared mission of spiritual hope in "Stairway to Heaven." Just as important to Led Zeppelin's taste for myth, though, was what was *not* on the album: any discernible title. The four runic symbols that function as both the record's real name and as representations of the personalities in the band had no clear denotation, but that made them more evocative, more a possibility than a meaning. (Page designed his own zoso-looking symbol and would never explain its significance—he told Plant only, but Plant forgot what it meant—while Bonham's pattern of intersecting circles, band members later noticed, resembled the logo for a beer the drummer liked.) In other words, Led Zeppelin's handling of myth gained weight from being both elusive and self-referential, as if those wielding the myth were also the ones the myth heralded. Also, the vagueness managed to reflect the rising sense of moral ambiguity in those years. (In Erik Davis's terrific volume about *Led Zeppelin IV*, he noted: "Zeppelin is a special sort of *Lord of the Rings*, one where you get to *root for both sides*.")

In the case of Jimmy Page, his use of symbolism had a special edge. As far back as his time in the Yardbirds, Page had expressed an interest in esoteric occultism. By this point in Led Zeppelin's history, that interest had transformed into an obsession with the British mystic and rogue Aleister Crowley, who tried messing in some pretty heavy juju, including an interest in Satanism, in the early 1900s. Page himself was never a satanist, but he was attracted to Crowley's philosophy. "His whole thing," the guitarist once said, "was total liberation and really getting down to what part you played. What you want to do, do it." Page had Crowley's primary law, "Do What Thou Wilt," inscribed in the run-off groove of the original LP releases of *Led Zeppelin III*. Years later, Page admitted that his concentration on Crowley was unfortunate, but in the band's lifetime occultism proved a source of both silly speculations and painful rumors. The most wearing—and trite— of these was that Page and the other members of Led Zeppelin (except for John Paul Jones, the quiet one) had sold their souls to the devil in exchange for tremendous fame and success.

Tales like this may hold a dark appeal for some—the soul-selling legend certainly didn't hurt Robert Johnson's stature over the years—but in the end it's all romantic know-nothingism. Robert Johnson never met any devils at midnight crossroads for the same reason that Jimmy Page and Led Zeppelin could never have made a supernatural deal for fame had they wanted to: There's no devil to make deals with. Any bargains are bargains with the self—but then, that might be enough. Crowley's dictum of "Do What Thou Wilt," when seen as a rationale for self-made law rather than for mere ambition, is in the end a pretty extreme pronouncement—that sort of sentiment has had untold awful reverberations across history. It would also have a terrible effect in the life and death of Led Zeppelin.

Houses of the Holy, the band's 1973 album (also the first with a proper title) has often been described as among Led Zeppelin's lesser works. In this case, though, with tracks like "The Rain Song," "No Quarter" and "The Ocean," and with some of the most expressive vocals Robert Plant ever recorded, "lesser" counts as a fairly short increment. Nobody, though, expressed similar doubts over Led Zeppelin's sixth studio release, the expansive *Physical Graffiti*, from 1975. When the group began writing and rehearsal sessions for the album, they realized they had stored up a worthy collection of earlier unreleased tracks that might fit interestingly alongside some of the longer and more diverse material that Page and Plant had been writing. The result—fifteen tracks spread over two LPs—created a textural and thematic breadth that was unlike anything else the band ever attempted. In particular, "Kashmir"—a song about journeying and not arriving, that made use of Indian and Arabic scales—was the band's single most ambitious recording. The track opens with a swirling drone and begins a steady mounting tension that, though the song's sections shift and evolve, never lets up. It's ineluctable; it pulls the listener across a relentless soundscape. Led Zeppelin would be criticized for producing songs and performances and riffs that built and built without resolution, but in "Kashmir" it was plain that the group's music wasn't about ideals of fulfillment or completion or satisfaction. The song itself was about a drive that Plant and Page made through southern Morocco, down a nonstop road through a never-ending desert. The song's music was also about a drive toward a way-off horizon that couldn't be resisted. Led Zeppelin wasn't making songs with conventional buildups and resolutions—they never had. They weren't interested in endings that were endings; they were interested in never reaching an ending.

Physical Graffiti and the 1975 concert performances displayed Led Zeppelin at an energetic artistic peak. After a tenth tour of America, and a series of triumphant May concerts at London's Earls Court—which many regard as the best the band ever played—the group was set to leave England for a time to avoid paying Britain's onerous taxes (up to 95 percent of the group's songwriting royalties). The day after the last Earls Court date, Robert Plant and his wife Maureen and their three children set out on a trip to Marrakesh, Morocco. Page and Charlotte Martin, with their daughter Scarlet, joined the Plants in June. The two families traveled through July, as the two songwriters began conceiving material for a new album, and they all wound up on the Greek island of Rhodes. On August 3, Page left to check on some property in Sicily; he planned to meet up with everybody in Paris in a few days' time. The next day, Maureen Plant was driving her family and Scarlet Page in a rented car down a narrow road on the island, when she lost control. The car hit a tree hard. Robert thought his wife was dead. His children were badly injured, though Scarlet Page was unhurt. Plant's ankle was severely broken. Charlotte Martin had been following in the car behind. She called Richard Cole back in London. The medical care on the island might not be enough for Maureen, who had lost a lot of blood and might die. Cole arranged to get Plant and his family to England, where Maureen would have to remain in the hospital for weeks. Plant, however, had to leave immediately, due to tax laws.

The band regrouped in California in September. Doctors had told Plant he would not be able to walk for months. In fact, they couldn't promise he would ever walk again unaided. Certainly, the group would not be able to tour for a year or more, if ever again. Page and Grant understood that the idleness and depression the band faced could do lasting damage to their creative momentum. Plant and Page sequestered themselves in Malibu and began writing material that was leaner and more hard-hitting. In November Led Zeppelin traveled to Munich and recorded *Presence*. Released in April 1976, *Presence* conveyed the sense of a band up against bad odds, fighting back. The opening two tracks, "Achilles Last Stand" (about the car accident) and "For Your Life" (about hell and drugs and terror, and about how life inside the band may have been developing), featured the best solos Page would ever play—abstract, desperate, raging. "*Presence* was pure anxiety and emotion," Page said later. "I mean, we didn't know if we'd ever be able to play in the same way again. It might have been a very dramatic change, if the worst had happened to Robert. *Presence* is our best in terms of uninterrupted emotion."

Over the years, *Presence* hasn't sold as well as most of the band's catalog. It's more or less the forgotten album; its feelings are too hard, too intense and probably too insular to stay close to for very long. In effect, Led Zeppelin accomplished something akin to Eric Clapton's achievement on Derek and the Dominos' *Layla*: They forged the spirit and purpose of blues into a new form, without relying on blues scales and structures. It's clearly singular in Led Zeppelin's body of work, and it's likely the best album the band ever made.

"It was really like a cry of survival . . . ," Plant said. "There won't be another album like it, put it like that. It was a cry from the depths, the only thing that we could do."

On January 1, 1976, Robert Plant was able to take his first steps without the help of a crutch or cane since the accident on Rhodes. Led Zeppelin didn't resume live performances, though, until their eleventh US tour, in 1977. Around this time, popular music had begun to change considerably—or at least a segment of it had tried to change. In New York and London, a new aesthetic and social perspective began to emerge, known as punk (or new wave). Punk would be many things—a different rhythmic and thematic sensibility, a new political means, a new generation's action of refusal—but crucially it was also a critique of rock & roll itself. In the view of punks, the 1970s established rock acts had veered to the mainstream and had grown comfortable and out of touch while living in conditions of privilege and grandiosity. This charge was leveled at many groups and artists, but at none so vehemently as Led Zeppelin, whose stadium tours, well-heeled decadence and persistent catering to a mass American audience seemed a betrayal of sorts. "I don't have to hear Led Zeppelin," said Clash bassist Paul Simonon. "Just looking at their record covers makes me want to throw up."

The funny part was that Led Zeppelin was one of the few prominent 1970s bands that professed an affinity for the new music. John Paul Jones said: "Punk did remind us of how we sounded early on—all brash and confident." In early 1977 the band visited London's Roxy Club to see the Damned live. Bonham, drunk, wandered onstage. "Get this drummer off-stage," he said of the Damned's Rat Scabies. "He's better than I am." A few minutes later, said Sex Pistols bassist Glen Matlock, Bonham had moved behind Scabies's drum kit, angry. "He was shouting, 'Where's the fucking band gone? They've only been playing for fifteen minutes—we play for three fucking hours because we're real men and not a bunch of wimps. Where's that Mouse Scabies? I'll show him how to play . . . .'" Matlock recalled that Led Zeppelin had to carry Bonham out of the club, all the while Bonham was "still shouting for Mouse Scabies to come out."

Whatever the group thought of punk, it had no bearing on the 1977 US tour. Page and Grant conceived it as the effort that would reassert Led Zeppelin as the dominant band of the decade—but it didn't go that way. The tour started on April 1, in Dallas, and was slated to extend for forty-nine concerts across America, for 1.3 million ticket holders. According to Richard Cole, Page, much of the road crew and Cole himself were using heroin regularly during the visit, and Page sometimes seemed weakened as a result. On the third night of the Chicago shows, Page was forced to leave the stage from severe stomach pain, and the show was canceled. After a couple of rest breaks, the band headed to the San Francisco Bay Area, for a pair of massive Oakland Stadium concerts promoted by Bill Graham. Trouble, though, had been building—actually, storing up for years. Peter Grant had always been protective of Led Zeppelin, but early along the way that protection turned into an impregnable shield designed to guarantee the band and its company a sense of impunity. "We made our own laws," Richard Cole told Stephen Davis in *Hammer of the Gods*. "If you didn't want to fucking abide by them, don't get involved."

Things were even worse on this tour. Grant was going through a painful divorce, and his temper was flaring easily. In addition, Richard Cole had brought in John Bindon as a security coordinator for the tour. Bindon had played hard-guy roles in films like *Performance*, *Quadrophenia* and *Get*

Carter, but some who met him around Led Zeppelin found him more frightening in real life. Plant, Page and Jones had all complained about Bindon's and Cole's handling of people, but that didn't curtail much of it. British writer Nick Kent, in *Mojo*, described Cole, in particular, as "a genuinely terrifying" person. "One night . . .," Kent wrote, "I saw him harassing a timid thirteen-year-old girl who'd come to the group's hotel simply to get an autograph of Robert Plant. The more frightened and hysterical she became, the more Cole seemed to enjoy it."

In his autobiography, *Bill Graham Presents: My Life Inside Rock and Out*, Graham recounted Cole calling him the day before the first of the Oakland weekend shows, demanding immediate delivery of a $25,000 advance on the shows' earnings. When Graham brought the money to the band's hotel, he wrote, he realized what the call was really about: "This was *drug* money." The next day, July 23, when the band's road crew and security force arrived at the coliseum, Graham was further disturbed: "I heard about the ugliness of their security, how they were just waiting to kill. They had these bodyguards who had police records in England. They were thugs."

Graham soon saw those reputations played out. When one of Graham's crew made what Grant took as a remark about his weight, Bindon approached the man and knocked him out. After the show, another of Graham's staff, Jim Matzorkis, saw a boy removing one of the band's plaques off a trailer door and took the plaque back from him, explaining that they needed it for the next day's show. The boy was Grant's son. Bonham saw the incident and reported it to Grant, who went looking for Matzorkis. Graham tried to intervene, but when Grant and Bindon found Matzorkis taking shelter in a trailer, they threw Graham out, shut the door and began to work the staffer over seriously. Graham tried to get back into the room to stop the beating, but Cole guarded the door, wielding a pipe. Matzorkis later said that when Bindon tried to gouge his eye out, he summoned his strength and escaped the trailer, bleeding. Graham had the man rushed to the hospital.

The next day, before Led Zeppelin took the stage, one of the band's lawyers required that Graham sign a letter of indemnification, releasing the group and its organization of any responsibility for the beating. Graham signed; he didn't want to risk the chance of a riot at the coliseum if the band wouldn't play. But he also knew that signing the letter didn't bind any of Matzorkis's legal options. Robert Plant tried to reach some sort of conciliation, but Graham wouldn't speak to him. Disheartened and angry about the whole matter, Jimmy Page played guitar sitting down for the entire show. The next morning an Oakland SWAT team surrounded Led Zeppelin's hotel and police officers arrested Grant, Cole, Bindon and John Bonham. They were all charged with assault, and Jim Matzorkis filed a $2 million civil suit.

The day after the arrests, July 26, the group traveled to New Orleans for the next show. As they were checking into the hotel, Plant received a call from his wife. Plant's six-year-old son Karac was seriously ill—a respiratory infection. Two hours later Maureen called back to tell Plant that their son was dead. Plant, Bonham and Cole caught the next flight back to England.

After the events of July 1977, Led Zeppelin was in pieces. The death of Plant's son stopped all band undertakings immediately. Bonham and Cole were the only members of Led Zeppelin's inner circle to attend Karac Plant's funeral in Birmingham. According to Cole—whose accounts are sometimes questionable—Plant was confused and hurt that the others hadn't joined him on this day. Plant, Cole claimed, said: "Maybe they don't have as much respect for me as I do for them. Maybe they're not the friends I thought they were." Grant maintained that he had been forced to stay behind in America to cancel the remaining tour dates, though according to Chris Welch in his biography of the manager, Grant later realized that his absence from Plant's side at that time created a distance between them that never truly healed.

Jimmy Page had to fend off rumors that his flirtations with the occult had backfired and created a curse, and that Led Zeppelin was now paying the cost. "I don't see how the band would merit a karmic attack," Page responded. "All I or we have attempted to do is go out and really have a good time and please people at the same time." But Plant later acknowledged that he had been forced to reevaluate everything. "After losing my son," he said, "I found that the excesses that surrounded Led Zeppelin were such that nobody knew where the actual axis of all this stuff was. Everybody was insular, developing their own world. The band had gone through two or three really big—huge—changes: changes that actually wrecked it before it was born again. The whole beauty and lightness of 1970 had turned into a sort of neurosis."

Certainly, the imbroglio in Oakland had tarnished what proved to be Led Zeppelin's last dates in America. Grant hired a Bay Area lawyer to settle the case, but when that proved difficult, he threatened the lawyer's practice; Grant didn't want Led Zeppelin's money audited. In February 1978 Bonham, Grant, Cole and Bindon pled *nolo contendere* to the assault charges—they denied guilt but accepted punishment—and each received a suspended sentence of less than two years and a fine of less than $1,000. Bill Graham was disillusioned. "As far as I was concerned," he said, "every one of those guys in that band was accountable for that shit, because they allowed it to go on." Robert Plant later said of Oakland: "It was an absolute shambles. It was so sad that I would be expected to go on and sing 'Stairway to Heaven.' . . . I had to sing it in the shadow of the fact that the artillery we carried with us was prowling around backstage with a hell of an attitude. It was a coming together of these two dark forces which had nothing to do with the songs that Page and I were trying to churn out."

Bill Graham's account of the Oakland incident was published in 1992 (Graham died in October 1991, in a helicopter accident near Vallejo, California). Chris Welch has described how, after reading the book, Grant called up his friend, fellow manager Ed Bicknell. Grant was in tears. "It's terrible," he said; "this book has come out and it tells the full story." Bicknell asked Grant if the account was true. "Yes," said Grant, "it is, but I don't want to be thought of as a bad person."

Grant and the other members of Led Zeppelin agreed to give Plant as much time and distance as he needed to grieve and come to his own decisions. "I felt quite remote from the whole thing," Plant told *Uncut* in 2005. "I wasn't comfortable with the group at all. We'd gone right through the hoop and, because my hoop was on fire, I didn't know if it was worth it anymore." On another occasion Plant said that Page's and others' drug use was also an issue: "Addiction to powders was the worst way to see yourself, a waste of your time and everybody's time. You make excuses to yourself why things aren't right or about what's happening to your potential. You lie to yourself first and rub your nose later. It was time to get out."

But by late 1978, Plant was ready to try again. The band recorded a new album in Stockholm. This time, Plant and Jones largely took the directional helm. "There were two distinct camps by then," John Paul Jones said, "and we were in the relatively clean one." However, with the exception of "In the Evening," "Carouselambra" and "I'm Gonna Crawl" (none of them especially well arranged), the new album, *In Through the Out Door*, was a misfire—the only one among the band's studio works. What was absent, clearly, was Jimmy Page's fucked-up quality, except Page was too fucked up to deliver it. (*In Through the Out Door* became best known for selling in such massive numbers out of the box that it single-handedly rescued the flagging 1979 American music industry.)

Led Zeppelin returned to live performing in July and August 1979, close to the time of the new album's release. They played a pair of warm-ups in Copenhagen, then staged their return spectacle at two August Knebworth Festival extravaganzas. Plant was uneasy with the scale of the setting and the band's performance—"a shit gig," he said years later—but these were clearly Jimmy Page's shows; his stage manner and guitar work on "Achilles Last Stand," "In the Evening," "Kashmir" and "Whole Lotta Love," as featured on the 2003 *Led Zeppelin* DVD box set, are joyous and transfixing. Grant wanted the band to return to America right away—maybe as a way of redeeming their bad end there—but Plant was adamantly opposed. He didn't want to be apart from his family more than necessary (in January, Maureen had given birth to the couple's second son, Logan Romero Plant). Instead, the singer agreed to a two-week summer 1980 tour through part of Europe. At the June 27 show in Nuremberg, John Bonham collapsed from physical exhaustion. The tour ended in Berlin on July 7, after Page canceled shows scheduled for France. Finally, Plant relented: He'd give Grant the American tour he wanted, but only if it were for four weeks. "I reckoned once Robert got over there and got into the swing," Grant said, "he'd be okay."

You can't talk about the end of Led Zeppelin—indeed, you can't talk meaningfully about Led Zeppelin, for better and worse—without considering John Bonham. He was in some ways the center of the band's story—the force that literally propelled the band and the problem that also stopped it. Bonham had grown up in the Black Country and found himself, a friend of his once said, in a music scene that was at the time a drinking culture. The trouble was, Bonham was a horrible drunk. Many people described him as the friendliest and most down-to-earth member of Led Zeppelin when he was sober, but after a few drinks, he could be belligerent as hell. Richard Cole believed that Bonham's temperament stemmed from the strain of being away from his wife and children. In *Mojo*, Nick Kent related a memory Bryan Ferry had of a night in Bonham's company in Los Angeles: "Ferry recalled Bonham bursting into tears and pleading to go home back to his family in the Midlands, so terrified had he become of his own insatiable appetites while on the road."

Some of Bonham's behavior, though, was pitiless. One time, according to *Hammer of the Gods*, on board the chartered Starship jet, he staggered out of the plane's bedroom cabin drunk, grabbed a stewardess and announced his intent to rape her. Grant and Cole had to pull him off. Another time Bonham showed up at LA's most famous rock & roll bar, the Rainbow, drank ten black Russians in rapid succession, glowered around the room, and when a young woman publicist recognized him and smiled at him, he lunged at her, punched her in the face, then went back to his drinks.

These incidents seemingly weren't alarming enough to convince anybody to intervene in Bonham's dissolution, although it's not clear that anything would have helped. Everybody close to the drummer attested to how much they loved the man, how they valued his better side and marveled at his talents. He incorporated the influences of Gene Krupa, Buddy Rich, Ginger Baker, Bernard Purdie, Max Roach and Alphonse Mouzon, but broke through it all with his own breathtaking feel. Moreover, his interplay with Page amounted to the best drummer-guitar rapport in rock & roll history. "John always felt his importance was minimal," Plant said, "but if you take him off any of our tracks, the track loses its sex, its potency and power. He . . . never had any idea how important he was, and he was very insecure because of it."

On September 24, 1980, Led Zeppelin met to begin rehearsals for the upcoming American tour. Bonham had overcome a heroin problem and was taking a drug to help with anxiety and depression—but he had also been drinking vodka the whole day, and the alcohol only renewed his depression. Plant remembered Bonham as being tired and disconsolate: "He was saying, 'I don't want to do this. You play the drums and I'll sing.'" Bonham drank through rehearsal, until there wasn't any point in continuing to play. Then the band convened back at Jimmy Page's new house in Windsor. Bonham had several more double vodkas—he'd drunk over forty measures of vodka in twelve hours—and passed out around midnight. He was moved into a spare bedroom by an assistant. The next day, in the afternoon, John Paul Jones went to wake Bonham, accompanied by Plant's assistant, Benji LeFevre. They found Bonham dead; he had rolled over in his sleep, taken water and vomit into his lungs and choked. Jones later told Cameron Crowe that Bonham's death looked "shockingly arbitrary."

They wouldn't say as much for a little over two months, but it all finished right then. This was not a band in which any of the parts could be replaced. It was a band that breathed together until it couldn't. "It was so . . . *final*," Plant later said. "I never even thought about the future of the band or music."

There was hubris in Led Zeppelin's story, and there were bad endings. There were harsh judgments and wrecked feelings—some self-incurred and deserved, some not. There was also a kind of awful innocence and intensity, and through it all a magnificent brilliance.

Mainly, there was a heaviness to bear. Robert Plant—the one person in the band's history who seemed to have deepened the most, though at the greatest price—kept his distance from the band's history and music for many years. Jimmy Page, on the other hand, loved the band's music and history, and stayed close to it in various ways—remastering albums, assembling collections of unreleased live music for CD and DVD, and playing Led Zeppelin's music onstage whenever the chance seemed right. (Page overcame his drug problems in 1983.) John Paul Jones, meantime, lived quietly, working as an arranger and producer and recording resourceful music without fanfare. (He also overcame his drug problem in 1983.) Peter Grant stayed mostly distant from the musicians he had fought for, developed a drug problem and overcame it, then died of a heart attack in November 1995 at age sixty. John Bindon, who had figured in some of Led Zeppelin's worst moments, was tried and acquitted in a gory 1978 murder and died of cancer in 1993. Richard Cole—who parted from Grant on strained terms just before Led Zeppelin's 1980 European tour—made a career for a few years telling stories about the band, admitting that he may not have been the best influence in their lives, though he always seemed rather proud of that. Page, Plant and Jones played together again in public on a handful of occasions after 1980—at the Live Aid benefit concert in 1985, at a celebration of Atlantic Records' fortieth anniversary in 1988, at the band's 1995 induction into the Rock and Roll Hall of Fame—but none of the occasions satisfied the three men. They knew what was missing.

In the years after the band's demise, when Robert Plant and Jimmy Page talked about each other, it was generally with respect, though it was also as if some hidden wound lay between them. In 1994 Plant received an invitation from MTV to play the network's *Unplugged* series. He knew the setting would call for revisiting some Led Zeppelin songs, so he invited Page to share the event with him. The two used the occasion to create a genuine collaboration, an adventure in mixing old and new forms: folk music, electronic loops, Moroccan spiritual drones, funereal blues, Egyptian and Western orchestration and Indian tonalities, filtered through the prism of some of Led Zeppelin's songs that dug the deepest (including several from the undervalued *Led Zeppelin III*). Page and Plant didn't invite John Paul Jones for the event—which hurt Jones and seemed churlish, especially given that they named their new endeavor after a song of his, "No Quarter." By then, though, it should have been apparent that if you're looking for grace in the Led Zeppelin legacy, it's best to examine sounds over manners. *No Quarter* proved to be among the best music Jimmy Page and Robert

Plant ever made together, and for a time they played these new sounds around the world.

Then that magic, too, was over. The pair's 1998 follow-up, *Walking into Clarksdale*, with more traditional rock & roll quartet instrumentation, seemed to renege on the new territory mapped out in *No Quarter*. Page and Plant toured the world yet again, playing the *Clarksdale* material alongside Led Zeppelin songs, but this time the two were closing prospects off rather than opening them up. Plant declined to continue the tour in 1999. Then, in 2007, the band re-formed to play at a tribute to Atlantic Records founder Ahmet Ertegun in London, with John Bonham's son Jason on drums, and they were once more the best band in the world.

Yet even if they never play together again, it's understandable. Led Zeppelin's music was always about possibilities: for sound, for an audience, for flawed people making something that might be better than themselves, for an audience that needed to hear that flawed people might transcend themselves. That music changed things far more than anybody ever expected, or might have wanted, even those who made the music. It is still an immediate music—it's too big, too overwhelming, to wear off or end, and too pleasurable to refuse. These messed-up men created something that still lays a claim on the times. That is Led Zeppelin's shadow, and it will outlast the souls who made it.

THE MADNESS AND WONDER
OF PINK FLOYD

There was no reason these men should ever stand together again. Roger Waters, David Gilmour, Nick Mason and Rick Wright—the four musicians who had carried Pink Floyd forward after Syd Barrett had fallen from reason in 1968—had not appeared on a stage together since June 1981, and it hardly seemed possible they ever would again. Waters and Gilmour had rather famously shown contempt for one another for a quarter century—each felt the other had tried to dishonor his life's work and hinder his future. After Waters started his own solo career in 1984, he went on to disparage the bandmates he had worked with for so long. Guitarist and singer David Gilmour, he said, "doesn't have any ideas," and drummer Nick Mason "can't play." (Waters had long before thrown keyboardist Rick Wright out of the band.) Gilmour gave as good as he got. When he first took his own version of the band on tour, he appropriated Waters's most famous prop, a gigantic pig balloon, and attached testicles to it, which some read as a commentary on how he viewed the band's former bassist. ("So they put balls on my pig," Waters said. "Fuck them.")

The long squabble resulted in the deepest, ugliest split in rock & roll's history, and almost certainly the most irreparable. On that warm London night in early July 2005, when the four men finally gathered again as Pink Floyd in London's Hyde Park at the historic Live 8 concert, it's unlikely that all the past anger and hurt was easily forgotten or healed, but that's partly what made the moment so moving. They played and sang despite their bitterness, in part because the evening's cause—to try to persuade the world's richest countries to forgive the debts of the poorest countries—was in keeping with belief systems they genuinely shared.

But there was another reason for assembling that night, that ran deeper in their history. They had a different kind of debt to pay that could never be paid, but it had to be admitted. Syd Barrett, a man who had been mysterious and lonely for decades, had been the heart of Pink Floyd in their earliest days—he wrote their songs, gave them their style, made them a force in the British music scene—but in 1968, Waters, Mason and Wright threw him out of the band after he slipped into mental disintegration. None of them had seen him since a surprise encounter in 1975 that left them stunned and in tears, but over the years he continued to define them, as they evolved the style he had left them, and as they began to think and write about the darkness that had eclipsed him. They owed Barrett something—in a way, everything—and if they failed to honor him that night at Live 8, before the world, they could never meaningfully attempt it again. That's because they knew Pink Floyd would not exist past this night, and perhaps they sensed that in the much-too-near future, neither would Barrett, the man who gave the band its original name and purpose.

The story of Pink Floyd is the story of the themes that raised and obsessed and tore at the band for almost four decades. That is, it's a story of madness, alienation, absence, hubris and a self-willed grace. There's really nothing else quite like it in popular music history. From the time they helped ignite pop-cultural upheaval in London in the late 1960s to that touching final public moment at Live 8, Pink Floyd always meant something in their moment. Indeed, the album that transfigured their fame in 1975, *Dark Side of the Moon*, managed to reflect the doubts and fears of a generation that had to cope with the loss of the ideals of the 1960s, and did it so effectively that it immediately established Pink Floyd as one of the biggest, best-loved bands in rock & roll history. Five years later, the epic and bleak *The Wall* only made them bigger (both *The Wall* and *Dark Side of the Moon* still rank high among best-selling albums worldwide). But *The Wall*—a story about a bitter, fucked-up loner rock star who could not bear the world around him—proved even darker than it first seemed, as its author, Roger Waters, increasingly could not bear the band around him. "If one of us was going to be called Pink Floyd," he told *Rolling Stone* in 1987, "it's me," though the rest of Pink Floyd had other ideas.

Despite both triumphs and wounds, the band's members couldn't escape a certain bond—not just a hatred for one another, but also a realization that without the community they once had, their music could never have mattered. Certainly, the group's five members shared some strong common formations. Most of them were either born in or grew up around Cambridge—a well-off university town that was steeped in antiquity, yet that also prized a progressive streak that was as artistic as it was political—and most of them appeared headed for careers in the arts. But what would shortly bring Waters, Barrett, Mason and Wright together was a passion for the promising sounds of rock & roll, blues and R&B, best heard in late-night programs emanating from Western Europe's Radio Luxembourg. Like other key British pop musicians—including John Lennon, Keith Richards, Eric Clapton and Jimmy Page—Pink Floyd would take the spirit of experimentation that they gained from art school and apply it to the raw form of rock & roll, with results that would transform the culture around them.

Waters left Cambridge in 1962 to take architecture courses at Regent Street Polytechnic in London. There he met fellow student Mason, who had grown up around music, art and politics and had been playing drums for years. Waters was already playing guitar—in fact, he sometimes practiced in class when he didn't want to study. In 1963 he and Mason joined an existing group, Sigma 6, where they met keyboard player Wright, who loved jazz and classical music. Wright and Mason were still fairly earnest about their possible architectural futures, but not Waters. He was already trying the patience of his lecturers. "I could have been an architect, but I don't think I'd have been very happy," he told journalist Caroline Boucher in 1970. "I hated being under the boot."

Syd Barrett—another young guitarist and art student who had been regarded back in Cambridge as rebellious—arrived in London in September 1964, to study painting. Waters and Barrett had known each other back in Cambridge, where Barrett was part of the bohemian art school set, learning about French existentialism, the 1950s Beat movement and Eastern religion, and where he was already studying guitar with his friend David Gilmour. Barrett had a passion for the melodic form of the Beatles' music and for the blues-steeped pop of the Rolling Stones, but he was also given to unusual guitar tunings and an odd slide guitar technique (which he may have learned from Gilmour), and he would become interested in finding a looser form of spontaneity when playing rock & roll. By the time Barrett joined up with Waters in London—the two had vowed in Cambridge to form a band one day—Sigma 6 had become the Abdabs, then the Tea Set. There would be personnel changes along the way—including the departure of a bassist, leaving that role to Waters—but by the autumn of 1965 they had settled on a four-man lineup: Waters on bass, Wright on keyboards, Mason on drums and Barrett on lead guitar and vocals. Barrett also gave the group a new identity: the Pink Floyd Sound, derived from the first names of two obscure blues musicians, Pink Anderson and Floyd Council (and from the names of Barrett's cats). "It was great when Syd joined," Wright said, according to writer Barry Miles, who would also be a witness to the band's rise. "Before him we'd play the R&B classics, because that's what all groups were supposed to be doing then. . . . With Syd, the direction changed, it became more improvised around the guitar and keyboards. Roger started to play the bass as a lead instrument and I started to introduce more of my classical feel."

After that, the first phase of the Pink Floyd story played out quickly—for better and worse. The better part came out of a confluence of the band's ambitions and the fast-rising movement in London's arts scene and youth culture. The Beatles and the Rolling Stones, among numerous other artists, were transforming the aesthetics and purposes of mid- and late-1960s British pop—how it sounded, what it could say, how it emboldened or unsettled listeners—and this impact carried past radio, to how people made and viewed art, how they dressed, and how they gathered and inter-acted in public situations. As a result, experimentation and a daring new sense of social play increasingly became a part not just of popular culture but of daily life. In London, from 1965 to 1968, this all became enmeshed in a movement sometimes known as the London Underground or the Spontaneous Underground. Whether they intended to or not, Pink Floyd, more than anybody—more than the Beatles, for example—became the *sound,* the central house band, of this movement. That's because Pink Floyd, billed sometimes as "London's farthest-out group," developed them-selves and their music in the midst of it all, live, night after night, with a population that was far more than a mere audience. Behind all that, there was a diligent attempt by various movers, such as producer Joe Boyd, ESP record label owner Steve Stollman, Indica bookstore and gallery operator Barry Miles and organizer John "Hoppy" Hopkins, to arrange events that brought music, poetry, performance art and kinetic art together with a par-ticipatory audience, with some of the partakers experimenting with mar-ijuana, hashish and psychedelics, primarily LSD. It all became intertwined enough that for some—both advocates and detractors—the music seemed inseparable from the drug experience. (Roughly similar gatherings had taken place the year before at the Acid Tests in Los Angeles and the Bay Area, with Ken Kesey's Merry Pranksters and the Grateful Dead, though the London scene was much more fashion- and art-conscious.) These events—sometimes called happenings or raves—were frequently unadvertised, promoted by word-of-mouth and invitation.

Pink Floyd worked their way into the heart of this scene through a series of key live appearances, starting in early 1966 at London's Marquee and spreading by the end of that year to the All Saints Church, the Roundhouse and the short-lived all-night UFO Club, playing for crowds that included Paul McCartney, John Lennon, Mick Jagger, Christine Keeler, Pete Townshend, Donovan, Marianne Faithfull and Yoko Ono (the latter whose performance art appeared at the 14-Hour Technicolor Dream rave at Alexandra Palace in early 1967). There were other acts popular in this circuit, including Soft Machine, Arthur Brown, Procol Harum, Tomorrow, the Pretty Things, the Third Ear Band and the jazz group AMM, but Pink Floyd set themselves apart with two features: an increasingly complex and resourceful cycle of light projections that appeared to envelop and react to the band as it played, and their abstract style of improvisation that could appear formless and unruly one moment, then precise, pounding and exhilarating the next. Artist Duggie Fields, who was a close friend of Barrett's, said: "A group of their friends was their audience first, then suddenly they got an enormous following in a very short space of time, shorter than it took for the Rolling Stones to happen." Of course, other artists—such as the Yardbirds and blues and jazz bands—had been playing extended improvisations in clubs as well, but largely those acts extemporized within well-formed metric structures.

By the end of 1966, Pink Floyd had signed a rather lucrative deal with EMI (5,000 British pounds), which allowed them unlimited time to record their first album at the label's Abbey Road studios. (They would in fact end up recording during the same early 1967 stretch that the Beatles were making *Sgt. Pepper's Lonely Hearts Club Band.* Paul McCartney had been a fan of Pink Floyd's Spontaneous Underground shows and told Barry Miles he thought the band represented a "new synthesis of electronic music and rock & roll.") EMI assigned the group to Norman Smith, who had been the Beatles' sound engineer up through *Rubber Soul.* Smith appeared a strange fit—reportedly he wasn't initially fond of the band's instrumental experiments "Astronomy Domine" and "Interstellar Overdrive"—and in later years he disparaged the group. "I could barely call it music," he said. Smith also found working with Syd Barrett exhausting, seeing him as hard to communicate with and not receptive to suggestions.

Still, what resulted from those sessions was something wonderful and enduring. With Pink Floyd's debut, *The Piper at the Gates of Dawn* (Barrett had named the album after a passage from Kenneth Grahame's *The Wind in the Willows),* the band loomed as a potentially matchless force in British rock & roll, though Syd Barrett was clearly the group's imaginative center. He had been paying close attention to the other transformative music of that time—the Beatles' *Revolver,* the Byrds' *Fifth Dimension,* the Mothers of

Invention's *Freak Out!,* the Kinks' *Face to Face,* John Coltrane's *A Love Supreme* and *Om,* the debut works of the Fugs and Love—and though it all had its influence, he nonetheless rapidly emerged as an original. He wrote Lewis Carroll– and Hilaire Belloc–indebted wordplay, and he wrote songs about fantasy and childhood and horror and the I Ching, all paired with remarkably inveigling and intuitive melodies. He was the primary reason Pink Floyd was now the most notable new band in British rock & roll, and he loved being a part of the cultural adventure that surrounded them.

Then, just as 1967's Summer of Love was under way, the Spontaneous Underground came under fatal fire as the British press mounted attacks against the morality of the movement and the London police began making more frequent arrests for drug possession. EMI stated in a press release: "The Pink Floyd does not know what people mean by psychedelic pop and are not trying to create hallucinatory effects on their audiences." Jenny Fabian, who has done some of the best writing about the London scene, told Nick Mason, in his book *Inside Out: A Personal History of Pink Floyd,* that Floyd "were the first authentic sound of acid consciousness. . . . They'd be up on stage like supernatural gargoyles playing their spaced-out music, and the same color that was exploding over them was exploding over us. It was like being taken over, mind, body and soul."

This question about the band's psychedelic sources was about to take on a painful resonance. At the peak of Pink Floyd's early creative powers, with a remarkable album—that would define the London Underground season in a vivid and undying way—now finished and set for summer 1967 release, Syd Barrett began to fall apart. The onset was sudden. As the group's "See Emily Play" soared into the Top Ten, Pink Floyd was set for three consecutive July appearances on the British weekly program *Top of the Pops*; Barrett looked increasingly haggard and wary as the weeks progressed, until finally he walked off the third show, frantic and angry.

That was just the start. At the International Love-In at the Alexandra Palace that same month, Barrett had to be hauled onstage by Waters, but he never played his guitar. In the first week of August, just as *The Piper at the Gates of Dawn* was being released, Pink Floyd's managers, Peter Jenner and Andrew King, canceled the band's English tour due to Barrett's "nervous exhaustion" and sent the singer on vacation with a doctor to a Spanish island. While there, Barrett screamed in horror when there was a storm and spent some nights sleeping in a graveyard. In November, Pink Floyd embarked on its first American tour. Onstage at San Francisco's Winterland,

Barrett stood with his arms hanging limp, occasionally blowing into a whistle. On TV appearances, he refused to mime the words to the band's songs. At a Los Angeles show, Barrett detuned his guitar and stared at some space past the audience. When Barrett was found asleep in the band's LA motel, a cigarette burning into his fingers (an instance later depicted in the film *The Wall*), the band insisted that it was time to leave America. Back in England, on tour with the Jimi Hendrix Experience, Barrett sometimes disappeared for his band's set. Years later Nick Mason told Barry Miles in *Pink Floyd: The Early Years:* "You're trying to be in this band . . . and things aren't really working out and you don't really understand why. You can't believe that someone's deliberately trying to screw it up and yet the other half of you is saying 'This man's crazy—he's trying to *destroy* me!'"

There has been a lot of argument, conjecture and myth making over the years about what went so terribly wrong for Syd Barrett in such a short amount of time. Many have attributed his disintegration to a steady overconsumption of LSD. He had taken the drug since his days in Cambridge, and in 1966 he lived in an apartment with people who ingested the hallucinogen regularly and purportedly fed it to Barrett whether he was aware of it or not. ("We never ventured inside," said Mason. "It was not a world the rest of us frequented.") Others—including Roger Waters—believe that the psychedelics likely triggered a dormant schizophrenia in Barrett. Author Tim Willis, however, when researching 2002's *Madcap: The Half-Life of Syd Barrett, Pink Floyd's Lost Genius,* discovered that Barrett had never been diagnosed with schizophrenia or given medications, "on the grounds that he has an 'odd' mind rather than a sick one."

Barrett's decline was made more confusing because the singer didn't simply plummet in a steady decline. He had fully lucid and creative times. But by Christmas 1967, after Barrett again stood still onstage at a major show, just staring, it was apparent that things could no longer continue in the same way. At the beginning of 1968, the band brought in Barrett's old Cambridge friend, David Gilmour, to take his place on guitars and vocals. The hope had been that Barrett might continue as a songwriter—similar to the way that Brian Wilson still wrote material for the Beach Boys but no longer toured with them—but even that seemed unfeasible. The band was having difficulty with Barrett's newer material—"Vegetable Man" and "Scream Thy Last Scream" were songs they thought emanated from madness—and they later buried the recordings of those songs rather than release them. A crucial instance in Barrett's final days with his band took place during a rehearsal session for a new offering, "Have You Got It Yet?"

The song was designed like a riddle, with a shifting arrangement, and each time Barrett put the question to the band he was essentially telling them that they could never figure him out. A few days after Gilmour joined, the band minus Barrett was en route to that night's performance when somebody asked, "Shall we pick up Syd?" The response was: "Fuck it, let's not bother." The band drove on and performed his songs that night without him, and never played with him again. As Pink Floyd worked on its next album, Barrett would sit in the studio's lobby with his guitar, waiting to be called in to the sessions. He also stood before the stage one night at a club, glaring as David Gilmour sang his songs. The instance unnerved Gilmour so much that he came close to quitting the band that night.

Some saw the ejection of Barrett from the band that he had catapulted to fame as a tragedy and betrayal. Peter Jenner and Andrew King were so upset by the turn of events that they dropped management of the band and stuck with Barrett. They thought the band had no future without him, and told them so. (Nick Mason later admitted, "If we'd parted with him earlier, we'd have sunk without a trace.") This rupture was the most pivotal point in the band's history. It changed what Pink Floyd could and would be, and it also haunted the band forever, in ways that resonated in their later work and troubled community. At the end of Pink Floyd's second album, *A Saucerful of Secrets,* the band included Barrett's farewell song, "Jugband Blues." It's doleful, even humorous, but its heartaching lyrics have always been seen as Barrett's self-diagnosis of his own delusion: "It's awfully considerate of you to think of me here / And I'm much obliged to you for making it clear / That I'm not here . . . / And I'm wondering who could be writing this song." But those lines could work on another level as well, as Barrett's way of saying to the band: How could anybody so damaged or dispensable write a song this beautiful and original?

At some point during Barrett's deterioration, the band and its management arranged for him to visit with famed psychiatrist R. D. Laing, known for his unorthodox approach to the treatment of mental illness, particularly schizophrenia and psychosis. Band members would drive Barrett to Laing's door, but he would refuse to leave the car. After listening to tapes of Barrett speaking, Nick Mason wrote in *Inside Out,* Laing did "make one challenging observation: yes, Syd might be disturbed, or even mad. But maybe it was the rest of us who were causing the problem, by pursuing our desire to succeed, and forcing Syd to go along with our ambitions. Maybe Syd was actually surrounded by mad people."

·   ·   ·

One of the persistent myths that attached itself over the years to the ouster of Syd Barrett was that Barrett resented the others for wanting to move Pink Floyd into a more pop-wise, commercially certain direction. It's true that Barrett certainly hated—and suffered from—the pressures to follow "Arnold Layne" and "See Emily Play" with surefire hit concoctions (he reportedly didn't like the idea of focusing on singles), but despite his gift for guiding the band in anarchic instrumentals, he was clearly foremost a pop songwriter: All of Barrett's last recordings for Pink Floyd were concise and poetic (plus great), and the only reason some were never released was because Barrett kept them for himself, or because the band didn't have the nerve to face their former songwriter's convoluted genius.

In any event, Barrett was no longer a contributor to the band. Roger Waters, having set aside his higher education and any other ambitions, now made Pink Floyd his purpose, and he was determined that the group continue. "He was the one," David Gilmour told Barry Miles, "who had the courage to drive Syd out, because he realized that as long as Syd was in the band, they wouldn't keep it together, the chaos factor was too great. Roger always looked up to Syd and felt very guilty about the fact that he'd blown out his mate." June Bolan, who worked for Jenner's management firm and used to drive a van for Pink Floyd, thought that Waters in effect saved the ensemble's future. "Having had two or three years of a band," she told Nicholas Schaffner, "and suddenly one member falls by the wayside, why should your lifeblood, your livelihood, be stopped? Roger was determined that it wasn't going to fall apart because Syd wasn't there anymore, and he would show everybody. . . . And he did it against all adversity, because nobody gave him credence for being a creator."

Others, though, also credited the band's new guitarist and lead singer, Gilmour, with recasting Pink Floyd's direction. In contrast to Syd Barrett, Gilmour was less inclined to a John Coltrane– or Ornette Coleman–like approach to inventing forays of melody and harmony in the moment, sometimes in contrary motions, and favored a more clearly structural and melodic approach to improvisation that gave room to the dominant mellifluence of his guitar. It was both this collaboration and competition between Waters and Gilmour that would now largely drive Pink Floyd in the direction of their triumphs, though it would also make for their troubles. In his early seasons in the band, Gilmour was already reacting to Waters's domineering manner, describing him as "a pushy sort of person" to a British music paper. It was a forecast of bitter years to come.

The band's second album, *A Saucerful of Secrets* (1968), was a worthy successor to *Piper at the Gates of Dawn*—part whimsical and part forlorn pop, alongside two dark-edged sonic explorations, "Set the Controls for the Heart of the Sun" and the title track, both of which proved to have great life in concert for years. The latter, in particular, set forth possibilities that the band would extend throughout their career as a sort of signature mode, a different approach to improvisation. "Instead of the standard song structure . . .," Mason later wrote, "Roger and I mapped it out in advance, following the classical music convention of three movements. This was not unique to us, but it was unusual. With no knowledge of scoring, we designed the whole thing on a piece of paper, inventing our own hieroglyphics."

For the next few years, the band made music that was as close to twentieth-century avant-garde methods as it was to rock & roll. "Pink Floyd is about pushing forward and taking risks," Waters said, and the music they made bore out his boast. *Ummagumma* and *Atom Heart Mother* featured lengthy experiments in serial atonality and orchestral composition, and EMI felt at a loss at times for what to do with such records, especially in America. (For *Atom Heart Mother*, Pink Floyd presented the record company with cover art featuring a photo of a grazing cow, with no mention of the band's name. "Are you trying to destroy this company?" one dismayed label executive screamed at them.) That Pink Floyd's albums continued to prove hits in England (all of the group's albums have placed in the British Top Ten) was testament to a number of things—including that much of the British pop audience at that time was receptive to the postpsychedelic form emerging as progressive rock (though Pink Floyd's version of the form didn't much resemble the classical borrowings of Emerson, Lake and Palmer or the heavy fantasias of Yes), and that the band had accrued a considerable amount of unstinting goodwill from its days as the sound of the London Underground. It also owed to the band's matchless sense of stagery. "In the future," Syd Barrett said in a 1967 interview, "groups are going to have to offer more than a pop show. They are going to have to offer a well-presented theater show." Pink Floyd would pursue that vision tirelessly, with shows that featured increasingly sophisticated light effects and giant props (including a massive octopus that once emerged from a lake during an outdoor show). In the late 1960s, these theatricals sometimes accompanied lengthy thematic suites, *The Man* and *The Journey*, that were early tastes of Roger Waters's appetite for full-length conceptual works.

With Pink Floyd, there was a sense that this was a band working toward something—some surprising amalgam of music and ideas that would stand as an unparalleled work and that would define the band's place in modern arts.

• • •

In 1971 the band began to home in on that promise. Their music had made a crucial turn earlier in the year, with the writing and recording of "Echoes," a twenty-five-minute piece that occupied half of the album *Meddle*. What was key about "Echoes" was how it was assembled—from small bits and experiments—to form a cohesive whole that felt like a live exploratory performance reflecting the band's state of mind. (Roger Waters later called it an "epic sound poem.") In December, beginning a new album, Waters—who was by now the band's main songwriter and in effect the group leader—told the other members of Pink Floyd that he wanted the band to make a work that focused on one subject: What are the forces and stresses in modern life that alienate people from one another and from their hopes? Together, they came up with a list of disturbances that included aging, violence, fear of death, religion, ideology, war, capitalism (all band members were left of center in their politics, though Waters more so than the others) and madness. The latter concern, in particular, had gripped Waters recently, as he began to reflect on the providence of Syd Barrett. (He had already written a song along those lines, "Brain Damage.") Waters's aim, he told the others, was for the new work to be unified by the theme it was exploring, though Gilmour and Wright also thought it was important to hold it all together with the music's tone.

The new album, with the working title *Eclipse*, would take a long time. Other obligations, such as tours and a soundtrack (*Obscured by Clouds*, for Barbet Schroeder's 1972 film *La Vallée*), disrupted the progress. More important, Waters wanted to get the lyrics right—he wanted them simple, clear, direct, not laden in obscure metaphors—and Gilmour was intent on fashioning music that would lure listeners into the assembly of dark meditations. Like "Echoes," this was music that would meld moments and motifs into seamless layers for an interconnected effect. Their deliberations paid well: In March 1973 Pink Floyd released *Dark Side of the Moon*, an immediate modern masterwork. Interlaced with spoken passages that addressed the songs' subjects in candid (and sometimes disturbing) ways, and held together by the craftiest segues in popular music history, the record set new standards for how an album might sound and play and matter in the lives of a mass of listeners, with an effect that had not been accomplished since the Beatles' productions. The album also realized its thematic ambitions—it was that genuinely rare creation: a thoughtful and imaginative statement about grim modern realities that managed to soothe you with its nightmares.

Dark Side of the Moon (the title was a tribute to Syd Barrett, an acknowl-
edgment of where his band left him) was—and remains—Pink Floyd's
best-loved, most enduring moment. It captured a wide audience, and not
merely in its time: Since its release, *Dark Side of the Moon* has sold around 35
million copies and remained on *Billboard*'s chart for 591 consecutive weeks
(the longest run of any work), continuing to appear in the charts off and on
ever since. But if the record marked Pink Floyd's apotheosis, it also put in
motion processes that would have an increasingly depressing effect. For all
its worthiness and art, *Dark Side of the Moon* was also clearly a perfectly cast
product: The music's explorations had been refined until the end result
resembled a polished object with the widest appeal possible. This might have
been rewarding for a band that had always fallen short of mass acceptance
(especially in America), but given Pink Floyd's roots and earlier avant-
garde methods, the music's well-mannered effect couldn't help but seem like
something of a compromise. Also, the mass acceptance brought with it a
mass audience that now knew the band for this considerable hit, but not for
the sensibility that had led up to the new music—which was something Pink
Floyd's members weren't prepared for. "We were used to all these reverent
fans who'd come and you could hear a pin drop," David Gilmour told
David Fricke in 1982. "We'd try to get really quiet, especially at the beginning
of 'Echoes' or something that has tinkling notes, trying to create a beautiful
atmosphere, and all these kids would be there shouting 'Money'!"

After Pink Floyd finished their 1973 tours, they gathered in October to
start work on the next album. Given the success they had just enjoyed, they
could now do anything they wanted. The trouble was, they didn't really want
to do anything. "At that point," Waters later said, "all our ambitions were
realized." At first, the group decided to make an altogether different kind of
album, *Household Objects,* in which none of the sounds would be made by
musical instruments. After two months of hammering nails and breaking
lightbulbs, the band had no idea of where to take the project. At one point
or another, each of the four members had talked to the group's management
about leaving the band. Finally, in the middle of a band argument about all
the misdirection, Waters hit on a feasible approach: Why not make the
record about the distance and malaise that was going on between them?
"Our bodies were there," he later said, "but our minds and feelings somewhere else." Indeed, if *Dark Side of the Moon* was about social alienation,
Wish You Were Here was about a more personal form of estrangement: the
absence of friends, inspiration, even of the mutual community they had
once found in one another. The effort produced the two best songs that

post-Barrett Pink Floyd would ever record—"Wish You Were Here" (with a melody by David Gilmour) and "Shine On You Crazy Diamond." Tellingly, both were songs about Syd Barrett, whom Waters then thought of as a "symbol of all the extremes of absence some people have to indulge in because it's the only way they can cope with how fucking sad modern life is—to withdraw completely." Waters would also later say that "Wish You Were Here" could just as easily have been addressed to the rest of the band members, whom he was no longer feeling as close to. Or it could even be, he said, about his battle within himself.

One day in early June 1975, while listening to a playback of "Shine On You Crazy Diamond," the group spotted an unfamiliar figure in the studio—an overweight, bald man—examining their equipment. After watching the stranger for several minutes, Waters turned to Rick Wright and said: "Do you know who that guy is? Think, *think*." Wright studied the visitor's face, then flashed: It was Syd Barrett. Waters later said he was in tears over the Barrett they now encountered, who was no longer a symbol but a flesh-and-blood person who seemed terribly solitary. The conversation was awkward. Barrett told the band he was ready to help them again with their music. As they spoke, "Shine On You Crazy Diamond," with its depiction of the man now visiting his former band, played around them, over and over, describing a once vibrant man, now empty-eyed. If Barrett recognized himself in the song, he made no mention. This was also the day of David Gilmour's wedding. Barrett accompanied the others to the reception, then disappeared. None of them ever saw him again.

Pink Floyd did not take *Wish You Were Here* on the road in the same way it had *Dark Side of the Moon* or the albums that immediately followed. This had been the band's most personal work—a face-on reckoning with not just prospects of separation and absence, but with unrecoverable loss and indelible guilt, and it was perhaps material they did not want so soon to live with for nights on end.

After *Wish You Were Here*, almost everything about Pink Floyd's story turns ugly—which isn't to say unworthy or unrewarding, because there was fascinating work that would yet emerge—but ugly just the same. In a way, that was the point—Roger Waters was intent on writing about psychological and social disfigurements—but just as often it was an inadvertent result of the band's internal life.

With 1977's *Animals*—a set of dark and funny fables about oppression and revolt—Waters secured his command of the band. He was now writing almost all the songs' words and music, singing lead vocals increasingly and telling the others when and what to play. There had been a long-running argument in the band: Gilmour favored more emphasis on the albums' musical contexts, but Waters increasingly thought the words should be paramount. With *Animals,* Waters pared back any comfortable arrangements or textures, and that gave Gilmour cause to worry about future recordings. Also, the guitarist wasn't sure that Waters was charismatic enough to carry too many of the band's new performances onstage. "We didn't have a Roger Daltrey or Mick Jagger," Gilmour told Nicholas Schaffner in *Saucerful of Secrets: The Pink Floyd Odyssey.* "All we had was a bass player that would stomp around scowling and making faces."

The liabilities of Waters as a front man became painfully evident soon enough. *Animals,* like every remaining album Roger Waters would make from this point on, was a decidedly odd work—moralizing, musically repetitive, forbidding, smug—yet it was also daring. The six-month tour that accompanied the album, though, was miscast from start to end. Playing exclusively in stadiums to massive audiences, with immense props—including a ghostly looking helium balloon in the shape of a pig that floated over audiences and exploded into flames—it was as if Pink Floyd was determined to live out their recent concerns about alienation by implanting an emotional distance between the audience, the music and themselves. The tour wore on Waters. He found the large concert arenas dehumanizing, and he began to see much of the audience as inconsistent with his music's message. It all culminated in an incident at the last show in Montreal, Canada, when Waters—fed up with a fan who was loudly and repeatedly requesting a song—spat in the fan's face. David Gilmour was so disgusted that he refused to return to the stage for an encore. When asked in 1980 what he thought the role was for a rock audience, Waters replied: "Passive. Like they're in a theater. You bloody well sit there. I hate audience participation." It was a far cry from the days of the London Underground.

That act of spitting on a fan was another of those pivotal events in Pink Floyd's history. Waters was so disillusioned after the 1977 tour that he swore Pink Floyd would never perform big concerts again unless the band was behind a wall. In January 1978 he came to the band with the idea of enacting that vision: He wanted to construct a multimedia epic that told the story of a musician cut off from his audience and his feelings, who in effect lived behind a wall that he could not overcome. (Waters also offered the band the chance to record *The Pros and Cons of Hitchhiking* instead, but they firmly refused.) Waters's writing had grown more personal over the recent albums, but this new project, *The Wall*, would ante up that invest-ment. The songs about the rock star's anger and pain and loss emerged from Waters's own experience (his father, Eric Fletcher Waters, was a con-scientious objector who had been conscripted in World War II and killed in battle in Italy, like the father in the story), which is no doubt why he became so obsessive about monitoring every aspect of the work-in-progress. He did, however, give some leeway to producer Bob Ezrin, whom he recruited to help him work with the rest of the band. But the producer soon grew critical of how Waters treated his bandmates. When Rick Wright wouldn't cut short a vacation to travel to Los Angeles to finish some key-board parts, Waters insisted that management fire the keyboardist. (Wright would remain as a paid musician, but he was no longer a member of Pink Floyd.) "Roger is a bully," Ezrin later said. "He has a way of instilling self-doubt in everyone—by deferring his own self-doubt."

The Wall occupied Pink Floyd for more than three years. It would find life as the band's most ambitious album, as a stage extravaganza (which indeed featured a wall 160 feet wide and 35 feet tall that was built up during each night's show, then destroyed at the climax) and as a film (starring the Boom-town Rats' Bob Geldof). In its essential purpose, *The Wall* was brilliant: Like *Dark Side of the Moon*, it examined forces of alienation, though this time Waters focused on the various ideologies—such as education, the family, the military—that aimed to manage consciousness. In practice, though . . . Clearly, for millions of Pink Floyd's fans *The Wall* succeeded (the Record Industry Association of America lists it as the fourth best-selling album of all time), but for many others it proved too sprawling, agitated and out of balance, whether on record or on stage. Plus, the film version, directed by Alan Parker, was simply excruciating. Waters—who wrote the screenplay but was banned from the film's set because Parker found him too intru-sive—later admitted that the movie was "unremitting in its onslaught upon the senses." (Asked what *Pink Floyd: The Wall* was about at a press conference, producer Alan Marshall replied: "It's about some mad bastard and this wall.")

Waters followed *The Wall* with *The Final Cut*, and this time he made no bones about who was in charge. The album's subtitle reads: "A requiem for the postwar dream, by Roger Waters, performed by Pink Floyd." The album is Waters's condemnation of Cold War–era Western political, economic and military values, and an indictment of Britain under Margaret Thatcher in particular. Gilmour didn't like the new songs; like the work on *Animals*, they were made up of older tunes that had been discarded, and he thought the lyrics lacked any intricacy. Waters told Gilmour that unless he relented and accepted the work, the album would appear as a Waters solo effort. (Gilmour subsequently removed his name as a producer.) "We were all fighting like cats and dogs," Waters later said. "We were finally realizing—or accepting, if you like—that there was no band." Months after *The Final Cut*'s release in November 1983, Pink Floyd was slated for live performances, but Waters canceled the dates. "The future of Pink Floyd depends very much on me," he told *Rolling Stone*.

Gilmour and Nick Mason saw it differently. In 1986 they decided to make a new Pink Floyd album without Waters, and they brought Rick Wright back for the project. "I haven't spent twenty years building up my name," Gilmour said. "I've spent twenty years building up Pink Floyd's name." Waters erupted at the news. He sued to dissolve the band—which would end Pink Floyd as a recording or touring entity—but Gilmour and Mason fought back. (In the end, Gilmour and Mason got the rights to Pink Floyd's name, Waters got to keep *The Wall*—and the rights to the floating pig.) The new Pink Floyd's first album without Waters, *A Momentary Lapse of Reason* (coproduced by Bob Ezrin), was also the first Pink Floyd album that climbed to Number One in both England and the United States, and their 1988–89 tour was the biggest in the band's history, grossing $135 million. Waters was dismayed at their success. "I was slightly angry that they managed to get away with it," he said years later, "that the great unwashed couldn't tell the fucking difference." For all the ways in which Waters may have been wrong for so long in how he treated the band, he ended up right about the one important thing: Pink Floyd didn't matter without him. *A Momentary Lapse of Reason,* 1994's *The Division Bell,* and the "restored" Pink Floyd's two live albums, *Delicate Sound of Thunder* and *P.U.L.S.E.,* had none of the sense of consequence of the band's earlier albums. Unfortunately, Waters's solo albums—*The Pros and Cons of Hitch Hiking, Radio K.A.O.S.* and *Amused to Death*—had no real life outside the context of his former band. Pink Floyd needed Roger Waters's acerbic point of view, and Waters needed his former band's sonic grace, but they were cut off from each other's purposes.

With all the bad blood, all the ways they tried to demean each other's abilities and integrity, it was clear they could never work together again. When Roger Waters staged *The Wall* near the site of the fallen Berlin Wall, with a cast of numerous talented singers and musicians—Joni Mitchell, Van Morrison, Sinéad O'Connor and Cyndi Lauper, among them—he pointedly declined to invite Pink Floyd's members to join him. "I have no more respect for them," Waters said.

That was in 1990.

•   •   •

In 2005 Bob Geldof called David Gilmour and asked if Pink Floyd would consider uniting once more with Roger Waters to play the upcoming London Live 8 concert. No, said Gilmour. Word got to Roger Waters, who called Gilmour and said he thought they should do it—that the cause mattered more than their differences. "I think he was surprised to hear from me," Waters said. Gilmour thought about it for a day and gave in.

Pink Floyd was clearly the most anticipated performance in that long day of anticipated performances—this version of the group had not played together in twenty-four years—and the expectation was remarkably well rewarded. It wasn't simply that they managed to overcome a history of rancor longer than the history of the original band itself, nor was it that they sounded fucking terrific that made the event so affecting. It was, instead, the moment that honored their reason for being in the first place. Halfway through their set, Waters said: "It's actually quite emotional standing up here with these three guys after all these years. Standing to be counted with the rest of you. Anyway, we're doing this for everyone who's not here, but particularly, of course, for Syd."

Then Pink Floyd played their best song, "Wish You Were Here," in likely the best version they had ever managed. Bringing their voices into harmony for probably the last time, David Gilmour and Roger Waters sang together, measuring the time, loss, longing and desolation over the years. They could have been singing to each other—speaking across abandoned dreams and lost ground—but they weren't. It was unlikely they would ever go past this point. They were wonderful but hardly comfortable together. Their transcendent event was that they had acknowledged a loss bigger than their own injuries, and at this late date, that was probably all they could do.

One year later, almost to the day, the man who inspired that moment died. In the years immediately after he was expelled from the band, Syd Barrett went on to make two albums, *The Madcap Laughs* and *Barrett*, largely produced by his former band members. David Gilmour later recalled that it was hard producing *Barrett*—his performances were erratic, he preferred little accompaniment, his songs were hard to make sense of, both lyrically and melodically. Over the years, these eccentric records have been held up as proofs of Barrett's madness. To some, that has made them seem dark and appealing. To others, it has simply made them too painful to bear. "I can't imagine anyone liking them," Rick Wright once said. But those records—which in fact shine on, brilliantly—are also proofs of something else: that Syd Barrett's innate, matchless genius had a hard time losing its flame.

The members of Pink Floyd never had any further contact with Barrett after the day in 1975 when he visited their studio. His family wouldn't allow it; hearing about his former band upset him too much. The band, however, made sure he always received his royalty payments in full and on time; the music he wrote for Pink Floyd still sold considerably. In his last few years, Barrett suffered from diabetes—his vision diminished and some of his fingers were amputated—and he was diagnosed with pancreatic cancer only a short time before his death on July 7, 2006.

Syd Barrett never returned to making music after the mid-1970s, but according to his younger sister Rosemary he did begin making art again. She told Mike Watkinson and Pete Anderson, the authors of a Barrett biography, that he would photograph a flower, make a large painting of the flower, photograph the painting, then destroy the painting. "Once something was over, it was over," she said. "He felt no need to revisit it." It was something like what had happened to him during his time with Pink Floyd: He created things that had a life for a phase, and then for reasons that may never be known, all that was left of those things were memories that in time had to be lost. Pink Floyd was one of those things that he made, but in time that too had to be lost. It never really belonged to anybody, but nobody understood that better than Syd Barrett, who long ago grew tired of leaving his shadow in the world and had to let it go.

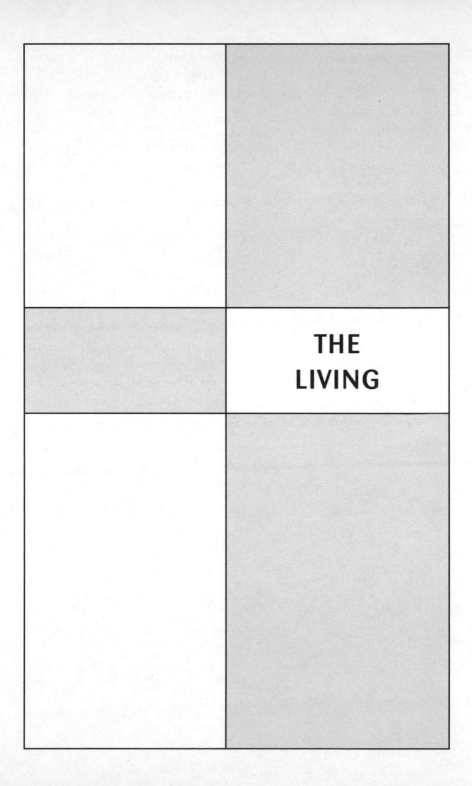

**THE
LIVING**

BOB DYLAN:
NOT THERE, THEN THERE

In 1997 critic Greil Marcus turned out a fascinating and essential book, *Invisible Republic: Bob Dylan's Basement Tapes*, about Bob Dylan's most mysterious body of music and its relation to departed dreams, forsworn histories and questions of community—important concerns in this troubled land that we still call America. (The volume has since been retitled, rather unfortunately, *The Old, Weird America: The World of Bob Dylan's Basement Tapes*.)

In the mid-1960s, Dylan outraged the folk movement that had once exalted him for his social anthems by strapping on an electric guitar and playing howling music that effectively killed off any remaining notions that folk was the imperative new art form of American youth. In the process, he conferred on rock a greater sense of consequence and a deeper expressiveness. But this also meant that he upended rock & roll by recasting it as a protean medium that could mock an entire society's values and politics, and might even, in the end, help redeem (or at least affront) that society. In July 1966, following a tumultuous concert tour of the UK, with his backing group the Hawks, Dylan suffered a motorcycle accident near his home in Woodstock, New York. He was taken to Middletown Hospital, with a concussion and broken vertebrae of the neck. He retreated to his home in Woodstock, with his wife and children, and spent months holed up with his friends from the Hawks—now renamed the Band—in their nearby basement studio. Dylan and the Band played music in seclusion for several months—recording over one hundred tracks—and though several of those songs (most famously, "I Shall Be Released," "Tears of Rage," "Too Much of Nothing," "You Ain't Goin' Nowhere" and "The Mighty Quinn") were later covered by other artists, Dylan himself rarely rerecorded the tracks for subsequent albums and would perform only a handful of them live in later performances. In 1967 Dylan returned to his official recording career with

John Wesley Harding, an album that effectively finished rock's psychedelic era and set in motion a whole new season of roots revivalism. But those songs that had been recorded in seclusion, later known as "the basement sessions," became Dylan's legendary apocrypha and were bootlegged many times in many forms over the years. Finally, in 1975, Dylan authorized the release of *The Basement Tapes,* a partial set of those 1967 recordings.

Marcus's *Invisible Republic* is about *all* that Dylan and the Band truly made and left behind in that long hermetic season—a season when much of the rest of the nation was in a political and generational uproar that would soon lead to outright (sometimes bloody) cultural war. Whether Dylan and the Band knew it or not, Marcus comments, they were not only recapitulating and remaking America's musical story in that time, they were also echoing important aspects of the nation's history—both its past and its future. Often as not, though, they were doing so by way of off-the-cuff, improvised, time-killing (maybe even occasionally inebriated) performances. Dylan would remember a song, start it, and it would become something else. Or he would start with nothing but the moment and the inventions of his own language, and then see where that would go. Through it all, some interesting themes and images seemed to recur or play off one another. As Marcus notes, the basement recordings are full of strange parables, biblical references, half-finished tales of humor, flight, death and abandonment. It is all rough-hewn and primitively recorded—as if a ghost were taking it all down in its impalpable memory—and yet there is something about those songs that seems timeless, as if all the tumult going on in the world outside—a tumult that Dylan helped make possible with his earlier mind-challenging style of rock & roll—was simply far, far removed. At the same time, you *do* hear America—its joys, its losses, its fears and betrayals—in those basement recordings as you hear it nowhere else in Dylan's music, not even in his early, more explicitly political anthems.

It is Marcus's contention that, in effect, Dylan and the Band were creating another version of America in this music and in their fraternity. His point is that though Dylan and the Band were in a way isolated from America at this time, they also couldn't escape it. It was in their music, in their memory, in the reality that was around them—the ongoing horror of the Vietnam War—and it was certainly in the world that, one way or another, they would have to go back to. It had always been there, and it would always remain there.

"In the basement theater . . . ," Marcus writes, "[there] were doors all around the room . . . ; all you had to do was find the key. Each time a new key opened a door, America opened up into both the future and the past. . . . [When] Dylan spoke of an America that was wide open, he meant open to what was to come, not to what had been, open to the question of who and what Americans might become, not to the question of who and where they came from. There is no nostalgia in the basement recordings. . . . In the basement the past is alive to the degree that the future is open, when one can believe that the country remains unfinished, even unmade; when the future is foreclosed, the past is dead. How the future depends on the past is more mysterious."

Invisible Republic's most powerful and intriguing passage is on a song that is possibly the basement sessions'—if not Bob Dylan's—most cryptic and transfixing, "I'm Not There." The song is a truly remarkable performance— half-mumbled, spectral-sounding and holding (and hiding) secrets that can't be given a fully comprehensible utterance. The song is available only on bootlegs; Dylan himself is reported to have no affection for it. "'I'm Not There,'" he once told a journalist, "is a song that's not there." But the song *is* there— or at least something is—and once you hear it, its plaints and rhythms and dreamlike musings never leave your memory. "In . . . 'I'm Not There,'" Marcus writes, "you can sense the presence of something . . . sins committed, perhaps even without intent, that will throw the world out of joint, crimes that will reverberate across space and time in ways that no one can stop. What language do you speak when you speak of things like this?"

I've always heard "I'm Not There" as the sorrow of a man cut off from someone he loves and cannot help and cannot reach. Marcus hears it as something far more frightening: "In the last lines of the song . . . so bereft that . . . the song's . . . five minutes . . . seem like no measurable time, you no longer quite believe that anything so strong *can* be said in words: '*I wish I was there to help her*—but I'm not there, I'm gone.' There is a singer and a woman in the song; he can't reach her, and he can't reach her because he won't. . . . *No one*, you say to the singer, can be left as alone as you have left this woman, and be as abandoned as you have finally abandoned her. . . . [The] singer is not simply the only person who can reach the woman in the song, he is the last person who can reach her. The town has already abandoned her. . . . A town that can leave anyone so far outside of itself . . . may be in and of itself a crime." The community that Marcus (and maybe Dylan as well) is talking about is not unlike so many of the communities that have always populated this land, and still populate it.

I have sometimes thought that what informed Dylan's retreat into Woodstock and the fraternity of the Band was a way of finding what could be recovered after one had learned too much about the meanness of not just the world outside, but also about the dark, troubled depths of one's own history and desire. There is a spooky, unforgettable bootleg video of a visit between Dylan and John Lennon, as they sit in the back of a limousine, winding their way through London in postdawn hours. It was shot in 1966 (for the singer's still unreleased, astonishing film, *Eat the Document*), during Dylan's wild and dangerous UK tour with the Hawks, and in the roughly twenty minutes that the episode lasts, you can see that Dylan was a man clearly close to some sort of a breakdown. At first he and Lennon are funny and acerbic—not to mention competitive—in their exchanges, though it also seems apparent that Dylan has been up the entire night, maybe drinking, maybe taking drugs. Suddenly, he starts to come undone. He is sick of having a camera in front of him at every moment, and more than that, he is *literally* sick. He turns pale, rolls down the window, begs the driver to get him back to the hotel as quickly as possible. Lennon, meantime, is cautious, trying to stay clever, though he looks clearly horrified at what he is witnessing. Had Dylan kept up that pace—that pace of indulgence, that pace of making music that challenged almost every aspect of the world, music that outraged his old fans and caused his new fans to want him to push even *harder*—he might well have been dead within a season or two. The psychic costs of that sort of artistry, of that force of invention, can be unimaginable. It was as if Dylan danced extremely close to the lip of an abyss. *We* wanted to know what he saw there—we wanted to know so that we could have that knowledge without running the ungodly risk of facing that abyss ourselves. Dylan probably got as close to that edge as one can and still remain alive, and finally he decided that the glimpse alone was not worth his obliteration. Dylan, it seems, saw too much too fast, and was afraid of ever getting that close again to chaos. All the music he would later make seems to be a reaction against how he felt in that morning limousine ride.

So when Dylan suffered his 1966 motorcycle accident, he drew back. The accident could have killed him, but so could the life he'd been living. Still, periods of retreat can sometimes be as painful to recall as whatever led to the retreat in the first place. Dylan once told biographer Robert Shelton: "Woodstock was a daily excursion to nothingness." The Band's guitarist Robbie Robertson, in conversation with Marcus for the purpose of his book, seems to confirm Dylan's comment: "A lot of stuff, Bob would say, 'We should *destroy* this.'" In that nothingness, though, Dylan made some of his best music, and—not for the last time—reinvented himself.

Greil Marcus's *Invisible Republic* uncovers the basement sessions' mysteries—at least as much as anyone, short of Dylan, is likely to uncover them (Dylan has never talked at length about those recordings). The one question Marcus really doesn't address in his book is: Are these recordings the final place where Bob Dylan ever expressed himself as both a voice *about* and *of* America? For my part, I have also heard that same voice in some of Dylan's most disparaged works—at moments in *Knocked Out Loaded*, *Down in the Groove*, even in the overly maligned *Self Portrait* (an album Marcus hates). It's that voice calling back to a lost home and a lost time—a place the singer can never reach again and can also never remove from his heart and memory.

At one time we heard it as a voice that enlightened us to something that was new, the unknown that was now possible. Perhaps, though, that voice was all along telling us about a different unknown: what we've had, what we've lost and what we may—or may never—get to hold close again.

Despite the enduring influence of Bob Dylan's 1960s work, until 1997 the modern pop world had lost much of its fascination with him. In the late 1980s and in the 1990s, artists like Bruce Springsteen, Prince, Madonna, Public Enemy, Nine Inch Nails, Kurt Cobain, Beck, Pearl Jam, U2, Courtney Love, Tupac Shakur and Notorious B.I.G. all produced (more or less) vital work that transformed what popular music is about and what it might accomplish, and some of that work affected the culture at large, fueling ongoing social and political debate. Dylan hadn't made music equal to that effect for many years, nor had he really tried to. At best, he tried occasionally to render work that tapped into pop's commercial and technological vogues (such as 1985's *Empire Burlesque* and 1989's *Oh Mercy*), or he mounted tours designed to interact with the massive audiences that his backing bands attracted (such as his 1980s ventures with the Grateful Dead and Tom Petty and the Heartbreakers). At moments, he seemed to be casting about for a sense of connection and intent, as if he had lost his focus and was adrift. Other times, he produced records that many observers regarded as haphazard and uncommitted (like *Knocked Out Loaded*, *Down in the Groove* and 1990's *Under the Red Sky*—though to my tastes, all of those records hold instances of incomparable brilliance).

Meantime, through the late 1980s and much of the 1990s, as he flew under the radar of pop and mainstream media, Dylan was in fact pulling off one of his more extraordinary acts of reclamation. In interviews since then, he has told the story of an event—a moment of awareness—that came to him onstage in Locarno, Switzerland. He said that a phrase struck him—

"I'm determined to stand whether God will deliver me or not"—and that in that moment, he realized that it was his vocation to rededicate himself to his music and its performance. Yet Dylan didn't make any public pronouncements about this realization and how it had changed his purpose as a singer, musician and songwriter. In much of the 1990s, Dylan played out his essential art more onstage than on record (though his early 1990s acoustic recordings of older folk songs, *Good as I Been to You* and *World Gone Wrong*, were flat-out extraordinary). He overhauled his band a few times, always burnishing the lineup, and he and that band toured frequently, playing numerous one-night stands in concert halls and theaters. Dylan also took a more active part in *playing* the music and began brandishing his own style of lead guitar, focusing on shaping phrases that sprang from the songs' hidden melodic motifs. Indeed, Dylan seemed to adopt a viewpoint similar to the one favored by jazz trumpeter and bandleader Miles Davis for most of his career: namely, that the truest vital experience of music resides in the moment of its performance, in the living act of its formation and in the spontaneous yet hard-earned discoveries that those acts of creation yield. The next time the musicians play the same song, it is not really the same song. It is a new moment and creation, a new possibility, a newfound place on the map, soon to be left behind for the next place.

By 1997 Dylan had been touring almost incessantly for over a generation. Beyond his stylistic, political, philosophical and personal changes, beyond the sheer weight of his legend, he continued to play music simply because, in any season, on almost any given night, it was what he would prefer to be doing; it wasn't just a career action, but instead, a necessary way of living—as if he had returned to the restless troubadour life that he effectively renounced following his motorcycle accident. His reclamation remained, for the most part, one of the best-kept secrets in modern music—that is, until the middle of 1997, when two events brought the world's attention back to him. The first happened in late May 1997, when Bob Dylan entered a Manhattan hospital after suffering severe chest pains. Early reports claimed that the singer had suffered a heart attack (it turned out that Dylan had incurred histoplasmosis, a severe but treatable fungal heart infection), and the evening news and cable entertainment programs treated the illness as a prelude to an obituary. Dylan didn't die, of course, but he was hit harder with the illness than he let be generally known. For the rest of us, the episode served as an admonition of sorts: Bob Dylan had changed the world, and the world had all but forgotten him.

The second turnaround event was an affirmation of Dylan's songwriting and singing talent. In late 1997, Dylan released his first album of new songs in over six years, *Time Out of Mind*—a work that proved as devastating as it did captivating. In the album's opening moments, "Love Sick," a guitar uncoils and rustles, and Dylan starts an announcement: "I'm walking . . ." He pauses, as if he were looking over his shoulder, counting the footsteps in his own shadow, then continues: ". . . through streets that are dead." And for the next seventy minutes-plus, we walk with him, through one of the most transfixing storyscapes in recent music or literature.

Though some critics saw *Time Out of Mind* as a report on personal romantic dissolution—like *Blood on the Tracks*, twenty-two years earlier—*Time*'s intensity is broader and more complex than that. It *is* in part about what remains after love's wreckage: Dylan sings "Love Sick" in the voice of an older man, talking to himself about the last love he could afford to lose. For singing this haunted by abandonment, you have to seek the lingering ghosts of Robert Johnson, Billie Holiday, Hank Williams and Frank Sinatra. But *Time Out of Mind* went beyond that. By the time of the album's sixteen-minute closing epic of fatigue, humor and gentle and mad reverie, "Highlands," Dylan has been on the track of departure for so long that he arrives someplace new—someplace not quite like any other place he has ever taken us before. *Time Out of Mind* keeps company with hard fates, and for all the darkness and hurt it divulges, its final effect is hard-boiled exhilaration. It is the work of a man looking at a new frontier—not the hopeful frontier seen through the eyes of an ambitious youth, but the unmapped frontier that lays beyond loss and disillusion.

Time Out of Mind was an end-of-the-century work from one of the few artists with the voice to give us one. And, like Dylan's best post-1970s songs—including "The Groom's Still Waiting at the Altar," "Man in the Long Black Coat," "Under the Red Sky," "Dark Eyes," "Every Grain of Sand," "Death Is Not the End," "Blind Willie McTell" and "Dignity"—*Time*'s songs aren't that much of a deviation from such earlier touchstones as "Like a Rolling Stone" and "I Shall Be Released." That is, they are the testament of a man who isn't aiming to change the world so much as he's simply trying to find a way to abide all the heartbreaks and disillusion that result from living in a morally centerless time. In the end that stance may be no less courageous than the fiery iconoclasm that Dylan once proudly brandished.

In the seasons that followed *Time Out of Mind*, Dylan gave some of the best live performances of his life. As often as not, his most affecting and victorious performances on these occasions were "Tangled Up in Blue" (from *Blood on the Tracks*) and "Love Sick." Both are songs about what lies past lost dreams and ruined faith—though the two songs are ages apart in perspective and miles apart in tone. As he closed in on the ending century, Dylan performed "Tangled Up in Blue" with more ferocity and openness than any other song in his set. He pushed into his stinging flurry of acoustic guitar riffs and strums as if trying to break the song wide open and find its last meanings, and audiences reacted as if they were hearing something of their own story in the turmoil of the music, and the lyric's account of flight and renewal. "Love Sick" is the other end of the story, twenty-odd years down a hard line. Onstage, Dylan sang the song in the voice of an older man, wanting to let go of his hopes so he can also let go of his hates, and damning himself for not being able to abandon his memory.

Even so, nothing about his past seemed to confine him. On September 11, 2001, Dylan released another collection of new songs, *Love and Theft*—his forty-third album. *Love and Theft* was another work to present Dylan at the full peak of his musical, lyrical and vocal strengths. The album sounds at moments like Dylan was unearthing new revelations with an impulsive wit and language—in much the same way he did on his early hallmark, *Highway 61 Revisited*—though *Love and Theft* also seems to derive from ancient wellsprings of American vision and concealment, much like *John Wesley Harding* or those legendary 1967 basement sessions. Dylan, however, bristled at such comparisons. *Love and Theft*, as he put it, plays by its own rules. Which is to say that while the album may trade in occasional riffs of guitar or wordplay that recall the singer's earlier glories, it arrives as a blend of world-weariness, humor and sad-eyed compassion that bears comparison to little else in contemporaneous music. But then, all of Dylan's key works—whether wondrous or dubious—have played by the singer's own sense of standards or by his inclination to disrupt standards.

It has always been tempting, of course, to read much of Dylan's music as a key to his current life and sensibility. He did not divulge much about the details of his life or the changing nature of his beliefs, and so when he made records like *Nashville Skyline*, *Self Portrait* and *New Morning*—records that extolled the value of marriage and family as the redemptive meaning of life, and that countless critics cited as Dylan's withdrawal from "significance"— many fans assumed that these works also suggested the truths of Dylan's own private life. Later, in the mid-1970s, when Dylan's marriage began to come apart, and he made *Blood on the Tracks* and *Desire*—with those records' accounts of romantic loss and disenchantment—his songs seemed to be confessions of his suffering, and the pain appeared to suit his artistic talents better than domestic bliss had. Maybe . . . but also maybe not. The truth is, there is still virtually nothing that is publicly known about the history of Bob Dylan's marriage to Sara Lowndes—how it came together, how it survived for a time, or how and why it ultimately failed.

From the moment he became a name that the nation began to heed, Dylan maintained that he can't (or *won't*) be known through his personal history. Early on, he told interviewers he rode boxcars and had worked as a carney, drove a bakery truck and worked construction, though he was barely twenty-one. He mythologized his past from the get-go—it was all "hokum—hophead talk" he says now, but it was a way of keeping people out of the private details of his life. He also claimed, from 1965's "Like a Rolling Stone" and on, that the meanings behind his songs were inscrutable even to himself, or out of the reach of his consciousness and memory. This attitude, of course, had the effect of imbuing Dylan with the powers of mystery and legend: He became seen as the key to understanding how a known world turned upside down at an important time, yet that key has never been willing to turn its own lock. That is, until the publication of *Chronicles, Volume One*—a collection of memoir-meditations so open and revealing that it can rank alongside the writings of Henry Miller. In it Dylan has chosen to share some of the more eventful passages in his life, and the results prove every bit as mind-bending as his best music. It is the story of how a person lives in his own mind as he figures out the world around him—ultimately, a story of the spirit.

Chronicles is also telling in the narratives it selects to lay out. Dylan goes deep into a handful of crucial periods—his early, prerecording years in New York, when he's figuring out what he wants to say in songs and how to say it; his self-imposed late-1960s exile in Woodstock, New York, in a time when America was ready to burn down; and his mid-1980s malaise, as he recorded *Oh Mercy*. These are all periods when Dylan was on the verge of pivotal discoveries, or reeling from their aftereffect. If you're looking for divulgences about Dylan's rumored drug-dazed flameout in 1966, at the peak of his fame, or about his guarded love affairs and marriages, you won't find those remembrances here. Yet what he does reveal about himself is far more interesting. For one, *Chronicles* makes plain that Dylan isn't the distant figure who became more internalized after the height of his fame in the mid-1960s. Just the opposite: He has always watched his world—our world—closely. He assayed it voraciously, and he assessed those who walked across its stage. He remembers *everything* and *everybody*. As a result, we're inside Dylan's head like we've never been before, and it's a mesmerizing place, full of extraordinary views on philosophy and politics, and maybe most surprisingly, history: antediluvian history, American history and the history of the times he's lived in. Indeed, Dylan has lived fully in his times and understood them. It's part of what makes his book such an important document.

Chronicles opens—and it closes—circa 1961–62, in New York City. Dylan, still underage, has come to Greenwich Village from the Midwest, where he filled his head with everything he could discover about the dark, uncontainable world of American folk music. He tells this part of his story in vivid language—plainspoken yet as distinctive as any of his best lyrics—and in transfixing detail. He conjures up rooms full of living history, full of the famous and the unknown, and he tells us how they walked, talked, looked and why they mattered, from Harry Belafonte and Woody Guthrie to Jack Dempsey and Tiny Tim (the latter with whom Dylan shared French fries when they were both playing music in exchange for meals). Through it all, Dylan has intimations that something big might crack open inside him. "I could transcend the limitations," he writes. "It wasn't money or love that I was looking for. I had a heightened sense of awareness, was set in my ways, impractical and a visionary to boot. My mind was strong like a trap and I didn't need any guarantee of validity." In moments like this you get a sense of Dylan's pride—and his ego. He knows he's changed modern culture—it's evident even when he tries to deny that effect—and his assessments of his power are hardly misplaced. But in 1962, as he's readying to record his first album, something is still missing for him. He has glimpses of a new vision coalescing—some original way to build songs and inhabit them with his mind—but these glimpses come in fitful bursts. He doesn't know for sure what he's looking for, but he looks everyplace—in the ancient histories of Tacitus and Thucydides; in the poems of Ovid, Milton and Edgar Allan Poe; in the form-breaking paintings of Pablo Picasso and modernist Red Grooms; in the dangerous, radical songwriting of Bertolt Brecht and Kurt Weill and in the ghostly voice of the late blues singer Robert Johnson.

In that period, Dylan settled into the New York Public Library, reading American newspapers on microfilm from 1855 to 1865—the years that America fell divided in the Civil War, and kinsman killed kinsman. "You wonder," he writes, "how people so united by geography and religious ideals could become such bitter enemies. After a while you become aware of nothing but a culture of feeling, of black days, of schism, evil for evil, the common destiny of the human being getting thrown off course. It's all one long funeral song. . . . The age that I was living in didn't resemble this age, but yet it did in some mysterious and traditional way. Not just a little bit, but a lot. . . . Back there, America was put on the cross, died and was resurrected. There was nothing synthetic about it. The godawful truth of that would be the all-encompassing template behind everything that I would write."

Near *Chronicles'* end, after having moved on to the other periods the book covers, Dylan returns to the same time and place, fills in a little more detail. The moment when he would see how to grasp his art and encounter the times inches closer here. He meets seventeen-year-old Suze Rotolo, with whom he has a famed, tempestuous romance, and who takes him to the city's museums, where he sees works by Goya, El Greco, Kandinsky and Picasso. The latter particularly grabs him. "Picasso had fractured the art world and cracked it wide open," he notes. "He was revolutionary. I wanted to be like that." Rotolo also introduces him to the groundbreaking paintings and constructions of Red Grooms, whose art had elements of satire and protest in it, but also rendered the inhabitants of the everyday world in ways uncommon to art. Grooms's work jolts Dylan. "There was a connection in Red's work to a lot of the folk songs I sang . . . ," he writes. "What the folk songs were lyrically, Red's songs were visually—all the bums and cops, the lunatic bustle, the claustrophobic alleys. . . . He incorporated every living thing into something and made it scream. . . . Subconsciously, I was wondering if it was possible to write songs like that." These moments and others—discovering the dangerous, radical songwriting of Bertolt Brecht and Kurt Weill; John Hammond introducing him to the ghostly voice of blues singer Robert Johnson; reading the French Symbolist poet Arthur Rimbaud; thinking it might be possible to write a long-form song with the momentum of a poem like Allen Ginsberg's *Howl*—all build up. Dylan hasn't moved yet beyond folk, hasn't even written his early anthems, but he knows he's about to grab a chimera by the horns and ride it into the unknown. "I had a vivid idea of where everything was," he says. "The future was nothing to worry about. It was awfully close."

Six years later, Dylan is now living in Woodstock, New York—a remote and bucolic place. "Truth was," he says, "that I wanted to get out of the rat race." He was looking for seclusion, time alone with his wife Sara Lowndes (never mentioned by name in *Chronicles*) and their three children. He wanted time to live a normal American life. But this was 1968. There was no normal American life. The country resembled the Civil War that Dylan had meditated on earlier. "The war in Vietnam was sending the country into a deep depression," he writes. "If you saw the news, you'd think the whole nation was on fire. It seemed like every day there was a new riot in another city, everything on the edge of danger and change. . . ."

It wasn't just the edge of change. Change was in fact happening in serious ways, and to some observers what Dylan did a few years before gave voice to this change, emboldened its cause. Dylan does not want anything to do with this view, but it doesn't matter. People came to his home. They invaded it. They wanted Dylan active in their causes, they wanted him at the barricades. "These gate-crashers, spooks, trespassers, demagogues were all disrupting my home life . . . ," he writes. "Everything was wrong, the world was absurd. It was backing me into a corner. Even persons near and dear offered no relief." He takes his family back to Greenwich Village, but the same thing happens there. That future that Dylan headed hopefully into in 1962 had played out unexpectedly. His mystique and fame worked against him, as did his role in modern times. He'd made music that was daring and risky, that ignited all kinds of things—and now he hated the place he found himself in as a result. He didn't want to be seen as a revolutionary, as the voice of a generation—"the Big Bubba of Rebellion," he writes, "Leader of the Freeloaders, Kaiser of Apostasy . . ." The revolutionaries, he reasoned, are as destructive as what they are opposing. Dylan determined not to make any more art that might invoke the fires outside, and decided to shut down his creative self. "Art is unimportant next to life," he says, "and you have no choice. I had no hunger for it anymore, anyway." Dylan goes on to claim that he made *Nashville Skyline* and *Self Portrait* as a means of disenchanting his audience, as a way of pushing them away.

This is fascinating stuff, and Dylan relates it all in a powerful voice, both broken and full of rage. It's also fascinating because of what Dylan elides as we turned that page from 1962 to 1968. In the intervening years, he had made music that not only put him on the map but that remade the map, and that raised the stakes everywhere around him. He doesn't mention any of that here, but then he doesn't need to. There would be no book to read if all that hadn't happened. But there are other omissions far more curious. During this same period he issued *John Wesley Harding*—a masterful record that, like his earlier work, changed the current rock & roll temper, inspiring the Beatles and Rolling Stones, among numerous others, to return to a more fundamental method of music making. Dylan doesn't talk about any of this work in *Chronicles*, except maybe in a brief, oblique reference. Instead of mentioning this, he centers on 1970's *New Morning*, a pleasant enough middling effort. "I felt like these songs could blow away in cigar smoke, which suited me fine . . . ," he writes. "[The] album itself had no specific resonance to the shackles and bolts that were strapping the country down, nothing to threaten the status quo." Interestingly, some of *New Morning*'s songs began as something else altogether—as contributions to *Scratch*, a dark metaphysical play by poet and playwright Archibald MacLeish, but the venture came to unsettle Dylan. "The play spelled death for society with humanity lying facedown in its own blood," he writes. "MacLeish's play was . . . signaling something through the flames. The play was up to something and I didn't think I wanted to know." (*Scratch* was, in fact, suggested by the famous Stephen Vincent Benet short story "The Devil and Daniel Webster.") Maybe it's fitting that America's most eventful poet of that time— Dylan, not MacLeish—could no longer bear the prospects of chaos. The country was mad around him, and he found that trying to maintain a sane sanctuary—in his home and in his mind—was maddening enough in itself. Dylan settled for whatever *New Morning* achieved for him. He would rebound later, of course, but that's another story.

Instead he moves ahead seventeen years, to 1987, another time of misery. He's no longer sure he should write, no longer sure he should play. Soon, he finds rejuvenation listening to a jazz singer in a low-end bar in San Rafael, California, where Dylan is rehearsing for a tour with the Grateful Dead. But this isn't salvation. Neither is the making of another fair-to-middling record, *Oh Mercy*, which is the chapter's putative subject. When real salvation happens here, it's in the form of an epiphany that stretches back to his Village days, when holding a guitar was a vital act that could lead to mind-blowing possibilities. This is *Chronicles'* most elegiac chapter, and it unfolds like a symphony. Again Dylan passes over an awful lot of ground to bring us here. He doesn't mention *Blood on the Tracks*, his 1975 work that many regard as his best album, and he doesn't talk about his controversial religious period, which produced the epochal *Slow Train Coming*. Rather, he talks about feeling lost in the wilderness, making his way through, biding his time, as he renewed his vision. This is as powerful as anything Dylan may have written about, say, *Blonde on Blonde* or any of his other clear brilliant victories. To be sure, *Chronicles'* stories are about real invention and inspiration, but they are also about demoralization, about how withdrawal or half-measures or even failures can work their own saving grace. Dylan tells these stories in an unwavering voice, from an internal vantage that few, if any, ever expected from him. He uncovers these moments, measures and owns them, and then he moves on. It's a remarkable achievement, and like Henry Miller's best personal writings, it is a story that opens up the times that it portrays, and then reveals the possibilities of the human spirit. They aren't always easy possibilities. After all, it's life only, but it's never been written this way before.

LEONARD COHEN'S
LIFE OF DEPRESSION

In 1994 songwriter and singer Leonard Cohen—who had long been, at the same time, one of the most respected and most underappreciated artists in modern music—disappeared from the popular music world. For that matter, disappeared from public life altogether. His withdrawal took place without fanfare and certainly without expectation. In the late 1980s and early 1990s, with such works as *I'm Your Man* and *The Future*, Cohen had enjoyed the most successful period in his long recording career and was also enjoying unexpected newfound acclaim. Numerous artists—including Jeff Buckley, Jennifer Warnes, Nick Cave, Tori Amos, Suzanne Vega, Willie Nelson and Frank Black—were covering his songs in tribute albums or on their own records, and various filmmakers (such as Oliver Stone and Atom Egoyan) were featuring his work in their movies. At age fifty-eight, Leonard Cohen seemed—somewhat improbably—at the top of his game. But then he simply walked away, leaving behind his legendary love affairs; his two-storey home in Los Angeles; and, it seemed, his recording and literary careers as well.

As it turned out, Cohen had decided to take up residence at a Zen monastery on Mount Baldy, an hour northeast of Los Angeles. The site is a Boy Scout camp, 6,500 feet up the mountain, and was run by Cohen's longtime Zen master and elderly friend, Kyozan Joshu Sasaki, also known as Sasaki Roshi. In time, Cohen was ordained a monk in Roshi's order. After that, more and more biographers and journalists began writing about Cohen's music and literature as finished bodies of work. We should not expect to hear anything more of him, several of us surmised, apart from the occasional poem that he released to friends for publication on the internet.

Then, just as unassumingly as he took leave of everything, Cohen also took leave of the monastery in 1999 and returned to his life with family and friends. In the fall of 2001, he released a new album, *Ten New Songs*, that was, in many ways, unlike anything he had recorded before and was among the best works of that year. In contrast to the often-acerbic themes that dominated *I'm Your Man* and *The Future*, Cohen's new album was about the sad-eyed acceptance and full-hearted love that come after the fires of suffering and the advent of age. It is not about a fearsome future, but rather about a tolerant present—and in that way, it amounts to a brave story of sorts. Deep in the folds of the album there are hints about the mysteries that had surrounded Cohen in the 1990s: Why did he leave the world behind when the world finally seemed ready for him? And why did he then return with what might arguably be called his bravest vision of deliverance since his brilliant, form-breaking 1960s novel, *Beautiful Losers*?

The answer is: Something happened to Leonard Cohen while he was gone—something that changed him. It's also something he'll say only so much about.

It is 1988, a pleasant summer early evening in Los Angeles. I meet Cohen at the upstairs quarters of his mid-Wilshire–area duplex home, for an interview. At this point, Cohen is between dates on an expansive American tour, in support of his most recent (and surprisingly popular) album, *I'm Your Man*. It is quickly becoming apparent to many people that *I'm Your Man* and the present tour will change everything in Cohen's long career, seemingly for the better.

I had met or spoken with Cohen at occasional points since the recording of his 1979 album *Recent Songs*. Some of our conversations had taken place in tequila bars—as mariachi bands wandered the room—and some in recording studios or backstage, after concerts. Until this 1988 evening, though, our longest talks had been one or two transatlantic telephone interviews, at rather odd hours. At one point we were talking about romantic and sexual love—a subject that has always deeply informed Cohen's work. *Recent Songs* was, in no small part, an album that, like his prior collaboration with Phil Spector, *Death of a Ladies' Man*, contemplated the passions and difficulties of his long relationship with Suzanne Elrod, the mother of his two children (daughter Lorca and son Adam). Cohen, like many of us, is sometimes inclined to take personal experiences and view the world through their prism, and on one of those late nights, talking about his recent music and his current view of romance, he commented: "People are lonely, and their attempts at love, in whatever terms they've made those attempts, they've failed. And so people feel they don't want to get ripped off again, they don't want to get burned again. They get defensive and hard and cunning and suspicious. And of course they can never fall in love under those circumstances. By falling in love, I don't necessarily mean, nor do I necessarily exclude, falling in love with the cheerleader—though that's a good way, too. I mean just to be able to surrender, for a moment, your particular point of view, the trance of your own subjectivity, and to accommodate someone else. That has become difficult for people.

"This is our predicament today," he continued. "There's no point in bringing to your relationships the whole catastrophe that everybody's already experienced. We know it's fragile and we know it's painful, but you cannot bring that. You can't introduce that into every relationship." He paused. "The situation between men and women," he said, "is irredeemable. There's nothing to say about it. It has come to the end."

Because I was going through my own romantic disillusion at the time, I started to agree, then Cohen laughed. "Drunk," he said. "Drunk again."

This early evening in 1988, though, drinks aren't on the menu. Instead, as Cohen ushers me into his simply appointed kitchen, he is intent on making a fine chicken soup. Around the kitchen are a few small religious icons and portraits—some symbols of Cohen's own Judaism, a few bits of Hindu and Buddhist statuary and art, and a picture of Kateri Tekakwitha, the famed Iroquois Indian who figures controversially into Canada's early history of Catholic conversions, and who looms over the mysterious heart of Cohen's novel *Beautiful Losers*.

There are many things that can be said truthfully about Leonard Cohen. For one, he is far more hilarious than most people might expect from his dour image and songs—even though he has been, at times, a genuinely depressed individual and much of his work evinces that. But there is one thing about Cohen that, for me, stands out above any other artist, politician, author, actor, philosopher or celebrity I've ever met: He is an exemplar of immaculate manners, courtesy and thoughtfulness, and it is apparent that these attributes come naturally to him. They are not there for show: They are part of who he is and how he conducts himself in the world.

As Cohen attends to his soup, we begin our first of many long conversations over the years about his life and career. It is sometimes overlooked that Cohen possesses one of the longest-running careers of any serious artist working in popular music—a career that, in vital ways, predates those of the Beatles, Bob Dylan, the Rolling Stones, and even Ray Charles, Johnny Cash and Elvis Presley. Which isn't to say that Cohen recorded music before any of these other artists did, but that he was certainly creating a major body of enduring work before most of them became known (and for the record, he was indeed playing guitar in a country-western band well before Elvis Presley ever wandered into Sam Phillips's Memphis Sun Studios).

Cohen was born in 1934, in Montreal. He was the only son of Nathan and Masha Cohen (Leonard also has an older sister, Esther). He shows me a picture of his parents: They look formal yet warm. The Cohens were, in fact, a somewhat prominent and affluent family in Montreal's large Jewish community. Though the family observed Judaism's traditions and holy days, they weren't zealous or insulated when it came to religion. As a result, Cohen also found himself fascinated by the Catholic culture that pervaded in much of Montreal. "The experience I had of Catholicism," he says, "was very sweet. When I spoke to my Catholic friends, they—being in a rebellious condition of youth—had a critical position of their backgrounds that would indicate to me the oppressive quality of the religion that they experienced. I didn't experience any of those oppressive qualities. I just saw the child, the mother, the sacrifice, the beauty of the ritual. And when I began to read the New Testament, I found a radical model that touched me very much: 'Love your enemy; blessed are the meek, for they shall inherit the earth.' I felt these tenets were a radical refinement of certain principles that exist very powerfully in Judaism also."

This mix of a sense of Jewish identity, suffering and mysticism, and an interest in Christian iconography and obsessions with redemption would figure prominently—and with a kindly equanimity—throughout Cohen's lifetime of work and would also enlighten his later fascination with Zen Buddhism. Many critics have traced Cohen's other notable passions—sorrow and loss—to the grief he experienced at age nine, when his father died, following a long debilitating condition that resulted from serious injuries incurred in World War I. Other biographers trace both Cohen's musical manners and his lifelong bouts with melancholy to his Russian-born mother. Masha apparently sang constantly around the home, in a lovely and haunting melismatic voice, and also suffered from (and was treated for) depression.

Cohen, though, isn't so sure that this background alone shaped his development. "It's true that my father's death was my first real experience with loss," he says, "but I never thought much about my family. My mother was a very sweet and compassionate woman. She was also a refugee and witnessed the destruction of her own milieu in Russia, so I think she was justifiably melancholy about something, in the sense of a Chekhovian character; it was both comic and self-aware. But the truth is, my family seemed to be like everybody else's family: They seemed to be perfectly acceptable, decent people, in fact honorable people. Nothing seemed to happen, really. No conflicts. I may be just speaking out of profound ignorance of what really affected me, but I don't have any recollection of any family problems. We're conditioned to look back at our childhood with a very severe and scrutinizing and judgmental view to find out why we're suffering, when in truth we might not be suffering because of those matters.

"I think that, like the families of many of my friends, my family gave me an encouragement to be noble and good. As a result, all my close friends had this sense of huge possibility for themselves. There was something in the air, I guess, that encouraged a number of us to think in a kind of messianic mode about ourselves. We had the sense that there was something important in our lives. This was before television. There was room for a personal mythology to develop."

Those aspirations to mythology and possibility—along with an appetite for women—came early and forcibly to Cohen. Both passions characterized his writing, and even in his late teens and early adulthood his poems and prose began to draw the attention and praise of many of Canada's leading critics, teachers and writers—including the famed iconoclastic poet Irving Layton, whose own fixations with themes of deliverance and sex bore great influence on Cohen's growth. Looking back, Cohen believes that Montreal's lack of any recognized centrality to the world of art, literature and ideas may have turned out to be a boon for him and his Canadian compatriots. "When I was at college [at Montreal's McGill University] and I started to write and meet the other writers in the city, we had the sense that what we were doing was very important because *there was no audience*. We weren't in London or New York—we didn't have the weight of the literary establishment around to say what was possible and what was not possible. It was completely open-ended. We had the sense of an historic occasion every time we gathered and had a glass of beer. We all thought we were famous by the age of sixteen or seventeen, and I think that equipped a number of us with a very strong sense of identity. Irving Layton feels that's essential for a writer to survive—a strong sense of identity—because otherwise you get wrecked. The atmosphere of our meetings and gatherings in Montreal cafés and private houses was that this was the most important thing that was going on in Canada—that we were the legislators of mankind, that we had a redemptive function in some way. We were going to restore vitality through the language, confer meaning on our experience and the experience of our country. Many very wild and extravagant notions were entertained."

Cohen also credits an experience he had at a summer camp—where the director was a socialist and a folksinger—as decisive in his artistic progress. "He played good guitar," says Cohen of the director, "and he introduced me to folksinging via unionism left-wing thought. I learned about the People's Song organization. I found out about a whole leftist position, a resistance position. I'd never known there was anything to resist. Things seemed perfectly okay to me, but I found out that there was a division of thought on this—that there were people who were dispossessed and there were those who spoke for the dispossessed. My imagination was touched and my sense of justice was activated, but mostly I loved the position in the songs, and I started learning them and how to sing them. I got a guitar, and after the camp season was finished, I started learning songs. I went down to Harvard during the summer, to the folk song library and listened, and I began acquiring the knowledge of a lot of folk music. At the same time, I got interested in conventional poetry, in particular the Spanish poet Federico Lorca—but I didn't see much difference between songs and poems. So later I didn't have to make any great leap between writing and singing. I saw that what mattered was that the figure stands and raises his voice in the name of something, and that kind of figure is the one I've had in my heart or my imagination from the very beginning. Whether it was folk music or a poem, it was the word, and I cast my lot with that kind of idea. Later, with writer friends, we gathered together around the guitar, around the folk song, and in the course of those gatherings, people wrote their own songs from time to time. I wrote some of my own songs. That's what we did every night; we drank and we sang folk songs. It had no commercial application, but it was pervasive."

In 1956 Cohen self-published his first poetry collection, *Let Us Compare Mythologies*. "At that time nobody would think in a million years of submitting their poetry to some publisher," he says. "There was no authority, there was no establishment, there was no academy that would judge whether you were a poet or not. We were self-appointed. We spoke with authority and we published our own poems, and the poems we published were in mimeographed magazines. That's where our poems were published. Eventually we graduated to the printing press." *Mythologies* met with critical acclaim, and Cohen's next volume, *The Spice-Box of Earth* (1961), fixed his position as Canada's major new literary voice.

Meantime, Cohen wanted to see the world outside Montreal and wanted to explore different forms of writing. Also, he had to face the inescapable problem of how a poet makes a living: While Cohen's recognition as an emerging major writer was heartening, poetry simply could not provide him with a living. "I tried law school," he tells me with a laugh. "I failed there. I was asked to leave. And I tried factory work. I had no money by this time. I wasn't taking any money from my family; there was very little money left. Also, there was a lot of resistance to giving me money. People thought I was a junkie or a bohemian; I had blown my cover by this time. So I was working here or there—even as an elevator man in New York. Finally, I applied to the Canada Council, and I got a grant on the basis of *Let Us Compare Mythologies.* That gave me a small amount of money, enough to travel to the ancient capitals. I wanted to go to Athens, Rome and Jerusalem. I stopped off in London, and while I was there I wrote the first draft of *The Favorite Game,* my first novel." *The Favorite Game,* published in 1963, was a semiautobiographical account of Cohen's development as a youthful writer, sensualist and worrier—more or less his equivalent to James Joyce's *Portrait of the Artist as a Young Man.*

In the late 1950s, Cohen visited the Greek isle of Hydra (which Henry Miller had written about so memorably in *The Colossus of Maroussi*), and fell in love with the landscape, the warm climate, the culture and its people. In 1960 he bought a three-storey house on the island for $1,500. (Cohen still owns and maintains the home.) While there, he also met and lived with a fetching Norwegian woman named Marianne Ihlen and her son. This relationship began a pattern that followed Cohen throughout his life: He would find himself drawn in by the assurances and bliss of domestic and sexual commitment, but he would also feel confined by the realities of such a life. That is, he craved the order that relationships gave him but he also needed to work against how that order limited him.

For the next few years, Cohen went back and forth between Greece and Canada. He even visited Cuba, shortly after Fidel Castro's successful revolution—though he had to flee Havana when he was suspected of being a possible American spy. In his time on Hydra, he began to think about a new novel—eventually entitled *Beautiful Losers*—something that would stretch his own artistic boundaries and perhaps those of literature as well.

Hydra life went on with Marianne, and Cohen spent his afternoons sitting in the isle's sun typing, playing records by Elvis Presley, Ray Charles, Nina Simone and Edith Piaf on a portable phonograph machine. "I remember playing Elvis Presley once to a group of expatriates and saying, 'This guy has changed it all. Listen to this.' They thought I was kidding. . . . During all this time, I was writing *Beautiful Losers*, and I knew that it was living work while I was doing it—though I was doing it more or less with sunstroke. In fact, as I was typing it, I melted several LPs on my little portable record player—several Ray Charles records. I had to keep buying them, because they would just melt, it was so hot and bright. I was writing in the sun on a little folding table in the back of my house. In the spring it would be filled with thousands of daisies, and they'd wither as the summer progressed. I'd just be sitting there in this mad kind of skeletal situation after the spring and I was writing with sunstroke and I eventually . . . I finally broke down. I think I was slightly demented and frenzied during the whole creation of the thing. But I knew that it was alive, because I'd read it to my friends. They would laugh or they would be on the edge of their seats. I knew that something was unfolding and there was a joyous activity behind it also. But as I say, slightly crazed. Which freed the writing tremendously."

Beautiful Losers was published in 1966. Looking back on the literary atmosphere and cultural battles that were already flaring in this period— a time in which some of Henry Miller's works and Allen Ginsberg's *Howl* remained notorious and still subject to suppression in some communities—it seems startling that *Beautiful Losers* managed to find its way to print uncensored: It is a genuinely daring, groundbreaking and startlingly sexual work about a man's search for identity, memory, purpose and transcendence amid a dizzying weave of romantic, religious and historical betrayals—and the book's unexpected and bewildering end can genuinely lift the top of your head off. Just as Allen Ginsberg's *Howl* opened up new territories and new courage in American literature in 1955, Leonard Cohen's *Beautiful Losers* opened up new perspectives about form and time in modern fiction—and many writers and critics still cite it as a major event in postwar literature. Over forty years after its publication, *Beautiful Losers* remains a mesmerizing and astonishing work, and it makes plain that if Cohen had desired, he had the opportunity to reach for the sort of literary standing accorded such authors as Norman Mailer, Thomas Pynchon and Henry Miller.

To date, Cohen has never written another novel, and as wonderful as much of his later work has proven, there is a go-for-broke audacity in *Beautiful Losers* that is matchless. But Cohen's creative ambitions were already changing by the time the novel was published. "I'd finished *Beautiful Losers* and I'd got some very good reviews for it," he says, "but it only sold a few thousand books, both in Canada and the United States, and I couldn't make a living. It was like facing a hard truth. I really worked at this; I'd produced two novels, three books of poems, and I couldn't pay my rent. This was serious, because I had people that depended on me by that time."

Cohen would later tell the *New York Times,* "All my writing has guitars behind it," and by the mid-1960s, Cohen realized that the ambitions of literature and the effects of popular music were indeed hardly antithetical. If anything, they were merging. "I have to admit," he says, "that, living in Greece most of the time, I had been completely unaware of the whole renaissance in music that was taking place in the early and middle '60s. Still, I was playing a lot of guitar and I thought, 'It's all right being a writer— I always want to be a writer—but I think I'd like to go to Nashville and make some country-western records.' On my way to Nashville I stopped in New York, and that's when I first heard about people like Phil Ochs and Judy Collins and Bob Dylan and Joan Baez and Dave Van Ronk. That's when I realized that the thing that many of us had been doing in Montreal years before had become public.

"You see, I had been drifting around the world, speaking from the heart and occupying a certain mythological life. Consequently I felt very close to the singers on the New York scene. I also felt somewhat pissed off that they'd got there before me. They'd actually put out their songs and were there. Most of their music didn't blow my mind, as the expression was at the time, because I'd been writing verse for a long time and I'd already opted out of the system that they were criticizing. I was already living the life that they were living—perhaps even more securely and more comfortably than they were. Also, I was coming from that poetry background, in which the marketplace was bullshit. In Montreal we hadn't been thinking, 'How can we get on the bestseller list?' That was like the last place you want to be—that would mean that it's over. Still, I was sorry I didn't know about it, or I would've joined them a lot earlier. It was that sense of having been out of it—that's what bothered me more than anything. It wasn't acute, but I was somewhat pissed off. These people got there and they were cashing in on it at all levels."

Cohen begins to set the table for our meal, then continues. "When I heard Dylan, I *knew* that we were dealing with a poet. From the beginning I understood that this was a writer of high significance, someone that really spoke with a true voice of feeling. I recognized that immediately because that's all I cared about. That was the life I was living—that life where you stood by what you wrote. It was a matter of life and death and you didn't fool around with it. *Beautiful Losers* was written long before I heard of Dylan, and it has that same kind of extravagance, that same kind of surrealism. It was arguably as heavy as anything else that was going down at that time. Then I bumped into Lou Reed at Max's Kansas City, and he said, 'You're the guy that wrote *Beautiful Losers*. Sit down.' I was surprised and delighted to learn that I had some credentials on the scene, and I was welcomed warmly by Lou Reed and by Bob Dylan and by Phil Ochs. All those guys knew what I'd written. So I realized I hadn't really missed the boat or that my work had been for naught, because these songwriters—along with the poets back in Canada—became the first real academy in my life. I had influenced the scene in some tiny way even before I started with song."

In 1967 singer Judy Collins recorded one of Cohen's earliest (and still most recognized) songs, "Suzanne"—a meditation on the elusiveness of any clear paths to salvation—and the tune enjoyed widespread fame. Around that same time, legendary producer and A&R person John Hammond (who had signed such artists as Count Basie, Billie Holiday, Bob Dylan and Aretha Franklin, among others, and would later sign Bruce Springsteen) visited Cohen's new single-room residence at the Chelsea Hotel to hear the writer's musical material. "Hammond," says Cohen, "was what they used to call in the nineteenth century a gentleman. A very impressive man, without an ego. In my hotel room I played him a few tunes, and he said, 'You've got it.' I dared to hope that he meant not just the contract, but the right to consider myself as belonging in that incredible catalog of people that he'd signed. A hundred levels below, perhaps, but still, he allowed me to step into that stream."

Cohen released his first album, *Songs of Leonard Cohen*, in 1968. He claims not to have much affection for the final work (he feels that producer John Simon "sweetened" the sound too much), but the record clearly established a reputation for Cohen as somebody who spoke for those who feel lost and are in search of any saving grace, whether it be religion or sex. A fellow tenant of Cohen's at the Chelsea Hotel—legendary archivist Harry Smith, who compiled the hugely influential *Anthology of American Folk Music*—ran into Cohen one day at the hotel and said: "Leonard, I know a lot of people are congratulating you on the lyrics, but I want you to know, the tunes are really good." Cohen places his soup before us and smiles at the memory of Smith's compliment. "It's true," he says. "Nobody was mentioning the tunes; it was all about the lyrics, and all my 'seriousness.'"

Despite his newfound reputation, Cohen says he found himself increasingly forlorn, and his relationship with Ihlen was fading. "People talk about loneliness," Cohen says, "but I really passed days without speaking to anybody. Sometimes weeks where the only contact I would have was with the woman I bought cigarettes from, and a day could be redeemed by her smile. It was a difficult period, and it didn't stop being difficult for a long time. The songs on those first few albums are the record of how I got back. I didn't have much money, and even after my first record came out I had, theoretically, access to interesting groups of people. But I still found myself walking the streets, trying to find someone to have a cup of coffee with. I don't know how it happened like that. It just seemed to be the way things were set up. So that was the material of my life—and I understood that a lot of other people must be in this predicament. I began to develop this idea that a catastrophe had or was taking place, because I couldn't see why I couldn't make contact."

Also, says Cohen, he felt at odds with much of the social rhetoric of the time. "I was a little older than most of the other people in that scene, and there was a political stance that I was not that comfortable with. It seemed to be too real and too unreal at the same time. Those were not really the issues that we legislators of mankind were meant to concern ourselves with. I recognized the fraternal quality in this expression, but I didn't really feel part of it for a number of reasons. It just went against my grain to burn an American flag. The position on Vietnam was one thing—it was completely legitimate and even necessary to resist the war. But much of the rhetoric I found ugly: calling police 'pigs,' 'Amerika' with a *k*. I mean, America is *not* Nazi Germany. It may be terrible, but that sense of perspective, the distortion of that perspective, offended me, and I could never really buy the violent rhetoric. To me, America was the greatest experiment in human history. As bad as it is, it's where things have been the best, so to see Americans in this convulsion . . . My feeling was, this is not appropriate behavior for Americans. You don't pull down your own country. Those things I couldn't accept. That's why I wrote very early on, in *Parasites of Heaven* (a poetry collection from 1966), 'Shouldn't we study etiquette before we study magic?' We were being told magic was going to save everything, but I was offended by a lot of what I considered misunderstanding of personal responsibility. Just because a guy was a landlord didn't mean you smeared shit on the walls and left without paying the rent. I always had a sense that there's a certain fundamental respect that has to be paid to the organization of society, and that it could collapse under a certain kind of attack."

In 1969 Cohen met twenty-four-year-old Suzanne Elrod—the woman with whom he would share his longest and most tempestuous relationship. The two moved to Nashville, and Cohen recorded his next few albums— *Songs From a Room*, *Songs of Love and Hate* and *Live Songs*—with producer Bob Johnston (who also produced work by Johnny Cash, Marty Robbins, the Byrds and Simon and Garfunkel, and produced Bob Dylan's *Blonde on Blonde*, *John Wesley Harding* and *Nashville Skyline*). "Bob Johnston was one of the most lovable guys I ever bumped into," says Cohen. "He was open to everything."

Cohen's subsequent recordings—*New Skin for the Old Ceremony, Death of a Ladies' Man, Recent Songs* and *Various Positions*—were even stronger works: They were affecting and sometimes stark portrayals of the struggle for romantic faith amid sexual warfare and spiritual hope in the face of cultural dissolution. In addition, with *Various Positions* Cohen shifted his musical range. He began composing less on guitar and more on keyboards and synthesizers. As a result, his melodies and harmonic progressions acquired remarkable new grace and depth ("Hallelujah" and "Coming Back to You" are models of involving and revelatory song structure). Also, with 1988's *I'm Your Man*, Cohen fully embraced pop's increasing passion for electronic orchestration and rhythms, making for music that was gleaming, spooky and catchy all in the same instant, and that matched the mordant, dark-humored tone of his new lyrics about world-weary hearts making their way through a landscape of geopolitical calamities. Cohen says: "There was a lot of resistance even among the people I worked with to using electronic sounds. For me, though, it was like writing a sonnet—you had to work within the limitations that the medium offers. That called on me as the composer to move the invention somewhere else."

Although Cohen's music grew more imaginative and appealing—and his ever-deepening voice grew warmer and more intimate sounding—his records sold modestly in the United States (though several of his albums became substantial and lasting hits in England and much of Europe). Legend has it that when Cohen first played *Various Positions* for Columbia Records pooh-bah Walter Yetnikoff in 1984, Yetnikoff said, "Leonard, we know you're great but we just don't know if you're any good"—and declined to release the album in the States.

On this mid-evening in 1988, after Cohen has cleared the dinner dishes away, we remain at his small kitchen table. I ask him whether all the years of the public's indifference and his record company's apathy had left him somewhat disheartened or embittered. "Well," he says, smiling, "I must preface any answer by saying that I feel lucky that I've been able to make a living at all. I've been able to live a good life, I've been able to go where I wanted, help the people I wanted, and I haven't had to worry about things really. And I know that I am in a very kindly minority of artists that have been able to survive doing the thing that they're doing. I'm grateful for having had this kind of career, which didn't involve any of the burdens of celebrity. Beyond that, there have been times when I've thought I was being given a raw deal by a record company, when I thought that even from the point of view of a product they were not taking advantage of it. I have had those stabs of anger or resentment, but nothing so devastating, for instance, as an argument with one's mate. Nothing of that kind of weight. But I have been pissed off from time to time, yeah.

"But, you know, I didn't think very big in the early days. It's only recently I got greedy. I was happy that I'd made that first record and that some people loved it. But I admit I came from a position where I thought I was unassailable as a writer. I was already a world historic figure, in my own mind, at eighteen. As time went along, my confidence began to be shaken."

Was it shaken because of the way in which the albums were received?

"It's just that my life was quite unhappy," he replies. "I didn't feel I was really connecting, I didn't feel the work had that mark of real craft. I felt my gift was waning—that my life was being led away from a certain kind of devotional path: consecration, dedication. I was being corrupted by something. It wasn't money, it wasn't fame, it wasn't women. It's just that there was something in the air. A sense of moral failure began to accumulate, and I wasn't having any fun at all. I didn't feel that I was in the service of the great powers that had empowered me, that had called me to work. The work lost its redemptive quality completely. Things seemed pretty shut down; I didn't know where to turn. I knew I wasn't giving my so-called career any real attention. But those were not the things that concerned me. What was concerning me was that it was a moment-to-moment struggle to pretend to be okay, and that got quite acute."

What helped Cohen begin to recover, he says, was his growing interest in Zen Buddhism—in particular the version taught by Japanese master Sasaki Roshi. Cohen had first met Roshi in 1971, and had tried to study with him at his monastery but found the rigorous discipline and conceptualism too difficult. Still, he kept going back—and in some ways, he says, he was attracted as much to Roshi's spirit and manner as to the teachings of Zen. "Long before I knew Roshi, I was drawn to the aesthetics of what I thought Zen was. You know, the clean lines, the open spaces, the clouds, the haiku. That is, I was drawn to some translated cultural presentation of what I thought Zen was. But one of Roshi's sidelines is completely overthrowing those versions of what Zen might be standing for. When I bumped into Roshi, I became deeply touched by his capacity to allow you to feel friendship: the deep kind of friendship with which he greets you and everybody else—it just stops the mind from spinning. You experience the mind as it stops spinning, and you don't even know this. You just feel marvelously concentrated and attentive to the tea he's pouring you or the cake that he's offering you or the drink that he's fumbling for, because he's all too human. I was very touched by that, and by his profound hospitality.

"With Roshi, I began to investigate—I don't want to say seriously but with a certain sense of urgency—how the self arises. What it is, how it dies, and how it is reborn. That probably saved my life. I was beginning to experience some very severe depression. In my rather superficial way that has been the stabilizing element in my life, this study of the self, and my association with this teacher has been a very important association. Just before I left him recently [this was in 1988], Roshi said, 'Cohen, eighteen years I know you. I never try to give you my religion. I just pour your sake.' And that's true. He never tried to make a Buddhist out of me. He had no interest in that."

Roshi also taught Cohen a valuable lesson, he says, that transformed all his later music: "It was during the time I was making *Various Positions*. Roshi was in the studio with me in New York. I'd been traveling with him as his secretary, and I was taking advantage of my time in New York to record. He came to a recording session, and this was a time when all the news about me was bad and depressing—razor blades and all that stuff. The next morning we were having breakfast, and I said to him, 'What did you think, Roshi?' He said, 'Leonard, you should sing more sad.' Everybody was telling me quite the contrary—not that I knew any alternative or something. But he saw that I hadn't gone where I could go, with my voice, with my trip. It was like the deepest and, at the same time, the most pragmatic advice. He saw that my voice could go low, that I could get deep into the material consciously—that I could explore things. I still don't feel like I've taken his advice to where it could go. I still hear him saying: 'You should sing more sad.' Because that's what it is, you know? If that's who you are."

During this same period in 1988, I also visit Cohen in Manhattan. He is on tour to support *I'm Your Man*—which does better than any other album Cohen has released in the United States and is a major hit in parts of Europe. When Columbia Records grants Cohen an award for the album's successful international sale, Cohen replies: "Thank you. I have always been touched by the modesty of your interest in my work."

At his sold-out July 1988 concert at Carnegie Hall, it is apparent in his delivery of songs like "Ain't No Cure for Love," "Coming Back to You" and "Dance Me to the End of Love" that Cohen has fully taken to heart his Zen master's advice to "sing sadder." But it is *I'm Your Man*'s signal song, "First We Take Manhattan"—a sinister and tense depiction of social collapse and a terrorist's revenge—that seems to stir Cohen's audiences the most. The song unfolds with a thrilling sense of menace, though it carries an undertow of bitter humor. Performed live, it's as if the song were a call to battle, at the heart of a show full of divulgences about heartbroken acquiescence and charitable grief.

I share some of these reactions with Cohen when we meet in his room at the Mayfair Hotel, just off lower Central Park. It is a terribly hot and sticky afternoon and yet Cohen is dressed both obliviously and impeccably, in a dark, double-breasted pinstripe suit, with a crisp white shirt and a smart tie. I envy his ability to look so gentlemanly and handsome in such horrid weather. Cohen insists that I take the most comfortable chair in the room, then calls room service to order me an ice-cold drink. He settles into a stiff-backed chair and places his fingers to his lips, as if thinking carefully about how he wants to reply to my comments. "These are extreme times," he says, after a few moments. As he begins talking, he stands up, unzips his slacks, takes them off, and folds them carefully over the back of another chair. This is all done matter-of-factly and is clearly a sensible thing to do. It's such a sweltering day, why would he want to wrinkle the pants to a nice suit? Still, Cohen keeps his jacket and tie and shoes and socks on as he settles back into his chair.

Meantime, Cohen keeps talking. "You see, I think we are now living amidst a plague of biblical proportions, on various levels. I think the world is breaking down. I think our order, our manners, our political systems are breaking down. And I think that redemptive love may be breaking down as well." I've heard a similar viewpoint from him before. Is this the depressed Cohen speaking or an enlightened realist? He continues: "I don't want to sit here and sound like I'm speaking from the point of view of a prophet—I'm not saying '*repent*.' I don't presume to say what we should repent for—or even if we should. I am making this comment simply as somebody who has been observing this breakdown develop, as somebody who believes that something massive has happened to us, but we didn't necessarily notice it when it happened. I am also not saying this as a warning. There is no point in trying to forestall the apocalypse. The bomb has already gone off. We are now living in the midst of its aftermath. The question we should be facing isn't how we might avoid this. Rather, the question is: How can we live with this knowledge with grace and kindness, knowing that the end has already come?

"So," he adds, "that's how I arrived at that kind of ominous, geopolitical menace that the man in 'First We Take Manhattan' presents. We can no longer buy the version of reality that is presented to us in the public world.

There's hardly any public expression that means anything to anybody. There's not a politician speaking who touches you. There's hardly a song you hear—"

Just then there is a knock at the door. "Excuse me," says Cohen. He stands up and carefully pulls his pinstripe slacks back on, opens the door and signs the bill for my cold soda. He closes the door, hands me my drink, takes his pants back off and sits down. He flashes me a warm smile at this point. There is nothing coy or ironic in the gesture—it's a truly gentle and compassionate expression. I realize that Leonard Cohen has just given me—and not for the first time—an example of how one behaves with grace and etiquette, even though he's filled with the dreadful knowledge that we are all living on borrowed time.

That was the last time I'd see or speak with Cohen for several years. Though much of what he had to say on that day was full of apprehension, I failed to understand that he wasn't speaking simply from an interesting philosophical or political perspective. It wasn't until his next collection, *The Future*, in 1992, that I realized that the sense of sociopolitical foreboding in Cohen's recent albums might be prophetic (whether he owned up to it or not), and that his new songs were also revealing—maybe more clearly than ever before—a distress that lay deep inside his own mind, heart and history. In the album's opening title track, Cohen seemed to traverse lines of all sorts that he had not crossed before:"Get ready for the future / It is murder."

I have always liked songs and art that are both honest and merciless, but I have to admit that "The Future" scared the fuck out of me—maybe because I was trying to figure out for myself at that time how one manages to live with unbearable expectations. A year later, I read a terrific article about Cohen in *The New Yorker* by Leon Wieseltier. The article is entitled "The Prince of Bummers," and in it Wieseltier made the following relevant observations: "Some artists are wide, some artists are deep. There is no denying that Cohen's stylish, self-regarding abjection is present in almost everything he writes and sings. His records are not distinguished by a vastness of feeling. But the feelings that he studies he masters. Cohen does not digress, but he plumbs. And his specificity is a source of his strength . . . when he sings about a man overrun by his passions, it is not gladly. The ruined man does not praise ruin. It is one of the central themes of his songs that he wishes to be rescued from disorder, or at least to be vouchsafed the reason for it. There may be little uplift in Cohen, but neither is there an infatuation with meaninglessness."

I decide I'd like to catch up with Cohen and see how he is holding up. But before I can, Cohen has seemingly disappeared—or moved on to a place where questions about his art might have no further usefulness. Maybe that makes a certain sense. After all, *The Future* was about realizing that the future might not be something that reasonable or friendly voices would want to talk about.

It was now nine years later, the late summer of 2001. I was knocking once more on the same door, at the same duplex house in Los Angeles. The man who answers the door is still an elegant gentleman. Though it's morning, he has a beautiful suit on, and he still insists on offering his visitor the most comfortable seat in his house. Of course, Leonard Cohen has also changed a bit: He is sixty-six when I visit this time, and he wears his pepper gray hair in a shaven crop—a holdover from his habits as a Zen monk.

Cohen left Roshi's Mount Baldy monastery in 1999, after a six-year residency. We are meeting now because he has finished a new album, *Ten New Songs*. It may be the loveliest album Cohen has ever made, and perhaps his most gracious as well. Conceptually, it seems miles apart from the fearful fatalism that ruled *I'm Your Man* and *The Future*. When I share this observation with Cohen, he simply says: "*The Future* came out of suffering. This came out of celebration."

Cohen says he'd been working on sets of lyrics for years, during his time at the monastery. "Many of those long hours in the meditation hall when I was being invited to do something or other with my mind, I was never quite clear what that was. So I found myself working on rhymes and verses. It was a very concentrated kind of activity and a very delicious activity." Cohen goes on to discuss that he didn't compose the album's music this time around. Rather, Sharon Robinson (a longtime friend who was a backup vocalist on some of Cohen's earlier albums and tours) took on that chore. When Cohen first returned from the monastery, he had no immediate plans for recording. Then one night he ran into Robinson at the Beverly Center. He began to renew his acquaintance with her and her family (Cohen is the godfather to her son), and before long he handed Robinson some lyrics he had been writing over the years and asked her if she saw any musical possibilities in them. The two began swapping tunes and arrangements on hard drives. Though Cohen's original plan was to record the album with a full band, in the end he was so moved by Robinson's own demos that he retained them for his basic tracks. Consequently, *Ten New Songs* is entirely written and played by Robinson and Cohen—"Two people in one mind," as Cohen's then-manager Leanne Ungar put it. Says Cohen: "This incredible friendship produced this little masterpiece. I'm talking frank: I think it's a fine piece of work and I don't think I did it, so, I can speak this way. Sharon did most of it. Occasionally I would make some adjustments. There would be a movement in the melody that I didn't think I could handle or that I didn't think served the song. And I'd often say, 'Sharon, does this tune have more than four notes? You know the limitations I have.'" Cohen laughs at his own reputation as a restricted singer. "To be honest," he says, "I recognize that my vocals have a certain authenticity, and that my voice is very relaxed. I can now move around the melody maybe in a way that I haven't done before, with a deeper sense of commitment. At the same time, I feel that Sharon's tracks also made that possible for me."

Cohen picks up a pack of Vantage cigarettes and lights one. He will smoke them almost nonstop through our conversations. "I started smoking again, about a year ago," he says, almost apologetically. "Got to quit again, naturally. People say, 'Your voice has gotten very low.' I say, 'Yeah, fifty thousand cigarettes will do it—and a lot of whiskey.'"

I ask Cohen the obvious questions: Why did he withdraw from his career and move to the monastery? Did he see his action as a retreat, or as a step forward?

Cohen studies his cigarette, as if measuring how to reply. "It had occurred to me," he says after a few moments, "that I would have made my last . . . penetration in the marketplace. I figured the writing activity would continue on some level, but the whole market application felt remote to me at the time that I went to the monastery. And yet there was no sense of dissatisfaction with my career. On the contrary. If anything, it was like, 'Well, so this is what it's like to succeed.' You know, I was fifty-eight by this time, and I had the respect of my peers and another generation or two, and people were writing kindly about me. But my daily predicament was such that there wasn't much nourishment from that kind of retrospection. I went up to the monastery in 1993, after my last tour, with the feeling of, 'If this works, I'll stay.' I didn't put a limit on it, but I knew I was going to be there for a while.

"Also, I was there because I had the good fortune to study with Roshi. He's the real thing, man. He is a hell-raiser—there's not an ounce of piety about him. Anybody with him knows that he's addressing in you that mechanism that is involved with life and death and salvation. You know the place where he is and where he's been and what he's given his life to, because who wants to be living up there with a bunch of dumb Americans who don't get it? This guy is smart enough to be rich, and yet he lives in a little shack, up there in the snow. He's a very exalted figure. When you're with him, you're in the presence of something that is so refined and so wild at the same time, so free and yet so responsible. But I was never looking for a new religion. I was perfectly satisfied with my old religion. I had no crisis of faith or a sense that it was time to renounce the things of the world. Nothing of that order."

The phone in the hallway rings. Cohen pauses to hear who might be calling, but the caller hangs up when the machine answers. Cohen smiles. "I offer a prayer of gratitude when no one leaves a message."

I ask Cohen if he can give me a definition of Zen, as he has come to understand it. "I'd be very hard pressed to do that," he replies. "Because I don't know what it is. I'm not trying to be coy or Zenlike by saying that. I've studied with a teacher, but he's never represented himself as being definitive. The tradition in Zen is that each teacher arises with his own radical model and presents it in his own radical, innovative, original way. If anything, it is the transmission of one teacher to another who has the authority to present this radical vision of reality."

Would Cohen consider himself a teacher—or ever want to be one? He shakes his head vigorously. "I don't have the authority—either based on transmission or on vocation or aptitude or desire—to teach."

Cohen begins to tell the story of the occasion that he told his master Roshi that he wanted to leave the monastery and return to his life. "We were very close friends, Roshi and I. We were the two oldest guys up there, even though there were many years separating us. I had been cooking for him and looking after him for some time. So when I asked his permission to leave . . . *disappointed* is not the right word. He was sad—just like you would be if a close friend went away. But there was no question of him refusing me the permission. It was a matter of respect. He asked me why I wanted to leave. I said, 'I don't know why.' He said, 'How long?' I said, 'I don't know, Roshi, how long.' He said, 'Don't know. Okay.'"

Cohen stubs out his cigarette and sits quietly. After a few moments he offers to fix me lunch. I learned long ago that it is impossible not to partake of food when you visit Leonard Cohen's home.

After lunch, Cohen takes me to his recording studio, built above the garage behind his house. "This is a delightful space to work in," he says—and it indeed captures lights and shadows and sound in ways that almost any writer would desire in a room. Cohen brings along his cigarettes, lights one up and settles into a sofa. He pauses for a long moment before speaking. "I can't talk about what really happened to me up there because it's personal. I don't want to see it all in print. The truth is, I went up there for the same reason by and large that I have done everything: to address this relentless depression that I'd had all my life. I would say everything I've done—you know, wine, women, song, religion, meditation—were all involved in that struggle to somehow penetrate this depression that was the background of all my activities.

"By imperceptible degrees something happened at Mount Baldy," says Cohen, many cigarettes later, "and my depression lifted. It hasn't come back for two and a half years. . . . Roshi said something nice to me one time. He said that the older you get the lonelier you become and the deeper the love you need. Which means that this hero that you're trying to maintain as the central figure in the drama of your life, this hero is not enjoying the life of a hero. You're exerting a tremendous maintenance to keep this heroic stance available to you, and the hero is suffering defeat after defeat, and they're *not* heroic defeats; they're ignoble defeats. Finally one day you say, 'Let him die—I can't invest any more in this heroic position.' From there, you just live your life as if it's real—as if you have to make decisions even though you have absolutely no guarantee of any of the consequences of your decisions."

I ask Cohen if he worries that by losing some of his depression he may have also lost a valuable muse. After all, as even he's noted at times, depression has long been perceived as one of the defining motivating forces in all his work.

"The truth," he says, "is that all those earlier records and books were written *despite* whatever depression or inner conflict was going on. *Ten New Songs* is really the first piece of work for me that doesn't have that background. If anything, it's born out of the absence of crisis.

"But yes, depression has often been the general background of both my work and my daily life. There really was no alternative available most of the time. But my feeling is that whatever I did was in spite of that, not because of it. It wasn't the depression that was the engine of my work. That just happened to be the condition of my life. Whatever my personal inclinations and proclivities were, they weren't necessarily conditioned by the depression. In other words, if I had a brave thought, it wasn't because I was depressed. Nor was that brave thought—if indeed it was brave—produced by the depression. That was just the sea I swam in. There are people who say that the engine of the whole creative operation is depression or melancholy. I don't know whether I bought into that or not, because I didn't have the luxury for those kinds of speculations at the time. But yes, I thought it was an acceptable theory.

"But my real activity is writing, composing. Since that depression has lifted—and I don't know whether it's permanent or temporary—I still have the same appetite to write. In other words, the appetite to write was not a function of the depression. Nor has the intensity or the attention to the activity changed at all. And I don't think the work has diminished. It's just that there isn't that same background of anguish. This isn't to say that life becomes simpler. The struggle to get things right is still intense, but the background is completely different. It doesn't mean that when you're pushing that boulder up the hill, it's an easier task because you're not depressed. It still involves every muscle you've got and every strategy you can summon. But the whole landscape is different because the background is not anguish. You know, I've still got to find the rhyme for 'orange.' The fact that I'm not depressed does not make that any easier. Nor does it mean that all your work falls to pieces and you can no longer associate yourself with the suffering of the world.

"I mean, something wonderful happened to me. I don't know what it was. I just know that life is worth living, and I'm in a position to enjoy the next phase."

I go back to see Cohen a few more times over the next weeks. I keep inventing reasons—more questions that I claim need to be addressed—but the truth is, I just like being in his company and hearing him talk. I like the way he insists that I eat something, or the moment in which he pulls out an ancient sutra and reads it to me, in a voice as lovely and captivating as his singing voice. Also, I value hearing his tales about some of the wonderful musician friends of his who are long dead—such as Tim Buckley, David Blue, Phil Ochs and Tim Hardin—but whose work will never die. "I remember seeing Tim Hardin," he says, "at a club once, dressed in a silk scarf and stinking drunk. I thought: 'This success thing is going to kill some of these guys—it's going to kill people. Stepping out of a limousine, with their pockets full of money and white silk scarves—this can't be good for the trip.' And yeah, it got a lot of people—and other people it didn't touch. Didn't really touch Joni Mitchell, didn't really touch Van Morrison, didn't really touch Dylan. I mean, look at the whole new phase of fertility that Dylan has entered. He could change the whole scene around again, easily."

Another night, Cohen and I talk about his reputation as a ladies' man. He says: "I wrote a song a while back called 'I Was Never Any Good at Loving You.' And I think it's true. I don't think I came across as a particularly good lover. I'm much better at friendship. But I had a strong sexual drive that overpowered every other consideration. I had no idea who the people were that I was sleeping with. I mean, my appetite for intimacy—and not just physical intimacy but the intimacy that went with that activity—was so intense that I was just interested in the essence of those things. It was just an appetite. And consequently misunderstandings and suffering from both parties arose."

Is the appetite still strong for Cohen?

"No. A while back I was visiting my old friend, the poet Irving Layton. He's close to ninety now. We were having a smoke and he said, 'Leonard, have you noticed any decline in your sexual interest?' I said, 'I have, Irving.' He said, 'I'm relieved to hear that, Leonard.' I said, 'So I take it, Irving, you've experienced some decline in your sexual interest?' He said, 'Yes, I have.' I said, 'When did you begin to notice this decline in your sexual interest?' He said, 'Oh, about the age of sixteen or seventeen.'

"And it's true in a certain way. It's never that hot as it is in those years. I don't know whether sex was ever magic for me. It was unavoidably intense—the hunt—but it never really worked. It wasn't particularly enjoyable. It was just an unavoidable urgency that left me no options."

I wonder about how his familial relationships have developed—particularly those with his daughter Lorca and his son Adam. Has that been enjoyable? "Yes," he says, "and that completely caught me by surprise, because I tried to flee from commitments of all kinds. So when the legitimate question of commitment arose, it just overthrew me. I tried to escape as quickly as I could, but the mother of my children outmaneuvered me, pitifully. And . . . I always loved them as infants, but . . . it was hard. I found the whole predicament somewhat intolerable, although because of my tribal conditioning, I did what I could, and it wasn't that bad. But as my children grew up and—and now that I find myself living close to my kids, in the neighborhood here, the relationships are very nourishing. Better than the relationships I was able to have with my own parents."

One of the last times I visit Cohen, we talk about whether, by hanging up his robes, he felt he had in fact abdicated being a Zen monk. "No," he replies, "I don't know what it means. Some years ago before I became a monk, I said to Roshi, 'I become monk, Roshi? I should become monk?' He said, 'No, no need. You already Zen monk.' So, you know, these things are outside of this realm of investigation. I don't know whether or not I've hung up my robes. Roshi's going to be ninety-five, and I'll soon be sixty-seven. It's already old men talking to one another, and now it's time to train the new generations."

I ask Cohen if he intends to continue to make records and publish books. "Yes, I'd like to continue working," he says. "I hope I don't fall over tomorrow. I have a whole new set of songs I'm working on, and I've returned to writing on guitar. Also, I'd like to publish my writings from Mount Baldy. I'd like it to be a big thick book.

"It isn't that in my life I had some inner vision that I've been trying to present. I just had the appetite to work. I think the appetite for activity was much more urgent than the realization of any search or vision. I felt that this was my work, and that it was the only work I could do."

Cohen puts on his suit jacket and walks me outside. I'm waiting for a ride to pick me up. As he waits with me, he says: "This sounds like the most hackneyed nineteenth-century platitude, but in the midst of my own tiny personal troubles, I was able to turn to art, or whatever you want to call it. I was able to turn to art, and in the making of art find solace and strength. I mean, this sounds terrible, but I turned to the thing I knew how to do and I made some songs out of it. And in the making of those songs, much of the pain in my life was dissolved, from time to time. And that is one of the things that I see that art does, is that it heals."

He stares at the bright sun above, bearing down on us. "I'm nearing my late sixties now," he says. "I like what Tennessee Williams said: 'Life is a fairly well written play except for the third act.' I feel I'm at the beginning of the third act. And I'm finding the beginning of the third act is kind of pleasant because you have the experience of the other two acts and you more or less have your health. Of course, by the end of the third act, which nobody can predict, it can be pretty hairy. So you know, this right here is a good stage, a good point to be: the beginning of the third act.

"I don't pretend to have salvation or the answers or anything like that. I'm not saved. But on the other hand, I'm not spent."

ACKNOWLEDGMENTS
AND MEMORIAM

Writing doesn't always accrue debts, but in my case, I have more than a few I should admit to.

I began writing about popular music in 1974, with a review of Bob Dylan and the Band, for a Portland, Oregon, underground newspaper. It was an opportunity that came unexpectedly—an invitation from an editor—and that occasion changed everything for me. I had grown up with rock & roll and I had been transformed by it—it informed the real ideals that I've lived by more than most other influences, including family. Another important passion, though, preceded rock & roll: a love for reading. As a child, I found mirth and wonder in the comic book tales of Carl Barks, who wrote and drew the great Donald Duck and Uncle Scrooge adventures for Disney. Later, around the time my father was dying, I found something else in authors like Herman Melville and Edgar Allan Poe. I wasn't any more somber than most kids, but there must have been something about reading writers for whom there were no great certainties of consolation that took hold for me. In any event, that hold has never lost its grip. A trust in disquiet can be heartening in its own ways.

As it turned out, rock & roll—which I had grown up with—proved a wonderful medium for mixing mirth and disquiet, for many of us. It told of desires and losses, it upended cultural and political values with abandon, and it felt fucking great to hear it and to be with others when they heard it. When I received a chance to write about this thing that I loved, I understood what a gift that was. I'd been reading rock and jazz critics for years; their writings opened new rich territories to me. I saw them as trailblazers, creating a literature that worked in a vital yet uneasy relation to the music itself. Often, those writers inspired me as much as the music itself. Many of them wrote for *Rolling Stone*, *The Village Voice*, Boston's *Real Paper*, the jazz magazine *Down Beat*, or other now defunct publications, including *Eye*, *Cheetah*, *Trouser Press*, *Bomp!*, the original *Crawdaddy* and the original *Creem*. All of these critics and journalists were in print long before I was, and all (but one or two) were a few years older.

Among those historians, journalists and critics who affected me most in that time, and who had a formative sway on rock & roll (and jazz) literature, are the following: Alfred Aronowitz, Whitney Balliett, Lester Bangs, Joachim Berendt, Stanley Booth, Samuel Charters, Robert Christgau, Nik Cohn, Jonathan Cott, Cameron Crowe, Ben Edmonds, Leonard Feather, Ben Fong-Torres, Charlie Gillett, Ralph J. Gleason (a cofounder of *Rolling Stone*), Richard Goldstein, Peter Guralnick, Nat Hentoff, Robert Hilburn, Chris Hodenfield, Jan Hodenfield, Stephen Holden, Jerry Hopkins, Lenny Kaye, Nick Kent, Jon Landau, Alan Lomax, Michael Lydon, Greil Marcus, Dave Marsh, Richard Meltzer, John Mendelsohn, Dan Morgenstern, John Morthland, Paul Nelson, Robert Palmer, Ira Robbins, Lillian Roxon, Bud Scoppa, Arnold Shaw, Greg Shaw, Derek Taylor, Nick Tosches, Ed Ward, Ian Whitcomb, Jon Wiener, Paul Williams, Ellen Willis, and Langdon Winner.

Other music (and music-related) writers whose work I've admired and learned from over the years include Michael Azerrad, J. D. Considine, Stephen Davis, Anthony DeCurtis, Michael Eric Dyson, Bill Flanagan, David Fricke, Simon Frith, Deborah Frost, David Gans, Nelson George, Sid Griffin, Edna Gunderson, Dream Hampton, Clinton Heylin, Gerri Hirshey, Nick Hornby, Barney Hoskyns, Blair Jackson, Alan Kozinn, John Leland, Alan Light, Kurt Loder, Ian MacDonald, Joe McEwen, Kristine McKenna, Dennis McNally, Chris Morris, Charles Shaar Murray, Philip Norman, Jon Pareles, Steve Pond, Ann Powers, Simon Reynolds, Tim Riley, Jon Savage, Fred Schruers, Joel Selvin, Rob Sheffield, Danyel Smith, Neil Strauss, Michael Sugg, Greg Tate, Ken Tucker, Richie Unterberger and Sarah Vowell. I also want to express gratitude for the pleasures and influence gained from Britain's *Mojo* magazine and its groundbreaking work as a music history source, and for David Barker's $33\frac{1}{3}$ book series (Continuum Publishing) and its indispensable portrayals of music that matters in our lives.

However, the people who have had the most direct bearing on my writing, who have only improved it, are the editors and editorial assistants I've known over the years: Eric Bates, Nathan Brackett, Will Dana, Jim DeRogatis, Susan Ellingwood, Jason Fine, Andrew Greene, James Henke, Peter Herbst, Sid Holt, James Kaminsky, Mark Kemp, Joe Levy, Bob Love, Susan Murcko, Barbara O'Dair, Tobias Perse, Bob Wallace, David Wild, Sean Woods and, of course, Jann Wenner.

·   ·   ·

I came to know a few of the writers listed above to varying degrees over the years, but none as memorably as Paul Nelson, who died in June 2006, at age seventy. Rock & roll criticism certainly would have developed without Paul's influence—the music that emerged in the 1950s and 1960s was itself a literature that demanded literary assessment—but early on he brought an elegant style and an innovative perspective to the form. He helped found the first magazine that documented the American folk music revival, *Little Sandy Review*, and he and another friend helped instill in a young Bob Dylan a knowledge of folk music and the work of Woody Guthrie, in the early 1960s in Minnesota. In the late 1960s, Nelson was among the first serious American critics writing about the intense transformations in rock & roll, but he brought to that writing a keen understanding of film and literature—and of their critical traditions and arguments—that helped form an understanding of how this ever-changing popular music form was enriching modern culture and raising the stakes in the society around (and outside) it. He also, perhaps better than anybody else, found a voice to illuminate the mystery at the heart of a song, and in the heart of the person who made that song. In the early 1970s, Paul worked for a time as an A&R man at Mercury Records, where he helped inform Rod Stewart's early masterpieces, and where he signed the New York Dolls. Later, as a music critic—and then reviews editor—at *Rolling Stone*, he wrote pieces that helped establish the meaning and standing of artists as diverse as the Sex Pistols and Willie Nelson.

I came to know Paul as his critical career was ending—that is, as he shut the book on it after a season of personal crisis that was only intensified by some discord with *Rolling Stone*. I was intimidated by him early on—which, I think, was sensible, given his feats, and that he was among America's best critical writers. I'm not sure why he befriended me, though maybe it owed something to us both having an attachment to the work of detective novelist Ross Macdonald, whom Nelson knew well. (Macdonald's writings about family, history and transgression in modern California helped me better understand and accept the place after I moved here in 1977.) In any event, Paul gave me the chance to write feature reviews about Lou Reed and Joy Division for *Rolling Stone* in the early 1980s, and when I underwent panic and a genuine emotional breakdown while working on the latter piece, Paul allowed me that crash, which in itself helped me to recover and finish my work. I think that kindness saved me at a crucial point.

Later, I would visit Paul in New York, and a couple of times he stayed with me in Los Angeles. On those occasions, we would stay up late, watching older films—noir, farce, horror, western—one after another, sometimes until near dawn. (The only music we listened to together was by female pop and jazz vocalists Chris Connor, Jeri Southern, Helen Merrill and Julie London, and jazz trumpeter and singer Chet Baker, Paul's favorite artist.) Paul introduced me to the westerns of Budd Boetticher and the stately comedies of Clarence Brown, and I still have the collection of numerous movies he recorded for me on VHS. One occasion, though, above all others stays with me. I was visiting Paul at one of his sequences of apartments—this one in Queens. By this time, he had left journalism entirely and had sold off much of his valuable hard-boiled fiction collection to cover living expenses (but also to buy new books and films). On this evening, we were talking about recent difficult romantic collapses we had gone through—the sort that deplete your dreams, that you can't imagine getting past. As bad as I might have felt, I couldn't help noting that there was something particularly bottomless in the way Paul talked about his disenchantment on that night. I felt I was hearing a submission, a giving up, that no matter how broken I could imagine myself being, I couldn't yet imagine hearing in my own voice. That same night, Paul introduced me to *The Seventh Victim*, a 1943 film produced by Val Lewton and directed by Mark Robson. It's a strange story—creepy and heartbreaking—that's ostensibly about a missing woman and the ploys of a set of sophisticated Manhattan Satan worshippers, but what the film is really about is the appeal of death over the pain of life. The missing woman is found, of course, and is in fear of her life, literally. That is, in her depression, she can't tell whether she sees death as a terror or a blessing. She finally comes to an understanding, abruptly, in what is one of the most uncommon and haunting endings in film history. (A line from John Donne's "Holy Sonnet VII" accompanies the moment: *"I runne to death, and death meets me as fast, and all my pleasures are like yesterday."*)

After the early 1990s, I lost touch with Paul. He moved at least a time or two more, and he stopped having phone numbers. I could have made a better effort, I should have, but Paul steadily receded from his former presence in the world. I ran into him one summer night in 1999, around two in the morning, on the streets of Lower Manhattan. I was overjoyed to see him, but he seemed distant—not unfriendly, but absent. He said he was working at a video store in the West Village and that he was finishing a screenplay. He didn't have a home phone number to give me. I gave him mine, but I never heard from him, and before much longer I moved back to Los Angeles.

Paul died in the summer of 2006, at an Upper East Side apartment that he sublet illegally. According to Neil Strauss's feature-length account in a December 2006 issue of *Rolling Stone*, Paul had barely been eating for some time, and a summer heat wave almost certainly contributed to his end. Strauss's article was entitled "The Man Who Disappeared"—an apt summary of Paul's long-running abdication of his vocation and, finally, his life. I don't believe that there was anything contrary or intentionally self-destructive about his long good-bye. Rather, I think something in Paul just broke along the way, and after that he managed the loss in his life with a hard-earned grace.

All of us who knew Paul Nelson valued him. He was a gentle and compassionate man with a pointed but sympathetic wit, and an unsparing intellect. He elevated rock & roll criticism before the form even had a life, and line for line, paragraph for paragraph, he was one of the most elegant critics and journalists that America produced since 1960. I benefited from knowing him and from being edited by him, but I became a more conscientious writer simply by reading him. His command of the written word, how he used it to illuminate his times and to advocate the promise of the intrepid new artists who were remapping twentieth-century culture, gave us all something to live up to.

I'd like to give special thanks to Leah Miller, Edith Lewis and Patricia Romanowski at Free Press, who helped make this better page by page, and to my editor, Dominick Anfuso, whose support, patience and kindness have been invaluable to me. In addition, my deep-felt gratitude to my long-suffering agent, Richard Pine; to Doubleday and Anchor Books, who previously published some of the chapters now collected here; and to Jann Wenner and *Rolling Stone*, for making much of this material possible in the first place, and for making it better.

Finally, my love and thanks to the family who let me in their door: Samantha, Preston (a fine writer in the making) and Tessa Schock. How could I ever get any work done without you?

PERMISSION CREDITS

INDEX

ABOUT THE AUTHOR

MIKAL GILMORE is a journalist and music aficionado who has written for *Rolling Stone* magazine since the 1970s. His first book, *Shot in the Heart,* is a National Book Critics Circle and *L.A. Times* Book Prize–winning memoir about his older brother Gary, the first man to be executed in Utah after pleading guilty to murder.